Honda CBR125R
Service and Repair Manual

by Matthew Coombs
with additional information on fuel injected models by Martynn Randall

Models covered
CBR125R-4. 124.7cc. 2004
CBR125R-5. 124.7cc. 2005
CBR125RW-6. 124.7cc. 2006
CBR125RW-7. 124.7cc. 2007
CBR125RW-8. 124.7cc. 2008
CBR125RW-9. 124.7cc. 2009
CBR125RW-A. 124.7cc. 2010

(4620-208-10AK1)

T0339325

ABCDE
FGHIJ

© Haynes Publishing 2012

A book in the **Haynes Service and Repair Manual Series**

ISBN **978 0 85733 553 1**

Printed in Malaysia

Haynes Publishing
Sparkford, Yeovil, Somerset BA22 7JJ, England

Haynes North America, Inc
859 Lawrence Drive, Newbury Park, California 91320, USA

Printed using NORBRITE BOOK 48.8gsm (CODE: 40N6533) from NORPAC; procurement system certified under Sustainable Forestry Initiative standard. Paper produced is certified to the SFI Certified Fiber Sourcing Standard (CERT - 0094271)

Contents

Contents

Acknowledgements

Our thanks are due to Bransons Motorcycles of Yeovil and Total Triumph of Taunton who supplied the machines featured in the illustrations throughout this manual. We would also like to thank NGK Spark Plugs (UK) Ltd for supplying the colour spark plug condition photographs, the Avon Rubber Company for supplying information on tyre fitting and Draper Tools Ltd for some of the workshop tools shown.

Thanks are also due to Honda (UK) Ltd. who supplied model photographs.

Honda's long running NSR125 was finally killed off by tough emission regs at the end of 2003. This 124cc two-stroke had filled Honda's position in the learner bike market as far back as 1986 when the first NS125F was introduced. What was needed was a four-stroke liquid-cooled and catalysed replacement which could capture the youth market whilst at the same time satisfying strict new Euro-2 emission laws. This was no easy task, because no 125cc four-stroke is going to the have the acceleration and 'out and out' fun feel of a revvy two-stroke. Honda's job was to package it in such a way that it sold on looks alone.

Styling was borrowed from the well established CBR supersport range, with a riding position to make any new rider look and feel like they're on something a lot bigger. With learner riders in mind, weight was kept down to 115 kg and a low seat height ensured the new CBR125R could be easily handled by all sizes of rider. An RC211V inspired Repsol Honda liveried model was released in 2005. Equipped with disc brakes front and rear, 6-spoke alloy wheels with low-profile tyres, a box-section swingarm linked to monoshock rear suspension, and a full fairing with twin headlights, the new machine looked every bit like its CBR600F stable mate.

The new 2-valve sohc 4-stroke liquid-cooled engine is produced at Honda's Thailand factory. It has a balancer shaft to smooth out vibration and power delivery. Drive from the 6-speed gearbox is handled by chain and sprockets. Low emissions are taken care of by an air induction system to ensure full burning of the exhaust gases and a catalytic converter in the exhaust pipe to clean up harmful pollutants.

About this Manual

The aim of this manual is to help you get the best value from your motorcycle. It can do so in several ways. It can help you decide what work must be done, even if you choose to have it done by a dealer; it provides information and procedures for routine maintenance and servicing; and it offers diagnostic and repair procedures to follow when trouble occurs.

We hope you use the manual to tackle the work yourself. For many simpler jobs, doing it yourself may be quicker than arranging an appointment to get the motorcycle into a dealer and making the trips to leave it and pick it up. More importantly, a lot of money can be saved by avoiding the expense the shop must pass on to you to cover its labour and overhead costs. An added benefit is the sense of satisfaction and accomplishment that you feel after doing the job yourself.

References to the left or right side of the motorcycle assume you are sitting on the seat, facing forward.

We take great pride in the accuracy of information given in this manual, but motorcycle manufacturers make alterations and design changes during the production run of a particular motorcycle of which they do not inform us. No liability can be accepted by the authors or publishers for loss, damage or injury caused by any errors in, or omissions from, the information given.

CBR125R-4 2004 model

The CBR125R is the environmentally-friendly four-stroke successor to Honda's two-stroke NSR125R, aimed at maintaining the sporting image while becoming more suitable for today's learner riders. It uses a single cylinder liquid-cooled engine. Drive to the single overhead camshaft, which actuates the two valves via a pair of rocker arms, is by chain from the left-hand end of the crankshaft. A balancer shaft driven directly off the crankshaft keeps things smooth. The clutch is a conventional wet multi-plate unit and the gearbox is 6-speed. Drive to the rear wheel is by chain and sprockets.

A single 28 mm CV carburettor supplies fuel and air to the engine. An electronic ignition system ignites the mixture via a single spark plug. A catalyst is incorporated in the exhaust system, which features a stainless steel silencer.

The twin-spar steel frame uses the engine as a stressed member. Front suspension is by oil-damped 31 mm forks. Rear suspension is by a progressively damped single shock absorber. The box-section steel swingarm pivots through the frame.

The front brake system has a twin-piston sliding caliper acting on a conventional disc, and the rear brake system has a single piston sliding caliper acting on a conventional disc.

Available in black, blue and red colours.

CBR125R-5 2005 model

There were no significant changes from the RR-4 (2004) model.

A Repsol replica paint scheme was added to the original black, blue and red colour options.

CBR125RW-6 2006 model

There are no significant changes from the RR-5 (2005) model.

Available in black, orange, red and Repsol replica colours.

CBR125RW-7 and RW-8 2007/8 models

The 2007 model was updated with fuel injection, a catalytic converter built into the exhaust system, and minor bodywork revisions and revised lighting. Colours were red, blue, black, white. There were no changes for 2008.

CBR125RW-9 and RW-A 2009/10 models

No change apart from new colours of white with blue, black with silver, and black with red.

Bike spec

Engine

Type	Four-stroke, single cylinder
Capacity	124.7 cc
Bore	58.0 mm
Stroke	47.2 mm
Compression ratio	11.0 to 1
Cooling system	Liquid-cooled
Clutch	Wet multi-plate
Transmission	Six-speed constant mesh
Final drive	Chain and sprockets
Camshaft	SOHC, chain-driven
Fuel system	
CBR125R-4, R-5 and RW-6 models	28 mm CV carburettor
CBR125RW-7, RW-8, RW-9 and RW-A models	PGM-FI fuel injection
Exhaust system	Two-piece, incorporating a catalytic converter
Ignition system	Computer-controlled digital transistorised with electronic advance

Chassis

Frame type	Twin spar steel
Rake and Trail	25°, 88 mm
Fuel tank	
Capacity (including reserve)	10 litres
Reserve volume (when gauge needle goes into red zone)	approx. 2.1 litres
Front suspension	
Type	31 mm oil-damped telescopic forks, non-adjustable
Travel	109 mm
Rear suspension	
Type	Single shock absorber (non-adjustable), box-section aluminium swingarm
Travel (at axle)	120 mm
Wheels	17 inch, 6-spoke alloys
Tyres	
Front	80/90-17MC (44P)
Rear	100/80-17MC (52P)
Front brake	Single 276 mm disc with twin piston Nissin sliding caliper
Rear brake	Single 220 mm disc with single piston Nissin sliding caliper

Dimensions and weights

Overall length	1920 mm
Overall width	
CBR125R-4, R-5 and RW-6 models	675 mm
CBR125RW-7, RW-8, RW-9 and RW-A models	680 mm
Overall height	
CBR125R-4, R-5 and RW-6 models	1070 mm
CBR125RW-7, RW-8, RW-9 and RW-A models	1065 mm
Wheelbase	1294 mm
Seat height	776 mm
Ground clearance	172 mm
Weight (dry)	115 kg
Weight (with fuel, oil and coolant)	124 kg
Maximum weight (carrying) capacity	180 kg

Professional mechanics are trained in safe working procedures. However enthusiastic you may be about getting on with the job at hand, take the time to ensure that your safety is not put at risk. A moment's lack of attention can result in an accident, as can failure to observe simple precautions.

There will always be new ways of having accidents, and the following is not a comprehensive list of all dangers; it is intended rather to make you aware of the risks and to encourage a safe approach to all work you carry out on your bike.

Asbestos

● Certain friction, insulating, sealing and other products - such as brake pads, clutch linings, gaskets, etc. - contain asbestos. Extreme care must be taken to avoid inhalation of dust from such products since it is hazardous to health. If in doubt, assume that they do contain asbestos.

Fire

● Remember at all times that petrol is highly flammable. Never smoke or have any kind of naked flame around, when working on the vehicle. But the risk does not end there - a spark caused by an electrical short-circuit, by two metal surfaces contacting each other, by careless use of tools, or even by static electricity built up in your body under certain conditions, can ignite petrol vapour, which in a confined space is highly explosive. Never use petrol as a cleaning solvent. Use an approved safety solvent.

● Always disconnect the battery earth terminal before working on any part of the fuel or electrical system, and never risk spilling fuel on to a hot engine or exhaust.
● It is recommended that a fire extinguisher of a type suitable for fuel and electrical fires is kept handy in the garage or workplace at all times. Never try to extinguish a fuel or electrical fire with water.

Fumes

● Certain fumes are highly toxic and can quickly cause unconsciousness and even death if inhaled to any extent. Petrol vapour comes into this category, as do the vapours from certain solvents such as trichloro-ethylene. Any draining or pouring of such volatile fluids should be done in a well ventilated area.
● When using cleaning fluids and solvents, read the instructions carefully. Never use materials from unmarked containers - they may give off poisonous vapours.
● Never run the engine of a motor vehicle in an enclosed space such as a garage. Exhaust fumes contain carbon monoxide which is extremely poisonous; if you need to run the engine, always do so in the open air or at least have the rear of the vehicle outside the workplace.

The battery

● Never cause a spark, or allow a naked light near the vehicle's battery. It will normally be giving off a certain amount of hydrogen gas, which is highly explosive.

● Always disconnect the battery ground (earth) terminal before working on the fuel or electrical systems (except where noted).
● If possible, loosen the filler plugs or cover when charging the battery from an external source. Do not charge at an excessive rate or the battery may burst.
● Take care when topping up, cleaning or carrying the battery. The acid electrolyte, evenwhen diluted, is very corrosive and should not be allowed to contact the eyes or skin. Always wear rubber gloves and goggles or a face shield. If you ever need to prepare electrolyte yourself, always add the acid slowly to the water; never add the water to the acid.

Electricity

● When using an electric power tool, inspection light etc., always ensure that the appliance is correctly connected to its plug and that, where necessary, it is properly grounded (earthed). Do not use such appliances in damp conditions and, again, beware of creating a spark or applying excessive heat in the vicinity of fuel or fuel vapour. Also ensure that the appliances meet national safety standards.
● A severe electric shock can result from touching certain parts of the electrical system, such as the spark plug wires (HT leads), when the engine is running or being cranked, particularly if components are damp or the insulation is defective. Where an electronic ignition system is used, the secondary (HT) voltage is much higher and could prove fatal.

Remember...

✗ **Don't** start the engine without first ascertaining that the transmission is in neutral.
✗ **Don't** suddenly remove the pressure cap from a hot cooling system - cover it with a cloth and release the pressure gradually first, or you may get scalded by escaping coolant.
✗ **Don't** attempt to drain oil until you are sure it has cooled sufficiently to avoid scalding you.
✗ **Don't** grasp any part of the engine or exhaust system without first ascertaining that it is cool enough not to burn you.
✗ **Don't** allow brake fluid or antifreeze to contact the machine's paintwork or plastic components.
✗ **Don't** siphon toxic liquids such as fuel, hydraulic fluid or antifreeze by mouth, or allow them to remain on your skin.
✗ **Don't** inhale dust - it may be injurious to health (see Asbestos heading).
✗ **Don't** allow any spilled oil or grease to remain on the floor - wipe it up right away, before someone slips on it.
✗ **Don't** use ill-fitting spanners or other tools which may slip and cause injury.
✗ **Don't** lift a heavy component which may be beyond your capability - get assistance.

✗ **Don't** rush to finish a job or take unverified short cuts.
✗ **Don't** allow children or animals in or around an unattended vehicle.
✗ **Don't** inflate a tyre above the recommended pressure. Apart from over-stressing the carcass, in extreme cases the tyre may blow off forcibly.
✔ **Do** ensure that the machine is supported securely at all times. This is especially important when the machine is blocked up to aid wheel or fork removal.
✔ **Do** take care when attempting to loosen a stubborn nut or bolt. It is generally better to pull on a spanner, rather than push, so that if you slip, you fall away from the machine rather than onto it.
✔ **Do** wear eye protection when using power tools such as drill, sander, bench grinder etc.
✔ **Do** use a barrier cream on your hands prior to undertaking dirty jobs - it will protect your skin from infection as well as making the dirt easier to remove afterwards; but make sure your hands aren't left slippery. Note that long-term contact with used engine oil can be a health hazard.
✔ **Do** keep loose clothing (cuffs, ties etc. and long hair) well out of the way of moving mechanical parts.

✔ **Do** remove rings, wristwatch etc., before working on the vehicle - especially the electrical system.
✔ **Do** keep your work area tidy - it is only too easy to fall over articles left lying around.
✔ **Do** exercise caution when compressing springs for removal or installation. Ensure that the tension is applied and released in a controlled manner, using suitable tools which preclude the possibility of the spring escaping violently.
✔ **Do** ensure that any lifting tackle used has a safe working load rating adequate for the job.
✔ **Do** get someone to check periodically that all is well, when working alone on the vehicle.
✔ **Do** carry out work in a logical sequence and check that everything is correctly assembled and tightened afterwards.
✔ **Do** remember that your vehicle's safety affects that of yourself and others. If in doubt on any point, get professional advice.
● If in spite of following these precautions, you are unfortunate enough to injure yourself, seek medical attention as soon as possible.

Frame and engine numbers

The frame serial number is stamped into the right-hand side of the steering head. The engine number is stamped into the crankcase on the left-hand side. Both of these numbers should be recorded and kept in a safe place so they can be given to law enforcement officials in the event of a theft. There is also a VIN plate on the right-hand side of the frame just behind the steering head and a colour code label on the left-hand side. The carburettor has an ID number stamped into its body.

The frame serial number, engine serial number, and colour code should also be kept in a handy place (such as with your driver's licence) so they are always available when purchasing or ordering parts for your machine.

Models are identified by their model code (e.g. R-4 or R-5). The model code is printed on the colour code label.

Model code	Production year
CBR125R-4	2004
CBR125R-5	2005
CBR125RW-6	2006
CBR125RW-7	2007
CBR125RW-8	2008
CBR125RW-9	2009
CBR125RW-A	2010

Buying spare parts

Once you have found all the identification numbers, record them for reference when buying parts. Since the manufacturers change specifications, parts and vendors (companies that manufacture various components on the machine), providing the ID numbers is the only way to be reasonably sure that you are buying the correct parts.

Whenever possible, take the worn part to the dealer so direct comparison with the new component can be made. Along the trail from the manufacturer to the parts shelf, there are numerous places that the part can end up with the wrong number or be listed incorrectly.

The two places to purchase new parts for your motorcycle – the franchised or main dealer and the parts/accessories store – differ in the type of parts they carry. While dealers can obtain every single genuine part for your motorcycle, the accessory store is usually limited to normal high wear items such as chains and sprockets, brake pads, spark plugs and cables.

Used parts can be obtained from breakers yards for roughly half the price of new ones, but you can't always be sure of what you're getting. Once again, take your worn part to the breaker for direct comparison, or when ordering by mail order make sure that you can return it if you are not happy.

Whether buying new, used or rebuilt parts, the best course is to deal directly with someone who specialises in your particular make.

The colour code label is on the left-hand side of the frame

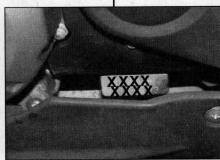

The engine number is stamped into the left-hand side of the crankcase

The VIN plate (arrowed) is on the right-hand side of the frame

The frame number is stamped into the right-hand side of the steering head

Engine oil level

Before you start:

✔ Start the engine and let it idle for 3 to 5 minutes.
Caution: Do not run the engine in an enclosed space such as a garage or workshop.
✔ Stop the engine and support the motorcycle upright on level ground. Allow it to stand for a few minutes for the oil level to stabilise.

The correct oil:

● Modern, high-revving engines place great demands on their oil. It is very important that the correct oil for your bike is used.

● Always top up with a good quality motorcycle oil of the specified type and viscosity and do not overfill the engine. Do not use engine oil designed for car use.

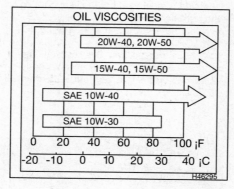

OIL VISCOSITIES

20W-40, 20W-50
15W-40, 15W-50
SAE 10W-40
SAE 10W-30

Oil type	API grade SG or higher
Oil viscosity	SAE 10W30 (see viscosity chart for alternatives)

Caution: Do not use chemical additives or oils labelled 'ENERGY CONSERVING' – such additives or oils could cause clutch slip.

Bike care:

● If you have to add oil frequently, check the engine joints, oil seals and gaskets for oil leakage. If not, the engine could be burning oil, in which case there will be white smoke coming out of the exhaust (see *Fault Finding*).

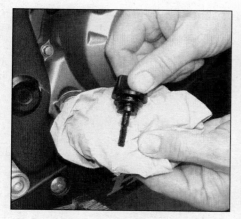

1 The oil level dipstick is incorporated with the filler cap, which is on the right-hand side of the engine. Unscrew the cap and wipe the dipstick clean.

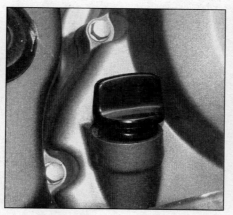

2 Insert the dipstick so that the cap contacts the engine, but do not screw it in.

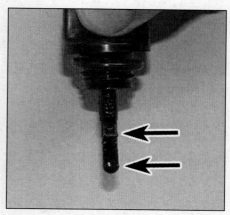

3 Remove the dipstick and check the oil mark - it should lie between the upper and lower level lines (arrowed).

4 If the level is on or below the lower line, top up the engine with the recommended grade and type of oil to bring the level almost up to the upper line. Do not overfill.

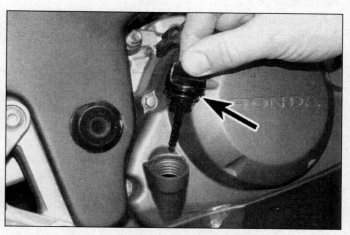

5 On completion, make sure the O-ring (arrowed) on the underside of the cap is in good condition and properly seated. Fit a new one if necessary. Wipe it clean and smear new oil onto it. Fit the cap, making sure it is secure in the cover.

Brake fluid levels

⚠️ *Warning: Brake hydraulic fluid can harm your eyes and damage painted surfaces, so use extreme caution when handling and pouring it and cover surrounding surfaces with rag. Do not use fluid that has been standing open for some time, as it is hygroscopic (absorbs moisture from the air) which can cause a dangerous loss of braking effectiveness.*

Before you start:

✔ The front brake fluid reservoir is on the right-hand handlebar. The rear brake fluid reservoir is located under the seat cowling on the right-hand side.
✔ Make sure you have a supply of DOT 4 hydraulic fluid.
✔ Wrap a rag around the reservoir being worked on to ensure that any spillage does not come into contact with painted surfaces.

Bike care:

● The fluid in the front and rear brake master cylinder reservoirs will drop as the brake pads wear down. If the fluid level is low check the brake pads for wear (see Chapter 1), and replace them with new ones if necessary (see Chapter 7). Do not top the reservoir(s) up until the new pads have been fitted, and then check to see if topping up is still necessary – when the caliper pistons are pushed back to accommodate the extra thickness of the pads some fluid will be displaced back into the reservoir.
● If either fluid reservoir requires repeated topping-up there is a leak somewhere in the system, which must be investigated immediately.
● Check for signs of fluid leakage from the hydraulic hoses and/or brake system components – if found, rectify immediately (see Chapter 7).
● Check the operation of both brakes before taking the machine on the road; if there is evidence of air in the system (spongy feel to lever or pedal), it must be bled (see Chapter 7).

Front brake fluid level
(photos 1-5)

Rear brake fluid level
(photos 6-11)

1 With the bike on its sidestand set the handlebars so the reservoir is level and check the fluid level through the window in the reservoir body – it must be above the LOWER level line (arrowed).

2 If the level is on or below the LOWER line, undo the two reservoir cover screws and remove the cover, diaphragm plate and diaphragm.

3 Top up with new clean DOT 4 hydraulic fluid, until the level is up to the UPPER line (arrowed) on the inside of the reservoir. Do not overfill and take care to avoid spills (see **Warning** above).

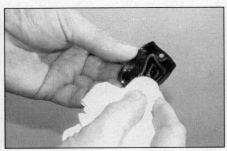

4 Wipe any moisture off the diaphragm with a tissue.

5 Ensure that the diaphragm is correctly seated before installing the plate and cover. Secure the reservoir cover with its screws.

6 The rear brake fluid level is visible through the reservoir body – it must be between the UPPER and LOWER level lines (arrowed).

7 If the level is on or below the LOWER line undo the bolt securing the fluid reservoir to the frame and draw the reservoir out.

8 Undo the two reservoir cover screws and remove the cover, diaphragm plate and diaphragm.

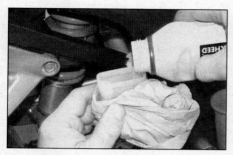

9 Top up with new DOT 4 hydraulic fluid, until the level is up to the UPPER line. Do not overfill and take care to avoid spills (see **Warning**).

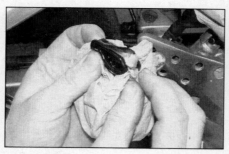

10 Wipe any moisture off the diaphragm with a tissue.

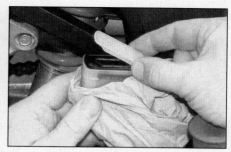

11 Ensure that the diaphragm is correctly seated before installing the plate and cover. Secure the cover with its screws. Fit the reservoir onto its mount and tighten the bolt.

Tyres

The correct pressures:

● The tyres must be checked when **cold**, not immediately after riding. Note that incorrect tyre pressures will cause abnormal tread wear and unsafe handling. Low tyre pressures may cause the tyre to slip on the rim or come off.
● Use an accurate pressure gauge. Spend as much as you can justify on a quality gauge.
● Proper air pressure will increase tyre life and provide maximum stability and ride comfort.

Front	Rear
29 psi (2.00 Bar)	33 psi (2.27 Bar)

Tyre care:

● Check the tyres carefully for cuts, tears, embedded nails or other sharp objects and excessive wear. Operation of the motorcycle with excessively worn tyres is extremely hazardous, as traction and handling are directly affected.
● Check the condition of the tyre valve and ensure the dust cap is in place.
● Pick out any stones or nails which may have become embedded in the tyre tread. If left, they will eventually penetrate through the casing and cause a puncture.
● If tyre damage is apparent, or unexplained loss of pressure is experienced, seek the advice of a tyre fitting specialist without delay.

Tyre tread depth:

● At the time of writing UK law requires that tread depth must be at least 1 mm over 3/4 of the tread breadth all the way around the tyre, with no bald patches. Many riders, however, consider 2 mm tread depth minimum to be a safer limit. Honda recommend a minimum of 1.5 mm on the front and 2 mm on the rear. Refer to the tyre tread legislation in your country.
● Many tyres now incorporate wear indicators in the tread. Identify the location marking on the tyre sidewall to locate the indicator bar and replace the tyre if the tread has worn down to the bar.

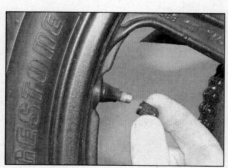

1 Remove the dust cap from the valve and do not forget to fit it after checking the pressure.

2 Check the tyre pressures when the tyres are **cold**.

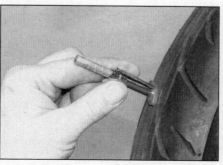

3 Measure tread depth at the centre of the tyre using a depth gauge.

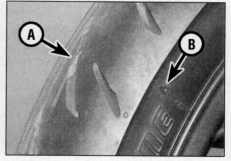

4 Tyre tread wear indicator (A) and its location marking (B) on the edge or sidewall (according to tyre manufacturer).

Coolant level

Warning: DO NOT remove the radiator pressure cap to add coolant. Topping up is done via the coolant reservoir tank filler. DO NOT leave open containers of coolant about, as it is poisonous.

Before you start:

✔ Make sure you have a supply of coolant available (use either an ethylene glycol based pre-mixed coolant, or prepare a mix of 50% distilled water and 50% corrosion inhibited ethylene glycol anti-freeze).

✔ Always check the coolant level when the engine is at normal working temperature. Take the motorcycle on a short run to allow it to reach normal temperature.

Caution: Do not run the engine in an enclosed space such as a garage or workshop.

✔ Stop the engine and support the motorcycle upright on level ground.

Bike care:

● It is important that anti-freeze is used in the system all year round, and not just in the winter. Do not top the system up using only water, as the system will become too diluted.

● Do not overfill the reservoir tank. If the coolant is significantly above the UPPER level line at any time, the surplus should be siphoned or drained off to prevent the possibility of it being expelled out of the overflow hose.

● If the coolant level falls steadily, check the system for leaks (see Chapter 1). If no leaks are found and the level continues to fall, it is recommended that the machine is taken to a Honda dealer for a pressure test.

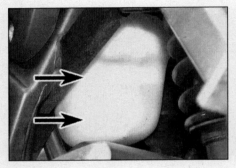

1 The coolant reservoir is visible from the left-hand side. With the motorcycle vertical, the coolant level should lie between the upper and lower level lines (arrowed) marked on the back of the reservoir.

2 If the coolant level is on or below the LOWER line, remove the rider's seat (see Chapter 8). Remove the reservoir filler cap.

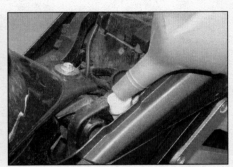

3 Top the reservoir up with the recommended coolant mixture to the UPPER level line, using a suitable funnel if required. Fit the cap securely and install the seat.

Suspension, steering and final drive

Suspension and Steering:

● Check that the front and rear suspension operates smoothly without binding (see Chapter 1).
● Check that the steering moves smoothly from lock-to-lock.

Drive chain:

● Check that the chain isn't too loose or too tight, and adjust it if necessary (see Chapter 1).
● If the chain looks dry, lubricate it (see Chapter 1).

Legal and safety

Lighting and signalling:

● Take a minute to check that the headlight, tail light, brake light, licence plate light, instrument lights and turn signals all work correctly.
● Check that the horn sounds when the button is pressed.
● A working speedometer, graduated in mph, is a statutory requirement in the UK.

Safety:

● Check that the throttle grip rotates smoothly when opened and snaps shut when released, in all steering positions. Also check for the correct amount of freeplay (see Chapter 1).
● Check that the brake lever and pedal, clutch lever and gearchange lever operate smoothly. Lubricate them at the specified intervals or when necessary (see Chapter 1).
● Check that the engine shuts off when the kill switch is operated. Check the starter interlock circuit (see Chapter 1).
● Check that the sidestand return springs hold the stand up securely when retracted.

Fuel:

● This may seem obvious, but check that you have enough fuel to complete your journey. If you notice signs of fuel leakage rectify the cause immediately.
● Ensure you always use unleaded fuel, minimum 91 RON (Research Octane Number).

Chapter 1
Routine maintenance and servicing

Contents

Degrees of difficulty

| **Easy,** suitable for novice with little experience | | **Fairly easy,** suitable for beginner with some experience | | **Fairly difficult,** suitable for competent DIY mechanic | | **Difficult,** suitable for experienced DIY mechanic | | **Very difficult,** suitable for expert DIY or professional | |

Engine

Spark plug type	
Standard	
NGK	CR8E
Denso	U24ESR-N
For continuous high speed use	
NGK	CR9E
Denso	U27ESR-N
Spark plug electrode gap	0.7 to 0.8 mm
Engine idle speed:	
Carburettor models	1400 ± 100 rpm
Fuel injected models	1450 ± 100 rpm
Valve clearances (COLD engine)	
Intake valve	0.06 mm (0.04 to 0.08 mm range)
Exhaust valve	0.27 mm (0.25 to 0.29 mm range)

Chassis

Drive chain slack	25 to 35 mm
Throttle cable freeplay	2 to 6 mm at twistgrip flange
Clutch cable freeplay	10 to 20 mm at lever ball end
Tyre pressures (cold)	see *Pre-ride checks*
Steering head bearing pre-load (see Section 17)	1.0 to 1.5 N

Lubricants and fluids

Engine oil	see *Pre-ride checks*
Engine oil capacity	
Oil change	1.0 litres
Following engine overhaul	1.3 litres
Coolant type	50% distilled water, 50% corrosion inhibited ethylene glycol anti-freeze
Coolant capacity	
Radiator and engine	0.72 litres
Reservoir	0.28 litres
Brake fluid	DOT 4
Drive chain	SAE 80 or 90 gear oil or aerosol chain lubricant suitable for O-ring chains
Steering head bearings	Multi-purpose grease with EP2 rating
Bearing seal lips	Multi-purpose grease
Gearchange lever/rear brake pedal/footrest pivots	Multi-purpose grease
Clutch lever pivot	Multi-purpose grease
Sidestand pivot	Multi-purpose grease
Throttle twistgrip	Multi-purpose grease
Front brake lever pivot and piston tip	Silicone grease
Cables	Aerosol cable lubricant

Torque settings

Crankshaft end cap	8 Nm
Engine oil drain plug	25 Nm
Fork clamp bolts (top yoke)	23 Nm
Fuel valve nut	27 Nm
Handlebar clamp bolts	27 Nm
Handlebar end-weight screw	9 Nm
Rear axle nut	59 Nm
Spark plug	12 Nm
Steering head bearing adjuster nut	
Initial setting	27 Nm
Final setting	1 Nm
Steering stem nut	88 Nm
Timing inspection cap	6 Nm
Tappet locknut	10 Nm

Note: *The Pre-ride checks outlined in the owner's manual cover those items which should be inspected before every ride. Also perform the pre-ride inspection at every maintenance interval (in addition to the procedures listed). The intervals listed below are the intervals recommended by the manufacturer for the models covered in this manual.*

Pre-ride
☐ See 'Pre-ride checks' at the beginning of this manual.

After the initial 600 miles (1000 km)
Note: *This check is usually performed by a Honda dealer after the first 600 miles (1000 km) from new. Thereafter, maintenance is carried out according to the following intervals of the schedule.*

Every 600 miles (1000 km)
☐ Check, adjust, clean and lubricate the drive chain (Section 1)

Every 2500 miles (4000 km) or 6 months
☐ Check the spark plug (Section 2)
☐ Clean the air filter element and crankcase breather (Section 3)
☐ Check and adjust the valve clearances (Section 4)
☐ Check and adjust the engine idle speed – Carburettor models only (Section 5)
☐ Check the brake pads for wear (Section 6)
☐ Check the brake system and brake light switch operation (Section 6)
☐ Check the fuel system and hoses (Section 7)
☐ Check and adjust the throttle and choke cables (Section 8)
☐ Check and adjust the clutch cable freeplay (Section 9)
☐ Check the sidestand and starter interlock circuit (Section 10)
☐ Check the front and rear suspension (Section 11)
☐ Check the condition of the wheels, wheel bearings and tyres (Section 12)
☐ Lubricate the clutch, gearchange and brake levers, brake pedal, sidestand pivot, and the throttle and choke cables (Section 13)

Every 5000 miles (8000 km) or 12 months
Carry out all the items under the 2500 mile (4000 km) check, plus the following:
☐ Change the engine oil (Section 14)
☐ Check the cooling system (Section 15)
☐ Check the tightness of all nuts, bolts and fasteners (Section 16)
☐ Fit a new spark plug (Section 2)

Every 7,500 miles (12,000 km) or 18 months
Carry out all the items under the 2500 mile (4000 km) check, plus the following:
☐ Clean the engine oil strainer (Section 14)
☐ Check and adjust the steering head bearings (Section 17)
☐ Check the pulse secondary air injection (PAIR) system – Carburettor models only (Section 18)
☐ Fit a new air filter element (Section 3)

Every two years
☐ Change the brake fluid (Section 6)
☐ Change the coolant (Section 15)

Non-scheduled maintenance
☐ Check the battery (Section 19)
☐ Fit new brake master cylinder and caliper seals (Section 6)
☐ Fit new brake hoses (Section 6)
☐ Clean the fuel strainer (Section 7)
☐ Fit new fuel system hoses (Section 7)
☐ Change the front fork oil (Section 11)
☐ Re-grease the swingarm pivot (Section 11)
☐ Re-grease the steering head bearings (Section 17)

1 This Chapter is designed to help the home mechanic maintain his/her motorcycle for safety, economy, long life and peak performance.

2 Deciding where to start or plug into the routine maintenance schedule depends on several factors. If your motorcycle has been maintained according to the warranty standards and has just come out of warranty, start routine maintenance as it coincides with the next mileage or calendar interval. If you have owned the machine for some time but have never performed any maintenance on it, start at the nearest interval and include some additional procedures to ensure that nothing important is overlooked. If you have just had a major engine overhaul, then start the maintenance routine from the beginning. If you have a used machine and have no knowledge of its history or maintenance record, combine all the checks into one large service initially and then settle into the specified maintenance schedule.

3 Before beginning any maintenance or repair, the machine should be cleaned thoroughly, especially around the oil filter, valve cover, body panels, drive chain, suspension, wheels, etc. Cleaning will help ensure that dirt does not contaminate the engine and will allow you to detect wear and damage that could otherwise easily go unnoticed.

4 Certain maintenance information is sometimes printed on labels attached to the motorcycle. If the information on the labels differs from that included here, use the information on the label.

Maintenance procedures

1 Drive chain and sprockets

Check chain slack

1 A neglected drive chain won't last long and will quickly damage the sprockets. Routine chain adjustment and lubrication isn't difficult and will ensure maximum chain and sprocket life.

2 To check the chain, place the bike on its sidestand and shift the transmission into neutral. Make sure the ignition switch is OFF.

3 Push up on the bottom run of the chain and measure the slack midway between the two sprockets, then compare your measurement to that listed in this Chapter's Specifications **(see illustration)**. As the chain stretches with wear, adjustment will periodically be necessary (see below). Since the chain will rarely wear evenly, roll the bike forward so that another section of chain can be checked (having an assistant to do this makes the task a lot easier); do this several times to check the entire length of chain, and mark the tightest spot.

Caution: Riding the bike with excess slack in the chain could lead to damage, particularly if it reaches 50 mm.

4 In some cases where lubrication has been neglected, corrosion and dirt may cause the links to bind and kink, which effectively shortens the chain's length and makes it tight **(see illustration)**. Thoroughly clean and work free any such links, then highlight them with a marker pen or paint. Take the bike for a ride.

5 After the bike has been ridden, repeat the measurement for slack in the highlighted area. If the chain has kinked again and is still tight, replace it with a new one (see Chapter 7). A rusty, kinked or worn chain will damage the sprockets and can damage transmission bearings. If in any doubt as to the condition of a chain, it is far better to install a new one than risk damage to other components and possibly yourself.

6 Check the entire length of the chain for damaged rollers, loose links and pins, and missing O-rings and replace it with a new one if necessary. Note: Never install a new chain on old sprockets, and never use the old chain if you install new sprockets – replace the chain and sprockets as a set.

7 Inspect the drive chain slider on the front of the swingarm for excessive wear and damage and replace it with a new one if necessary.

Adjust chain slack

8 Position the bike so that the tightest spot of the chain is at the centre of its bottom run. Support the bike on the sidestand.

9 Slacken the rear axle nut **(see illustration)**. Slacken the locknut on the adjuster on each side of the swingarm **(see illustration)**.

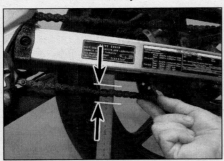

1.3 Push up on the chain and measure the slack

1.4 Neglect has caused the links in this chain to kink

1.9a Slacken the axle nut (A) and the locknut (B) . . .

1.9b . . . on each side

1.10a Turn each adjuster by an equal amount . . .

1.10b . . . then check the alignment marks as described

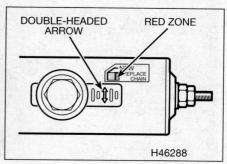

1.12 Check the alignment of the arrow with the decal – here the index point is in the green zone, so the chain is OK

10 To reduce chain slack turn the adjuster nut on each side evenly and clockwise until the amount of freeplay specified at the beginning of the Chapter is obtained at the centre of the bottom run of the chain **(see illustration)**. Following adjustment, check that the same index line on each chain adjustment marker is in the same position in relation to the back edge of the slot in the swingarm **(see illustration)**. It is important the alignment is the same on each side otherwise the rear wheel will be out of alignment with the front. Also make sure that the front face of each adjuster nut is butted against the end of the swingarm. If there is a difference in the positions, adjust one of them so that its position is exactly the same as the other. Check the chain freeplay again and readjust if necessary.

11 To increase chain slack turn the adjuster nut on each side of the swingarm evenly and anti-clockwise, then push the wheel forwards in the swingarm until the nut butts the end of the swingarm, then apply the same principles given in Step 10 for checking alignment.

12 Also check the alignment of the double-headed arrow on the adjustment marker with the wear decal on the left-hand side of the swingarm **(see illustration)**. When the arrow meets the red REPLACE CHAIN zone, the drive chain has stretched excessively and must be replaced with a new one (see Chapter 7). In illustration 1.10b the arrow is

in the 'replace chain' zone, though the wear decal is missing.

13 When adjustment is complete, counter-hold the adjuster nuts to prevent them turning and tighten the locknuts against them. Tighten the axle nut to the torque setting specified at the beginning of the Chapter. Recheck the adjustment as above, then place the machine on an auxiliary stand and spin the wheel to make sure it runs freely.

Clean and lubricate the chain

14 If required, wash the chain using a dedicated aerosol cleaner, or in paraffin (kerosene) or a suitable non-flammable or high flash-point solvent that will not damage the O-rings, using a soft brush to work any dirt out if necessary. Wipe the cleaner off the chain and allow it to dry. If the chain is excessively dirty remove it from the machine and allow it to soak in the paraffin or solvent (see Chapter 7).

Caution: Don't use petrol (gasoline), an unsuitable solvent or other cleaning fluids which might damage the internal sealing properties of the chain. Don't use high-pressure water to clean the chain. The entire process shouldn't take longer than ten minutes, otherwise the O-rings could be damaged.

15 The best time to lubricate the chain is after the motorcycle has been ridden. When the chain is warm, the lubricant will penetrate the

joints between the side plates better than when cold. **Note:** *Honda specifies SAE 80 to SAE 90 gear oil or an aerosol chain lube that it is suitable for O-ring (sealed) chains; do not use any other chain lubricants – the solvents could damage the chain's sealing rings.* Apply the lubricant to the area where the sideplates overlap – not the middle of the rollers **(see illustration)**.

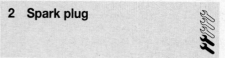

⚠️ *Warning: Take care not to get any lubricant on the tyres or brake system components. If any of the lubricant inadvertently contacts them, clean it off thoroughly using a suitable solvent or dedicated brake cleaner before riding the machine.*

Check sprocket wear

16 Remove the front sprocket cover **(see illustration)**. Check the teeth on the front sprocket and the rear sprocket for wear **(see illustration)**. If the sprocket teeth are worn excessively, replace the chain and both sprockets with a new set.

2 Spark plug

Check and adjustment

1 Make sure your spark plug socket is the correct size before attempting to remove

1.15 Apply the lubricant to the top of the lower chain run, so centrifugal force will work it into the chain when the bike is moving

1.16a Two bolts retain the sprocket cover

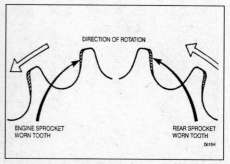

1.16b Check the sprockets in the areas indicated

2.3 Pull the cap off the spark plug

2.5 Unscrew and remove the plug

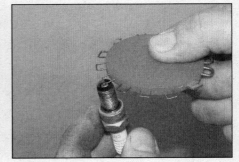

2.7a Using a wire type gauge to measure the spark plug electrode gap

2.7b Adjusting the gap using the fitting provided on the tool

the plugs – a suitable one is supplied in the motorcycle's tool kit which is stored under the seat.

2 Remove the right-hand fairing side panel (see Chapter 8).

3 Pull the cap off the spark plug **(see illustration)**.

4 Clean the area around the base of the spark plug to prevent any dirt falling into the engine.

5 Using either the plug removing tool supplied in the bike's toolkit or a deep spark plug socket, unscrew and remove the plug from the cylinder head **(see illustration)**.

6 Check the condition of the electrodes, referring to the spark plug reading chart at the

end of this manual if signs of contamination are evident.

7 Clean the plug with a wire brush. Examine the tips of the electrodes; if a tip has rounded off, the plug is worn. Measure the gap between the two electrodes using a feeler gauge or a wire type gauge **(see illustration)**. The gap should be as given in the Specifications at the beginning of this chapter; if necessary adjust the gap by bending the side electrode **(see illustration)**.

8 Check the threads, the washer and the ceramic insulator body for cracks and other damage.

9 If the plug is worn or damaged, or if any deposits cannot be cleaned off, replace the plug with a new one.

10 Thread the plug into the cylinder head until the washer seats **(see illustration)**. Since the cylinder head is made of aluminium, which is soft and easily damaged, thread the plug as far as possible by hand. Once the plug is are finger-tight, the job can be finished with a spanner on the tool supplied or a socket drive **(see illustration 2.5)**. If a new plug is being installed, tighten it by 1/2 a turn after the washer has seated. If the old plug is being reused, tighten it by 1/8 to 1/4 turn after the washer has seated, or if a torque wrench can be applied, tighten the spark plug to the

torque setting specified at the beginning of the Chapter.

11 Fit the spark plug cap, making sure it locates correctly onto the plug **(see illustration 2.3)**. Install the fairing side panel (see Chapter 8).

> **HAYNES HiNT** *Stripped plug threads in the cylinder head can be repaired with a Heli-Coil insert – ask a dealer about this service.*

Renewal

12 At the prescribed interval, whatever the condition of the existing spark plug, remove the plug as described above and install a new one.

3 Air filter and crankcase breather

Air filter

Caution: If the machine is continually ridden in wet or dusty conditions, the filter should be cleaned more frequently.

1 Remove the fuel tank (see Chapter 4A or 4B).

2 Undo the five screws securing the air filter cover **(see illustration)**. Remove the cover.

2.10 Thread the plug into the head by hand to prevent cross-threading

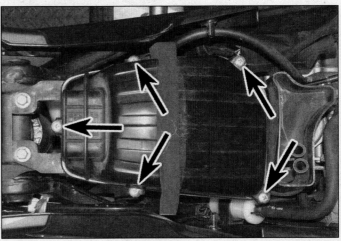

3.2 Undo the screws (arrowed) and remove the cover . . .

3.3 . . . and the filter element

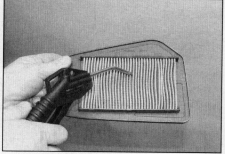

3.4 Direct the air in the opposite direction of normal flow

3.5 Make sure the element is correctly seated then install the cover

3 Remove the filter element from the housing, noting how it fits **(see illustration)**.

4 Tap the filter element on a hard surface to dislodge any dirt, then use compressed air to clear the element, directing the air in the opposite way to normal flow, i.e. from the underside **(see illustration)**. Do not use any solvents or cleaning agents on the element.

5 Fit the filter element into the housing, making sure it is properly seated, then fit the cover and secure it with its screws **(see illustration)**.

6 Install the fuel tank (see Chapter 4A or 4B).

7 At the prescribed interval remove the filter element (Steps 1 to 3) and replace it with a new one whatever its apparent condition.

Crankcase breather

Caution: If the machine is continually ridden in wet conditions or at full throttle, the crankcase breather should be drained more frequently.

8 Locate the crankcase breather drain tube on the underside of the bike, then release the clamp and slide it up the hose **(see illustration)**. Place a suitable container under the hose, then remove the plug from the end of the hose and allow any deposits to drain into the container.

4 Valve clearances

Note: *When setting the position of the crankshaft for the engine timing (Steps 4 and 5), be sure*

3.8 Release the clamp (arrowed), then remove the plug and drain the hose

that you have the correct timing mark on the flywheel – the T which denotes top dead centre (TDC) for engine timing is on its side and can be easily confused with the F mark, also on its side, which denotes the firing (ignition timing) point.

Special tool: *A set of feeler gauges is necessary for this job **(see illustration 4.6)**.*

1 The engine must be completely cool for this maintenance procedure, so let the bike stand overnight before beginning.

2 Remove the spark plug (see Section 3). Remove the valve cover (see Chapter 2).

3 Unscrew the timing inspection cap and the crankshaft end cap from the alternator cover on the left-hand side of the engine **(see illustration)**. Check the condition of the cap O-rings and replace them with new ones if necessary.

4 To check the valve clearances the engine must be turned to position the piston at top dead centre (TDC) on its compression stroke so

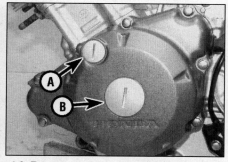

4.3 Remove the timing inspection cap (A) and the crankshaft end cap (B)

that the valves are closed. The engine can be turned using a suitable socket on the alternator nut and turning it in an anti-clockwise direction only **(see illustration 4.5a)**.

5 Turn the engine anti-clockwise until the line next to the T mark on the rotor aligns with the static timing mark, which is a notch in the inspection hole rim, and the index line on the camshaft sprocket is parallel and flush with the cylinder head top surface (the line will be below the sprocket bolts) **(see illustrations)**. There should now be some freeplay in each rocker arm (i.e. they are not contacting the valve stem). If the index line is parallel but not flush with the head, i.e. it is above the sprocket bolts not below them, rotate the engine anti-clockwise one full turn (360°) until the line next to the T mark again aligns with the static timing mark, the index line on the sprocket is flush with the head, and there is some freeplay in the rockers.

4.5a Turn the engine anti-clockwise using the nut . . .

4.5b . . . until the line next to the T mark aligns with the notch (arrowed) . . .

4.5c . . . and the camshaft sprocket line is as shown

4.6 Insert the feeler gauge between the base of the adjuster on the arm and the top of the valve stem as shown

4.7 Slacken the locknut then turn the adjuster using a screwdriver until the gap is correct

4.9 Fit the caps using new O-rings and smear them and the threads with grease

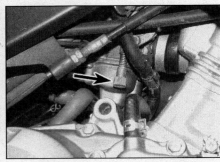

5.3 Idle speed adjuster (arrowed)

6 With the engine in this position, check the clearance of each valve by inserting a feeler gauge of the same thickness as the correct valve clearance (see Specifications) in the gap between the rocker arm and the valve stem **(see illustration)**. The intake valve is on the back of the cylinder head and the exhaust valve is on the front. The gauge should be a firm sliding fit – you should feel a slight drag when you pull the gauge out.

7 If the gap (clearance) is either too wide or too narrow, slacken the locknut on the adjuster in the rocker arm and turn the adjuster as required using a screwdriver until the gap is as specified and the feeler gauge is a sliding fit, then hold the adjuster still and tighten the locknut **(see illustration)**. Recheck the clearance after tightening the locknut.

8 When the clearances are correct install the

valve cover (see Chapter 2) and the spark plug (Section 2).

9 Install the timing inspection cap and crankshaft end cap using new O-rings if required, and smear the O-rings and the cap threads with clean oil **(see illustration)**. Tighten the caps to the torque setting specified at the beginning of the Chapter.

10 On completion, check and adjust the idle speed (see Section 5).

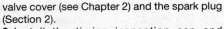

5 Idle speed

Note: *This procedure applies only to carburettor models – on fuel injected models, the idle speed is controlled by the engine management ECU, and is not adjustable.*

6.3 Twist and flex the hoses to check for cracks and deterioration

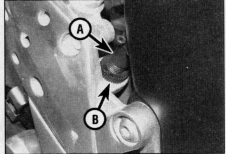

6.5 Hold the rear brake light switch body (A) and turn the adjuster ring (B) as required

1 The idle speed should be checked at the specified interval. It should also be checked and if necessary adjusted after the valve clearances have been adjusted.

2 The engine should be at normal operating temperature, which is usually reached after 10 to 15 minutes of stop-and-go riding. Place the motorcycle on its sidestand, and make sure the transmission is in neutral.

3 The idle speed adjuster is a knurled knob located on the right-hand side of the carburettor and accessed from between the frame and the engine **(see illustration)**. With the engine running, turn the knob until the engine idles at the speed specified at the beginning of the Chapter. Turn the screw clockwise to increase idle speed, and anti-clockwise to decrease it.

4 Snap the throttle open and shut a few times, then recheck the idle speed. If necessary, repeat the adjustment procedure.

5 If a smooth, steady idle can't be achieved, check the spark plug, air filter element and valve clearances (Sections 2, 3 and 4). If the problem persists, there could be an air leak in the intake duct between the carburettor and the cylinder head, or a problem within the carburettor itself – refer to Fault Finding at the end of the book, and to Chapter 4.

6 Brake system

Brake system check

1 A routine general check of the brake system will ensure that any problems are discovered and remedied before the rider's safety is jeopardised.

2 Check the brake lever and pedal for loose fixings, improper or rough action, excessive play, bends, and other damage. Replace any damaged parts with new ones (see Chapter 6). Clean and lubricate the lever and pedal pivots if their action is stiff or rough (see Section 13).

3 Make sure all brake component fasteners are tight. Check the brake pads for wear (see below) and make sure the fluid level in the reservoirs is correct (see Pre-ride checks). Look for leaks at the hose connections and check for cracks in the hoses and unions **(see illustration)**. If the lever or pedal is spongy, bleed the brakes (see Chapter 7).

4 Make sure the brake light operates when the front brake lever is pulled in. The front brake light switch, mounted on the underside of the master cylinder, is not adjustable. If it fails to operate properly, check it (see Chapter 9).

5 Make sure the brake light is activated just before the rear brake takes effect. The switch is mounted behind the rider's right-hand footrest bracket. If adjustment is necessary, hold the switch and turn the adjuster ring on the switch body until the brake light is activated when required **(see illustration)**. If the brake light comes on too late or not at all, turn the ring clockwise (when looked at from the top) so the

6.6a Front brake pad wear indicator (arrowed)

6.6b Rear brake pad wear indicator (arrowed)

15 Replace all the seals in each caliper as a set – a rebuild kit for each caliper is available; master cylinder seals are supplied as a kit along with a new piston and spring (see Chapter 7).

7 Fuel system

⚠️ **Warning: Petrol (gasoline) is extremely flammable, so take extra precautions when you work on any part of the fuel system. Don't smoke or allow open flames or bare light bulbs near the work area, and don't work in a garage where a natural gas-type appliance is present. If you spill any fuel on your skin, rinse it off immediately with soap and water. When you perform any kind of work on the fuel system, wear safety glasses and have a fire extinguisher suitable for a Class B type fire (flammable liquids) on hand.**

switch threads out of the bracket. If the brake light comes on too soon or is permanently on, turn the ring anti-clockwise so the switch threads into the bracket. If the switch doesn't operate the brake light, check it (see Chapter 9).

Brake pad wear check

6 Each brake pad has wear indicators in the form of cut-outs in the friction material. The wear indicators should be plainly visible by looking at the edges of the friction material from the best vantage point – on the front brake look at the bottom edge of the pad from below the caliper, and on the rear brake look at the rear edge of the pad from behind the caliper, but note that an accumulation of road dirt and brake dust could make them difficult to see **(see illustrations)**.

7 If the indicators aren't visible, then the amount of friction material remaining should be, and it will be obvious when the pads need replacing. Honda do not specify a minimum thickness for the friction material, but anything less than 2 mm should be considered worn. **Note:** *Some after-market pads may use different indicators to those on the original equipment pads.*

8 If the pads are worn to or beyond the wear indicator (i.e. the bottom of the cut-out on the front pads or the beginning of the cut-out on the rear pads) or there is little friction material remaining, they must be replaced with new ones, though it is advisable to fit new pads before they become this worn.

9 If the pads are dirty or if you are in doubt as to the amount of friction material remaining,

remove them for inspection (see Chapter 7). If the pads are excessively worn, check the brake discs (see Chapter 7).

10 Refer to Chapter 7 for details of pad removal and installation.

Brake fluid change

11 The brake fluid should be changed at the prescribed interval or whenever a master cylinder or caliper overhaul is carried out. Refer to Chapter 7, Section 11 for details. Ensure that all the old fluid is pumped from the hydraulic system and that the level in the fluid reservoir is checked and the brakes tested before riding the motorcycle.

Brake hoses

12 The hoses will deteriorate with age and should be replaced with new ones regardless of their apparent condition (see Chapter 7).

13 Always replace the banjo union sealing washers with new ones when fitting new hoses. Refill the system with new brake fluid and bleed the system as described in Chapter 7.

Brake caliper and master cylinder seals

14 Brake system seals will deteriorate over a period of time and lose their effectiveness, leading to sticky operation of the brake master cylinders or the pistons in the brake calipers, or fluid loss. Although seal replacement is not subject to a specific time or mileage interval, it is advised after a high mileage has been covered and particularly if fluid leakage or a sticking caliper action is apparent.

Carburettor models

1 Remove the fuel tank (see Chapter 4A). Check the fuel supply hose, the fuel valve vacuum hose and the fuel tank overflow and breather hoses **(see illustration)**, the crankcase breather hose **(see illustration)**, and the PAIR system hoses (see Section 18), for signs of leaks, deterioration or damage. In particular check that there are no leaks from the fuel hose or hose unions. Make sure each hose is secure on its union at each end and retained by a clamp. Replace any hose that is cracked or deteriorated with a new one (see Chapter 4A for fuel tank and air filter housing removal).

2 Check the fuel tank for signs of fuel leakage. If the joint between the fuel valve and the tank is leaking, ensure the nut is tight, to the torque setting specified if you have the correct tools (see Chapter 4A) **(see illustration)**; if the leak persists remove the valve and apply a suitable sealant to the threads (see Chapter 4A). If the joint between the level sensor and the tank is leaking make sure the nuts are tight; if the leak persists remove the sensor and fit a new O-ring (see Chapter 4A).

3 Inspect the carburettor, particularly around the float chamber on the bottom, for signs

7.1a Check the fuel system hoses (arrowed) . . .

7.1b . . . and the crankcase breather hose (arrowed) for damage

7.2 Fuel valve nut (arrowed)

7.3 Check around the float chamber (arrowed) for signs of fuel leakage

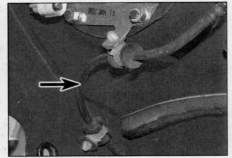

7.6 Inspect the fuel line (arrowed) and its connections

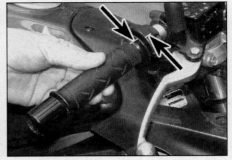

8.4 Throttle cable freeplay is measured in terms of twistgrip rotation

of leakage **(see illustration)**. If there are any leaks, remove the carburettor and fit new seals (see Chapter 4A).

4 Cleaning of the fuel strainer is advised after a particularly high mileage has been covered, although no interval is specified. It is also necessary if fuel starvation is suspected. Remove the fuel valve from the fuel tank to access the strainer (see Chapter 4A). Remove the strainer and flush it through from the inside. Check the gauze for damage and replace it with a new one if necessary. Fit the strainer back onto the valve using a new O-ring.

Fuel injected models

5 Raise the front of the fuel tank and support it as described in Chapter 4B.
6 Inspect the fuel line from the pump base to the throttle body **(see illustration)**. Renew the fuel line if it is cracked, damaged or leaking.
7 Check that there is no sign of leakage from the fuel pump joint with the tank.

8	Throttle and choke cables

Throttle cable

1 With the engine off, make sure the throttle grip rotates smoothly and freely from fully closed to fully open with the front wheel turned at various angles. The grip should return automatically from fully open to fully closed when released.
2 If the throttle sticks, this is probably due to a

cable fault. Remove the cable (see Chapter 4A) and lubricate it (see Section 13). Check that the inner cable slides freely and easily in the outer cable. If not, replace the cable with a new one.
3 With the cable removed, make sure the throttle twistgrip rotates freely on the handlebar – dirt combined with a lack of lubrication can cause the action to be stiff. If necessary, undo the handlebar end-weight screw and remove the weight, then slide the twistgrip off the handlebar. Clean any old grease from the bar and the inside of the tube. Smear some new grease of the specified type onto the bar, then refit the twistgrip. When fitting the end-weight, align the boss with the cut-out on the inner weight inside the handlebar. Clean the threads of the end-weight retaining screw, then apply a suitable non-permanent thread locking compound and tighten it to the torque setting specified at the beginning of the Chapter. Install the cable, making sure it is correctly routed (see Chapter 4A). If this fails to improve the operation of the throttle, the cable must be replaced with a new one. Note that in very rare cases the fault could lie in the carburettor/throttle body (see Chapter 4A or 4B).
4 With the throttle operating smoothly, check for a small amount of freeplay in the cable, measured in terms of the amount of twistgrip rotation before the throttle opens, and compare the amount to that listed in this Chapter's Specifications **(see illustration)**. If it's incorrect, adjust the cable as follows.
5 Initially adjust freeplay using the adjuster in the throttle cable where it leaves the throttle/switch housing on the handlebar. Slide the

rubber boot off the adjuster. Loosen the locknut and turn the adjuster in or out as required until the specified amount of freeplay is obtained (see this Chapter's Specifications), then retighten the locknut and fit the boot **(see illustration)**.
6 If the adjuster has reached its limit of adjustment, reset it to its start point by turning it fully in, so that freeplay is at a maximum, then adjust the cable at the carburettor/throttle body end as follows.
7 Remove the right-hand fairing side panel (see Chapter 8). The adjuster is on the cable bracket. Slacken the adjuster locknut, then screw the adjuster in or out as required, making sure the lower nut remains captive in the bracket, thereby threading itself along the adjuster as you turn it, until the specified amount of freeplay is obtained, then tighten the locknut **(see illustration)**. Subsequent adjustments can be made at the throttle end when required. If the cable cannot be adjusted as specified, replace it with a new one (see Chapter 4A). Check that the throttle twistgrip operates smoothly and snaps shut quickly when released.

> ⚠ **Warning: Turn the handlebars all the way through their travel with the engine idling. Idle speed should not change. If it does, the cable may be routed incorrectly. Correct this condition before riding the bike.**

Choke cable – R-4, R-5 and RW-6 models

8 With the engine off, make sure the choke knob moves smoothly and freely **(see illustration)**.

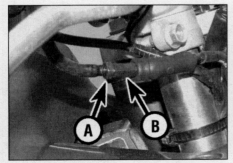

8.5 Slacken the locknut (A) and turn the adjuster (B) as required – throttle end

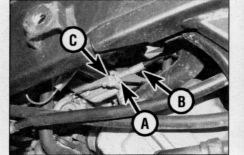

8.7 Throttle cable adjuster locknut (A), adjuster (B) and lower nut (C)

8.8 Check the action of the choke

9.3 Measure the amount of freeplay at the clutch lever end as shown

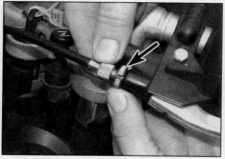

9.4 Slacken the lockring (arrowed) and turn the adjuster in or out as required

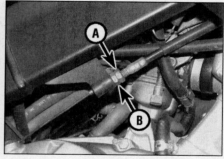

9.8 Slacken the locknut (A) and turn the adjuster nut (B) as required

9 If it is stiff or stuck, this is probably due to a cable fault. Remove the cable (see Chapter 4A) and lubricate it (see Section 13). Check that the inner cable slides freely and easily in the outer cable. If not, replace the cable with a new one.

10 If the choke is still stiff, the fault is in the choke plunger in the carburettor. Remove the carburettor and remove the choke plunger for inspection (see Chapter 4A).

9 Clutch

1 Check that the clutch lever operates smoothly and easily.

2 If the clutch lever operation is heavy or stiff, remove the cable (see Chapter 2) and lubricate it (see Section 13). If the cable is still stiff, replace it with a new one. Install the lubricated or new cable (see Chapter 2).

3 With the cable operating smoothly, check that it is correctly adjusted. Periodic adjustment is necessary to compensate for wear in the clutch plates and stretch of the cable. Check that the amount of freeplay at the clutch lever ball end is within the specifications listed at the beginning of the Chapter **(see illustration)**.

4 If adjustment is required, this can be done first at the lever end of the cable. Loosen the adjuster lockring, then turn the adjuster in or out until the required amount of freeplay is obtained **(see illustration)**. To increase freeplay, thread the adjuster into the lever bracket. To reduce freeplay, thread the adjuster out of the bracket.

5 Make sure that the slot in the adjuster and the lockring, are not aligned with the slot in the lever bracket – these slots are to allow removal of the cable, and if they are all aligned while the bike is in use the cable could jump out. Also make sure the adjuster is not threaded too far out of the bracket so that it is only held by a few threads – this will leave it unstable and the threads could be damaged. Tighten the lockring on completion.

6 If all the adjustment has been taken up at the lever, thread the adjuster all the way into the bracket to give the maximum amount of

freeplay, then back it out one turn – this resets the adjuster to its start point.

7 Now set the correct amount of freeplay using the adjuster at the clutch end of cable. The adjuster is set in a bracket above the clutch cover on the right-hand side of the engine.

8 Slacken the locknut, then turn the adjusting nut as required until freeplay at the lever ball end is as specified **(see illustration)**. To increase freeplay turn the adjusting nut anti-clockwise as you look down at it. To reduce freeplay turn the adjusting nut clockwise as you look down at it. Tighten the locknut on completion. Subsequent adjustments can now be made using the lever adjuster only.

10 Sidestand and starter safety circuit

1 Check the stand springs for damage and distortion **(see illustration)**. The springs must be capable of retracting the stand fully and holding it retracted when the motorcycle is in use. If a spring is sagged or broken it must be replaced with a new one.

2 Lubricate the stand pivot regularly (see Section 13).

3 Check the stand and its mount for bends and cracks. Stands can often be repaired by welding.

4 Check the operation of the starter safety circuit as follows:

● Make sure the transmission is in neutral, then retract the stand and start the engine.

10.1 Check the springs as described

Pull in the clutch lever and select a gear. Extend the sidestand. The engine should stop as the sidestand is extended.

● Make sure the transmission is in neutral and the sidestand is down, then start the engine. Pull the clutch lever in and select a gear. The engine should stop.

● Check that when the sidestand is down the engine can only be started if the transmission is in neutral.

● Check that when the sidestand is up and the transmission is in gear the engine can only be started if the clutch lever is pulled in.

5 If the circuit does not operate as described, check the sidestand switch, neutral switch, clutch switch, diodes, and the circuit wiring between them (see Chapter 9).

11 Suspension

1 The suspension components must be maintained in top operating condition to ensure rider safety. Loose, worn or damaged suspension parts decrease the motorcycle's stability and control.

Front suspension check

2 While standing alongside the motorcycle, apply the front brake and push on the handlebars to compress the forks several times **(see illustration)**. See if they move up-and-down smoothly without binding. If binding is felt, the forks should be disassembled and inspected (see Chapter 6).

11.2 Compress and release the front suspension

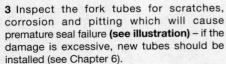

11.3 Check the tube for damage and signs of oil leakage

11.7 Compress and release the rear suspension

3 Inspect the fork tubes for scratches, corrosion and pitting which will cause premature seal failure **(see illustration)** – if the damage is excessive, new tubes should be installed (see Chapter 6).

4 Inspect the area above the dust seal for signs of oil leakage **(see illustration 11.3)**, then carefully lever the seal out using a flat-bladed screwdriver and inspect the area around the fork seal. If leakage is evident, the seals must be replaced with new ones (see Chapter 6). If there is evidence of corrosion between the seal retaining ring and its groove in the fork slider, spray the area with a penetrative lubricant, otherwise the ring will be difficult to remove if needed. Press the dust seal back into the top of the fork tube on completion.

5 Check the tightness of all suspension nuts and bolts to be sure none have worked loose, referring to the torque settings specified at the beginning of Chapter 6.

Rear suspension check

6 Inspect the rear shock absorber for fluid leakage and tightness of its mountings. If leakage is found, the shock must be replaced with a new one (see Chapter 6).

7 With the aid of an assistant to support the bike, compress the rear suspension several times **(see illustration)**. It should move up-and-down freely without binding. If any binding is felt, the worn or faulty component must be identified and checked (see Chapter 6). The problem could be due to either the shock absorber or the swingarm pivot.

8 Support the motorcycle on an auxiliary stand so that the rear wheel is off the ground. Grab the swingarm and rock it from side-to-side – there should be no discernible movement at the rear **(see illustration)**. If there's a little movement or a slight clicking can be heard, inspect the tightness of the swingarm and shock absorber mounting bolts and nuts, referring to the torque settings specified at the beginning of Chapter 6, and re-check for movement.

9 Next, grasp the top of the rear wheel and pull it upwards – there should be no discernible freeplay before the shock absorber begins to compress **(see illustration)**. Any freeplay felt in either check indicates worn bushes in the shock absorber or swingarm. The worn components must be identified and replaced with new ones (see Chapter 6).

10 To make an accurate assessment of the swingarm bushes, remove the rear wheel (see Chapter 7) and the bolt securing the shock absorber to the swingarm (see Chapter 6). Grasp the rear of the swingarm with one hand and place your other hand at the junction of the swingarm and the frame. Try to move the rear of the swingarm from side-to-side. Any wear (play) in the bearings should be felt as movement between the swingarm and the frame at the front. If there is any play, the swingarm will be felt to move forward and backward at the front (not from side-to-side). If there is any play in the swingarm remove it for inspection (see Chapter 6). If the bushes are worn a new swingarm must be fitted as the bushes are not available separately.

Front fork oil change

11 Although there is no set interval for changing the fork oil, note that the oil will degrade over a period of time and lose its damping qualities. Refer to Chapter 6, Sections 6 and 7 for details of front fork removal, oil draining and refilling. The forks do not need to be completely disassembled to change the oil.

Rear suspension lubrication

12 Although there is no set interval, the swingarm pivot bolt should be removed, cleaned and re-greased periodically as necessary (see Chapter 6, Section 12).

12 Wheels and tyres

Wheels

1 Cast wheels are virtually maintenance free, but they should be kept clean and checked periodically for cracks and other damage. Also check the wheel runout and alignment (see Chapter 7). Never attempt to repair damaged cast wheels; they must be replaced with new ones if damaged. Check that the wheel balance weights are fixed firmly to the wheel rim. If you suspect that a weight has fallen off, have the wheel rebalanced by a motorcycle tyre specialist.

11.8 Checking for play in the swingarm bushes

11.9 Checking for play in the rear shock mountings

12.4a Checking for play in the front wheel bearings

12.4b Checking for play in the rear wheel bearings

Tyres

2 Check the tyre condition and tread depth thoroughly – see Pre-ride checks. Check the valve rubber for signs of damage or deterioration and have it renewed if necessary by a tyre fitting specialist. Also, make sure the valve stem cap is in place and tight.

Wheel bearings

3 Wheel bearings will wear over a considerable mileage and should be checked periodically to avoid handling problems.
4 Support the motorcycle upright using

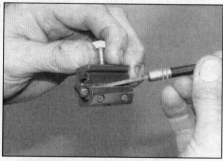

13.3a Fit the cable into the adapter . . .

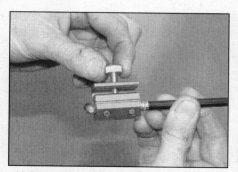

13.3b . . . and tighten the screw to seal it in . . .

an auxiliary stand so that the wheel being examined is off the ground. Check for any play in the bearings by pushing and pulling the wheel against the hub **(see illustrations)**. Also rotate the wheel and check that it turns smoothly and without any grating noises.
5 If any play is detected in the hub, or if the wheel does not rotate smoothly (and this is not due to brake or transmission drag), remove the wheel and inspect the bearings for wear or damage (see Chapter 7).

13 Stand, lever pivot and cable lubrication

Pivot points

1 Since the controls, cables and various other components of a motorcycle are exposed to the elements, they should be checked and lubricated periodically to ensure safe and trouble-free operation.
2 The footrest pivots, clutch and brake lever pivots, brake pedal and gearchange lever linkage and sidestand pivot should be lubricated frequently. In order for the lubricant to be applied where it will do the most good, the component should be disassembled

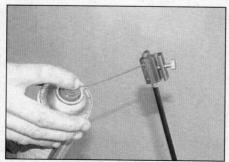

13.3c . . . then apply the lubricant using the nozzle provided inserted in the hole in the adapter

(see Chapter 6). The lubricant recommended by Honda for each application is listed at the beginning of the Chapter. If an aerosol lubricant is used, it can be applied to the pivot joint gaps and will usually work its way into the areas where friction occurs, so less disassembly of the component is needed (however it is always better to do so and clean off all corrosion, dirt and old lubricant first). If motor oil or light grease is being used, apply it sparingly as it may attract dirt (which could cause the controls to bind or wear at an accelerated rate). Note: A good lubricant for the control lever pivots is a dry-film lubricant (available from many sources by different names).

Cables

Special tool: A cable lubricating adapter is necessary for this procedure.
3 To lubricate the cables, disconnect the relevant cable at its upper end, then lubricate it with a pressure adapter and aerosol lubricant **(see illustrations)**. See Chapter 4A for throttle and choke cable removal procedure, and Chapter 2 for the clutch cable.

14 Engine oil and strainer

 Warning: Be careful when draining the oil, as the exhaust pipe, the engine, and the oil itself can cause severe burns.

Oil change

1 Consistent routine oil changes are the single most important maintenance procedure you can perform. The oil not only lubricates the internal parts of the engine, transmission and clutch, but it also acts as a coolant, a cleaner, a sealant, and a protector. Because of these demands, the oil takes a terrific amount of abuse and should

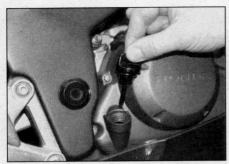

14.3 Unscrew the oil filler cap to act as a vent . . .

14.4a . . . then unscrew the oil drain plug . . .

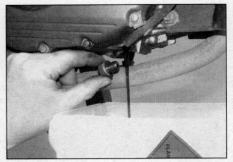

14.4b . . . and allow the oil to completely drain

be replaced as specified with new oil of the recommended grade and type.

 HAYNES HINT *Saving a little money on the difference in cost between a good oil and a cheap oil won't pay off if the engine is damaged.*

2 Before changing the oil, warm up the engine so the oil will drain easily. Place the bike on its sidestand on level ground. The oil drain plug is on the underside of the engine at the front. Remove the lower fairing (See Chapter 8).

3 Position a clean drain tray below the engine. Unscrew the oil filler cap from the clutch cover to vent the crankcase and to act as a reminder that there is no oil in the engine **(see illustration)**.

14.4c The sealing washer may need to be cut off

14.5b . . . and tighten it to the specified torque

4 Unscrew the oil drain plug and allow the oil to flow into the drain tray **(see illustrations)**. Check the condition of the sealing washer on the drain plug and replace it with a new one if it is damaged or worn; you may have to cut the old one off **(see illustration)**.

5 When the oil has completely drained, fit the plug into the engine, preferably using a new sealing washer, and tighten it to the torque setting specified at the beginning of the Chapter **(see illustrations)**. Do not overtighten it as the threads in the engine are easily damaged.

6 Refill the engine to the proper level using the recommended type and amount of oil (see Pre-ride checks). With the motorcycle vertical, the oil level should lie between the upper and lower level lines on the dipstick (see Pre-ride checks). Check the condition of the O-ring on the filler cap and replace it with a new one if it

14.5a Install the drain plug using a new sealing washer . . .

14.12 Withdraw the strainer, noting how it locates in the grooves and how the thin edge faces inwards

is damaged or worn. Install the filler cap **(see illustration 14.3)**.

7 Start the engine and let it run for two or three minutes. Shut it off, wait a few minutes, then check the oil level. If necessary, add more oil to bring the level close to the upper line, but do not go above it.

8 Check around the drain plug that there are no leaks.

9 The old oil drained from the engine cannot be re-used and should be disposed of properly. Check with your local refuse disposal company, disposal facility or environmental agency to see whether they will accept the used oil for recycling. Don't pour used oil into drains or onto the ground.

 HAYNES HINT *Check the old oil carefully – if it is very metallic coloured, then the engine is experiencing wear from break-in (new engine) or from insufficient lubrication. If there are flakes or chips of metal in the oil, then something is drastically wrong internally and the engine will have to be disassembled for inspection and repair. If there are pieces of fibre-like material in the oil, the clutch is experiencing excessive wear and should be checked.*

Strainer

10 Drain the engine oil (see Steps 2 to 5).

11 Remove the clutch cover (see Chapter 2).

12 Withdraw the strainer from its slot in the bottom of the engine, noting which way round it fits **(see illustration)**.

13 Wash the strainer in solvent making sure all debris is removed from the mesh. Check the mesh for holes and damage and replace it with a new one if necessary.

14 Coat the rubber rim of the strainer with clean oil, then slide it into the grooves in its chamber, making sure the thinner edge goes in first.

15 Install the clutch cover (see Chapter 2). Refill the engine with the correct amount of oil (see Steps 6 to 8).

15 Cooling system

Check

 Warning: The engine must be cool before beginning this procedure.

1 Check the coolant level in the reservoir (see Pre-ride checks).

2 Remove the lower fairing and the fairing side panels (see Chapter 8). Check the entire cooling system for evidence of leaks. Examine each rubber coolant hose along its entire length. Look for cracks, abrasions and other damage. Squeeze each hose at various points to see whether they are dried out or hard **(see illustration)**. They should feel firm, yet pliable, and return to their original shape when released. If necessary, replace them with new ones (see Chapter 3).

3 Check for evidence of leaks at each cooling system joint and around the pump on the right-hand side of the engine. Tighten the hose clips carefully to prevent future leaks. If the pump is leaking around the cover, check that the bolts are tight. If they are, remove the cover and replace the O-ring with a new one (see Chapter 3).

4 To prevent leakage of coolant from the cooling system to the lubrication system and vice versa, two seals are fitted on the pump shaft. On the front of the engine below the pump housing there is a drain hose **(see illustration)**. If either seal fails, the drain allows the coolant or oil to escape and prevents them mixing. The seal on the water pump side is of the mechanical type which bears on the rear face of the impeller. The second seal, which is mounted behind the mechanical seal is of the normal feathered lip type. If on inspection the drain shows signs of leakage remove the pump, and fit a new mechanical seal if there is coolant leakage, and a new oil seal as well if there is oil leakage or if the leakage is an emulsion-like mix of coolant and oil (see Chapter 3).

5 Check the radiator for leaks and other damage. Leaks in the radiator leave tell-tale scale deposits or coolant stains on the outside

15.2 Check all the coolant hoses as described

of the core below the leak. If leaks are noted, remove the radiator (see Chapter 3) and have it repaired or replace it with a new one – do not use a liquid leak stopping compound to try to repair leaks.

6 Check the radiator fins for mud, dirt and insects, which may impede the flow of air through the radiator. If the fins are dirty, remove the radiator (see Chapter 3) and clean it using water or low pressure compressed air directed through the fins from the inner side of the radiator. If the fins are bent or distorted, straighten them carefully with a screwdriver **(see illustration)**. If airflow is restricted by bent or damaged fins over more than 20% of the radiator's surface area, replace the radiator with a new one.

 Warning: Do not remove the pressure cap when the engine is hot. It is good practice to cover the cap with a heavy cloth and turn the cap slowly anti-clockwise. If you hear a hissing sound (indicating that there is still pressure in the system), wait until it stops, then continue turning the cap until it can be removed.

7 Remove the pressure cap from the radiator filler neck by undoing the locking screw, then turning the cap anti-clockwise until it reaches the stop **(see illustration)**. Now press down on the cap and continue turning it until it can be removed **(see illustration)**.

8 Check the condition of the coolant in the system. If it is rust-coloured or if accumulations of scale are visible, drain, flush and refill the system with new coolant (see below). Check

15.4 Check the pump drain hose (arrowed) for signs of leakage

the cap seal for cracks and other damage. If in doubt about the pressure cap's condition, have it tested by a Honda dealer or fit a new one.

9 Check the antifreeze content of the coolant with an antifreeze hydrometer. If the system has not been topped-up with the correct coolant mixture (see Pre-ride checks) the coolant will be too weak to offer adequate protection. If the hydrometer indicates a weak mixture, drain, flush and refill the system (see below).

10 Fit the cap by turning it clockwise until it reaches the first stop then push down on it and continue turning until it can turn no further. Tighten the locking screw **(see illustration 15.7a)**. Start the engine and let it reach normal operating temperature, then check for leaks again. As the coolant temperature increases, the electric fan (mounted on the back of the radiator) should come on automatically and the temperature should begin to drop. If it does not, refer to Chapter 3 and check the fan, fan switch and fan circuit.

11 If the coolant level is consistently low, and no evidence of leaks can be found, have the entire system pressure checked by a Honda dealer.

Change the coolant

 Warning: Allow the engine to cool completely before performing this maintenance operation. Also, don't allow anti-freeze to come into contact with your skin or the painted surfaces of the motorcycle. Rinse

15.6 Straighten any fins which are bent

15.7a Undo the locking screw . . .

15.7b . . . and remove the pressure cap as described

15.13 Remove the cap from the reservoir

15.14a Unscrew the drain bolt . . .

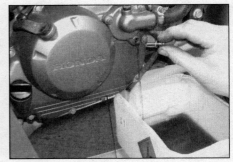

15.14b . . . and allow the coolant to drain

off spills immediately with plenty of water. Anti-freeze is highly toxic if ingested. Never leave anti-freeze lying around in an open container or in puddles on the floor; children and pets are attracted by its sweet smell and may drink it. Check with local authorities (councils) about disposing of anti-freeze. Many communities have collection centres which will see that anti-freeze is disposed of safely. Anti-freeze is also combustible, so don't store it near open flames.

Draining

12 Support the motorcycle upright on a level surface using an auxiliary stand. Remove the rider's seat, the lower fairing and the right-hand fairing side panel (see Chapter 8).

13 Remove the pressure cap from the top of the radiator by undoing the locking screw, then turning the cap anti-clockwise until it reaches a stop **(see illustration 15.7a)**. If you hear a hissing sound (indicating there is still pressure in the system), wait until it stops. Now press down on the cap and continue turning the cap until it can be removed **(see illustration 15.7b)**. Also remove the coolant reservoir cap **(see illustration)**.

14 Position a suitable container beneath the water pump on the right-hand side of the engine. Unscrew the drain bolt and allow the coolant to completely drain from the system **(see illustrations)**. Retain the old sealing washer for use during flushing.

15 Release the clamp and disconnect the overflow hose from the back of the radiator

filler neck and place it in the container to allow the reservoir to drain **(see illustration)**.

Flushing

16 Flush the system with clean tap water by inserting a hose in the radiator filler neck. Allow the water to run through the system until it is clear and flows out cleanly. If the radiator is extremely corroded, remove it (see Chapter 3) and have it cleaned by a specialist. Also flush the reservoir, then fit the radiator overflow hose back onto the filler neck.

17 Clean the drain hole in the water pump then install the drain bolt using the old sealing washer **(see illustration 15.23)**.

18 Using a suitable funnel inserted from the top, between the fuel tank and the fairing, fill the system to the base of the radiator filler neck with clean water mixed with a flushing compound **(see illustration 15.24)**. Make sure the flushing compound is compatible with aluminium components, and follow the manufacturer's instructions carefully. If you don't have a suitable funnel remove the fairing (see Chapter 8). Fit the radiator cap.

19 Start the engine and allow it to reach normal operating temperature. Let it run for about ten minutes.

20 Stop the engine. Let it cool for a while, then cover the pressure cap with a heavy rag and turn it anti-clockwise to the first stop, releasing any pressure that may be present in the system. Once the hissing stops, push down on the cap and remove it completely.

21 Drain the system once again.

22 Fill the system with clean water, then fit the radiator cap and repeat Steps 19 to 21.

Refilling

23 Install the drain bolt using a new sealing washer and tighten it **(see illustration)**.

24 Using a suitable funnel inserted from the top between the fuel tank and the fairing, fill the system to the base of the radiator filler neck with the proper coolant mixture (see this Chapter's Specifications) **(see illustration)**.
Note: *Pour the coolant in slowly to minimise the amount of air entering the system.* If you don't have a suitable funnel remove the fairing (see Chapter 8). Fill the reservoir to the UPPER level line (see Pre-ride checks). Carefully shake the bike to dislodge any trapped air.

25 Start the engine and allow it to idle for 2 to 3 minutes. Flick the throttle twistgrip part open 3 or 4 times, so that the engine speed rises to approximately 4000 to 5000 rpm, then stop the engine. Any air trapped in the system should bleed back to the radiator filler neck.

26 If necessary, top up the coolant level to the base of the radiator filler neck, then install the pressure cap. Also top up the coolant reservoir to the UPPER level line.

27 Start the engine and allow it to reach normal operating temperature, then shut it off. Let the engine cool then remove the pressure cap as described in Step 13. Check that the coolant level is still up to the base of the radiator filler neck. If it's low, add the specified mixture until it reaches the base of the filler neck. Refit the cap and tighten the locking screw.

15.15 Detach the hose (arrowed) and allow the reservoir to drain

15.23 Use a new sealing washer on the drain bolt

15.24 Fill the system slowly

28 Check the coolant level in the reservoir and top up if necessary.

29 Check the system for leaks. Install the fairing panels and seat (see Chapter 8).

30 Do not dispose of the old coolant by pouring it down the drain. Instead pour it into a heavy plastic container, cap it tightly and take it into an authorised disposal site or service station – see Warning at the beginning of this sub-Section.

Hose renewal

31 The hoses will deteriorate with age and should be replaced with new ones regardless of their apparent condition (see Chapter 3).

16 Nuts and bolts

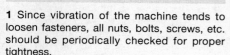

1 Since vibration of the machine tends to loosen fasteners, all nuts, bolts, screws, etc. should be periodically checked for proper tightness.

2 Pay particular attention to the following, referring to the relevant Chapter:

Spark plug
Engine oil drain plug
Lever and pedal bolts
Footrest and sidestand bolts
Engine mounting bolts/nuts
Shock absorber bolts/nut; swingarm pivot bolt/nut
Handlebar clamp bolts
Front fork clamp bolts (top and bottom yoke) and fork top bolts

Steering stem nut
Front axle nut
Rear axle nut
Front and rear sprocket bolts/nuts
Brake caliper and master cylinder mounting bolts
Brake hose banjo bolts and caliper bleed valves
Brake disc bolts
Exhaust system bolts/nuts

3 If a torque wrench is available, use it along with the torque settings given at the beginning of this and other Chapters.

17 Steering head bearings

Freeplay check and adjustment

1 Steering head bearings can become dented, rough or loose during normal use of the machine. In extreme cases, worn or loose steering head bearings can cause steering wobble – a condition that is potentially dangerous.

Check

2 Remove the lower fairing (see Chapter 8). Raise the front wheel off the ground using an auxiliary stand placed under the engine. Always make sure that the bike is properly supported and secure.

3 Point the front wheel straight-ahead and slowly move the handlebars from lock to lock. Any dents or roughness in the bearing races

will be felt and if the bearings are too tight the bars will not move smoothly and freely. Again point the wheel straight-ahead, and tap the front of the wheel to one side. The wheel should 'fall' under its own weight to the limit of its lock, indicating that the bearings are not too tight (take into account the restriction that cables and wiring may have). Check for similar movement to the other side.

4 If available, attach one end of a spring balance (graduated zero to 30 N) around the fork, and hold it at right-angles to the line between the two forks. With the steering straight-ahead, pull on the balance and check the reading at which the steering starts to turn **(see illustration)**. If the reading is below the minimum value specified in the pre-load range given in the Specifications at the beginning of the Chapter, the steering head is too loose, if the reading is above the maximum value specified the steering head is too tight. If the steering doesn't perform as described, and it's not due to the resistance of cables or hoses, then the bearings should be adjusted as described below.

5 Next, grasp the bottom of the forks and gently pull and push them forward and backward **(see illustration)**. Any looseness or freeplay in the steering head bearings will be felt as front-to-rear movement of the forks. If play is felt, adjust the bearings as described below.

 Make sure you are not mistaking any movement between the bike and stand, or between the stand and the ground, for freeplay in the bearings. Do not pull and push the forks too hard – a gentle movement is all that is needed. Freeplay between the fork slider and the fork tube due to worn bushes can also be misinterpreted as steering head bearing play – do not confuse the two.

Adjustment

Special tool: *A C-spanner will be required to locate in the notches of the bearing adjuster nut.*

6 As a precaution, remove the fuel tank (see Chapter 4A or 4B) and the fairing (see Chapter 8). Though not actually necessary, this will

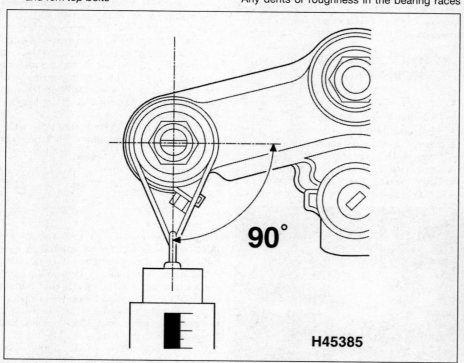

17.4 Steering head bearing tension check

H45385

17.5 Checking for play in the steering head bearings

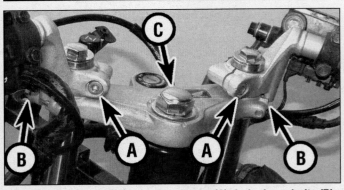

17.7 Slacken the handlebar clamp bolts (A), fork clamp bolts (B), and remove the steering stem nut (C)

17.8 Steering head bearing adjuster nut (shown with top yoke removed)

prevent the possibility of damage should a tool slip. Raise the front wheel off the ground using an auxiliary stand placed under the engine. Always make sure that the bike is properly supported and secure.

7 Slacken the handlebar clamp bolts and the fork clamp bolts in the top yoke, then remove the steering stem nut and its washer **(see illustration)**. Ease the top yoke upwards by just enough to gain access to the bearing adjuster nut.

8 Using either a C-spanner or a suitable drift located in one of the notches in the adjuster nut, turn the adjuster nut clockwise to tighten the head bearings or anti-clockwise to loosen them, and only moving it a small amount at a time **(see illustration)**. After each small adjustment recheck the freeplay as described above (Steps 3 to 5), before making further adjustments. The object is to set the adjuster nut so that the bearings are under a very light loading, just enough to remove any freeplay, but not so much that the steering does not move freely from side-to-side. If you have a spring balance (see Step 4), set the adjuster nut so that the steering starts to move at around the mid-point of the pre-load range given in the Specifications at the beginning of the Chapter.

Caution: Take great care not to apply excessive pressure because this will cause premature failure of the bearings.

9 If the bearings cannot be correctly adjusted, disassemble the steering head and check the bearings and races for wear (see Chapter 6, Sections 9 and 10).

10 With the bearings correctly adjusted, move the top yoke back into position and fit the steering stem nut and its washer. Tighten the steering stem nut, then the fork clamp bolts to the torque settings specified at the beginning of the chapter **(see illustration 17.7)**. Make sure the handlebars are correctly aligned by pulling them back against the stops then tighten the handlebar clamp bolts to the specified torque.

11 Check the bearing adjustment as described above and re-adjust if necessary.

12 Install the fuel tank (see Chapter 4A or 4B) and the fairing (see Chapter 8) if removed.

Lubrication

13 Over a considerable time the grease in the bearings will be dispersed or will harden allowing the ingress of dirt and water.

14 The steering head should be disassembled periodically and the bearings cleaned and re-greased (see Chapter 6, Sections 9 and 10).

18 PAIR (Pulse secondary air supply) system

1 To reduce the amount of unburned hydrocarbons released in the exhaust gases, a pulse secondary air supply (PAIR) system is fitted to carburettor models. The system consists of the control valve (mounted under the fuel tank), the reed valve (fitted in the valve cover) and the hoses linking them. The control valve is actuated by a vacuum taken off the intake duct between the carburettor and the cylinder head and transmitted by hose. Air is sourced from a hose connected to the frame, and is drawn through a filter fitted in line with the hose.

2 Under certain operating conditions, the vacuum in the hose opens up the PAIR control valve which then allows filtered air to be drawn through it and the reed valve and cylinder head passage and into the exhaust port. The air mixes with the exhaust gases, causing any unburned particles of fuel in the mixture to be burnt in the exhaust port/pipe. This process changes a considerable amount of hydrocarbons and carbon monoxide into relatively harmless carbon dioxide and water. The reed valve in the valve cover is fitted to prevent the flow of exhaust gases back up the cylinder head passage and into the air filter housing.

3 The system is not adjustable and requires little maintenance. Remove the fuel tank to access and inspect the components (see Chapter 4A). Check that the hoses are not kinked or pinched, are in good condition and are securely connected at each end **(see illustration)**. Replace any hoses that are cracked, split or generally deteriorated with new ones. Make sure the filter is not clogged **(see illustration)**.

4 Refer to Chapter 4A for further information on the system and for checks if it is believed to be faulty.

19 Battery

1 All models covered in this manual are fitted with a sealed MF (maintenance free) battery. Note: Do not attempt to remove the battery caps – removal will damage the caps, resulting in electrolyte leakage and battery damage. All that should be done is to check that the terminals are clean and tight and that the casing is not damaged or leaking. See Chapter 9 for further details.

2 If the machine is not in regular use, disconnect the battery and give it a refresher charge every month to six weeks or invest in a trickle charger (see Chapter 9).

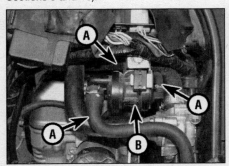

18.3a Check the PAIR system hoses (A) as described. PAIR control valve (B) . . .

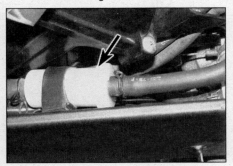

18.3b . . . and air filter (arrowed)

Chapter 2
Engine, clutch and transmission

Contents

Degrees of difficulty

| Easy, suitable for novice with little experience | | Fairly easy, suitable for beginner with some experience | | Fairly difficult, suitable for competent DIY mechanic | | Difficult, suitable for experienced DIY mechanic | | Very difficult, suitable for expert DIY or professional | |

Specifications

General

Type	Four-stroke single
Capacity	124.7 cc
Bore	58.0 mm
Stroke	47.2 mm
Compression ratio	11.0 to 1
Cylinder compression	195 psi (13.7 Bar) @ 530 rpm
Cooling system	Liquid cooled
Lubrication	Wet sump, trochoid pump
Clutch	Wet multi-plate
Transmission	Six-speed constant mesh
Final drive	Chain

Cylinder head

Warpage (max)	0.05 mm

Camshafts and rocker arms

Intake lobe height
  Standard . . . . 29.4556 to 29.5366 mm
  Service limit (min) . . . . 29.05 mm
Exhaust lobe height
  Standard . . . . 29.3756 to 29.4556 mm
  Service limit (min) . . . . 28.85 mm
Runout (max) . . . . 0.02 mm
Rocker arm bore diameter
  Standard . . . . 10.000 to 10.015 mm
  Service limit (min) . . . . 10.10 mm
Rocker arm shaft diameter
  Standard . . . . 9.972 to 9.987 mm
  Service limit (min) . . . . 9.75 mm
Rocker arm-to-shaft clearance
  Standard . . . . 0.013 to 0.043 mm
  Service limit (min) . . . . 0.10 mm

Valves, guides and springs

Valve clearances . . . . see Chapter 1
Stem diameter
  Intake valve
    Standard . . . . 4.975 to 4.990 mm
    Service limit (min) . . . . 4.863 mm
  Exhaust valve
    Standard . . . . 4.965 to 4.980 mm
    Service limit (min) . . . . 4.853 mm
Guide bore diameter – intake and exhaust valves
  Standard . . . . 5.000 to 5.012 mm
  Service limit (max) . . . . 5.040 mm
Stem-to-guide clearance
  Intake valve
    Standard . . . . 0.010 to 0.037 mm
    Service limit . . . . 0.065 mm
  Exhaust valve
    Standard . . . . 0.020 to 0.047 mm
    Service limit . . . . 0.075 mm
Seat width – intake and exhaust valves
  Standard . . . . 0.90 to 1.10 mm
  Service limit (max) . . . . 1.50 mm
Valve guide height above cylinder head
  Intake valve . . . . 11.5 to 11.7 mm
  Exhaust valve . . . . 12.3 to 12.5 mm
Valve spring free length– intake and exhaust valves
  Inner spring
    Standard . . . . 33.5 mm
    Service limit (min) . . . . 31.0 mm
  Outer spring
    Standard . . . . 35.7 mm
    Service limit (min) . . . . 34.0 mm

Cylinder bore

Bore
  Standard . . . . 58.000 to 58.0105 mm
  Service limit (max) . . . . 58.05 mm
Warpage (max) . . . . 0.05 mm
Ovality (out-of-round) (max) . . . . 0.010 mm
Taper (max) . . . . 0.010 mm

Piston

	Standard	Service limit (min)
Piston diameter (measured 6.5 mm up from skirt, at 90° to piston pin axis)	57.97 to 57.99 mm	56.67 mm
Piston-to-bore clearance	0.01 to 0.04 mm	0.65 mm*
Piston pin diameter	12.994 to 13.000 mm	12.70 mm
Piston pin bore diameter in piston	13.002 to 13.008 mm	13.045 mm
Piston pin-to-piston pin bore clearance	0.002 to 0.014 mm	0.075 mm

If the piston-to-bore clearance exceeds the service limit, the cylinder can be rebored – Honda supply +0.25, +0.50, +0.75 and +1.00 oversize pistons and rings. Following rebore, the piston-to-bore clearance must be as standard for a normal piston

Piston rings

Ring end gap (installed)
  Top ring
    Standard . . . .   0.10 to 0.25 mm
    Service limit (max) . . . .   0.40 mm
  Second ring
    Standard . . . .   0.35 to 0.50 mm
    Service limit (max) . . . .   0.70 mm
  Oil ring side-rail
    Standard . . . .   0.20 to 0.70 mm
    Service limit (max) . . . .   1.1 mm
Ring-to-groove clearance
  Top ring
    Standard . . . .   0.045 to 0.075 mm
    Service limit (max) . . . .   0.10 mm
  Second ring
    Standard . . . .   0.015 to 0.050 mm
    Service limit (max) . . . .   0.09 mm

Starter clutch

Starter driven gear hub OD
  Standard . . . .   39.622 to 39.635 mm
  Service limit (min) . . . .   38.734 mm

Clutch

Friction plates   5
Plain plates   4
Friction plate thickness
  Type A (outer plate)
    Standard . . . .   3.50 to 3.60 mm
    Service limit (min) . . . .   3.42 mm
  Type B (inner plates)
    Standard . . . .   2.92 to 3.08 mm
    Service limit (min) . . . .   2.85 mm
Plain plate warpage (max) . . . .   0.15 mm
Spring free length
  Standard . . . .   40.0 mm
  Service limit (min) . . . .   39.1 mm
Clutch housing ID
  Standard . . . .   23.000 to 23.021 mm
  Service limit (min) . . . .   23.54 mm
Clutch guide OD
  Standard . . . .   22.959 to 22.980 mm
  Service limit (min) . . . .   22.93 mm
Clutch guide ID
  Standard . . . .   16.991 to 17.009 mm
  Service limit (max) . . . .   17.04 mm
Input shaft OD at clutch guide
  Standard . . . .   16.966 to 16.984 mm
  Service limit (max) . . . .   16.586 mm

Primary drive gear

Gear backlash . . . .   0.010 to 0.050 mm

Oil pump

Inner rotor tip-to-outer rotor clearance (max) . . . .   0.15 mm
Outer rotor-to-body clearance
  Standard . . . .   0.15 to 0.21 mm
  Service limit (max) . . . .   0.26 mm
Rotor end-float
  Standard . . . .   0.05 to 0.10 mm
  Service limit (max) . . . .   0.12 mm

Crankshaft

Runout (max) . . . .   0.03 mm

Balancer shaft

Gear backlash . . . .   0.015 to 0.068 mm

Connecting rod

Small-end internal diameter
  Standard . . . . 13.016 to 13.034 mm
  Service limit (max) . . . . 13.06 mm
Small-end-to-piston pin clearance
  Standard . . . . 0.016 to 0.040 mm
  Service limit . . . . 0.10 mm
Big-end side clearance
  Standard . . . . 0.40 to 0.60 mm
  Service limit (max) . . . . 0.85 mm
Big-end radial clearance
  Standard . . . . 0.006 to 0.014 mm
  Service limit (max) . . . . 0.05 mm

Selector drum and forks

Selector fork end thickness
  Standard . . . . 4.93 to 5.00 mm
  Service limit (min) . . . . 4.82 mm
Selector fork bore ID
  Standard . . . . 10.000 to 10.018 mm
  Service limit (max) . . . . 10.03 mm
Selector fork shaft OD
  Standard . . . . 9.986 to 9.995 mm
  Service limit (min) . . . . 9.93 mm
Selector drum right-hand journal OD
  Standard . . . . 25.959 to 25.980 mm
  Service limit (min) . . . . 25.90 mm
Selector drum bore ID in right-hand crankcase
  Standard . . . . 26.000 to 26.021 mm
  Service limit (max) . . . . 26.50 mm

Transmission

Gear ratios (no. of teeth)
  Primary reduction . . . . 3.350 to 1 (67/20T)
  Final reduction . . . . 2.800 to 1 (42/15T)
  1st gear . . . . 3.455 to 1 (38/11T)
  2nd gear . . . . 1.941 to 1 (33/17T)
  3rd gear . . . . 1.450 to 1 (29/20T)
  4th gear . . . . 1.174 to 1 (27/23T)
  5th gear . . . . 1.041 to 1 (25/24T)
  6th gear . . . . 0.923 to 1 (24/26T)
Input shaft 5th and 6th gears ID
  Standard . . . . 17.016 to 17.034 mm
  Service limit (max) . . . . 17.08 mm
Input shaft OD at 5th gear point
  Standard . . . . 16.966 to 16.984 mm
  Service limit (min) . . . . 16.93 mm
Input shaft-to-gear clearance at 5th gear point
  Standard . . . . 0.032 to 0.068 mm
  Service limit (max) . . . . 0.10 mm
Output shaft 1st gear ID
  Standard . . . . 18.000 to 18.021 mm
  Service limit (max) . . . . 18.07 mm
Output shaft 2nd gear ID
  Standard . . . . 23.020 to 23.041 mm
  Service limit (max) . . . . 23.09 mm
Output shaft 3rd and 4th gears ID
  Standard . . . . 22.020 to 22.041 mm
  Service limit (max) . . . . 22.09 mm
Output shaft 1st gear bush OD
  Standard . . . . 17.959 to 17.980 mm
  Service limit (min) . . . . 17.9 mm
Output shaft 2nd gear bush OD
  Standard . . . . 22.984 to 23.005 mm
  Service limit (min) . . . . 22.47 mm
Output shaft 1st gear gear-to-bush clearance
  Standard . . . . 0.020 to 0.062 mm
  Service limit (max) . . . . 0.10 mm

Transmission (continued)

Output shaft 2nd gear gear-to-bush clearance
    Standard . . . . 0.015 to 0.057 mm
    Service limit (max) . . . . 0.10 mm
Output shaft 1st gear bush ID
    Standard . . . . 15.000 to 15.018 mm
    Service limit (max) . . . . 15.10 mm
Output shaft 2nd gear bush ID
    Standard . . . . 20.020 to 20.041 mm
    Service limit (max) . . . . 20.10 mm
Output shaft OD at 1st gear bush point
    Standard . . . . 14.966 to 14.984 mm
    Service limit (min) . . . . 14.90 mm
Output shaft OD at 2nd gear bush point
    Standard . . . . 19.978 to 19.989 mm
    Service limit (min) . . . . 19.92 mm
Output shaft-to-bushing clearance at 1st gear bush point
    Standard . . . . 0.016 to 0.052 mm
    Service limit (max) . . . . 0.10 mm
Output shaft-to-bushing clearance at 2nd gear bush point
    Standard . . . . 0.031 to 0.063 mm
    Service limit (max) . . . . 0.10 mm

Torque settings

Camshaft holder nuts . . . . 29 Nm
Camshaft sprocket bolts . . . . 9 Nm
Clutch nut . . . . 74 Nm
Crankcase bolts
    Large head bolts (right-hand side) . . . . 12 Nm
    Small head bolts (left-hand side) . . . . 10 Nm
Crankshaft end cap . . . . 8 Nm
Engine mounting bolt nuts . . . . 60 Nm
Front sprocket bolts . . . . 10 Nm
Gearchange mechanism stopper arm bolt . . . . 12 Nm
Oil pump cover bolts . . . . 5 Nm
Primary drive gear nut . . . . 64 Nm
Rocker shaft stopper bolts . . . . 9 Nm
Selector drum cam plate bolt . . . . 12 Nm
Starter clutch bolts . . . . 30 Nm
Timing inspection cap . . . . 6 Nm
Valve cover bolts . . . . 10 Nm

1 General information

The engine/transmission unit is a liquid-cooled single cylinder of unit construction. The two valves are operated by rocker arms actuated by a single overhead camshaft which is chain driven off the left-hand end of the crankshaft. The crankcase divides vertically.

The crankcase incorporates a wet sump, pressure-fed lubrication system which uses a single rotor trochoidal oil pump that is gear-driven off the primary drive gear on the right-hand end of the crankshaft. Oil is filtered by a strainer in the bottom of the crankcase.

The alternator is on the left-hand end of the crankshaft. The ignition timing trigger is on the outside of the alternator rotor, and the pulse generator coil is mounted in the alternator cover along with the stator.

The water pump is on the right-hand side of the engine, and is gear driven off the primary drive gear on the right-hand end of the crankshaft.

Power from the crankshaft is routed to the transmission via the clutch. The clutch is of the wet, multi-plate type and is gear-driven off the crankshaft. The clutch is operated by cable. The transmission is a six-speed constant-mesh unit. Final drive to the rear wheel is by chain and sprockets.

2 Component access

Operations possible with the engine in the frame

The components and assemblies listed below can be removed without having to remove the engine from the frame. If however, a number of areas require attention at the same time, removal of the engine is recommended.

Valve cover
Cam chain, tensioner and blades
Camshaft and rockers
Cylinder head
Cylinder barrel and piston
Clutch
Gearchange mechanism
Alternator
Starter clutch
Oil pump and oil strainer
Starter motor
Water pump

Operations requiring engine removal

It is necessary to remove the engine from the frame to gain access to the following components.

Crankshaft, connecting rod and bearings
Balancer shaft
Transmission shafts and bearings
Selector drum and forks

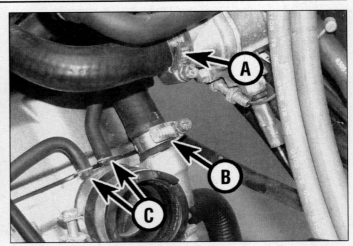

4.7a Detach the hoses (arrowed) from the water pump cover ...

4.7b ... thermostat cover (A) and cylinder head (B). Vacuum hoses (C)

3 Compression test

Special tool: *A compression gauge is required to perform this test.*

1 Poor engine performance may be caused by leaking valves, incorrect valve clearances, a leaking head gasket, a worn piston, worn piston rings or worn cylinder walls. A cylinder compression check will highlight these conditions.

2 The only tools required are a compression gauge (there are two types, one with a 10 mm threaded adapter to fit the spark plug hole in the cylinder head, the other has a rubber seal which is pressed into the spark plug hole to create a seal – the threaded adapter type is preferable), and a spark plug socket. Depending on the outcome of the initial test, a squirt-type oil can may also be needed.

3 Make sure the valve clearances are correctly set (see Chapter 1) and that the camshaft holder nuts are tightened to the correct torque setting (see Section 8).

4 Run the engine until it is at normal operating temperature. Remove the spark plug (see Chapter 1). Fit the plug back into the plug cap and ground the plug against the engine away from the plug hole – if the plug is not grounded the ignition system could be damaged.

5 Fit the gauge into the spark plug hole – if the rubber cone type is used keep the gauge pressed hard onto the hole throughout the test to maintain a good seal.

6 With the ignition switch ON, the throttle held fully open and the spark plug grounded, turn the engine over on the starter motor until the gauge reading has built up and stabilised.

7 Compare the reading on the gauge to the cylinder compression figure specified at the beginning of the Chapter (under General specifications).

8 If the reading is low, it could be due to a worn cylinder bore, piston or rings, failure of the head gasket, or worn valve seats. To determine which is the cause, pour a small quantity of engine oil into the spark plug hole to seal the rings, then repeat the compression test. If the figures are noticeably higher the cause is worn cylinder, piston or rings. If there is no change the cause is a leaking head gasket or worn valve seats.

9 Although unlikely, if the reading is high there could be a build-up of carbon deposits in the combustion chamber. Remove the cylinder head and scrape all deposits off the piston and the cylinder head.

4 Engine removal and installation

Caution: The engine is heavy. Engine removal and installation should be carried out with the aid of an assistant; personal injury or damage could occur if the engine falls or is dropped.

Removal

1 Support the bike either on its sidestand or using an auxiliary stand, making sure it is on level ground. Work can be made easier by raising the machine to a suitable working height on an hydraulic ramp or a suitable platform. Make sure the motorcycle is secure and will not topple over, and tie the front brake lever to the handlebar to prevent it rolling forwards.

2 Remove the lower fairing and fairing side panels, and to avoid the possibility of damage the fairing (see Chapter 8).

3 If the engine is dirty, particularly around its mountings, wash it thoroughly. This will make work much easier and rule out the possibility of caked on lumps of dirt falling into some vital component.

4 Drain the engine oil and coolant (see Chapter 1).

5 Disconnect the negative (–ve) lead from the battery (see Chapter 9).

6 Remove the fuel tank and the air filter housing (Chapter 4A or 4B). Either remove the carburettor/throttle body completely, or fully slacken the clamp screw securing it to the cylinder head intake duct, noting the orientation of the clamp, and ease the carburettor/throttle body out of the rubber leaving its cables and hoses still connected. Either way, plug the engine intake duct with clean rag to prevent contamination.

7 Release the clamps securing the cooling system hoses to the water pump cover, thermostat housing cover and cylinder head and detach them, noting their positions and routing **(see illustrations)**. Remove the radiator along with its hoses, noting their routing (see Chapter 3).

8 Remove the exhaust system (see Chapter 4A).

9 Pull the spark plug cap off the plug and secure it clear of the engine **(see illustration)**.

10 Detach the PAIR control valve vacuum hose and the fuel valve vacuum hose from the intake duct **(see illustration 4.7b)**. Also

4.9 Pull the cap off the spark plug

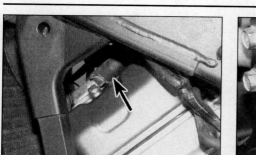

4.10 Detach the hose (arrowed) from the valve cover

4.11a Detach the lead from the starter motor terminal . . .

4.11b . . . and the mounting bolt

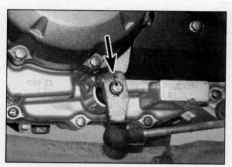

4.12a Make an alignment mark on the shaft (arrowed) . . .

4.12b . . . then unscrew the bolt and slide the arm off

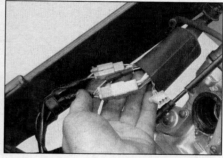

4.14 Free the wiring and disconnect the connectors

detach the PAIR air supply hose from the valve cover **(see illustration)**. Remove the fuel valve vacuum hose, noting its routing.

11 If required, remove the starter motor (see Chapter 9). Alternatively it can be left in place on the engine; pull back the rubber cover on its terminal, then unscrew the nut and disconnect the lead – spray it with some penetrating fluid first if it is corroded **(see illustration)**. Also unscrew the mounting bolt securing the earth lead and detach the lead **(see illustration)**.

12 Make a mark where the slot in the gearchange linkage arm aligns with the shaft **(see illustration)**. Unscrew the linkage arm pinch bolt and slide the arm off the shaft **(see illustration)**.

13 Remove the front sprocket (see Chap-

ter 7). Lay the drive chain against the front of the swingarm.

14 Free the wiring loom from the clip on the inside of the frame on the left-hand side, then draw the rubber boot off the connectors and disconnect the sidestand switch (green 2-pin) wiring connector, the alternator (natural 6-pin) wiring connector, and the neutral switch wiring connector **(see illustration)**. Free the sidestand switch wiring from the clip on the back of the engine and secure the wiring clear.

15 Slacken the locknut on the clutch cable adjuster, then thread the locknut and adjuster nut fully up the adjuster **(see illustration)**. Free the cable end from the release arm (create more slack if required using the adjuster on

the clutch lever bracket – see Chapter 1) then draw the cable forward out of the bracket **(see illustrations)**. Position the cable clear of the engine.

16 Position an hydraulic or mechanical jack under the engine with a block of wood between the jack head and sump. Make sure the jack is centrally positioned so the engine will not topple in any direction when the last mounting bolt is removed. Raise the jack to take the weight of the engine, but make sure it is not lifting the bike and taking the weight of that as well. The idea is to support the engine so that there is no pressure on any of the mounting bolts once they have been slackened, so they can be easily withdrawn. Note that it may be necessary to alter the position of the jack as

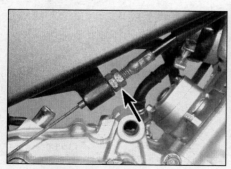

4.15a Thread the nuts (arrowed) up the adjuster . . .

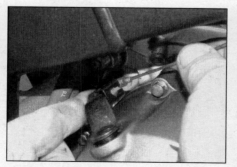

4.15b . . . then detach the cable end . . .

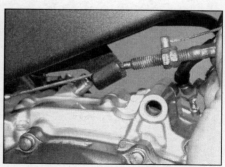

4.15c . . . and draw the cable out

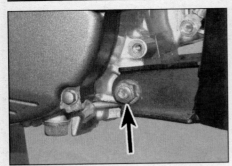

4.17a Unscrew the nut (arrowed) . . .

4.17b . . . and withdraw the bolt

4.17c Unscrew the bolts and remove the two hangers

some of the bolts are removed to relieve the stress transferred to the other bolts.

17 Unscrew the nut on the right-hand end of the engine front mounting bolt then withdraw the bolt **(see illustrations)**. Unscrew the bolts securing the engine hangers to the frame and remove them, noting how they fit **(see illustration)**.

18 Unscrew the nuts on the right-hand ends of the engine upper and lower rear mounting bolts **(see illustration)**.

19 Check that the engine is properly supported by the jack. Withdraw the upper and lower rear mounting bolts from the left-hand side **(see illustration)**.

20 The engine can now be removed from the frame (see **Caution** above). Check that all wiring, cables and hoses are free and clear, then carefully lower the jack and manoeuvre the engine clear. Fully lower the jack, then with the aid of an assistant remove the jack from under the engine and remove the engine.

Installation

Note: *It is advised to smear copper grease onto the engine mounting bolt shafts, not the threads, to prevent the possibility of them seizing in the engine or frame due to corrosion.*

21 Manoeuvre the engine into position under the frame and lift it onto the jack. Raise the engine to align all the mounting bolt holes, making sure that all cables and wiring are correctly routed and do not get trapped. Note that it may be necessary to adjust the jack as some of the bolts are installed to realign the other bolt holes.

22 Install the upper and lower rear mounting bolts from the left-hand side, then fit their nuts and tighten them finger-tight **(see illustrations 4.19 and 4.18)**.

23 Fit the engine hangers to the frame and tighten their bolts finger-tight **(see illustration 4.17c)**. Install the front mounting bolt from the left-hand side then fit the nut and tighten it finger-tight **(see illustrations 4.17b and a)**.

24 First tighten the engine hanger bolts. Now tighten the lower rear mounting bolt nut to the torque setting specified at the beginning of the Chapter. Next tighten the upper rear mounting bolt nut to the specified torque. Finally tighten the front mounting bolt nut to the specified torque.

25 Remove the jack from under the engine.

26 The remainder of the installation procedure is the reverse of removal, noting the following points:

● When fitting the gearchange linkage arm onto the gearchange shaft, align the slit in the arm with punch mark on the shaft **(see illustration 4.12a)**.
● Use a new gasket on the exhaust pipe.
● Make sure all wires, cables and hoses are correctly routed and connected, and secured by any clips or ties.
● Refill the engine with oil and coolant to the correct levels (see Chapter 1 and *Pre-ride checks*).
● Adjust the throttle and clutch cable freeplay.
● Adjust the drive chain (see Chapter 1).
● Start the engine and check that there are no oil or coolant leaks. Check the idle speed (see Chapter 1).

5 Engine overhaul – general information

1 Before beginning the engine overhaul, read through the related procedures to familiarise yourself with the scope and requirements of the job. Overhauling an engine is not all that difficult, but it is time consuming. Check on the availability of parts and make sure that

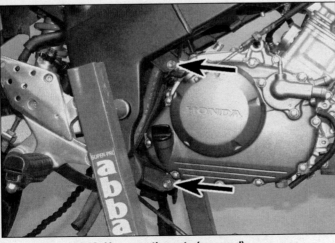

4.18 Unscrew the nuts (arrowed) . . .

4.19 . . . then withdraw the bolts and remove the engine

any necessary special tools are obtained in advance.

2 Most work can be done with a decent set of typical workshop hand tools, although a number of precision measuring tools are required for inspecting parts to determine if they are worn.

3 To ensure maximum life and minimum trouble from a rebuilt engine, everything must be assembled with care in a spotlessly clean environment.

Disassembly

4 Before disassembling the engine, thoroughly clean and degrease its external surfaces. This will prevent contamination of the engine internals, and will also make the job a lot easier and cleaner. A high flash-point solvent, such as paraffin (kerosene) can be used, or better still, a proprietary engine degreaser such as Gunk. Use old paintbrushes and toothbrushes to work the solvent into the various recesses of the casings. Take care to exclude solvent or water from the electrical components and intake and exhaust ports.

 Warning: The use of petrol (gasoline) as a cleaning agent should be avoided because of the risk of fire.

5 When clean and dry, position the engine on the workbench, leaving suitable clear area for working. Gather a selection of small containers, plastic bags and some labels so that parts can be grouped together in an easily identifiable manner. Also get some paper and a pen so that notes can be taken. You will also need a supply of clean rag, which should be as absorbent as possible.

6 Before commencing work, read through the appropriate section so that some idea of the necessary procedure can be gained. When removing components note that great force is seldom required, unless specified (checking the specified torque setting of the particular bolt being removed will indicate how tight it is, and therefore how much force should be needed). In many cases, a component's reluctance to be removed is indicative of an incorrect approach or removal method – if in any doubt, re-check with the text.

7 When disassembling the engine, keep 'mated' parts together that have been in contact with each other during engine operation. These 'mated' parts must be reused or replaced as an assembly.

8 A complete engine stripdown should be done in the following general order with reference to the appropriate Sections.
Remove the valve cover
Remove the camshaft holder
Remove the cylinder head
Remove the cylinder barrel and piston
Remove the cam chain and blades
Remove the starter motor (see Chapter 9)
Remove the clutch
Remove the gearchange mechanism
Remove the oil pump
Remove the water pump (see Chapter 3)

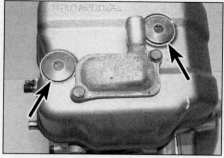

6.4a Unscrew the bolts (arrowed) . . .

Remove the alternator and starter clutch (see Chapter 9)
Separate the crankcase halves
Remove the selector drum and forks
Remove the transmission shafts
Remove the crankshaft and balancer shaft

Reassembly

9 Reassembly is accomplished by reversing the general disassembly sequence.

6 Valve cover

Note: *The valve cover can be removed with the engine in the frame. If the engine has been removed, ignore the steps which do not apply.*

Removal

1 Remove the fairing side panels (see Chapter 8).

2 Displace the radiator from its mounts and move it forwards (see Chapter 3) – there is no need to drain the cooling system or detach any hoses.

3 On R-4, R-5 and RW-6 models, detach the PAIR system hose from the valve cover **(see illustration 4.10)**.

4 Unscrew the two valve cover bolts and lift the cover off the cylinder head **(see illustrations)**. If it is stuck, do not try to lever it off with a screwdriver. Tap it gently around the sides with a rubber hammer or block of wood to dislodge it. Note the rubber washers for the bolts and remove them if they are loose **(see illustration 6.11)**.

6.10 Make sure the gasket locates in the groove and over the dowel (arrowed)

6.4b . . . and remove the cover

5 The rubber gasket is normally glued into the groove in the cover, and is best left there if it is reusable. If the gasket is in any way damaged, deformed or deteriorated, remove it **(see illustration 6.10)**.

6 Note the dowel that links the PAIR system air passage between the valve cover and cylinder head and remove it for safekeeping if it is loose (which is unlikely) **(see illustration 6.10)**.

7 If required, remove the PAIR system reed valve (see Chapter 4A).

Installation

8 If removed, install the PAIR system reed valve (see Chapter 4A).

9 If removed, fit the PAIR system dowel into the valve cover **(see illustration 6.10)**.

10 Examine the valve cover gasket for signs of damage or deterioration and fit a new one if necessary. If a new one is used, clean all traces of the old glue from the groove in the cover and clean it and the cylinder head mating surface with solvent. Fit the new gasket into the groove and over the dowel, using a suitable glue, sealant or grease to hold it in place **(see illustration)**.

11 Position the valve cover on the cylinder head, making sure the gasket stays in place **(see illustration 6.4b)**. If removed, fit the rubber washers into the cover, using new ones if required, and making sure they are installed with the metal side (possibly marked UP) facing up **(see illustration)**. Install the cover bolts and tighten them to the specified torque setting.

12 Install the remaining components in the reverse order of removal.

6.11 Make sure the washers are the correct way up

7.2a Undo the cap screw (arrowed) . . .

7.2b . . . and remove the O-ring

7.3a Slacken the mounting bolts (arrowed) slightly . . .

7 Cam chain tensioner

Note: *The cam chain tensioner can be removed with the engine in the frame. If the engine has been removed, ignore the steps which do not apply.*

Removal

1 Remove the left-hand fairing side panel (see Chapter 8).
2 Undo the tensioner cap screw and remove the O-ring **(see illustrations)**.
3 Slacken the tensioner mounting bolts slightly **(see illustration)**. Insert a small flat-bladed screwdriver in the end of the tensioner so that it engages the slotted plunger **(see illustration)**. Turn the screwdriver clockwise until the plunger is fully retracted and hold it in this position, then unscrew the tensioner mounting bolts and withdraw the tensioner from the engine **(see illustration)**. Release the screwdriver – the plunger will spring back out, but can be easily reset on installation.
4 Discard the gasket and O-ring as new ones must be used on installation. Do not attempt to dismantle the tensioner.

Installation

5 Check that the plunger moves smoothly when wound into the tensioner and springs back out freely when released **(see illustration)**. Ensure the tensioner and cylinder barrel surfaces are clean and dry.
6 Fit a new gasket onto the tensioner body **(see illustration)**. Insert a small flat-bladed screwdriver in the end of the tensioner so that it engages the slotted plunger **(see illustration)**. Turn the screwdriver clockwise until the plunger is fully retracted and hold it in this position, then install the tensioner with its mounting bolts and tighten them **(see illustration 7.3c)**. Release and remove the screwdriver.
7 Fit a new O-ring smeared with clean oil onto the tensioner, then fit the cap screw and tighten it **(see illustration)**.
8 Install the left-hand fairing side panel (see Chapter 8).

8 Camshaft holder, camshaft and rocker arms

Note: *The camshaft and rockers can be removed with the engine in the frame. Stuff clean rag into the cam chain tunnel to prevent*

7.3b . . . then insert the screwdriver and retract the plunger, . . .

7.3c . . . unscrew the mounting bolts and remove the tensioner

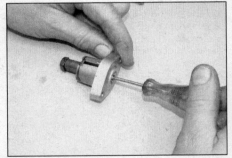

7.5 Check the action of the plunger

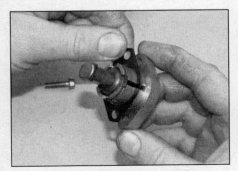

7.6a Fit a new gasket onto the tensioner . . .

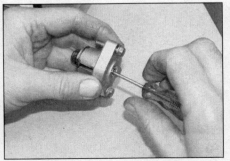

7.6b . . . then insert the screwdriver and retract the plunger

7.7 Fit a new O-ring then the cap screw

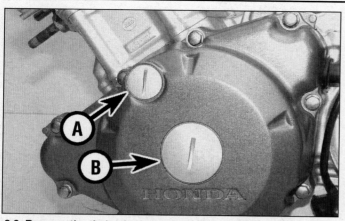

8.3 Remove the timing inspection cap (A) and the crankshaft end cap (B)

8.4a Turn the engine anti-clockwise using the nut . . .

anything dropping into the engine. When setting the position of the crankshaft for the engine timing (Steps 4 and 22), be sure that you have the correct timing mark on the flywheel – the T mark that denote top dead centre (TDC) for engine timing is on its side and can be easily confused with the F mark, also on its side, that denotes the firing (ignition timing) point.

Removal

1 Drain the coolant (see Chapter 1). Remove the radiator (See Chapter 3).
2 Remove the spark plug (see Chapter 1). Remove the valve cover (see Section 6).
3 Unscrew the timing inspection cap and the crankshaft end cap from the alternator cover on the left-hand side of the engine **(see illustration)**. Check the condition of the cap O-rings and replace them with new ones if necessary.
4 The engine must be turned so that the piston is at TDC (top dead centre) on its compression stroke. Turn the engine using a suitable socket on the alternator rotor nut, in an anti-clockwise direction only, until the line next to the T mark on the rotor aligns with the static timing mark,

8.4b . . . until the line next to the T mark aligns with the notch (arrowed) . . .

which is a notch in the inspection hole rim, and the index line on the camshaft sprocket is parallel and flush with the cylinder head top surface (the line will be below the sprocket bolts) **(see illustrations)**. There should now be some freeplay in each rocker arm (i.e. they are not contacting the valve stem). If the index line is parallel but not flush with the head, i.e. it is above the sprocket bolts not below them, rotate the engine anti-clockwise one full turn (360°) until the line next to the T mark again

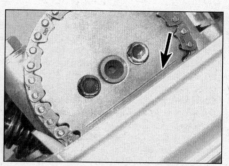

8.4c . . . and the camshaft sprocket line (arrowed) is as shown

aligns with the static timing mark, the index line on the sprocket is flush with the head, and there is some freeplay in the rockers.
5 Remove the cam chain tensioner (see Section 7).
6 Unscrew the bolts securing the cam chain sprocket **(see illustration)**. Slip the sprocket off its flange on the end of the camshaft and disengage it from the chain **(see illustration)**. Prevent the chain from dropping down its tunnel by securing it with a piece of wire.

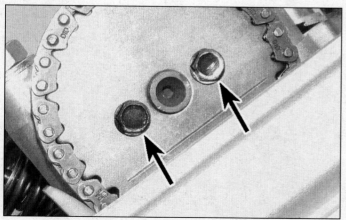

8.6a Unscrew the bolts (arrowed) . . .

8.6b . . . and remove the sprocket

8.7a Camshaft holder nuts (A), cylinder head bolts (B)

8.7b Lift the holder up off the studs, noting the dowels (arrowed)

7 Unscrew the camshaft holder nuts, slackening them evenly and a little at a time in a criss-cross sequence **(see illustration)**. Remove the nuts and their washers, and lift off the holder complete with the camshaft and rockers **(see illustration)**. Remove the two locating dowels from the studs or the underside of the holder if they are loose.
Caution: Make sure the holder lifts up squarely and evenly and does not stick on a dowel.
8 While the camshaft holder is out do not rotate the crankshaft – the chain may drop down and bind between the crankshaft and case, which could damage these components. Place a rag over the cylinder head.

Disassembly

9 Remove the circlip securing the camshaft in the holder, then draw the camshaft out **(see illustrations)**. Discard the circlip if it has deformed and fit a new one on assembly.
10 Mark each rocker arm according to its location in the holder. Unscrew the shaft stopper bolt, then hold the rocker arm and push the shaft out using a flat-bladed screwdriver in the slot in the end of the shaft, rotating the shaft as you do to ease removal **(see illustrations 8.19b and a)**. Slide the rocker back onto its shaft to prevent mixing up – both shafts and rocker arms are identical and are therefore interchangeable, but mark them according to their location so they can be installed in their original position.

8.9a Release the circlip . . .

8.9b . . . and withdraw the camshaft

Inspection

11 Check the bearing on each end of the camshaft – they must run smoothly, quietly and freely, and there should be no excessive play between the inner and outer races, or between the inner race and the camshaft, or between the outer race and the holder **(see illustration)**. If not, replace the camshaft with a new one – it comes fitted with bearings, and the bearings are not available separately. Check that the bearing housings in the holder are neither worn nor damaged.
12 Check the camshaft lobes for heat discoloration (blue appearance), score marks, chipped areas, flat spots and spalling **(see illustration 8.14)**. Measure the height of each lobe with a micrometer **(see illustration)**

and compare the results to the minimum height listed in this Chapter's Specifications. If damage is noted or wear is excessive, the camshaft must be replaced with a new one.
13 Check the amount of camshaft runout by supporting each end on V-blocks, and measuring any runout using a dial gauge. If the runout exceeds the specified limit the camshaft must be replaced with a new one.
14 Check the rocker arms for heat discoloration (blue appearance), score marks, chipped areas, flat spots and spalling where they contact the camshaft lobes **(see illustration)**. Similarly check the bottom of each clearance adjuster and the top of each valve stem. If damage is noted or wear is excessive, the rocker arms, camshaft and valves must be replaced with new ones as required.

8.11 Check the bearings (arrowed) as described

8.12 Measure the height of the camshaft lobes with a micrometer

8.14 Check the contacting surfaces on the rocker arms and camshaft lobes (arrowed)

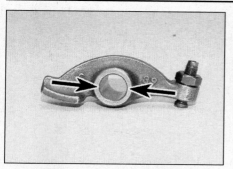

8.15a Measure the internal diameter of each bore . . .

8.15b . . . and the external diameter of each shaft

8.19a Slide the shaft into the holder and through the rocker . . .

15 Check for freeplay between each rocker arm and its shaft. The arms should move freely with a light fit but no appreciable freeplay. Measure the internal diameter of the arm bores and the corresponding diameter of the shaft **(see illustrations)**. Replace the arms and/or shafts with new ones if they are worn beyond their specifications. Check that the fork shaft holes in the holder are neither worn nor damaged.

16 Except in cases of oil starvation, the cam chain should wear very little. If the chain has stretched excessively, which makes it difficult to maintain proper tension, or if it is stiff or the links are binding or kinking, replace it with a new one. Refer to Section 9 for replacement.

17 Check the sprocket for wear, cracks and other damage, and replace it with a new one if necessary. If the sprocket is worn, the cam chain is also worn, and so probably is the sprocket on the crankshaft. If severe wear is apparent, the entire engine should be disassembled further for inspection.

18 Inspect the cam chain guide and tensioner blade (see Section 9).

Assembly

19 Lubricate each rocker shaft and arm with molybdenum disulphide oil (a 50/50 mixture of molybdenum disulphide grease and engine oil). Position each rocker arm in its location in the holder, making sure the adjuster is on the outside, and slide its shaft through, again using a flat-bladed screwdriver to rotate the shaft to ease installation and to align the stopper bolt hole with that in the holder **(see illustration)**. Fit the shaft stopper bolts and tighten them to the torque setting specified at the beginning of the Chapter **(see illustration)**.

20 Lubricate the camshaft bearings with clean engine oil and the camshaft lobes with molybdenum disulphide oil. Slide the camshaft into the holder, positioning the rocker arms so their contact faces on the inner ends locate against the camshaft lobes, and secure it with the circlip, using a new one if necessary **(see illustrations 8.9b and a)**.

Installation

21 Make sure the mating surfaces on the holder and the cylinder head are clean. If removed fit the dowels over the studs and push them into the head.

8.19b . . . then turn it to align the holes and fit the stopper bolt

22 Check that the line next to the T mark on the alternator rotor aligns with the notch in the inspection hole rim **(see illustration 8.4b)**. Turn the camshaft so that the tab on the sprocket flange is at the top.

23 Fit the camshaft holder assembly over the studs and onto the head, making sure the sprocket end of the camshaft is over the cam chain tunnel, and that the rocker arms locate correctly onto the valve stem ends, and locate it onto the dowels, making sure it is correctly seated on all sides **(see illustration 8.7b)**.

24 Smear clean engine oil onto the seating surfaces of the nuts. Fit the nuts with their washers and tighten them evenly in three stages and in a criss-cross sequence to the torque setting specified at the beginning of the Chapter **(see illustration)**.

25 Check again that the line next to the T mark on the alternator rotor aligns with

8.25 With everything correctly aligned fit the sprocket into the chain and onto the camshaft . . .

8.24 Fit the nuts with their washers and tighten them as described

the notch in the inspection hole rim **(see illustration 8.4b)**, and make sure the tab on the camshaft flange is at the top and the bolt holes are parallel with the head. Engage the cam chain sprocket with the chain, making sure the crankshaft does not rotate, that the front run of the chain between the sprockets is tight and that any slack is in the rear run so it will be taken up by the tensioner, that the index line is facing out and is flush with the cylinder head, i.e. below the bolt holes, and that the bolt holes align, and fit the sprocket onto the flange **(see illustration)**.

26 Fit the cam chain sprocket bolts and tighten them to the specified torque setting **(see illustration)**.

27 Use a piece of wooden dowel or other suitable tool to press on the back of the cam chain tensioner blade via the tensioner

8.26 . . . then install the bolts

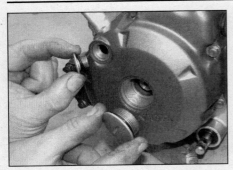

8.30 Fit the caps using new O-rings and smear them and the threads with grease

9.3 Removing the cam chain

9.6a Unscrew the bolt and remove the retainer . . .

bore in the cylinder barrel to ensure that any slack in the cam chain is taken up and transferred to the rear run of the chain. At this point check that all the timing marks are still in exact alignment as described in Step 4 **(see illustrations 8.4b and c)**. Note that it is easy to be slightly out (one tooth on the sprocket) without the marks appearing drastically out of alignment. If the marks are out unscrew the sprocket's bolts and slide the sprocket off the camshaft, then disengage it from the chain. Move the camshaft and/or crankshaft round as required, then fit the sprocket back into the chain and onto the camshaft, and check the marks again. With everything correctly aligned, tighten the bolts to the torque setting specified at the beginning of the Chapter.
Caution: If the marks are not aligned exactly as described, the valve timing will be incorrect and the valves may strike the pistons, causing extensive damage to the engine.
28 Install the cam chain tensioner (see Section 7).
29 Turn the engine anti-clockwise through two full turns and check again that all the timing marks still align (see Step 4) **(see illustrations 8.4a, b and c)**. Check the valve clearances and adjust them if necessary (see Chapter 1).
30 Install the timing inspection cap and crankshaft end cap using new O-rings if required, and smear the O-rings and the cap threads with clean oil **(see illustration)**.

Tighten the caps to the torque setting specified at the beginning of the Chapter.
31 Install the valve cover (see Section 6). Install the spark plug (see Chapter 1). Install radiator (see Chapter 3).

9 Cam chain, tensioner blade and guide blade

Note: *The cam chain and its blades can be removed with the engine in the frame. If the engine has been removed, ignore the steps which do not apply.*

Removal

Cam chain

1 Remove the camshaft holder (see Section 8).
2 Remove the alternator rotor and starter clutch (see Chapter 9).
3 Draw the cam chain off the crankshaft sprocket and out of the engine **(see illustration)**.

Tensioner blade

4 Remove the cylinder head (see Section 10).
5 Remove the alternator rotor and starter clutch (see Chapter 9).
6 Unscrew the tensioner blade retainer bolt and remove the retainer and the washer, then slide the blade off its pivot and draw

it out of the top of the cylinder barrel **(see illustrations)**.

Guide blade

7 Remove the cylinder head (see Section 10).
8 Draw the guide blade out of the top of the cylinder barrel, noting how it locates **(see illustration)**.

Inspection

Cam chain

9 Check the chain for binding, kinks and any obvious damage and replace it with a new one if necessary. Check the camshaft and crankshaft sprocket teeth for wear and replace the cam chain, camshaft sprocket and crankshaft sprocket with a new set if necessary – the drive sprocket on the crankshaft is pressed on, so the crankshaft will have to be taken to an engineering workshop or dealer equipped with an hydraulic press to remove it and to fit a new one.

Tensioner and guide blades

10 Check the sliding surface and edges of the blades for excessive wear, deep grooves, cracking and other obvious damage, and replace them with new ones if necessary.

Installation

11 Installation of the sprocket, chain and blades is the reverse of removal. Make sure the bottom of the guide blade sits in its seat and the lugs near its top locate in the cut-

9.6b . . . the washer . . .

9.6c . . . and the blade

9.8 Draw the guide blade out, noting how it locates

9.11a Make sure the bottom locates in its seat (arrowed) . . .

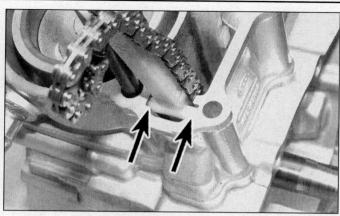

9.11b . . . and the lugs locate in the cut-outs (arrowed)

9.11c Make sure the hole in the retainer locates over the pivot

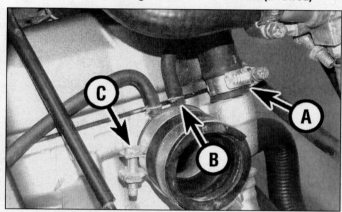

10.3 Detach the coolant hose (A), the PAIR vacuum hose (B) and if required the intake duct by slackening the clamp (C)

outs in the cylinder barrel **(see illustrations)**. Lubricate the tensioner blade pivot with clean oil, and make sure the retainer plate locates over the end of the pivot **(see illustration)**.

10 Cylinder head removal and installation

Note: *The cylinder head can be removed with the engine in the frame.*

Removal

1 Remove the carburettor/throttle body and the exhaust system (see Chapter 4A or 4B).
2 Remove the camshaft holder (see Section 8).
3 Slacken the clamp screw securing the coolant hose to the head and detach it, being prepared with a rag to catch any residual coolant **(see illustration)**.
4 Detach the PAIR control valve vacuum hose from the intake duct on R-4, R-5 and RW-6 models **(see illustration 10.3)**. If required slacken the clamp screw securing the intake duct and slip it off the head.
5 Unscrew and remove the two bolts in the cam chain tunnel **(see illustration 8.7a)**.
6 Hold the cam chain up and pull the cylinder head up off the barrel, then pass the cam chain

down through the tunnel **(see illustration)**. Do not let the chain fall into the engine – lay it over the front of the barrel and secure it with a piece of wire. If the head is stuck, tap around the joint faces with a soft-faced mallet. Do not attempt to free it by inserting a screwdriver between the head and barrel mating surfaces – you'll damage them.
7 Remove the cylinder head gasket and discard it as a new one must be used **(see illustration 10.11)**. If they are loose, remove the dowels from the cylinder barrel or the underside of the cylinder head **(see illustration 10.10)**.
8 Check the cylinder head gasket and the mating surfaces on the cylinder head and

cylinder barrel for signs of leakage, which could indicate warpage. Refer to Section 11 and check the cylinder head gasket surface for warpage.
9 Clean all traces of old gasket material from the cylinder head and cylinder barrel. If a scraper is used, take care not to scratch or gouge the soft aluminium. Be careful not to let any of the gasket material fall into the cylinder bore or the oil and coolant passages.

Installation

10 Lubricate the cylinder bore with engine oil. If removed, fit the dowels into the cylinder barrel **(see illustration)**. Make sure the cam

10.6 Carefully lift the head up off the barrel

10.10 Install the dowels (arrowed) . . .

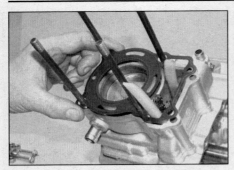

10.11 . . . then lay the new gasket on the barrel

10.13 Fit the cylinder head bolts after the camshaft holder

10.14 Locate the tab between the unions (arrowed)

chain guide blade is correctly seated (see Section 9).

11 Ensure both cylinder head and cylinder

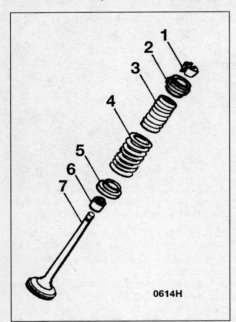

0614H

11.2 Valve components

1	Collets	5	Spring seat
2	Spring retainer	6	Valve stem oil
3	Inner valve spring		seal
4	Outer valve spring	7	Valve

barrel mating surfaces are clean. Lay the **new** head gasket over the studs, the cam chain and blades and onto the barrel, locating it over the dowels and making sure all the holes are correctly aligned **(see illustration)**. Never reuse the old gasket.

12 Carefully fit the cylinder head over the studs and the cam chain guide blade and onto the barrel, feeding the cam chain up through the tunnel as you do, and making sure it locates correctly onto the dowels **(see illustration 10.6)**. Secure the chain in place with a piece of wire to prevent it from falling back down.

13 Install the camshaft holder and tighten its nuts (see Section 8), then before fitting the cam chain sprocket onto the camshaft fit the two cylinder head bolts and tighten them **(see illustration)**. Finish the installation of the camshaft holder components.

14 If removed fit the intake duct and tighten its screw, aligning it so the tab locates between the vacuum take-off unions as shown **(see illustration)**. Connect the vacuum hose and coolant hose **(see illustration 10.3)**. Install the carburettor/throttle body and the exhaust system (see Chapter 4A or 4B).

11 Cylinder head and valve overhaul

Special tool: *A valve spring compressor*

(suitable for motorcycle engines) is essential for this operation.

1 Valve overhaul involves removing the valves and associated components from the cylinder head, cleaning them and checking them for wear. Valve seat recutting or valve guide replacement, if necessary, is a job for an engineer, but the valves can be ground in and all components reassembled in the home workshop.

Disassembly

2 Label and store the valves along with their related components in such a way that they can be returned to their original locations without getting mixed up **(see illustration)**. Labelled plastic bags or a plastic container with two compartments are ideal.

3 Compress the valve spring on the first valve with a spring compressor, making sure it is correctly located onto each end of the valve assembly **(see illustration)**. On the top of the valve the adaptor needs to be about the same size as the spring retainer – if it is too small it will be difficult to remove and install the collets **(see illustration)**. On the underside of the head make sure the plate on the compressor only contacts the valve and not the soft aluminium of the head **(see illustration)** – if the plate is too big for the valve, use a spacer between them. Do not compress the springs any more than is absolutely necessary.

4 Remove the collets, using a magnet or a screwdriver with a dab of grease on it **(see**

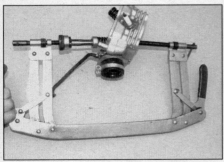

11.3a Compressing the valve springs using a valve spring compressor

11.3b Make sure the compressor locates correctly both on the top of the spring retainer . . .

11.3c . . . and on the bottom of the valve

11.4a Remove the collets . . .

11.4b . . . the spring retainer . . .

11.4c . . . the springs . . .

illustration). Carefully release the valve spring compressor and remove the spring retainer, noting which way up it fits, the springs and the valve **(see illustrations)**. If the valve binds in the guide and won't pull through, push it back into the head and deburr the area around the collet groove with a very fine file or whetstone **(see illustration)**.

5 Pull the valve stem seal off the top of the valve guide with pliers and discard it (the old seals should never be reused), then remove the spring seat noting which way up it fits **(see illustrations)**.

6 Repeat the procedure for the other valve. Remember to keep the parts for each valve together so they can be reinstalled in the same location.

7 Clean the cylinder head with solvent and dry it thoroughly. Compressed air will speed the drying process and ensure that all holes and recessed areas are clean. **Note:** *Do not*

11.4d . . . and the valve

use a wire brush mounted in a drill motor to clean the combustion chambers as the head material is soft and may be scratched or eroded away by the wire brush.

8 Clean all of the valve springs, collets, retainers and spring seats with solvent and dry

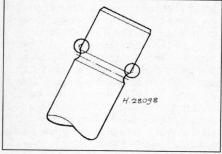

11.4e If the valve stem won't pull through the guide, deburr the area above the collet groove

them thoroughly. Do the parts from one valve at a time so that no mixing of parts between valves occurs.

9 Scrape off any deposits that may have formed on the valve, then use a motorised wire brush to remove deposits from the valve heads and stems. Again, make sure the valves do not get mixed up.

Inspection

10 Inspect the head very carefully for cracks and other damage. If cracks are found, a new head is required.

11 Using a precision straight-edge and a feeler gauge set to the warpage limit listed in the specifications at the beginning of the Chapter, check the head gasket mating surface for warpage. Take six measurements, one along each side and two diagonally across. If the head is warped beyond the limit specified at the beginning of this Chapter, consult a Honda dealer or take it to a specialist repair shop for advice on having the surface skimmed.

12 Examine the valve seats in the combustion chamber. If they are pitted, cracked or burned, the head will require work beyond the scope of the home mechanic. Measure the valve seat width and compare it to this Chapter's Specifications **(see illustration)**. If it exceeds the service limit, or if it varies around its circumference, overhaul is required.

13 Working on one valve and guide at a time, measure the valve stem diameter **(see illustration)**. Clean the valve's guide using

11.5a Pull the seal off the valve stem . . .

11.5b . . . then remove the spring seat

11.12 Measure the valve seat width

11.13a Measure the valve stem diameter with a micrometer

11.13b Measure the valve guide with a small bore gauge, then measure the bore gauge with a micrometer (arrowed)

a guide reamer to remove any carbon build-up – insert the reamer from the underside of the head and turn it clockwise only. Now measure the inside diameter of the guide (at both ends and in the centre of the guide) with a small bore gauge, then measure the gauge with a micrometer **(see illustration)**. Measure the guide at the ends and at the centre to determine if they are worn in a bell-mouth pattern (more wear at the ends). Subtract the stem diameter from the valve guide diameter to obtain the valve stem-to-guide clearance. If the stem-to-guide clearance is greater than listed in this Chapter's Specifications, replace whichever component is beyond its service limit with a new one – take the head to an engineer for valve guide replacement. If the valve guide is within specifications, but is worn unevenly, it should be replaced with a new one. Repeat for the other valve.

14 Carefully inspect each valve face, stem and collet groove area for cracks, pits and burned spots.

15 Rotate the valve and check for any obvious indication that it is bent, in which case it must be replaced with a new one. Check the end of the stem for pitting and excessive wear. The presence of any of the above conditions indicates the need for valve servicing.

16 Check the end of each valve spring for wear and pitting. Measure the spring free lengths and compare them to the specifications **(see illustration)**. If any spring is shorter than specified it has sagged and must be replaced with a new one. Also place the spring upright on a flat surface and check

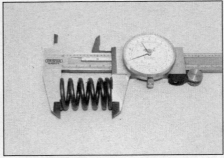

11.16 Measure the free length of the valve springs and check them for bend

it for bend by placing a ruler against it, or alternatively lay it against a set square. If the bend in any spring is excessive, it must be replaced with a new one.

17 Check the spring seats, retainers and collets for obvious wear and cracks. Any questionable parts should not be reused, as extensive damage will occur in the event of failure during engine operation.

18 If the inspection indicates that no overhaul work is required, the valve components can be reinstalled in the head.

Caution: Clean the head thoroughly before installation to remove any metal particles or abrasive grit that may still be present from the valve service operations. Use compressed air, if available, to blow out all the holes and passages.

Reassembly

19 Unless a valve service has been performed, before installing the valves in the head they should be ground in (lapped) to ensure a positive seal between the valves and seats. This procedure requires coarse and fine valve grinding compound and a valve grinding tool (either hand-held or drill driven – note that some drill-driven tools specify using only a fine grinding compound). If a grinding tool is not available, a piece of rubber or plastic hose can be slipped over the valve stem (after the valve has been installed in the guide) and used to turn the valve.

20 Apply a small amount of coarse grinding compound to the valve face. Smear some molybdenum disulphide oil (a 50/50 mixture of molybdenum disulphide grease and engine

oil) to the valve stem, then slip the valve into the guide **(see illustration 11.4d)**. **Note:** *Make sure each valve is installed in its correct guide and be careful not to get any grinding compound on the valve stem.*

21 Attach the grinding tool to the valve and rotate the tool between the palms of your hands. Use a back-and-forth motion (as though rubbing your hands together) rather than a circular motion (i.e. so that the valve rotates alternately clockwise and anti-clockwise rather than in one direction only). If a motorised tool is being used, take note of the correct drive speed for it – if your drill runs too fast and is not variable, use a hand tool instead. Lift the valve off the seat and turn it at regular intervals to distribute the grinding compound properly. Continue the grinding procedure until the valve face and seat contact area is of uniform width, and unbroken around the entire circumference **(see illustration and 11.12)**.

22 Carefully remove the valve and wipe off all traces of grinding compound, making sure none gets in the guide. Use solvent to clean the valve and wipe the seat area thoroughly with a solvent soaked cloth.

23 Repeat the procedure with fine valve grinding compound, then use solvent to clean the valve and flush the guide, and wipe the seat area thoroughly with a solvent soaked cloth. Repeat the entire procedure for the other valve. On completion thoroughly clean the entire head again, then blow through all passages with compressed air. Make sure all traces of the grinding compound have been removed before assembling the head.

24 Coat the valve stem with molybdenum disulphide oil (a 50/50 mixture of molybdenum disulphide grease and engine oil), then install it into its guide, rotating it slowly to avoid damaging the seal **(see illustration 11.4d)**. Check that the valve moves up-and-down freely in the guide.

25 Working on one valve at a time, lay the spring seat in place in the cylinder head with its shouldered side facing up **(see illustration)**.

26 Fit a **new** valve stem seal onto the guide, using finger pressure, a stem seal fitting tool or an appropriate size deep socket, to push the seal squarely onto the end of the valve guide until it is felt to clip into place **(see illustrations)**.

11.21 Make sure the contact areas are as described

11.25 Fit the spring seat using a rod to guide it if necessary

11.26a Fit a new valve stem seal . . .

11.26b ... and press it squarely into place

11.28 Locate each collet in its groove in the top of the valve stem

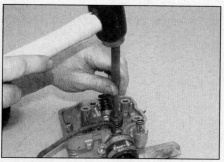

11.30 Seat the collets as described

27 Next, install the springs, with their closer-wound coils facing down into the cylinder head **(see illustration 11.4c)**. Fit the spring retainer, with its shouldered side facing down so that it fits into the top of the springs **(see illustration 11.4b)**.
28 Apply a small amount of grease to the collets to help hold them in place. Compress the valve springs with a spring compressor, making sure it is correctly located onto each end of the valve assembly (see Step 6) **(see illustrations 11.3a, 11.3b and 11.3c)**. Do not compress the springs any more than is necessary to slip the collets into place. Locate each collet in turn into the groove in the valve stem using a screwdriver with a dab of grease on it **(see illustration)**. Carefully release the compressor, making sure the collets seat and lock in the retaining groove.
29 Repeat the procedure for the other valve.
30 Support the cylinder head on wood blocks so the valves can't contact the work

HAYNES HiNT *Check for proper sealing of the valves by pouring a small amount of solvent into each of the valve ports. If the solvent leaks past either valve into the combustion chamber the valve grinding operation on that valve should be repeated.*

surface, then tap the end of each valve stem lightly to seat the collets in their grooves **(see illustration)**.
31 After the cylinder head and camshaft holder have been installed, check the valve clearances and adjust as required (see Chapter 1).

12 Cylinder barrel

Note: *The cylinder barrel can be removed with the engine in the frame.*

Removal

1 Remove the cylinder head (see Section 10).
2 Draw the cam chain guide blade out of the top of the barrel, noting how it locates **(see illustration 9.8)**.
3 Slacken the clamp screw securing the coolant hose to the barrel and detach it, being prepared with a rag to catch any residual coolant **(see illustration)**.
4 Hold the cam chain up and pull the cylinder barrel up off the crankcase, supporting the piston so the connecting rod does not knock against the engine, then pass the cam chain down through the tunnel **(see illustration)**.

Do not let the chain fall into the engine – lay it over the front and secure it with a piece of wire. If the barrel is stuck, tap around the joint faces with a soft-faced mallet. Do not attempt to free it by inserting a screwdriver between the barrel and crankcase mating surfaces – you'll damage them.
5 Remove the base gasket and discard it as a new one must be used. If they are loose, remove the dowels from the crankcase or the underside of the cylinder barrel **(see illustration 12.15)**.
6 Stuff clean rag into the cam chain tunnel and around the connecting rod to protect and support it and the piston and to prevent anything falling into the engine.
7 Clean all traces of old gasket material from the cylinder barrel and crankcase. If a scraper is used, take care not to scratch or gouge the soft aluminium. Be careful not to let any of the gasket material fall into the engine.

Inspection

Note: *Do not attempt to separate the cylinder liner from the cylinder barrel.*
8 Check the cylinder walls carefully for scratches and score marks.
9 Using a precision straight-edge and a feeler gauge set to the warpage limit listed in the specifications at the beginning of the Chapter,

12.3 Slacken the clamp (arrowed) and detach the hose

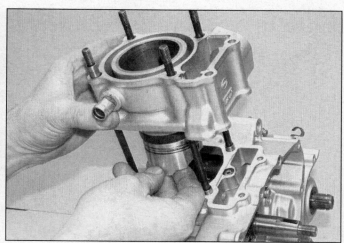

12.4 Carefully lift the barrel up off the crankcase

check the barrel top surface for warpage. Take six measurements, one along each side and two diagonally across. If the barrel is warped beyond the limit specified at the beginning of this Chapter, consult a Honda dealer or take it to an engineer for an opinion, though be prepared to have to buy a new one.

10 Using a telescoping bore gauge and a micrometer, check the dimensions of the cylinder to assess the amount of wear, taper and ovality. Measure near the top (but below the level of the top piston ring at TDC), centre and bottom (but above the level of the oil ring at BDC) of the bore, both parallel to and across the crankshaft axis **(see illustrations)**. Compare the results to the specifications at the beginning of the Chapter. If the cylinder is worn, oval or tapered beyond the service limit it can be re-bored – oversize (+0.25, +0.50, +0.75 and +1.00) piston and ring sets are available. Note that the engineer carrying out the re-bore must be aware of the piston-to-bore clearance (see Specifications).

11 If the precision measuring tools are not available, take the cylinder barrel to a Honda dealer or engineer for assessment and advice.

Installation

12 Check that the mating surfaces of the cylinder barrel and crankcase are free from oil or pieces of old gasket.

13 Check that all the studs are tight in the crankcase. If any are loose, or need to be replaced with new ones, remove them. Clean their threads and smear them with clean engine oil. Fit them into the crankcase with the marked end at the top, and tighten them using a stud tool, or by threading two of the camshaft holder nuts onto the top of the stud and tightening them together so they are locked on the stud, then tighten the stud by turning the upper of the two nuts. The distance between the top of each stud and the crankcase surface should be 169 mm.

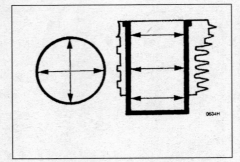

12.10a Measure the cylinder bore in the directions shown . . .

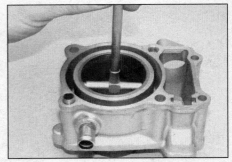

12.10b . . . using a telescoping gauge, then measure the gauge with a micrometer

14 If removed, fit the dowels over the studs and into the crankcase and push them firmly home **(see illustration 12.15)**.

15 Remove the rags from around the piston and the cam chain tunnel, taking care not to let the connecting rod fall against the rim of the crankcase, and lay the **new** base gasket in place, locating it over the dowels **(see illustration)**. The gasket can only fit one way, so if all the holes do not line up properly it is the wrong way round. Never re-use the old gasket.

16 Ensure the piston ring end gaps are positioned correctly before fitting the cylinder barrel (see Section 14) **(see illustration 14.10)**. If possible, have an assistant to support the cylinder barrel while the piston rings are fed into the bore.

17 Rotate the crankshaft so that the piston is at its highest point (top dead centre). It is useful to place a support under the piston so that it remains at TDC while the barrel is fitted, otherwise the downward pressure will turn the crankshaft and the piston will drop. Lubricate the cylinder bore, piston and piston rings with clean engine oil.

18 Carefully lower the barrel over the studs and onto the piston until the crown fits into the bore, holding the underside of the piston if you are not using a support to prevent it

dropping, and making sure it enters the bore squarely and does not get cocked sideways **(see illustration 12.4)**. Feed the cam chain up the tunnel and slip a piece of wire through it to prevent it falling back into the engine. Keep the chain taut to prevent it becoming disengaged from the crankshaft sprocket.

19 Carefully compress and feed each ring into the bore as the cylinder is lowered **(see illustration)**. If necessary, use a soft mallet to gently tap the cylinder down, but do not use force if it appears to be stuck as the piston and/or rings will be damaged.

20 When the piston and rings are correctly located in the bore, remove the support if used then press the cylinder barrel down onto the base gasket, making sure the dowels locate.

21 Hold the barrel down and turn the crankshaft to check that everything moves as it should.

22 Connect the coolant hose to its union and secure it with its clamp **(see illustration 12.3)**.

23 Install the cam chain guide blade, making sure the bottom of the blade sits in its seat and the lugs near its top locate in the cut-outs in the cylinder barrel **(see illustrations 9.8 and 9.11a and b)**.

24 Install the cylinder head (see Section 10).

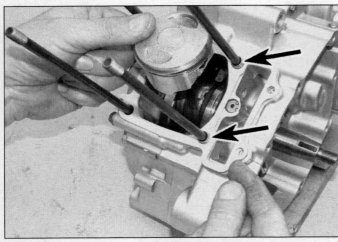

12.15 Lay the new gasket over the dowels (arrowed) and onto the crankcase

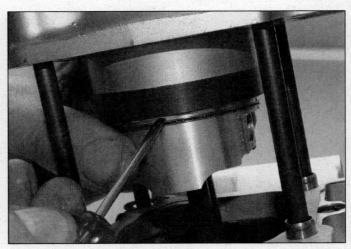

12.19 Carefully feed each ring into the bore as you lower the barrel

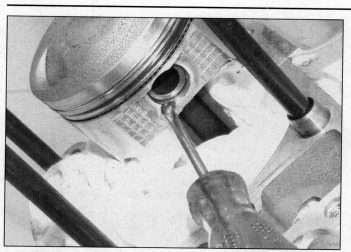

13.3a Prise out the circlip using a suitable tool in the notch . . .

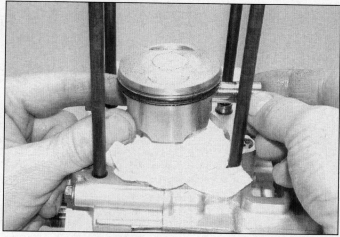

13.3b . . . then push out the pin and separate the piston from the rod

13 Piston

Note: *The piston can be removed with the engine in the frame.*

Removal

1 Remove the cylinder barrel (see Section 12). Check that the holes into the crankcase and the cam chain tunnel are completely blocked with rag.

2 Note that the piston crown is marked IN (though the mark is likely to be invisible until the piston is cleaned) and this mark faces the intake side of the cylinder.

3 Carefully prise out the circlip on one side of the piston using needle-nose pliers or a small flat-bladed screwdriver inserted into the notch **(see illustration)**. Push the piston pin out from the other side to free the piston from the connecting rod **(see illustration)**. Remove the other circlip and discard them as new ones must be used.

 If the piston pin is a tight fit in the piston bosses, heat the piston using a heat gun – this will expand the alloy piston sufficiently to release its grip on the pin. If the piston pin is particularly stubborn, extract it using a drawbolt tool, but be careful to protect the piston's working surfaces.

4 Using your thumbs or a piston ring removal and installation tool, carefully remove the rings from the piston **(see illustrations 14.9, 14.8a and b, 14.6c, b and a)**. Do not nick or gouge the piston in the process. Carefully note which way up each ring fits and in which groove as they must be installed in their original positions if being re-used. Look for identification marks

on the upper surfaces of the two compression rings, such as R on the top ring and RN on the second ring **(see illustration 14.8a)**.

5 Scrape all traces of carbon from the top of the piston. A hand-held wire brush or a piece of fine emery cloth can be used once most of the deposits have been scraped away. Do not, under any circumstances, use a wire brush mounted in a drill motor to remove carbon deposits; the piston material is soft and will be eroded away by the wire brush.

6 Use a piston ring groove cleaning tool to remove any carbon deposits from the ring grooves. If a tool is not available, a piece broken off an old ring will do the job. Be very careful to remove only the carbon deposits. Do not remove any metal and do not nick or gouge the sides of the ring grooves.

7 Once the deposits have been removed, clean the piston with solvent and dry it thoroughly. Make sure the oil return holes below the oil ring groove are clear.

Inspection

8 Carefully inspect the piston for cracks around the skirt, at the pin bosses and at the ring lands. Normal piston wear appears as even, vertical wear on the thrust surfaces. If the skirt is scored or scuffed, the engine

may have been suffering from overheating and/or abnormal combustion, which caused excessively high operating temperatures. Also check that the circlip grooves are not damaged.

9 A hole in the top of the piston, in one extreme, or burned areas around the edge of the piston crown, indicate that pre-ignition or knocking under load have occurred. If you find evidence of any problems the cause must be corrected or the damage will occur again (see *Fault Finding* in the Reference section).

10 Measure the piston ring-to-groove clearance by laying each piston ring in its groove and slipping a feeler gauge in beside it **(see illustration)**. Make sure you have the correct ring for the groove (see Step 4). Check the clearance at three or four locations around the groove. If the clearance is greater than specified, replace both the piston and rings as a set. If new rings are being used, measure the clearance using the new rings. If the clearance is greater than that specified, the piston is worn and must be replaced with a new one.

11 Check the piston-to-bore clearance by measuring the bore (see Section 12), then measure the piston 6.5 mm up from the bottom of the skirt and at 90° to the piston pin axis **(see illustration)**. Refer to the Specifications

13.10 Measure the piston ring-to-groove clearance with a feeler gauge

13.11 Measure the piston diameter with a micrometer at the specified distance from the bottom of the skirt

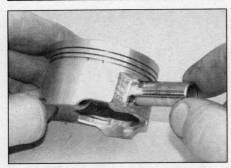

13.12a Fit the pin into the piston and check for any freeplay

13.12b Measure the external diameter of each end of the pin . . .

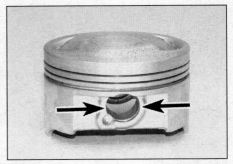

13.12c . . . and the internal diameter of the bore in the piston on each side (arrowed)

13.12d Measure the external diameter of the middle of the pin . . .

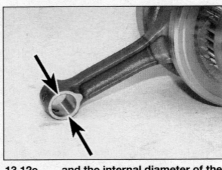

13.12e . . . and the internal diameter of the small-end of the connecting rod

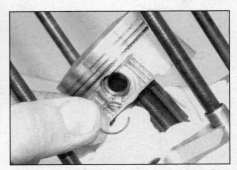

13.16 Use new circlips and make sure they locate correctly

at the beginning of the Chapter and subtract the piston diameter from the bore diameter to obtain the clearance. If it is greater than the specified figure, the piston must be replaced with a new one (assuming the bore itself is within limits).

12 Apply clean engine oil to the piston pin, insert it into the piston and check for any freeplay between the two **(see illustration)**. Measure the pin external diameter at each end **(see illustration)**, and the pin bores in the piston **(see illustration)**. Calculate the difference to obtain the piston pin-to-piston pin bore clearance. Compare the result to the specifications at the beginning of the Chapter. If the clearance is greater than specified, replace the components that are worn beyond their specified limits. Repeat the check and measurements between the middle of the pin and the connecting rod small-end **(see illustrations)**.

Installation

13 Inspect and install the piston rings (see Section 14).

14 Lubricate the piston pin, the piston pin bore and the connecting rod small-end bore with molybdenum disulphide oil (a 50/50 mixture of molybdenum disulphide grease and clean engine oil).

15 When fitting the piston onto the connecting rod make sure the IN mark on the piston crown faces the intake side (back) of the engine.

16 Fit a **new** circlip into one side of the piston (do not reuse old circlips). Line up the piston on the correct connecting rod and insert the piston pin from the other side **(see illustration 13.3b)**. Secure the pin with the other **new** circlip **(see illustration)**. When fitting the circlips, compress them only just enough to fit them in the piston, and make sure they are

properly seated in their grooves with the open end away from the removal notch.

17 Install the cylinder barrel (see Section 12).

14 Piston rings

Inspection

1 It is good practice to replace the piston rings with new ones when an engine is being overhauled. Before installing the new rings, check the end gaps with the rings installed in the bore, as follows.

2 Insert the top ring into the top of the bore and square it up with the bore walls by pushing it in with the top of the piston **(see illustrations)**. The ring should be

14.2a Fit the ring in its bore . . .

14.2b . . . and set it square using the piston . . .

14.2c . . . then measure the end gap using a feeler gauge

14.6a Fit the oil ring expander in its groove . . .

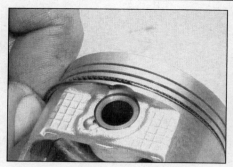

14.6b . . . then fit the lower side rail . . .

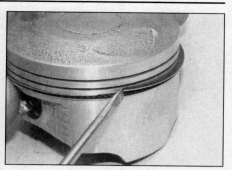

14.6c . . . and the upper side rail on each side of it

about 20 mm below the top edge of the bore. Slip a feeler gauge between the ends of the ring and compare the measurement to the specifications at the beginning of the Chapter **(see illustration)**.

3 If the gap is larger or smaller than specified, double check to make sure that you have the correct ring before proceeding; excess end gap is not critical unless it exceeds the service limit.

4 If the service limit is exceeded with new rings, check the bore for wear (see Section 12). If the gap is too small, the ring ends may come in contact with each other during engine operation, which can cause serious damage.

5 Repeat the procedure for the middle ring and the oil control ring side-rails, but not the expander ring.

Installation

6 Install the oil control ring (lowest on the piston) first. It is composed of three separate components, namely the expander and the upper and lower side-rails. Slip the expander into the groove, making sure the ends don't overlap, then fit the lower side-rail **(see illustrations)**. Do not use a piston ring installation tool on the side-rails as they may be damaged. Instead, place one end of the side-rail into the groove between the expander and the ring land. Hold it firmly in place and slide a finger around the piston while pushing the rail into the groove. Next, fit the upper side-rail in the same manner **(see illustration)**. Check that the ends of the expander have not overlapped.

7 After the three oil ring components have

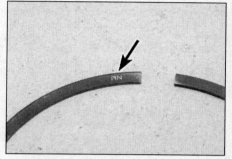

14.8a Note the marking on the ring (arrowed) and make sure it faces up

been installed, check to make sure that both the upper and lower side-rails can be turned smoothly in the ring groove.

8 The upper surface of the two compression rings should be marked with an identification letter at one end **(see illustration)**. Install the second (middle) ring next. Make sure that its identification letter near the end gap is facing up, thus ensuring that its tapered section is

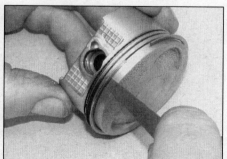

14.9 . . . and the top ring as described

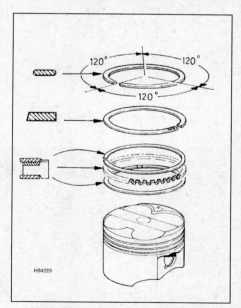

14.10 Piston ring installation details – stagger the ring end gaps as shown

14.8b Install the middle ring . . .

installed correctly. Fit the ring into the middle groove in the piston **(see illustration)**. Do not expand the ring any more than is necessary to slide it into place. To avoid breaking the ring, use a piston ring installation tool.

9 Finally, install the top ring in the same manner into the top groove in the piston **(see illustration)**. Make sure the identification letter (where present) near the end gap is facing up.

10 Once the rings are correctly installed, check they move freely without snagging and stagger their end gaps as shown **(see illustration)**.

15 Starter clutch and gears

Note: *The starter clutch can be removed with the engine in the frame. If the engine has been removed, ignore the steps which do not apply.*

Check

1 The operation of the starter clutch can be checked while it is in situ. Remove the starter motor (see Chapter 9). Check that the idle/reduction gear is able to rotate freely clockwise as you look at it via the starter motor aperture, but locks when rotated anti-clockwise. If not, the starter clutch is faulty and should be removed for inspection.

Removal

2 Remove the alternator rotor (see Chapter 9) – the starter clutch is bolted to the back of it.

15.3a Remove the collar . . .

15.3b . . . the idle/reduction gear . . .

15.3c . . . and the shaft

3 Remove the collar from the idle/reduction gear shaft, then remove the gear and the shaft **(see illustrations)**.

Inspection

4 With the alternator face down on a workbench, check that the starter driven gear rotates freely anti-clockwise and locks against the rotor in a clockwise direction **(see illustration)**. If it doesn't, the starter clutch should be dismantled for further investigation.
5 Withdraw the starter driven gear from the starter clutch, rotating it anti-clockwise as you do **(see illustration)**.
6 Check the condition of the sprags inside the clutch body and the corresponding surface on the driven gear hub **(see illustration)**. If they are damaged, marked or flattened at any point, they should be replaced with new ones. Measure the outside diameter of the hub and check that it has not worn beyond the service

limit specified **(see illustration)**. To remove the starter clutch assembly, hold the alternator rotor using a holding strap and unscrew the three bolts inside the rotor **(see illustration)**. The clutch outer and sprag piece are supplied as an assembly. Install the new assembly in a reverse sequence. Apply clean engine oil to the sprags. Apply a suitable non-permanent thread locking compound to the bolts and tighten them to the torque setting specified at the beginning of the Chapter.
7 Check the bush in the starter driven gear hub and its bearing surface on the crankshaft **(see illustration)**. If the bush shows signs of excessive wear (the groove in the surface of the bush for holding the oil will be barely visible) replace the driven gear with a new one.
8 Check the teeth of the reduction and idle gears and the corresponding teeth of the starter driven gear and starter motor drive

shaft. Replace the gears and/or starter motor if worn or chipped teeth are discovered on related gears. Also check the idle gear shaft for damage, and check that the gear is not a loose fit on it. Check the reduction gear shaft ends and the bores they run in for wear.

Installation

9 Lubricate the idle/reduction gear shaft with clean engine oil and insert it into its bore in the crankcase **(see illustration 15.3c)**. Slide the gear onto the shaft, meshing the teeth of the larger inner gear with those of the starter motor shaft **(see illustration 15.3b)**. Slide the collar over the shaft **(see illustration 15.3a)**.
10 Lubricate the outside of the starter driven gear hub and the bush in its centre with clean engine oil, then fit the gear into the clutch, rotating it anti-clockwise as you do so to spread the sprags and allow the hub to enter **(see illustration 15.5)**.

15.4 Check the operation of the starter clutch as described

15.5 Withdraw the driven gear

15.6a Check the sprags (A) and the driven gear hub (B)

15.6b Measure the diameter of the hub

15.6c The starter clutch is secured by the bolts (arrowed)

15.7 Check the bush (arrowed) for wear

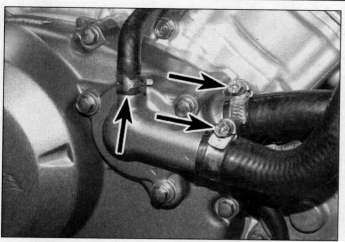

16.3 Release the clamps (arrowed) and detach the hoses

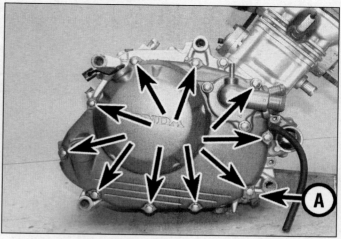

16.5 Unscrew the bolts (arrowed) and remove the cover – note the hose guide (A)

16.6 Unscrew the bolts (arrowed) and remove the pressure plate and springs

16.7a A peg spanner is needed to unscrew the nut . . .

16.7b . . . and the clutch must be held – this shows a commercially available holding tool

11 Install the alternator rotor (see Chapter 9), making sure the teeth on the starter driven gear mesh with those on the smaller outer gear teeth on the idle/reduction gear.

16 Clutch

Note: *The clutch can be removed with the engine in the frame. If the engine has been removed, ignore the steps which don't apply.*

Removal

1 Remove the lower fairing and the right-hand fairing side panel (see Chapter 8).
2 Drain the engine oil and the coolant (see Chapter 1).
3 Release the clamps securing the coolant hoses to the water pump and detach the hoses, noting which fits where **(see illustration)**.
4 Slacken the locknut on the clutch cable adjuster, then thread the adjuster nut away from the bracket. Free the adjuster from the bracket and detach the cable end from the release arm **(see illustrations 4.15a, b and c)**. Position the cable clear of the engine.

5 Working evenly in a criss-cross pattern, unscrew the clutch cover bolts, noting the guide for the water pump drain hose **(see illustration)**. Remove the cover, being prepared to catch any residual oil. Remove the gasket and discard it **(see illustration 16.27a)**. Remove the two dowels from either the cover or the crankcase if they are loose. Note the clutch lifter piece in the cover – make sure it does not drop out **(see illustration 16.26)**.
6 Working in a criss-cross pattern, gradually slacken the clutch spring bolts until pressure is released **(see illustration)**. To prevent the assembly from turning, cover it with a rag and hold it securely – the bolts are not very tight. If available, have an assistant hold the clutch while you unscrew the bolts. Remove the bolts, lifter plate and springs **(see illustrations 16.25b and a)**. Remove the bearing from the lifter plate if it is loose **(see illustration 16.16a)**.
7 To remove the clutch nut, a peg spanner (Honda tool pt. no. 07716-0020100) is required **(see illustration)**, or alternatively one can be made by cutting castellations into an old socket (see **Tool Tip**). Also the input shaft must be locked – this can be done in several ways: if the engine is in the frame, engage 6th

gear and have an assistant hold the rear brake on hard with the rear tyre in firm contact with the ground; alternatively, and if the engine has been removed, the Honda service tool (pt. no. 07GMB-KT7010) or a commercially available clutch holding tool (as shown) can be used to stop the clutch centre from turning **(see illustration)**. Unscrew the nut and remove the washer **(see illustration 16.24a)**.

A peg spanner can be made by cutting castellations into a socket of the correct size using a hacksaw.

16.8 Draw the complete clutch assembly off the shaft

16.9a Slide the guide off the shaft . . .

16.9b . . . followed by the washer

8 Grasp the complete clutch assembly and draw it off the shaft **(see illustration)**. Unless the plates are being replaced with new ones, keep the assembly together.

9 Slide the guide and the washer off the shaft **(see illustrations)**.

10 If required, grab hold of the pressure plate posts and draw the clutch plate assembly out of the clutch housing, noting how the friction plate tabs locate **(see illustration 16.21b)**. Place the clutch centre face down and remove the pressure plate from the back **(see illustration)**. Remove the clutch friction and plain plates, noting how they fit and keeping them in order, then remove the anti-judder spring and spring seat, noting which way round they fit **(see illustrations 16.20e, c, b and a)**. Note that of the friction plates, there are two types, the outermost plate (type A) having a larger internal diameter to the inner

ones (type B) – this is to accommodate the anti-judder spring and spring seat.

Inspection

11 After an extended period of service the clutch friction plates will wear and promote clutch slip. Measure the thickness of each friction plate using a Vernier caliper, noting that there is a difference in thickness of the outer (type A) plate to the rest **(see illustration)**. If any plate has worn to or beyond the service limits given in the Specifications at the beginning of the Chapter, or if any of the plates smell burnt or are glazed, the friction plates must be replaced with a new set.

12 The plain plates should not show any signs of excess heating (bluing). Check for warpage using a flat surface and feeler gauges **(see illustration)**. If any plate exceeds the maximum permissible amount of warpage, or

shows signs of bluing, all plain plates must be replaced with a new set.

13 Measure the free length of each clutch spring using a Vernier caliper **(see illustration)**. Place each spring upright on a flat surface and check it for bend by placing a ruler against it, or alternatively lay it against a set square. If any spring is below the minimum free length specified or if the bend in any spring is excessive, replace all the springs as a set. Also check the anti-judder spring and spring seat for damage or distortion and replace them with new ones if necessary.

14 Inspect the friction plates and the clutch housing for burrs and indentations on the edges of the protruding tabs on the plates and/or the slots in the housing **(see illustration)**. Similarly check for wear between the inner teeth of the plain plates and the slots in the clutch centre **(see illustration)**. Wear

16.10 Lift the pressure plate off the back of the assembly

16.11 Measuring clutch friction plate thickness

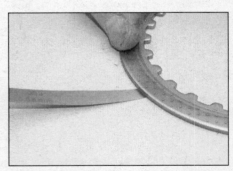

16.12 Check the plain plates for warpage

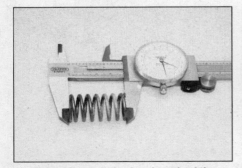

16.13 Measure the free length of the clutch springs and check them for bend

16.14a Check the friction plate tabs and housing slots . . .

16.14b . . . and the plain plate teeth and centre slots as described

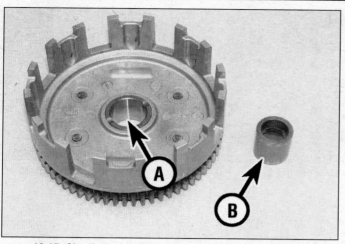

16.15 Check the bearing surfaces on the bush (A), the guide (B) and the shaft

16.16a Check the lifter plate and its bearing

of this nature will cause clutch drag and slow disengagement during gear changes as the plates will snag when the pressure plate is lifted. With care a small amount of wear can be corrected by dressing with a fine file, but if this is excessive the worn components should be renewed.

15 Inspect the bearing surfaces of the clutch housing bush and on the clutch guide and input shaft **(see illustration)**. Measure the internal diameter of the housing bush, the external and internal diameters of the guide and the external diameter of the input shaft where the guide sits, and compare the results to the specifications at the beginning of the Chapter. If there are any signs of wear, pitting or other damage the affected parts must be replaced with new ones.

16 Check the lifter plate and its bearing for signs of wear or damage and roughness **(see illustration)**. Check that the bearing outer race is a good fit in the centre of the lifter, and that the inner race rotates freely without any rough spots. Check the lifter piece and the corresponding cut-out in the release mechanism shaft for signs of wear or damage **(see illustration)**. Replace any parts necessary with new ones.

17 Check the release mechanism in the

clutch cover for a smooth action. If the action is stiff or rough, withdraw the shaft and remove the spring, noting how its ends locate **(see illustration)**. Clean and check the oil seal and the shaft bore in the cover. The seal can be replaced by levering the old one out with a seal hook or screwdriver and pressing the new one in **(see illustrations)**. Lubricate the shaft with molybdenum disulphide oil (a 50/50 mixture of molybdenum disulphide grease and engine oil) and the seal lips with grease before installing the shaft and fitting the spring. Make

sure the return spring ends locate correctly **(see illustration)**.

18 Check the teeth of the primary driven gear on the back of the clutch housing and the corresponding teeth of the primary drive gear on the crankshaft. Replace the clutch housing and/or primary drive gear with a new one if worn or chipped teeth are discovered – refer to Section 18 for the primary drive gear. Check the condition of the crankshaft oil seal in the cover and replace it with a new one if necessary – release the circlip, then lever the

16.16b Check the lifter piece and its seat cut-out in the shaft for wear

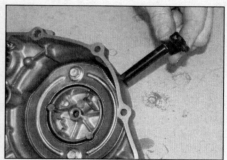

16.17a Withdraw the shaft from the cover

16.17b Lever out the seal . . .

16.17c . . . and press a new one into place

16.17d Make sure the spring is fitted so the top end locates in the hole in the shaft (arrowed)

16.18a Release the circlip . . .

16.18b . . . then lever out the seal

16.18c Press the new seal in using a suitable socket

16.20a Fit the anti-judder spring seat . . .

16.20b . . . and spring with its outer edge raised off the seat . . .

16.20c . . . then fit the friction plate with the larger internal diameter . . .

16.20d . . . so that it fits over the anti-judder components

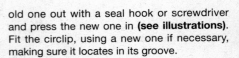

old one out with a seal hook or screwdriver and press the new one in (see illustrations). Fit the circlip, using a new one if necessary, making sure it locates in its groove.

Installation

19 Remove all traces of old gasket from the crankcase and clutch cover surfaces.

20 If the clutch plate assembly was disassembled, fit the spring seat onto the clutch centre, followed by the anti-judder spring, making sure its outer edge is raised off the spring seat – if it is touching the seat and the inner edge is raised, it is the wrong way round (see illustrations). Coat each clutch plate with engine oil, then build up the plates in the housing, starting with the outermost (type A) friction plate with the larger internal diameter so its fits around the anti-judder spring and seat (see illustration). Then fit a plain plate, then a type B friction plate, then alternating plain and friction plates until all are installed (see illustrations). Fit the pressure plate into the back of the pack, aligning the mark on the plate with that on the clutch centre, and making sure its castellations locate in the teeth of the inner plain plate (see illustrations). Grasp the pack and turn it on its side, then pull on the pressure plate posts and check for any freeplay between the clutch plates – there should be none; if there is, it means the pressure plate has not located properly.

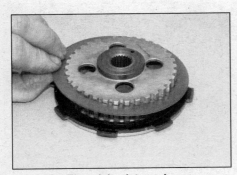

16.20e Fit a plain plate and so on . . .

16.20f . . . then fit the pressure plate, aligning the marks . . .

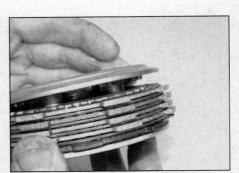

16.20g . . . and making sure the castellations engage

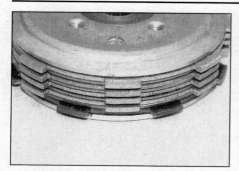

16.21a Align the friction plate tabs as shown

16.21b Fit the assembly into the housing, locating the tabs on the outer friction plate into the shallow slots in the housing

16.24a Fit the washer and clutch nut . . .

21 Align the tabs of the friction plates as shown **(see illustration)**. Turn the assembly over, grab hold of the pressure plate posts and fit the clutch plate assembly into the clutch housing, locating the friction plate tabs in the slots, making sure the tabs of the outermost plate locate in the shallow slots **(see illustration)**.

22 Slide the washer onto the shaft **(see illustration 16.9b)**. Smear the clutch guide inside and out with clean engine oil, then slide it onto the shaft **(see illustration 16.9a)**.

23 Slide the clutch assembly onto the guide on the shaft, making sure that the teeth of the primary driven gear on the back of the housing engage with those of the primary drive gear **(see illustration 16.8)**.

24 Fit the washer, then apply oil to the seating face of the clutch nut and thread it onto the shaft **(see illustration)**. Using the method employed on removal to lock the input shaft and the tool to fit the nut (see Step 7), tighten the nut to the torque setting specified at the beginning of the Chapter **(see illustration)**.

25 Fit the bearing into the lifter plate if removed, and lubricate it with oil **(see illustration 16.16a)**. Fit the clutch springs, lifter plate and bolts and tighten them evenly and a little at a time in a criss-cross sequence **(see illustrations)**.

26 Apply some oil to the lifter piece, then turn the release mechanism shaft in the cover until the cut-out is aligned and insert the lifter piece **(see illustration)**.

27 Fit the two dowels into the crankcase if removed, then fit a **new** gasket, locating it over the dowels **(see illustration)**. Lubricate the crankshaft end with oil. Make sure the oil strainer is installed. Install the cover, turning the water pump impeller as required to ease engagement of its gear with the primary drive gear **(see illustration)**. Install all the bolts finger-tight, not forgetting the hose guide, then tighten them evenly and a little at a time in a criss-cross pattern **(see illustration 16.5)**.

28 Engage the clutch cable end in the release lever arm, then locate the cable in its bracket and adjust freeplay (see Chapter 1) **(see illustrations 4.15c, b and a)**.

29 Fit the coolant hoses onto their unions on the water pump and secure them with the clamps – the hose from the bottom of the radiator fits onto the outer union on the front **(see illustration 16.3)**.

30 Fill the engine with the correct amount and type of oil and coolant (see Chapter 1). Install the fairing panels (See Chapter 8).

16.24b . . . and tighten it to the specified torque

16.25a Fit the springs . . .

16.25b . . . and the lifter plate, and tighten the bolts as described

16.26 Turn the shaft to align the cut-out then fit the lifter piece

16.27a Locate the new gasket over the dowels (arrowed) . . .

16.27b . . . then fit the cover

17.1 Slacken the lockring and turn the adjuster in

17.4a Free the outer cable from the adjuster . . .

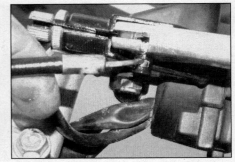

17.4b . . . and the inner cable from the lever

17 Clutch cable

1 Fully slacken the lockring on the adjuster at the handlebar end of the cable, then thread the adjuster fully in **(see illustration)**. This provides freeplay in the cable and resets the adjuster to the beginning of its span.
2 Remove the right-hand fairing side panel (see Chapter 8).
3 Slacken the locknut on the clutch cable adjuster, then thread the locknut and adjuster nut fully up the adjuster. Free the cable end from the release arm then draw the cable forward out of the bracket **(see illustrations 4.15a, b and c)**.
4 Align the slots in the adjuster and lockring at the handlebar end of the cable with that in

the lever bracket, then pull the outer cable end from the socket in the adjuster and release the inner cable from the lever **(see illustrations)**. Remove the cable from the machine, noting its routing through the guides.

Before removing the cable from the bike, tape the lower end of the new cable to the upper end of the old cable. Slowly pull the lower end of the old cable out, guiding the new cable down into position. Using this method will ensure the cable is routed correctly.

5 Installation is the reverse of removal. Apply grease to the cable ends. Make sure the cable is correctly routed through its guides. Adjust the amount of clutch lever freeplay (see Chapter 1).

18 Primary drive gear

Removal

1 Remove the clutch and separate the plate assembly from the clutch housing, then slide the housing back onto the shaft (see Section 16).
2 To unscrew the primary drive gear nut, a peg spanner (Honda pt. no. 07716-0020100) is required **(see illustration)**, or alternatively one can be made by cutting castellations into an old socket (see **Tool Tip** in Section 16). Wedge a stout piece of rag or rolled up strap between the teeth of the primary drive and driven gears where they mesh at the top – this will lock them together to prevent them turning **(see illustration)**. Slacken the primary drive gear nut. Remove the rag.
3 Slide the clutch housing off the shaft. Unscrew the primary drive gear nut and remove the washer, then slide the gear off the end of the crankshaft, noting how it locates on the Woodruff key **(see illustrations)**. Remove the key from its slot **(see illustration 18.7)**.
4 If the oil pump has been removed slide the inner washer off the shaft **(see illustration)**.

Installation

5 If a new primary drive gear is being installed it must be selected so that its colour code matches that of the crankcase – either

18.2a A peg spanner is needed to unscrew the nut

18.2b Using a piece of rolled strap to jam the gears while unscrewing the nut

18.3a Unscrew the nut and remove the washer . . .

18.3b . . . and the gear

18.4 The oil pump must be removed before the washer can be slid off

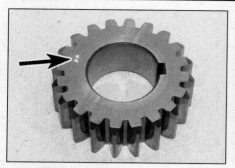

18.5a There should be a paint mark on the gear (arrowed) . . .

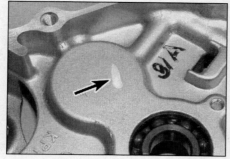

18.5b . . . and on the crankcase (arrowed)

18.7 Fit the key into its slot

yellow, blue or white **(see illustrations)**. After installation the backlash between the primary drive and driven gears must be checked (Step 9).

6 If the oil pump has been removed slide the inner washer onto the shaft **(see illustration 18.4)**.

7 Fit the Woodruff key into its slot in the crankshaft **(see illustration)**. Align the cut-out in the gear with the key, then slide the gear onto the shaft so it locates over the key **(see illustration 18.3b)**. Fit the washer and the nut **(see illustration 18.3a)**.

8 Slide the clutch housing onto the shaft so it meshes with the drive gear. Wedge the stout piece of rag where the gear teeth mesh at the bottom **(see illustration)**. Tighten the nut to the torque setting specified at the beginning of the Chapter **(see illustration)**.

9 If a new gear has been fitted mount a dial gauge so that its tip rests against and at right angles to the end of one of the driven gear teeth on the back of the clutch housing. Turn the clutch housing back and forth to measure the backlash between the teeth, making sure the drive gear does not move. Compare the reading to that specified at the beginning of the Chapter. If it differs from the standard amount, first make sure the colour codes for the crankcase and the gear are matched. If they do then either the crankshaft and/or the transmission input shaft bearings could be worn.

10 Install the clutch (see Section 16).

18.8a Wedge the rag or strap as shown . . .

18.8b . . . and tighten the nut to the specified torque

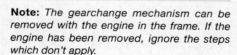

19 Gearchange mechanism

Note: *The gearchange mechanism can be removed with the engine in the frame. If the engine has been removed, ignore the steps which don't apply.*

Removal

1 Make sure the transmission is in neutral. Remove the clutch (see Section 16).

2 Make a mark where the slot in the gearchange linkage arm aligns with the shaft **(see illustration 4.12a)**. Unscrew the linkage arm pinch bolt and slide the arm off the shaft **(see illustration 4.12b)**.

3 Wrap a single layer of thin insulating tape around the gearchange shaft splines to protect the oil seal lips as the shaft is removed.

4 Note how the stopper arm spring ends locate and how the roller on the arm locates in the neutral detent on the selector drum cam, then unscrew the stopper arm bolt and remove the arm, the washer and the spring, noting how they fit **(see illustration)**.

5 Note how the gearchange shaft centralising spring ends fit on each side of the locating pin in the casing, and how the pawls on the selector arm locate onto the pins on the end of the selector drum behind the cam plate. Grasp the end of the shaft, then push the selector arm down until it clears the cam plate and withdraw the shaft/arm assembly **(see illustration)**.

19.4 Note how the spring ends and roller locate, then unscrew the bolt and remove the arm

19.5 Lower the arm and withdraw the shaft/arm assembly, noting how it fits

19.6a Hold the cam plate to prevent it turning and unscrew the bolt (arrowed)

19.6b Remove the plate locating pins from the drum

19.7a Check the selector arm pawls and cam plate pins . . .

6 If the crankcases are being separated, unscrew the cam plate bolt, locking the selector drum with a holding tool as shown or using a suitable tool wedged between the plate and the crankcase, and remove the washer **(see illustration)**. Remove the plate, noting that there are six small pins pressed into the back of it – they should not be loose but take care just in case **(see illustration 19.10a)**. There are also two pins that locate the plate on the end of the selector drum – they should stay in the end of the drum, but again take care as they could drop out. Remove them from the drum for safekeeping **(see illustration)**.

Inspection

7 Check the selector arm for cracks, distortion and wear of its pawls, and check for any corresponding wear on the pins on the selector drum cam plate **(see illustration)**.

Also check the stopper arm roller and the detents in the cam plate for any wear or damage, and make sure the roller turns freely **(see illustration)**. Replace any components that are worn or damaged with new ones.
8 Inspect the shaft centralising spring, the selector arm spring and the stopper arm return spring for fatigue, wear or damage. If any is found, they must be replaced with new ones. To replace the shaft spring, slide it off the end of the shaft, noting how its ends locate **(see illustration)**. Fit the new spring, locating the ends on each side of the tab. To replace the selector arm spring simply unhook its ends. Also check that the centralising spring locating pin in the crankcase is securely tightened. If it is loose, remove it and apply a non-permanent thread locking compound to its threads, then tighten it.
9 Check the gearchange shaft is straight and look for damage to the splines. If the

shaft is bent you can attempt to straighten it, but if the splines are damaged the shaft must be replaced with a new one. Also check the condition of the shaft oil seal in the left-hand side of the crankcase. If it is damaged, deteriorated or shows signs of leakage it must be replaced with a new one – lever out the old seal with a seal hook or screwdriver **(see illustration)**. Press or drive the new seal squarely into place using your fingers, a seal driver or suitable socket **(see illustration)**.

Installation

10 If removed, fit the cam plate locating pins into the end of the selector drum **(see illustration 19.6b)**. Locate the cam plate onto the pins **(see illustration)**. Apply a suitable non-permanent thread locking compound to the cam plate bolt and tighten it to the torque setting specified at the beginning of the Chapter **(see illustration)** – lock the

19.7b . . . and the stopper arm roller and cam plate detents

19.8 Centralising spring (A), selector arm spring (B)

19.9a Lever out the seal . . .

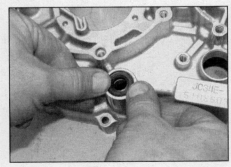

19.9b . . . and press a new one into place

19.10a Fit the cam plate onto the pins . . .

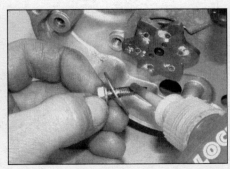

19.10b . . . then threadlock the bolt and tighten it to the specified torque

19.12 Stopper arm components

19.13 Correct assembly of the gearchange components

drum with a holding tool as on removal **(see illustration 19.6a)**.

11 Check that the shaft centralising spring is properly positioned **(see illustration 19.8)**. Apply some grease to the lips of the gearchange shaft oil seal in the left-hand side of the crankcase. Slide the shaft into place and push it all the way through the case until the splined end comes out the other side, and push the selector arm down so it fits behind the cam plate **(see illustration 19.5)**. Locate the selector arm pawls onto the pins on the selector drum and the centralising

spring ends onto each side of the locating pin in the crankcase.

12 Fit the stopper arm spring onto its post with the ends facing back and the curved end outermost. Fit the bolt through the stopper arm, then fit the washer **(see illustration)**. Apply a suitable non-permanent thread locking compound to the bolt. Install the arm, locating the roller onto the neutral detent on the selector drum and making sure the spring ends are positioned correctly **(see illustration 19.4)**. Tighten the bolt to the torque setting specified at the beginning of the Chapter.

13 Check that all components are correctly positioned **(see illustration)**. Install the clutch (see Section 16).

14 Remove the insulating tape from around the gearchange shaft splines. Slide the gearchange linkage arm onto the shaft, aligning its slit with the punch mark on the shaft **(see illustrations 4.12b and a)**. Install the pinch bolt and tighten it.

20 Oil pump

Note: *The oil pump can be removed with the engine in the frame. If the engine has been removed, ignore the steps which don't apply.*

Removal

1 Remove the clutch cover (see Section 16, Steps 1 to 5).

2 Unscrew the three bolts and remove the pump from the crankcase **(see illustration)**.

3 Remove the dowels from the crankcase if they did not come away with the pump.

4 If the primary drive gear has been removed slide the inner washer off the crankshaft **(see illustration 18.4)**.

Inspection

Note: *When removing the rotors from the oil pump, note whether the punch marks face into or out of the pump body. The marks serve as a guide to which way round to fit the rotors on installation. Refitting the rotors in their original positions will ensure that mated surfaces continue to run together.*

5 Remove the E-clip from the outer end of the shaft **(see illustration)**. Lift the gear off the cover on the inner face of the pump and withdraw the shaft from the pump **(see illustration)**. Slide the gear off the shaft and remove the drive pin **(see illustration)**.

6 Unscrew the bolts securing the cover to the pump body, then remove the dowels and the

20.2 Unscrew the bolts (arrowed) and remove the pump

20.5a Remove the E-clip . . .

20.5b . . . then remove the gear/shaft assembly

20.5c Slide the gear down off the shaft and remove the drive pin

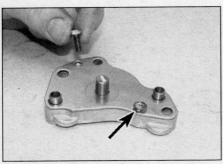

20.6a Unscrew the bolts (arrowed) . . .

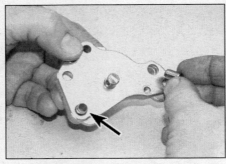

20.6b . . . then remove the dowels (arrowed) . . .

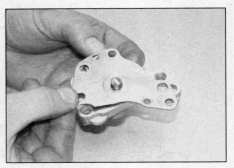

20.6c . . . the cover . . .

20.6d . . . and the rotors

20.9a Fit the shaft to align the rotors . . .

20.9b . . . then measure the inner rotor tip-to-outer rotor clearance as shown (inner cover shown removed for clarity)

cover **(see illustrations)**. Remove the inner and outer rotors, noting which way round they fit **(see illustration)**.

7 Clean all the components in solvent.

8 Inspect the pump body and rotors for scoring and wear. If any damage, scoring or uneven or excessive wear is evident, replace the components with new ones.

9 Fit the inner and outer rotors into the pump body with the punch marks facing out and aligned **(see illustration 20.14)**. Fit the shaft into the inner rotor **(see illustration)**. Measure the clearance between the inner rotor tip and the outer rotor with a feeler gauge and compare it to the service limit listed in the specifications at the beginning of the Chapter **(see illustration)**. If the clearance measured is greater than the maximum listed, replace the rotors with new ones.

10 Measure the clearance between the outer

rotor and the pump body with a feeler gauge and compare it to the maximum clearance listed in the specifications at the beginning of the Chapter **(see illustration)**. If the clearance measured is greater than the maximum listed, replace the outer rotor and pump body with new ones.

11 Lay a straight-edge across the rotors and the pump body and, using a feeler gauge, measure the rotor end-float (the gap between the rotors and the straight-edge **(see illustration)**. If the clearance measured is greater than the maximum listed, replace the rotors and pump body with new ones.

12 Check the pump drive gear, shaft and drive pin for wear or damage, and replace them with new ones if necessary. If wear and/or broken teeth are found on the gear check the primary drive gear teeth as well (Section 18).

13 If the pump is good, make sure all the components are clean, then lubricate them with new engine oil.

14 Fit the outer rotor into the pump body with the punch mark facing the same way as noted on removal **(see illustration 20.6d)**. Fit the inner rotor into the outer rotor with the punch mark facing the same way as noted on removal **(see illustration)**. Fill the pump with oil.

15 Fit the cover onto the pump body, then fit the locating dowels **(see illustrations 20.6c and b)**. Fit the bolts and tighten them to the torque setting specified at the beginning of the Chapter **(see illustration 20.6a)**.

16 Fit the drive pin and gear onto the shaft, locating the pin ends into the cut-outs in the gear **(see illustration 20.5c)**. Slide the drive shaft through the pump **(see illustration**

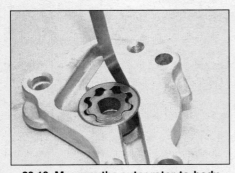

20.10 Measure the outer rotor-to-body clearance as shown

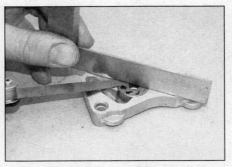

20.11 Measure rotor end-float as shown

20.14 Fit the inner rotor into the outer rotor

20.16a Note the flats on the shaft and inner rotor which must be aligned

20.16b Make sure the E-clip locates correctly in its groove

20.19 Make sure the dowels locate and the gears engage

20.5b), aligning the flats between the shaft and inner rotor **(see illustration)**. Fit the E-clip into its groove in the outer end of the shaft **(see illustrations)**.

17 Rotate the pump shaft by hand and check it turns the rotors smoothly and freely.

Installation

18 If the primary drive gear has been removed slide the inner washer onto the crankshaft **(see illustration 18.4)**.

19 Fit the pump, making sure the dowels locate in the crankcase, and the gears engage correctly (unless the primary drive gear has been removed), then install the bolts and tighten them **(see illustration)**.

20 Install the clutch cover (see Section 16, Steps 26 to 30).

21 Crankcase separation and reassembly

Note: *To separate the crankcase halves, the engine must be removed from the frame.*

Separation

1 To access the crankshaft and connecting rod assembly, balancer shaft, transmission shafts, selector drum and forks, and their bearings, the crankcase halves must be separated.

2 Before the crankcases can be separated the following components must be removed:

Starter motor (Chapter 9)
Neutral switch (Chapter 9)

Valve cover (Section 6)
Camshaft holder (Section 8)
Cylinder head (Section 10)
Cam chain and blades (Section 9)
Cylinder barrel (Section 12)
Piston (Section 13)
Alternator (Chapter 9)
Starter clutch gears (Section 15)
Clutch (Section 16)
Primary drive gear (Section 18)
Gearchange mechanism (Section 19)
Oil pump (Section 20)
Oil strainer (Chapter 1)

3 Fit a suitable 3 mm screw that is about 34 mm long through the washer and spring in the inner edge of the cam chain tunnel, and thread it into the hole in the bearing stopper pin below the spring to compress the spring until the circlip groove is exposed **(see illustration)**. Remove the circlip, then pull the washer/ spring/pin pin out using the head of the screw

to pull them **(see illustrations)**. Keep the screw in place for installation. Replace the circlip with a new one if it has deformed.

4 Remove the oil jet from its orifice in the top of the right-hand crankcase half **(see illustration)**.

5 Unscrew the four right-hand crankcase bolts evenly, a little at a time and in a criss-cross sequence until they are finger-tight, then remove them, noting the one fitted with a sealing washer **(see illustration)**. Note that a new sealing washer should be used on assembly.

> **HAYNES HiNT** *As each bolt is removed, store it in its relative position in a cardboard template of the crankcase halves. This will ensure all bolts and washers are returned to their original locations on reassembly.*

21.3a Thread the screw into the pin to compress the spring . . .

21.3b . . . then remove the circlip . . .

21.3c . . . and withdraw the pin by pulling on the screw head

21.4 Remove the oil jet

21.5 Right-hand crankcase bolts (arrowed)

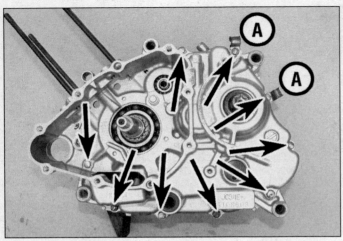

21.6 Left-hand crankcase bolts (arrowed) – note the wiring guides (A)

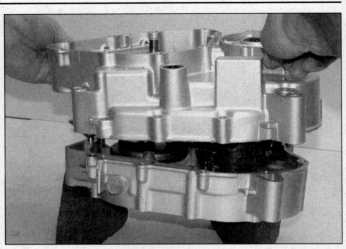

21.7 Carefully separate the crankcase halves

6 Unscrew the nine left-hand crankcase bolts evenly, a little at a time and in a criss-cross sequence until they are finger-tight, then remove them, noting the wiring guides secured by the upper rear bolts **(see illustration)**.

7 Place the engine on its right-hand side, laying it on wooden blocks so the shaft ends are clear of the bench. Carefully lift the left crankcase half off the right half, using a soft-faced hammer to tap around the joint to initially separate the halves if necessary **(see illustration)**. **Note:** *If the halves do not separate easily, make sure all fasteners have been removed. Do not try and separate the halves by levering against the crankcase mating surfaces as they are easily scored and will leak oil in the future if damaged.* The left-hand crankcase half will come away leaving the crankshaft, balancer shaft, transmission shafts and selector drum and forks in the right-hand half.

8 Note the thrust washer on the left-hand end of the transmission output shaft – if it is not there it is stuck to the bearing in the crankcase, in which case retrieve it and fit it back onto the shaft. Remove the two locating dowels from the crankcase if they are loose (they could be in either half) **(see illustration 21.13)**.

9 Refer to Sections 22 to 27 for the removal and installation of the components housed within the crankcases.

Reassembly

10 Remove all traces of sealant from the crankcase mating surfaces.

11 Ensure that all components and their bearings are in place in the right-hand crankcase half, and that all bearings and new oil seals are in the left-hand half (see Section 19 for the gearchange shaft oil seal and Section 25 for the transmission output shaft seal).

12 Generously lubricate the crankshaft and transmission shaft bearings and gears and the selector fork shafts and fork ends and the tracks in the selector drum with clean engine oil, then use a rag soaked in high flash-point solvent to wipe over the mating surfaces of both crankcase halves to remove all traces of oil.

13 If removed, fit the two locating dowels into the right-hand crankcase half **(see illustration)**. Make sure the thrust washer is in place on the left-hand end of the transmission output shaft.

14 Apply a small amount of suitable sealant (Three-Bond 1207B or equivalent RTV sealant – ask your dealer) to the mating surface of the left-hand crankcase half as shown, avoiding the oil passage in the top of the crankcase **(see illustration)**.

Caution: Apply the sealant only to the mating surfaces. Do not apply an excessive amount as it will ooze out when the case halves are assembled and may obstruct oil passages. Do not apply the sealant close to any of the oil passages.

15 Check again that all components are in position **(see illustration 21.13)**. Carefully fit the left-hand crankcase half down onto the right-hand crankcase half, making sure the

21.13 Make sure the thrust washer (A) and the dowels (B) are fitted

21.14 Apply the sealant as shown, avoiding the oil passage (arrowed)

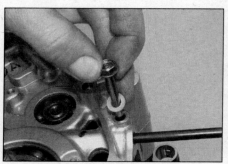

21.17 Fit a new sealing washer onto the upper bolt

21.21a Assemble the components and use the screw to compress the spring

21.21b The tip of the pin (arrowed) should be visible against the rim of the bearing

shaft ends and dowels all locate correctly **(see illustration 21.7)**.

16 Check that the left-hand crankcase half is correctly seated. Clean the threads of all the crankcase bolts. Turn the engine over.

Caution: The crankcase halves should fit together without being forced. If the casings are not correctly seated, remove the left-hand crankcase half and investigate the problem. Do not attempt to pull them together using the crankcase bolts as the casing will crack and be ruined.

17 Install the four right-hand crankcase bolts, fitting the two longer bolts in the upper holes, and fitting a new sealing washer with the uppermost bolt **(see illustration and 21.5)**. Secure the bolts finger-tight at first, then tighten them evenly and a little at a time in a criss-cross sequence – no torque setting is specified, but bolts of that size should tightened to 12 Nm.

18 Turn the engine over. Install the nine left-hand crankcase bolts, making sure they are fitted in their correct positions as there are four different lengths, and not forgetting to fit the wiring guides with the upper rear bolts **(see illustration 21.6)**. Secure the bolts finger-tight at first, then tighten them evenly and a little at a time in a criss-cross sequence – no torque setting is specified, but bolts of that size should tightened to 10 Nm.

19 With all crankcase fasteners tightened, check that the crankshaft, balancer shaft and transmission shafts rotate smoothly and easily. Check that the transmission shafts rotate freely and independently in neutral, then rotate the selector drum by hand and select each gear in turn whilst rotating the input shaft. If there are any signs of undue stiffness, tight or rough spots, or of any other problem, the fault must be rectified before proceeding further.

20 Fit the oil jet into its orifice in the top of the right-hand crankcase half **(see illustration 21.4)**.

21 If the bearing stopper pin assembly was taken apart after removal (Step 3), fit the spring into the pin and fit the washer, then fit the 3 mm screw used earlier through the washer and spring and thread it into the pin to compress the spring **(see illustration)**. Fit the bearing stopper pin into its hole **(see**

illustration 21.3c)**, locating the tip against the outer edge of the bearing **(see illustration)**. Fit the circlip, making sure it locates correctly, then undo the screw, allowing the spring and washer to settle against the circlip **(see illustrations 21.3b and a)**.

22 Install all other removed assemblies in a reverse of the sequence given in Step 2.

22 Crankcases and bearings

Crankcases

1 After the crankcases have been separated, remove the crankshaft and balancer shaft, the selector drum and forks and the transmission shafts, referring to the relevant Sections of this Chapter.

2 Clean the crankcases thoroughly with new solvent and dry them with compressed air. Blow out all oil passages with compressed air.

3 Remove all traces of old gasket sealant from the mating surfaces. Clean up minor damage to the surfaces with a fine sharpening stone or grindstone.

Caution: Be very careful not to nick or gouge the crankcase mating surfaces or oil leaks will result. Check both crankcase halves very carefully for cracks and other damage.

4 Small cracks or holes in aluminium castings can be repaired with an epoxy resin adhesive as a temporary measure or with one of the low temperature welding kits. Permanent repairs can only be done by TIG (tungsten inert gas or heli-arc) welding, and only a specialist in this process is in a position to advise on the economy or practical aspect of such a repair. If any damage is found that can't be repaired, replace the crankcase halves as a set.

5 Damaged threads can be economically reclaimed using a diamond section wire insert, for example of the Heli-Coil type (though there are other makes), which are easily fitted after drilling and re-tapping the affected thread.

6 Sheared studs or screws can usually be removed with extractors, which consist of a tapered, left-hand thread screw of very hard

steel. These are inserted into a pre-drilled hole in the stud, and usually succeed in dislodging the most stubborn stud or screw. If a stud has sheared above its bore line, it can be removed using a conventional stud extractor which avoids the need for drilling.

7 Install all components and assemblies, referring to the relevant Sections of this and the other Chapters, before reassembling the crankcase halves.

Bearing information

8 The crankshaft, balancer shaft, and transmission shaft bearings should all be replaced with new ones as part of a complete engine overhaul, or individually as required due to wear or failure.

9 Bearing failure occurs mainly because of lack of lubrication, the presence of dirt or other foreign particles, overloading the engine, break-up of one or more of the bearing components due to fatigue, or corrosion. Regardless of the cause of bearing failure, it must be corrected before the engine is reassembled to prevent it from happening again.

10 The bearings should rotate smoothly, freely and quietly, there should be no rough spots or excessive play between the inner and outer races, or between the inner race and the shaft it fits on, or between the outer race and its housing in the crankcase.

11 Dirt and other foreign particles get into the engine in a variety of ways. They may be left in the engine during assembly or they may pass through filters or breathers, then get into the oil and from there into the bearings. Metal chips from machining operations and normal engine wear are often present. Abrasives are sometimes left in engine components after reconditioning operations, especially when parts are not thoroughly cleaned afterwards. The best prevention for this cause of bearing failure is to clean all parts thoroughly and keep everything spotlessly clean during engine reassembly. Regular oil changes are also recommended.

12 Lack of lubrication or lubrication breakdown has a number of interrelated causes. Excessive heat (which thins the oil), overloading and oil leakage all contribute to lubrication breakdown. Blocked oil passages

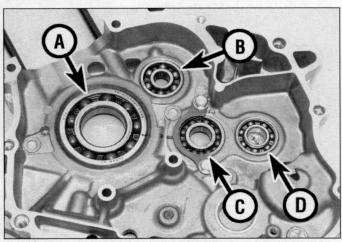

22.15a Main bearing (A), balancer shaft bearing (B), transmission input shaft bearing (C) and output shaft bearing (D) – right-hand crankcase half

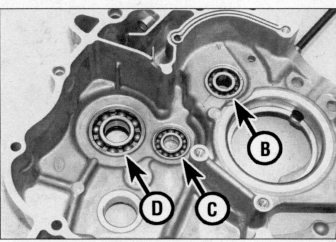

22.15b Balancer shaft bearing (B), transmission input shaft bearing (C) and output shaft bearing (D) – left-hand crankcase half

will starve a bearing of lubrication and destroy it.

13 Riding habits can have a definite effect on bearing life. Full throttle low speed operation, or labouring the engine, puts very high loads on bearings. Short trip riding leads to corrosion of bearings, as insufficient engine heat is produced to drive off the condensed water and corrosive gases produced. These products collect in the engine oil, forming acid and sludge. As the oil is carried to the engine bearings, the acid attacks and corrodes the bearing material.

14 Incorrect bearing installation during engine assembly will lead to bearing failure as well. To avoid bearing problems, clean all parts thoroughly before reassembly, and lubricate the new bearings with clean engine oil during installation.

Bearing removal and installation

Note: *If the correct bearing removal and installation tools are not available take the crankcases and crankshaft to a Honda dealer for removal and installation of the bearings – do not risk damaging either the cases or the crankshaft.*

Crankshaft (main) bearings

15 If the crankshaft (main) bearings have failed, excessive rumbling and vibration will be felt when the engine is running **(see illustrations)**.

16 Separate the crankcase halves (Section 21) and remove the crankshaft (Section 23).

17 To remove the right-hand main bearing from the crankcase, heat the bearing housing with a hot air gun, then tap the bearing out from the outside of the crankcase using a bearing driver or a suitable socket **(see illustration)**.

18 Smear the outside of the new bearing with clean oil. Note that it should be fitted with its marked side towards the inside of the engine. Heat the housing again and drive the bearing squarely in until it seats using a driver or socket that bears only on the bearing's outer race **(see illustration)**.

19 To remove the left-hand main bearing from the crankshaft, use an external bearing puller as shown to draw it off **(see illustration)**.

20 Smear the inside of the new bearing with clean oil. Note that it should be fitted with its marked side towards the crankshaft. Heat the bearing inner race and drive the bearing

squarely on until it seats using a tubular driver that bears only on the bearing's inner race.

Connecting rod (big-end) bearing

21 If the connecting rod (big-end) bearing has failed, there will be a pronounced knocking noise when the engine is running, particularly under load and increasing with engine speed. Refer to Section 23, Step 6 for checks that can be made.

22 The connecting rod and its bearing are an integral part of the crankshaft assembly which comes as a pressed-up unit – individual components are not available. If the big-end bearing fails replace the crankshaft/connecting rod assembly with a new one (see Section 23).

Balancer shaft bearings

23 If the balancer bearings have failed, excessive rumbling and vibration will be felt when the engine is running **(see illustrations 22.15a and b)**.

24 Separate the crankcase halves (Section 21) and remove the balancer shaft (Section 24).

25 To remove the bearings from the crankcase, heat the bearing housing with

22.17 Drive the bearing out from the outside . . .

22.18 . . . and drive it in from the inside until it seats

22.19 Using a puller to remove the bearing from the crankshaft

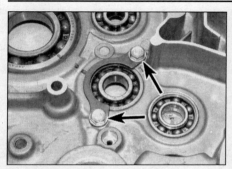

22.29 Unscrew the bolts (arrowed) and remove the plate

22.32a Locate the end of the puller behind the bearing . . .

22.32b . . . and use the slide-hammer to jar it out

a hot air gun, then tap the bearing out from the outside of the crankcase using a bearing driver or a suitable socket **(see illustration 22.17)**.

26 Smear the outside of the new bearing with clean oil and fit it with its marked side towards the inside of the engine, then heat the housing again and drive the bearing squarely in until it seats using a driver or socket that bears only on the bearing's outer race **(see illustration 22.18)**.

Transmission shaft bearings

27 If the transmission bearings have failed, excessive rumbling and vibration will be felt when the engine is running **(see illustrations 22.15a and b)**.

28 Separate the crankcase halves (Section 21) and remove the transmission shafts and the output shaft oil seal (Section 25).

29 Unscrew the two bolts securing the input shaft bearing retainer plate on the inside of the right-hand crankcase **(see illustration)**.

30 To remove the input shaft bearing from the right-hand crankcase and the output shaft bearing from the left-hand crankcase, heat the bearing housing with a hot air gun, then tap the bearing out from the outside of the crankcase using a bearing driver or a suitable socket **(see illustration 22.17)**.

31 Smear the outside of the new bearing with clean oil. Note that it should be fitted with its marked side towards the inside of the engine. Heat the housing again and drive the bearing squarely in until it seats using a driver or socket that bears only on the bearing's outer race **(see illustration 22.18)**.

32 To remove the input shaft bearing from the left-hand crankcase and the output shaft bearing from the right-hand crankcase, an expanding knife-edge bearing puller with slide-hammer attachment is required. Heat the bearing housing with a hot air gun, then fit the expanding end of the puller behind the bearing, then turn the puller to expand it and lock it in position **(see illustration)**. Attach the slide-hammer to the puller, then hold the crankcase firmly down and operate the slide-hammer to jar the bearing out **(see illustration)**.

33 Smear the outside of the new bearing with clean oil. Note that it should be fitted with its marked side towards the inside of the engine. Heat the housing again and drive the bearing squarely in until it seats using a driver or socket that bears only on the bearing's outer race **(see illustration 22.18)**.

34 Apply a suitable non-permanent thread locking compound to the bearing retainer plate bolts, then fit the plate and tighten the bolts **(see illustration 22.29)**.

23 Crankshaft and connecting rod

Note: *To remove the crankshaft the engine must be removed from the frame and the crankcase halves separated. The connecting rod is an integral part of the crankshaft assembly which comes as a pressed-up unit – individual components are not available.*

Removal

1 Remove the engine from the frame (see Section 4) and separate the crankcase halves (see Section 21).

2 Grasp the crankshaft and balancer shaft together and lift them both out of the crankcase **(see illustration)**. If the shafts are stuck, use a soft-faced hammer and gently tap on their right-hand ends.

Inspection

3 Clean the crankshaft with solvent. If available, blow the crank dry with compressed air. Check the balancer drive gear for wear or damage **(see illustration)**. If any of the gear teeth are excessively worn, chipped or broken, the crankshaft must be replaced with a new one. If wear or damage is found, also inspect the driven gear on the balancer shaft **(see illustration 24.3)**.

4 Place the crankshaft on V-blocks and check for runout using a dial gauge. Compare the reading to the maximum specified at the beginning of the Chapter. If the runout exceeds the limit, the crankshaft must be replaced with a new one.

5 Measure the connecting rod side clearance (the gap between the connecting rod big-end and the crankshaft web) with a feeler gauge. If the clearance is greater than the service limit listed in this Chapter's Specifications, replace the crankshaft with a new one.

6 Hold the crankshaft still and check for any radial (up and down) play in the big-end bearing by pushing and pulling the rod against the crank **(see illustration)**. If a dial gauge is

23.2 Lift the crankshaft and balancer shaft out together

23.3 Balancer drive gear (arrowed)

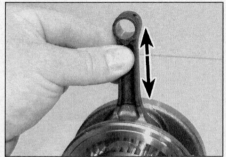

23.6 Check for any radial play in the big-end bearing

23.10a Align the lower punch marks, then engage the gears . . .

23.10b . . . so that the upper punch marks then align

available measure the amount of radial play and compare the reading to the maximum specified at the beginning of the Chapter. If the play exceeds the limit, the crankshaft must be replaced with a new one.

7 Refer to Section 13 and check the connecting rod small-end and piston pin for wear.

8 Have the rod checked for twist and bend by a Honda dealer if you are in doubt about its straightness.

9 Refer to Section 22 and check the crankshaft (main) bearings.

Installation

10 Engage the crankshaft with the balancer shaft, aligning the punch marks on the gear

24.3 Balancer driven gear (arrowed)

teeth and web as shown **(see illustrations)**. Carefully lower them into the right-hand crankcase, locating the shaft ends in the bearings **(see illustration 23.2)**.

11 Check that the crankshaft and balancer shaft rotate freely and easily.

12 Reassemble the crankcase halves (see Section 21).

24 Balancer shaft

Note: *To remove the balancer shaft the engine must be removed from the frame and the crankcases separated.*

24.4a Remove the circlip . . .

Removal

1 Remove the engine from the frame (see Section 4) and separate the crankcase halves (see Section 21).

2 Grasp the crankshaft and balancer shaft together and lift them both out of the crankcase **(see illustration 23.2)**. If the shafts are stuck, use a soft-faced hammer and gently tap on their right-hand ends.

Inspection

3 Clean the balancer shaft with solvent. If available, blow it dry with compressed air. Check the balancer driven gear for wear or damage **(see illustration)**. If any of the gear teeth are excessively worn, chipped or broken, the gear must be replaced with a new one. If wear or damage is found, also inspect the drive gear on the crankshaft **(see illustration 23.3)**.

4 If required remove the circlip, spring washer and plain washer, then draw the gear off the shaft, noting its alignment and how the rubber dampers and the springs fit **(see illustrations)**. Replace them with new ones if necessary. Make sure the circlip has not deformed.

5 If a new gear is being installed it must be selected so that its colour code, identified by paint marks on the gear **(see illustration 24.3)**, matches that on the crankcase **(see illustration 18.5b)** – either yellow, blue or white. After installation the

24.4b . . . the spring washer . . .

24.4c . . . and the plain washer . . .

24.4d . . . then draw off the gear and remove the springs and dampers

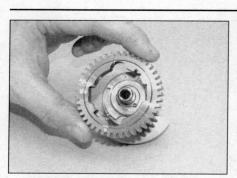

24.6a Align the gear on the shaft . . .

24.6b . . . then fit the dampers . . .

24.6c . . . and the springs

backlash between the primary drive and driven gears must be checked (Step 7).

6 Slide the gear onto the shaft with the shaped side facing out, making sure the holes for the springs and dampers are correctly aligned, and the pin locates in one of the small cut-outs, then fit the rubber dampers and springs **(see illustrations)**. Fit the plain washer and the spring washer, making sure the raised inner rim faces out, and secure them with the circlip, using a new one if necessary and making sure it locates correctly in its groove **(see illustrations 24.4c, b and a)** – you'll need to push the circlip hard against the spring washer to compress it so the circlip can locate in its groove.

7 If a new gear has been fitted, assemble the balancer shaft and crankshaft in the right-hand crankcase and join the crankcase halves, then mount a dial gauge on the top so that its tip rests against and at right-angles to the end of one of the driven gear teeth on the balancer shaft. Hold the crankshaft still and turn the balancer shaft back and forth to measure the backlash between the teeth. Compare the reading to that specified at the beginning of the Chapter. If it differs from the standard amount, first make sure the colour codes for the crankcase and the gear are the same. If they are, then either the crankshaft and/or the balancer shaft bearings could be worn.

8 Refer to Section 22 and check the balancer shaft bearings.

Installation

9 Engage the crankshaft with the balancer

shaft, aligning the punch marks on the gear teeth and web as shown **(see illustrations 23.10a and b)**. Carefully lower them into the right-hand crankcase, locating the shaft ends in the bearings **(see illustration 23.2)**.

10 Check that the crankshaft and balancer shaft rotate freely and easily.

11 Reassemble the crankcase halves (see Section 21).

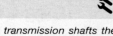

25 Transmission shaft removal and installation

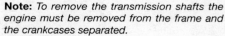

Note: *To remove the transmission shafts the engine must be removed from the frame and the crankcases separated.*

Removal

1 Remove the engine from the frame and separate the crankcase halves (see Section 21).

2 Remove the selector forks (see Section 27) – the drum can stay in place but remove it as well if required.

3 Grasp the input shaft and output shaft together and lift both shafts out of the crankcase – hold the bottom pinion on the output shaft to prevent it dropping off **(see illustration)**. If the shafts are stuck, use a soft-faced hammer and gently tap on their ends. Note that there is a thrust washer on the right-hand end of the output shaft which may stick to the bearing or fall off as you remove the shafts – retrieve the washer and fit it back onto the shaft.

4 Prise the output shaft oil seal out of the left-hand crankcase using a seal hook or screwdriver **(see illustration)**. Discard the seal as a new one must be used.

5 If necessary, the transmission shafts can be disassembled and inspected for wear or damage (see Section 26).

6 Refer to Section 22 and check the transmission shaft bearings.

Installation

7 Press or drive a new output shaft oil seal into the left-hand crankcase and lubricate its lips with oil **(see illustration)**.

8 Make sure the thrust washer is on the right-hand end of the output shaft and that it stays in place when installing the shafts – stick it in place with some oil or grease if it is likely to fall off **(see illustration)**.

9 Join the shafts together on the bench

25.3 Lift the transmission shafts out together

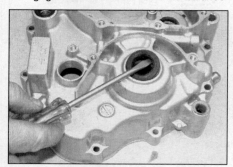

25.4 Remove and discard the oil seal

25.7 Drive the new seal into place – using a piece of wood as shown sets the seal flush with the rim

25.8 Use grease to stick the washer in place

25.9 Join the shafts so all related gears are engaged

so their related gears are engaged **(see illustration)**. Grasp the shafts together, holding the pinion and washer on the right-hand end of the output shaft to prevent them dropping off. Fit the shafts into the right-hand crankcase, locating their ends in the gears **(see illustration 25.3)**.

10 Make sure both transmission shafts are fully seated and their related pinions are correctly engaged.

11 Install the selector drum (if removed) and forks (see Section 27).

12 Position the gears in the neutral position and check the shafts are free to rotate easily and independently (i.e. the input shaft can turn whilst the output shaft is held stationary) before proceeding further. Also check that each gear can be selected by turning the input shaft with one hand and the selector drum with the other.

13 Make sure the thrust washer is in place on the left-hand end of the transmission output shaft.

1 Input shaft
2 5th gear pinion
3 Splined washer
4 Circlip
5 Combined 3rd/4th gear pinion
6 Circlip
7 Splined washer
8 6th gear pinion
9 2nd gear pinion
10 Thrust washer

26.1a Transmission input shaft components

14 Reassemble the crankcase halves (see Section 21).

26 Transmission shaft overhaul

1 Remove the transmission shafts from the crankcase (see Section 25). Always disassemble the transmission shafts separately to avoid mixing up the components **(see illustrations)**.

 HAYNES HiNT *When disassembling the transmission shafts, place the parts on a long rod or thread a wire through them to keep them in order and facing the proper direction.*

Input shaft
Disassembly

2 The thrust washer on the left-hand end of the shaft has a slightly out-of round section on

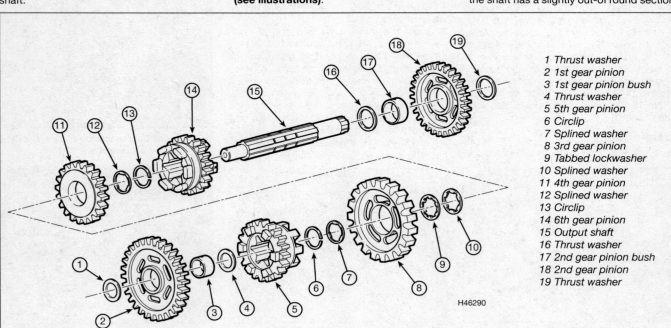

1 Thrust washer
2 1st gear pinion
3 1st gear pinion bush
4 Thrust washer
5 5th gear pinion
6 Circlip
7 Splined washer
8 3rd gear pinion
9 Tabbed lockwasher
10 Splined washer
11 4th gear pinion
12 Splined washer
13 Circlip
14 6th gear pinion
15 Output shaft
16 Thrust washer
17 2nd gear pinion bush
18 2nd gear pinion
19 Thrust washer

26.1b Transmission output shaft components

26.2a Note how the out-of-round section (arrowed) locates in the groove

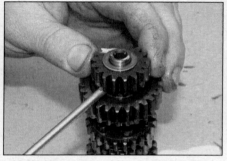

26.2b Use a screwdriver behind the 2nd gear pinion to lever the washer out of the groove

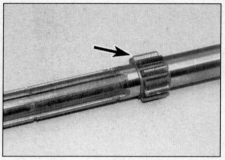

26.6 1st gear pinion (arrowed) is part of the shaft

its inner rim that locates in a groove in the shaft **(see illustration)**. To remove the washer slip one or two flat-bladed screwdrivers behind the 2nd gear pinion and lever it up so the washer is forced out of the groove and towards the end of the shaft **(see illustration)**. Slide the thrust washer and the 2nd gear pinion off the left-hand end of the shaft – note which way around the pinion is fitted; there should be a paint mark on the outer face but if one is not visible make your own **(see illustrations 26.18b and a)**.

3 Slide the 6th gear pinion off the shaft, followed by the splined washer **(see illustrations 26.17b and a)**.

4 Remove the circlip securing the combined 3rd/4th gear pinion, then slide the pinion off the shaft **(see illustrations 26.16b and a)**.

5 Remove the circlip securing the 5th gear pinion, then slide the splined washer and the pinion off the shaft **(see illustrations 26.15c, b and a)**.

6 The 1st gear pinion is integral with the shaft **(see illustration)**.

Inspection

7 Wash all of the components in clean solvent and dry them off.

8 Check the gear teeth for cracking, chipping, pitting and other obvious wear or damage. Any pinion that is damaged as such must be replaced with a new one.

9 Inspect the dogs and the dog holes in the gears for cracks, chips, and excessive wear especially in the form of rounded edges. Make sure mating gears engage properly. Replace the paired gears as a set if necessary.

10 Check for signs of scoring or bluing on the pinions, bushes and shaft. This could be caused by overheating due to inadequate lubrication. Check that all the oil holes and passages are clear. Replace any damaged pinions or bushes.

11 Check that each pinion moves freely on the shaft or its bush but without undue freeplay. On the output shaft check that each bush moves freely on the shaft but without undue freeplay. If the necessary equipment is available the individual components for which dimensions are given

in the Specifications at the beginning of this Chapter can be measured to assess the extent of wear.

12 The shaft is unlikely to sustain damage unless the engine has seized, placing an unusually high loading on the transmission, or the machine has covered a very high mileage. Check the surface of the shaft, especially where a pinion turns on it, and replace the shaft if it has scored or picked up, or if there are any cracks. Damage of any kind can only be cured by replacement.

13 Check the washers and circlips and replace any that are bent or appear weakened or worn. Use new ones if in any doubt. Note that it is good practice to renew all circlips when overhauling gearshafts.

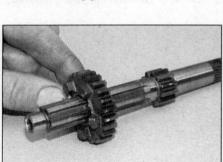

26.15a Slide the 5th gear pinion . . .

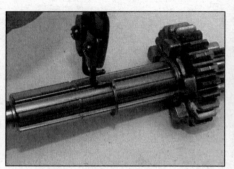

26.15c . . . and secure them with the circlip . . .

Reassembly

14 During reassembly, apply molybdenum disulphide oil (a 50/50 mixture of molybdenum disulphide grease and clean engine oil) to the mating surfaces of the shaft, pinions and bushes. When installing the circlips, do not expand their ends any further than is necessary. Install the stamped circlips and washers so that their chamfered side faces away from the thrust side.

15 Slide the 5th gear pinion onto the shaft with its dogs facing away from the integral 1st gear **(see illustration)**. Slide the splined washer onto the shaft, then fit the circlip, making sure that it locates correctly in the groove in the shaft **(see illustrations)**.

16 Slide the combined 3rd/4th gear pinion

26.15b . . . and the splined washer onto the shaft . . .

26.15d . . . making sure it locates properly in its groove

26.16a Slide the combined 3rd/4th gear pinion onto the shaft . . .

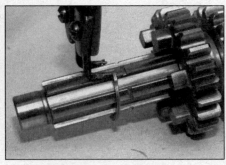

26.16b . . . and secure it with the circlip . . .

26.16c . . . making sure it locates properly in its groove

onto the shaft with the smaller 3rd gear pinion facing the 5th gear pinion **(see illustration)**. Fit the circlip, making sure it is locates correctly in its groove in the shaft **(see illustrations)**.

17 Slide the splined washer onto the shaft, followed by the 6th gear pinion, making sure its dogs face the 3rd/4th gear pinion **(see illustrations)**.

18 Slide the 2nd gear pinion onto the end of the shaft – the side with the paint mark faces out **(see illustration)**. Fit the shaped thrust washer onto the end of the shaft and press it down to the groove using a suitable socket until the out-of-round section on its inner rim locates in the groove **(see illustrations and 26.2a)**.

19 Check that all components have been correctly installed **(see illustration)**.

Output shaft

Disassembly

20 Slide the thrust washer off the left-hand end of the shaft, followed by the 2nd gear pinion, its bush and the thrust washer **(see illustrations 26.34d, c, b and a)**.

21 Slide the thrust washer off the right-hand end of the shaft, followed by the 1st gear pinion, its bush, the thrust washer and the 5th gear pinion **(see illustrations 26.33c, b and a, and 26.32b and a)**.

22 Release the circlip securing the 3rd gear pinion – the circlip does not have shaped ends to accommodate circlip pliers, so it is easier to remove it using two small screwdrivers to spread it clear of the groove then to pull the pinion behind it against it so it slides up the shaft **(see illustration)**. Slide the circlip, splined washer and the pinion off the shaft **(see illustrations 26.31c, b and a)**.

23 Slide the tabbed lockwasher off the shaft, then turn the splined washer to offset the splines and slide it off the shaft, noting how

26.17a Slide the splined washer . . .

26.17b . . . and the 6th gear pinion onto the shaft

26.18a Slide the 2nd gear pinion onto the shaft . . .

26.18b . . . then fit the thrust washer . . .

26.18c . . . and use a socket to drive it into the groove

26.19 The assembled input shaft should be as shown

26.22 Spread the circlip using a screwdriver then push the pinion behind it to move the circlip up the shaft

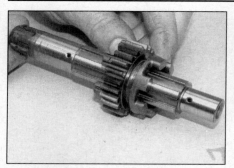

26.28a Slide the 6th gear pinion onto the shaft . . .

26.28b . . . and secure it with the circlip . . .

26.28c . . . making sure it locates in the groove

26.29a Slide the splined washer . . .

26.29b . . . and the 4th gear pinion onto the shaft

26.30a Slide the splined washer onto the shaft . . .

they fit together **(see illustrations 26.30c, b and a)**.

24 Slide the 4th gear pinion and the splined washer off the shaft **(see illustrations 26.29b and a)**.

25 Release the circlip securing the 6th gear pinion (see Step 22), then slide the circlip and pinion off the shaft **(see illustrations 26.28b and a)**.

Inspection

26 Refer to Steps 7 to 13 above.

Reassembly

27 During reassembly, apply molybdenum disulphide oil (a 50/50 mixture of molybdenum disulphide grease and clean engine oil) to the mating surfaces of the shaft, pinions and bushes. When installing the circlips, do not expand the ends any further than is necessary. Install the stamped circlips and washers so that their chamfered side faces away from the thrust side.

28 Slide the 6th gear pinion onto the right-hand end of the shaft, with its selector fork groove facing the right, then fit the circlip, using small screwdrivers as on removal to spread it, making sure it is locates correctly in its groove in the shaft **(see illustrations)**.

29 Slide the splined washer and the 4th gear pinion onto the shaft, with its dog holes facing the 6th gear pinion **(see illustrations)**.

30 Slide the splined washer onto the shaft and locate it in its groove, then turn it in the groove so that the splines on the washer align with the splines on the shaft and secure the washer in the groove **(see illustrations)**. Slide the tabbed lockwasher onto the shaft, so that the tabs locate under the inner rim of the splined washer **(see illustration)**.

31 Slide the 3rd gear pinion onto the shaft, with its dog holes facing away from the

26.30b . . . and locate it as shown

26.30c Slide the lockwasher onto the shaft and locate its tabs under the inner rim of the slotted washer

26.31a Slide the 3rd gear pinion . . .

26.31b . . . and the splined washer onto the shaft . . .

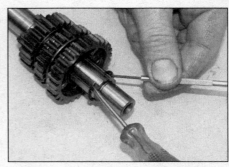

26.31c . . . and secure them with the circlip . . .

26.31d . . . making sure it locates in the groove

26.32a Slide the 5th gear pinion . . .

26.32b . . . and the thrust washer onto the shaft

26.33a Slide the bush . . .

26.33b . . . the 1st gear pinion . . .

4th gear pinion **(see illustration)**. Slide the splined washer on, then fit the circlip, using small screwdrivers as on removal to spread it, making sure it is locates correctly in its groove in the shaft **(see illustrations)**.

32 Slide the 5th gear pinion onto the shaft with its selector fork groove facing the 3rd gear pinion, followed by the thrust washer **(see illustrations)**.

33 Slide the 1st gear pinion bush onto the shaft, then slide the 1st gear pinion onto the bush with its shaped side facing the 5th gear pinion **(see illustrations)**. Fit the thrust washer onto the end of the shaft **(see illustrations)**.

34 Slide the thrust washer onto the left-hand end of the shaft, followed by the 2nd gear

26.33c . . . and the thrust washer onto the shaft

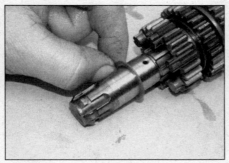

26.34a Slide the thrust washer onto the left-hand end . . .

26.34b . . . followed by the 2nd gear pinion bush . . .

26.34c . . . the 2nd gear pinion . . .

26.34d . . . and the thrust washer

26.35 The assembled output shaft should be as shown

pinion bush, then slide the 2nd gear pinion onto the bush with its shaped side facing the 6th gear pinion **(see illustrations)**. Fit the thrust washer onto the end of the shaft **(see illustrations)**.

35 Check that all components have been correctly installed **(see illustration)**.

27 Selector drum and forks

Note: *To remove the selector drum and forks the engine must be removed from the frame and the crankcases separated.*

Removal

1 Remove the engine (see Section 4) and separate the crankcase halves (see Section 21).

2 Before removing the selector forks, note that each fork carries an identification letter **(see illustration)**. The right-hand fork has PR, the centre fork PC, and the left-hand fork PL, with all marks facing the right-hand side of the engine. If no letters are visible, mark them yourself using a felt pen. The R and L forks fit into the output shaft and the C fork fits into the input shaft.

3 Support the selector forks and withdraw the shaft from the casing **(see illustration)**. Pivot each fork out of its groove in the selector drum.

4 Withdraw the selector drum from the right-hand side of the engine **(see illustration)**. Slide each fork out of its pinion and remove them **(see illustrations 27.11c, b and a)**. Once removed, slide the forks back onto the shaft to keep them in the correct order and way round.

Inspection

5 Inspect the selector forks for any signs of wear or damage, especially around the fork ends where they engage with the groove in the pinion. Check that each fork fits correctly in its pinion groove **(see illustration)**. Check closely to see if the forks are bent. If the forks are in any way damaged they must be replaced with new ones.

6 Measure the thickness of the fork ends and compare the readings to the specifications **(see illustration)**. Replace the forks with new ones if they are worn beyond their specifications.

7 Check that the forks fit correctly on the shaft. They should move freely with a light fit but no appreciable freeplay. Measure the internal diameter of the fork bores and the corresponding diameter of the fork shaft **(see illustration)**. Replace the forks and/or shaft with new ones if they are worn beyond their specifications. Check that the fork shaft holes in the casing are neither worn nor damaged.

8 Check the selector fork shaft is straight by

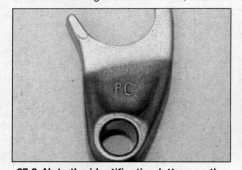

27.2 Note the identification letters on the forks

27.3 Withdraw the shaft and move the forks aside . . .

27.4 . . . then remove the selector drum

27.5 Check the fit of each fork in its pinion . . .

27.6 . . . and measure the fork end thickness

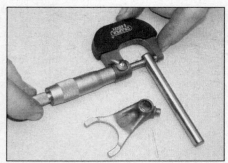

27.7 Measure the fork shaft OD and the fork bore ID

27.9 Check the guide pins and their grooves in the drum

27.10 Measure the diameters of the journal and its bore in the crankcase

27.11a Locate the PR fork . . .

27.11b . . . the PC fork . . .

27.11c . . . and the PL fork

27.13 Locate each fork guide pin in its groove in the drum

rolling it along a flat surface. A bent rod will cause difficulty in selecting gears and make the gearchange action heavy. Replace the shaft with a new one if it is bent.

9 Inspect the selector drum grooves and selector fork guide pins for signs of wear or damage **(see illustration)**. If either component shows signs of wear or damage the fork(s) and drum must be replaced with new ones.

10 Check that the selector drum rotates freely in each crankcase half and has no sign of freeplay between it and the casing. Measure the diameter of the right-hand journal and the corresponding internal diameter of the bore in the right-hand crankcase **(see illustration)**. Replace the drum and/or crankcases with new ones if they are worn beyond their specifications.

Installation

11 Lubricate each fork with oil. Locate each fork in turn in its pinion groove, making sure they are correctly positioned – see Step 2 **(see illustrations)**.

12 Lubricate the selector drum ends with clean engine oil. Slide the selector drum into position in the crankcase **(see illustration 27.4)**. Rotate it so that the hole for the neutral switch contact pin points to the bottom of the crankcase.

13 Pivot each fork round to locate its guide pin in its groove in the selector drum **(see illustration)**.

14 Lubricate the selector fork shaft with oil. With all three forks installed and aligned slide the shaft through each and into its bore in the crankcase **(see illustration 27.3)**.

15 Reassemble the crankcase halves (see Section 21).

28 Running-in procedure

1 Make sure the engine oil and coolant levels are correct (see *Pre-ride checks*). Make sure there is fuel in the tank.

2 Turn the engine kill switch to the ON position and shift the gearbox into neutral. Turn the ignition ON. Set the choke on R-4, R-5 and RW-6 models.

3 Start the engine and allow it to run at a moderately fast idle until it reaches operating temperature.

 Warning: If the oil pressure warning light doesn't go off, or it comes on while the engine is running, stop the engine

immediately. If an engine is run without oil, even for a short period of time, severe damage will occur.

4 Check carefully that there are no oil, coolant or fuel leaks and make sure the transmission and controls, especially the brakes, function properly before road testing the machine.

5 Treat the machine gently for the first few miles to make sure oil has circulated throughout the engine and any new parts installed have started to seat.

6 Even greater care is necessary if a new piston and rings or a new cylinder have been fitted, and the bike will have to be run in as when new. This means greater use of the transmission and a restraining hand on the throttle until at least 300 miles (500 km) have been covered. There's no point in keeping to any set speed limit – but don't labour the engine and gradually increase performance up to the 300 miles (500 km) mark. Experience is the best guide, since it's easy to tell when an engine is running freely.

7 Upon completion of the road test, and after the engine has cooled down completely, recheck the valve clearances (see Chapter 1) and check the engine oil and coolant levels (see *Pre-ride checks*).

Chapter 3
Cooling system

Contents

Degrees of difficulty

| Easy, suitable for novice with little experience | | Fairly easy, suitable for beginner with some experience | | Fairly difficult, suitable for competent DIY mechanic | | Difficult, suitable for experienced DIY mechanic | | Very difficult, suitable for expert DIY or professional | |

Specifications

Coolant
Mixture type and capacity	see Chapter 1

Fan switch
Cut-in temperature	100°C

Temperature gauge sensor - carburettor models
Resistance @ 50°C	134 to 179 ohms
Resistance @ 120°C	15 to 17.3 ohms

Engine coolant temperature sensor – fuel injection models
Resistance @ 80°C	47 to 57 ohms
Resistance @ 120°C	14 to 18 ohms

Thermostat
Opening temperature	74.5 to 77.5°C
Fully open	85°C
Valve lift	3.5 to 4.5 mm

Radiator
Cap valve opening pressure	16 psi (1.1 Bar)

Torque settings
Fan blade nut	1 Nm
Fan motor screws	3 Nm
Fan motor shroud bolts	9 Nm
Water pump impeller	10 Nm

2.2a Release the clip and fold the cover aside . . .

2.2b . . . then disconnect the fan motor wiring connector (arrowed)

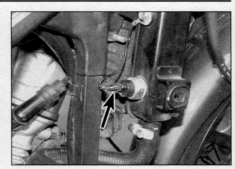

2.2c Also disconnect the wiring connector (arrowed) from the fan switch

1 General information

The cooling system uses a water/anti-freeze coolant to carry away excess heat from the engine and maintain as constant a temperature as possible. The cylinders are surrounded by a water jacket from which the heated coolant is circulated by thermo-syphonic action in conjunction with a water pump, which is driven by the primary drive gear. The hot coolant from the engine passes upwards to the thermostat and through to the radiator. The coolant then flows across the core of the radiator, then to the water pump and back to the engine where the cycle is repeated.

A thermostat is fitted in the system to prevent the coolant flowing through the radiator when the engine is cold, therefore accelerating the speed at which the engine reaches normal operating temperature. A temperature gauge sensor mounted in the thermostat housing transmits information to the temperature gauge on the instrument panel. A fan fitted to the back of the radiator aids cooling in extreme conditions by drawing extra air through. The fan motor is controlled by a thermo-switch mounted in the right-hand side of the radiator.

The complete cooling system is partially sealed and pressurised, the pressure being controlled by a valve contained in the spring-loaded radiator cap. By pressurising the coolant the boiling point is raised, preventing premature boiling in adverse conditions. The overflow pipe from the system is connected to a reservoir into which excess coolant is expelled under pressure. The discharged coolant automatically returns to the radiator by the vacuum created when the engine cools.

⚠ *Warning: Do not remove the pressure cap from the radiator when the engine is hot. Scalding hot coolant and steam may be blown out under pressure, which could cause serious injury. When the engine has cooled, place a thick rag, like a towel, over the pressure cap; slowly rotate the cap anti-clockwise to the first stop. This procedure allows any residual pressure to escape. When the steam has stopped escaping, press down on the cap while turning it anti-clockwise and remove it.*

Caution: Do not allow anti-freeze to come in contact with your skin or painted surfaces of the motorcycle. Rinse off any spills immediately with plenty of water. Anti-freeze is highly toxic if ingested. Never leave anti-freeze lying around in an open container or in puddles on the floor; children and pets are attracted by its sweet smell and may drink it. Check with the local authorities about disposing of used anti-freeze. Many communities will have collection centres which will see that anti-freeze is disposed of safely.

Caution: At all times use the specified type of anti-freeze, and always mix it with distilled water in the correct proportion. The anti-freeze contains corrosion inhibitors which are essential to avoid damage to the cooling system. A lack of these inhibitors could lead to a build-up of corrosion which would block the coolant passages, resulting in overheating and severe engine damage. Distilled water must be used as opposed to tap water to avoid a build-up of scale which would also block the passages.

2 Fan and fan switch

Cooling fan

Check

1 If the engine is overheating and the cooling fan isn't coming on, first check the fan fuse (see Chapter 9). If the fuse is good, check the switch as described below.

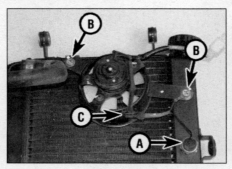

2.4 Disconnect the wiring connector (A), undo the screws (B) and free the wiring (C)

2 To test the cooling fan motor, remove the fuel tank (see Chapter 4A or 4B) and the right-hand fairing side panel. Release the rubber cover from its clip and fold it aside **(see illustration)**. Disconnect the fan motor wiring connector and the fan switch wiring connector **(see illustrations)**. Using a 12 volt battery and two jumper wires with suitable connectors, connect the battery positive (+) lead to the black/blue wire terminal on the fan side of the motor wiring connector, and the battery negative (–) lead to the fan switch wire terminal. Once connected the fan should operate. If it does not, and the wiring and connectors are all good, then the fan motor is faulty. Individual components are available for the fan assembly.

Replacement

⚠ *Warning: The engine must be completely cool before carrying out this procedure.*

3 Remove the radiator (see Section 5).
4 Disconnect wiring connector from the fan switch **(see illustration)**. Undo the screws securing the fan shroud to the radiator, noting the earth wire secured by the right-hand bolt, and remove the fan assembly. Free the fan wiring from its clamp.
5 Unscrew the fan blade nut and remove the blade. Undo the three screws securing the fan motor and separate it from the shroud **(see illustration)**.
6 Installation is the reverse of removal. Apply a suitable non-permanent thread locking compound to the fan blade nut and tighten it to the torque setting specified at the beginning of the Chapter. Also tighten the fan motor

2.5 Fan motor screws (arrowed)

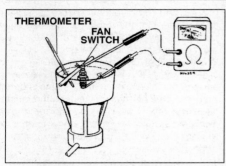

2.10 Fan switch test set-up

screws and the shroud bolts to the specified torque. Make sure the earth terminal is clean, and angle it down and to the left before tightening the bolt.

7 Install the radiator (see Section 5).

Fan switch

Check

8 If the engine is overheating and the cooling fan isn't coming on, first check the fan fuse (see Chapter 9). If the fuse is blown, check the fan circuit for a short to earth (see the wiring diagrams at the end of Chapter 9).

9 If the fuse is good, remove the right-hand fairing side panel (see Chapter 8). Disconnect the fan switch wiring connector **(see illustration 2.2c)**. Using a voltmeter check for voltage at the wiring connector with the ignition ON. There should be battery voltage. If there is no voltage check the wire from the switch back to the fusebox, via the fan motor, for continuity. If there is voltage check that the switch is tight in the radiator, and that the earth wire above the switch is secure and clean. Unscrew the earth wire bolt, detach the wire and check that it shows continuity to earth. If it doesn't locate the break or the detached wire or terminal and repair it.

10 If the wiring is good, or if the fan works but is suspected of cutting in at the wrong temperature or is on the whole time, remove the switch (Steps 12 and 13) and test it as follows: fill a small heatproof container with coolant and place it on a stove. Using an ohmmeter or continuity tester, connect the positive (+) probe of the meter to the wire terminal on the switch, and the negative (–) probe to the body of the switch **(see illustration)**. Using some wire or other support suspend the switch in the coolant so that just the sensing head up to the threads is submerged, and with the head a minimum of 40 mm above the bottom of the container. Also place a thermometer capable of reading temperatures up to 130°C in the coolant so that its bulb is close to the switch. **Note:** *None of the components should be allowed to directly touch the container.*

 Warning: This must be done very carefully to avoid the risk of personal injury.

11 Begin to heat the coolant, stirring it gently. Initially there should be no continuity, showing switch is open or off. When the temperature reaches around 100°C, the switch should close (turn on) and there should be continuity on the meter. Keep heating to a few degrees above 100, then turn off the heat. As the coolant cools to around 100°C the switch should open (turn off) and the meter should show no continuity. If there is more than a 2% error in the temperature at which the switch closes and opens, or if it shows continuity the whole time or no continuity the whole time, replace it with a new one (Steps 12 and 13).

Replacement

12 The switch is in the right-hand side of the radiator. Drain the cooling system (see Chapter 1).

13 Disconnect the wiring connector from the switch **(see illustration 2.2c)**. Unscrew the switch. Discard the O-ring as a new one must be used.

14 Installation is the reverse of removal. Fit a new O-ring onto the switch, and do not overtighten it. Fill the system with the specified coolant (see Chapter 1). Run the engine and check the switch for leaks before installing the fairing side panel.

---

3 Temperature gauge and sensor

Temperature gauge

Check

1 The circuit consists of the sensor mounted in the thermostat housing and the gauge in the instrument cluster. If the instruments malfunction first check the fuse (see Chapter 9).

2 If the gauge needle does not move as the engine warms up, remove the fuel tank and the air filter housing (see Chapter 4A or 4B). Disconnect the wiring connector from the sensor in the thermostat housing (see illustration 3.9 for carburettor-engined models); on models with fuel injection identify the green/blue wire in the connector (see illustration 5.15a in Chapter 4B). With the ignition ON, touch the wire against the frame or engine and check that the gauge needle moves around the gauge, then quickly disconnect the wire to avoid damaging the gauge. If the gauge moves, remove the sensor and check it (Steps 5 to 8).

3 If the gauge does not move check the wiring between the sensor and the gauge for continuity, referring to Chapter 9 for access to the instrument cluster wiring and for the wiring diagrams. Also check for continuity to earth between the sensor hex and the frame. If there is none make sure the sensor and the thermostat mounting bolt (see Section 4) are tight. If that is good, check voltage at the white/green wire to the gauge, and check for continuity to earth in the green wire. If the wiring is good the gauge is faulty.

Replacement

4 The temperature gauge is part of the instrument cluster and is covered in Chapter 9.

Temperature gauge sensor

Note: *On fuel injected models the ECT (engine coolant temperature) sensor performs the temperature gauge sensor function.*

Check

5 Drain the cooling system (see Chapter 1). The sensor is mounted in the thermostat housing (see illustration 3.9 for carburettor-engined models and illustration 5.15a in Chapter 4B for fuel injected models).

6 Remove the sensor (see Steps 9 and 10 below).

7 Fill a small heatproof container with coolant and place it on a stove. Using an ohmmeter, connect the positive (+) probe of the meter to the terminal on the sensor (on fuel injected models this is the terminal which the green/blue wire connects to), and the negative (-) probe to the body of the sensor. Using some wire or other support suspend the sensor in the coolant so that just the sensing head up to the threads is submerged and with the head a minimum of 40 mm above the bottom of the container **(see illustration 2.10)**. Also place a thermometer in the coolant so that its bulb is close to the sensor. **Note:** *None of the components should be allowed to directly touch the container.*

 Warning: This must be done very carefully to avoid the risk of personal injury.

8 Begin to heat the coolant, stirring it gently. When the temperature reaches around 50°C on carburettor models or 80°C on fuel injected models, turn the heat down and maintain the temperature steady for three minutes. The meter reading should be as shown at the beginning of this Chapter. It is not possible to raise the temperature of the coolant enough to check the resistance at the higher temperature given, but you should notice a gradual drop in resistance if you continue to heat the coolant. If the sensor does not perform as described, it must be assumed faulty and renewed.

Replacement

 Warning: The engine must be completely cool before carrying out this procedure.

9 Drain the cooling system (see Chapter 1). Remove the fuel tank and the air filter housing (see Chapter 4A or 4B). The sensor is mounted in the thermostat housing **(see illustration)**.

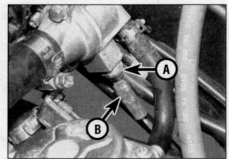

3.9 Temperature gauge sensor (A) and its wiring connector (B)

10 Disconnect the sensor wiring connector **(see illustration 3.9)**. Unscrew and remove the sensor.

11 Apply a suitable sealant to the threads of the sensor, making sure none gets on the sensor head. Install the sensor and tighten it. Connect the wiring.

12 Install the air filter housing and the fuel tank (see Chapter 4A or 4B). Refill the cooling system (see Chapter 1).

4 Thermostat

1 The thermostat is automatic in operation and should give many years service without requiring attention. In the event of a failure, the valve will probably jam open, in which case the engine will take much longer than normal to warm up. Conversely, if the valve jams shut, the coolant will be unable to circulate and the engine will overheat. Neither condition is acceptable, and the fault must be investigated promptly.

 Warning: The engine must be completely cool before carrying out this procedure.

Removal

2 Drain the coolant (see Chapter 1). Remove the fuel tank and the air filter housing (see Chapter 4A or 4B). The thermostat housing is on the inside of the right-hand frame spar.

3 Release the clamp and detach the PAIR system hose from the control valve **(see illustration)**.

4 To remove the thermostat, unscrew the two bolts securing the cover and detach it from the housing **(see illustrations)**. Withdraw the thermostat, noting how it fits **(see illustration)**.

5 To remove the thermostat housing, disconnect the temperature gauge sensor wiring connector **(see illustration 3.9)**. Release the clamps securing the hoses to the cover and housing **(see illustration)**. Detach the hose from the cover. Unscrew the bolt securing the housing to the frame, then detach the hoses from the housing.

Check

6 Examine the thermostat visually before carrying out the test. If it remains in the open position at room temperature, it should be replaced with a new one. Check the condition of the rubber seal around the thermostat and replace it with a new one if it is damaged, deformed or deteriorated.

7 Suspend the thermostat by a piece of wire in a container of cold water. Place a thermometer capable of reading temperatures up to 110°C in the water so that the bulb is close to the thermostat **(see illustration)**. Heat the water, noting the temperature when the thermostat opens, and compare the result with the Specifications given at the beginning of the Chapter. Also check the amount the valve opens after it has been heated for a few

minutes and compare the measurement to the specifications. If the readings obtained differ from those given, the thermostat is faulty and must be replaced with a new one.

8 In the event of thermostat failure, as an emergency measure only, it can be removed and the machine used without it (this is better than leaving a permanently closed thermostat in). **Note:** *Take care when starting the engine from cold as it will take much longer than usual to warm up. Ensure that a new unit is installed as soon as possible.*

Installation

9 To install the thermostat, first make sure the seal is fitted around it and is in good condition, otherwise fit a new thermostat – the seal is not available separately. Smear some fresh coolant over the seal. Install the thermostat with the hole at the top, making sure it locates correctly **(see illustration 4.4c)**. Fit the cover onto the housing, then install and tighten the bolts **(see illustrations 4.4b and a)**.

10 To install the thermostat housing, first connect the hoses to their unions on the housing, large hose first, then fit the housing and tighten the bolt **(see illustration 4.5)**. Fit the hose onto the cover, then tighten all the hose clamps. Connect the temperature gauge sensor wiring connector **(see illustration 3.9)**.

11 Connect the PAIR system hose to the control valve and fit the clamp **(see illustration 4.3)**.

12 Install the air filter housing and the fuel tank (see Chapter 4A or 4B). Refill the cooling system with fresh coolant (see Chapter 1).

4.3 Release the clamp (arrowed) and detach the hose

4.4a Unscrew the bolts (arrowed) . . .

4.4b . . . detach the cover . . .

4.4c . . . and remove the thermostat

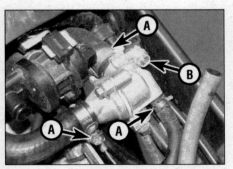

4.5 Release the hose clamps (A). Mounting bolt (B)

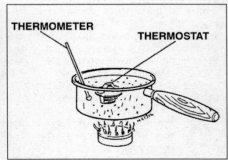

4.7 Thermostat testing set-up

5 Radiator

Note: *If the radiator is being removed as part of the engine removal procedure, detach the hoses from their unions on the engine rather than on the radiator and remove the radiator with the hoses attached to it. Note the routing of the hoses.*

Removal

 Warning: The engine must be completely cool before carrying out this procedure.

1 Remove the lower fairing and the fairing side panels (see Chapter 8). Drain the coolant (see Chapter 1). Remove the fuel tank (see Chapter 4A or 4B).

2 Release the rubber cover from its clip and fold it aside **(see illustration 2.2a)**. Disconnect the fan motor wiring connector and feed the wiring to the radiator, noting its routing **(see illustration 2.2b)**.

3 Slacken the clamps securing the hoses to the radiator and detach them, noting which fits where **(see illustrations)**.

4 Unscrew the radiator mounting bolts **(see illustration)**. Ease the radiator out to the right to free the mounting grommet from its lug on the frame, then remove the radiator **(see illustration)**. Note the arrangement of the collars and rubber grommets in the radiator mounts. Replace the grommets with new ones if they are damaged, deformed or deteriorated.

5 If necessary, remove the fan from the radiator (see Section 2). Check the radiator for signs of damage and clear any dirt or debris that might obstruct air flow and inhibit cooling. If the radiator fins are badly damaged or broken the radiator must be replaced with a new one.

Installation

6 Installation is the reverse of removal, noting the following.
● Make sure the rubber grommets are in place.
● Make sure the bolt collars are correctly installed in the grommets.
● Make sure that the fan wiring is correctly connected.
● Ensure the coolant hoses are in good condition (see Chapter 1), and are securely retained by their clamps, using new ones if necessary.
● On completion refill the cooling system with fresh coolant as described in Chapter 1.

Pressure cap check

7 If problems such as overheating or loss of coolant occur, check the entire system as described in Chapter 1. The radiator cap opening pressure should be checked by a Honda dealer with the special tester required to do the job. If the cap is defective, replace it with a new one.

5.3a Detach the two hoses (arrowed) from the right-hand side of the radiator . . .

5.3b . . . and the hose (arrowed) from the left-hand side

5.4a Unscrew the bolts (arrowed) . . .

5.4b . . . then draw the radiator to the right to free the grommet from the lug

6 Water pump

Check

1 The water pump is located on the lower right-hand side of the engine. Remove the lower fairing (see Chapter 8). Visually check the area around the pump for signs of leakage.

2 To prevent leakage of water from the cooling system to the lubrication system and vice versa, two seals are fitted on the pump shaft. On the front of the engine below the pump housing there is a drain hose **(see illustration)**. If either seal fails, the drain allows the coolant or oil to escape and prevents them mixing.

3 The seal on the water pump side is of the mechanical type which bears on the rear face of the impeller. The second seal, which is mounted behind the mechanical seal, is of the normal feathered lip type. If on inspection the drain shows signs of leakage remove the pump, and fit a new mechanical seal if there is coolant leakage, and a new oil seal as well if there is oil leakage or if the leakage is an emulsion-like mix of coolant and oil.

Removal

4 Drain the coolant (see Chapter 1).

5 Refer to Chapter 2, Section 16, Steps 1 to 5, and remove the clutch cover.

6 Unscrew the remaining pump cover bolts and remove the cover **(see illustration)**. Discard the O-ring as a new one must be used.

7 Wiggle the water pump impeller back-and-forth and in-and-out **(see illustration)**. If there is excessive movement, remove and disassemble the pump. Also check for

6.2 Check the drain hose (arrowed) for signs of leakage

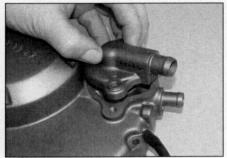

6.6 Remove the pump cover . . .

6.7 . . . and check the impeller

6.8a Counter-hold the shaft and unscrew the impeller

6.8b Remove the washer . . .

6.8c . . . then withdraw the shaft

6.8d Remove the washer . . .

Seal replacement

Note: *Do not remove the seals unless they need to be replaced with new ones – once removed they cannot be re-used.*

9 To remove the mechanical seal, an expanding knife-edged bearing puller with slide-hammer attachment is useful **(see illustration)**. Fit the expanding end of the puller behind the seal, then turn the puller to expand it and lock it. Attach the slide-hammer to the puller, then operate the slide-hammer to jar the seal out. Alternatively drive the seal out using a suitable drift inserted from the inner side of the cover **(see illustration)**.

10 Drive the oil seal out using a suitable drift inserted from the inner side of the cover. Note which way round the seal fits.

11 Fit the new oil seal into the cover and drive it in until it seats using a suitable socket.

12 Fit the new mechanical seal into the cover and drive it in until it seats using a suitable socket that bears only on the outer flange.

Installation

13 Fit the drive pin into its hole in the shaft **(see illustration 6.8f)**. Slide the gear onto the shaft with the cut-outs facing the drive pin and locate the gear onto it **(see illustration)**. Slide the washer against the gear **(see illustration 6.8d)**. Fit the shaft through the cover, rotating it to ease its passage through the seals **(see illustration 6.8c)**. Fit the washer onto the outer end of the shaft **(see illustration 6.8b)**. Thread the impeller on and tighten it to the torque setting specified at the beginning of

6.8e . . . the gear . . .

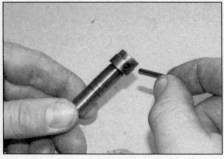

6.8f . . . and the drive pin

corrosion or a build-up of scale in the pump body.

8 Counter-hold the inner end of the pump shaft using a spanner on the flats, then unscrew the impeller and remove the washer

(see illustrations). Draw the shaft out of the cover and remove the washer **(see illustrations)**. Remove the gear and the drive pin from the shaft, noting how they fit **(see illustrations)**.

6.9a Remove the mechanical seal (arrowed) using a puller . . .

6.9b . . . or by driving it out from the back

6.13a Locate the gear onto the drive pin as shown

6.13b Thread the impeller onto the shaft and tighten it to the specified torque

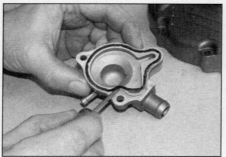

6.14a Fit the O-ring into the groove

6.14b Use a new sealing washer on the bottom bolt

the Chapter, counter-holding the shaft end as before **(see illustration)**. Rotate the pump by hand to make sure it turns freely (but take into account the friction of the seals).

14 Smear the new cover O-ring with grease and fit it into its groove in the cover **(see illustration)**. Fit the cover onto the pump **(see illustration 6.6)**. Install the bolts using a new sealing washer on the bottom one and tighten them **(see illustration)**.

15 Refer to Chapter 2, Section 16, Steps 27 to 29, and install the clutch cover.

16 Fill the engine with the correct amount and type of oil and coolant (see Chapter 1). Install the fairing panels (See Chapter 8).

7 Coolant reservoir

Removal

1 The coolant reservoir is located under the rider's seat on the left-hand side. Remove the seat cowling, and the right-hand fairing side panel (see Chapter 8). Remove the air filter housing (see Chapter 4A or 4B).

2 Place a suitable container for catching the coolant below the radiator. Release the clamp

and disconnect the overflow hose from the back of the radiator filler neck and place it in the container to allow the reservoir to drain **(see illustration)**.

3 Disconnect the feed hose from the bottom of the reservoir and the overflow hose from the top **(see illustration)**.

4 Unscrew the reservoir mounting bolt and manoeuvre the reservoir out, noting how it locates **(see illustration)**.

Installation

5 Installation is the reverse of removal. On completion refill the reservoir to the UPPER level line with the specified coolant mixture (see Chapter 1).

8 Coolant hoses and unions

Removal

1 Before removing a hose, drain the coolant (see Chapter 1).

2 Use a screwdriver to slacken the larger-bore hose clamps, then slide them back along the hose and clear of the union spigot. The small-bore hoses are secured by spring clamps

which can be expanded by squeezing their ears together with pliers.

Caution: The radiator unions are fragile. Do not use excessive force when attempting to remove the hoses.

3 If a hose proves stubborn, release it by rotating it on its union before working it off. If all else fails, cut the hose with a sharp knife. Whilst this means replacing the hose with a new one, it is preferable to buying a new radiator.

Installation

4 Slide the clamps onto the hose and then work the hose on to its union as far as the spigot where present.

> **HAYNES HiNT** *If the hose is difficult to push on its union, soften it by soaking it in very hot water, or alternatively a little soapy water on the union can be used as a lubricant.*

5 Rotate the hose on its unions to settle it in position before sliding the clamps into place and tightening them securely.

6 Refill the cooling system with fresh coolant (see Chapter 1).

7.2 Detach the hose (arrowed) and drain the reservoir

7.3 Detach the hoses (arrowed) . . .

7.4 . . . then unscrew the bolt (arrowed) and remove the reservoir

Chapter 4A
Fuel system and exhaust – carburettor models

Contents

Degrees of difficulty

Easy, suitable for novice with little experience 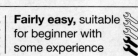	Fairly easy, suitable for beginner with some experience	Fairly difficult, suitable for competent DIY mechanic	Difficult, suitable for experienced DIY mechanic	Very difficult, suitable for expert DIY or professional

Specifications

Fuel

Grade . . . . Unleaded. Minimum 91 RON (Research Octane Number)
Fuel tank capacity (including reserve) . . . . 10 litres
Reserve volume (gauge needle goes into red zone) . . . . approx. 2.1 litres

Carburettor

Type CV
Size (throttle bore) . . . . 28 mm
ID number. VK6AB
Pilot screw setting (turns out). . . . . see Section 7
Float level. . . . . 13.0 mm
Idle speed. . . . . 1400 ± 100 rpm
Main jet 118
Pilot jet 38

Fuel level sensor

Sensor resistance. . . . . see Section 3

Torque settings

Fuel valve nut . . . . 27 Nm
PAIR reed valve cover bolts . . . . 5 Nm

1 General information and precautions

General information

CBR125R-4, R-5 and RW-6 models are equipped with a traditional carburettor. Later models are fuel-injected and covered in Chapter 4B.

The fuel system consists of the fuel tank, automatic fuel valve with fuel strainer, carburettor, fuel hose and control cables. The constant vacuum carburettor is operated by a single cable from the throttle twistgrip and has a manual choke operation, operated by cable via a knob on the top yoke.

Air is drawn into the carburettor via an air filter which is housed underneath the fuel tank.

The exhaust system is a one-piece design with a detachable silencer. A catalytic converter is located in the main exhaust pipe. The pulse secondary air system introduces fresh air into the exhaust port to improve exhaust end gas burning and reduce emissions.

A fuel gauge is incorporated in the instrument cluster, actuated by a level sensor which is situated in the base of the fuel tank.

Many of the fuel system service procedures are considered routine maintenance items and for that reason are covered in Chapter 1.

Precautions

⚠ **Warning: Petrol (gasoline) is extremely flammable, so take extra precautions when you work on any part of the fuel system. Always remove the battery (see Chapter 9). Don't smoke or allow open flames or bare light bulbs near the work area, and don't work in a garage where a natural gas-type appliance is present. If you spill any fuel on your skin, rinse it off immediately with soap and water. When you perform any kind of work on the fuel system, wear safety glasses and have a fire extinguisher suitable for a class B type fire (flammable liquids) on hand.**

Some residual fuel will remain in the fuel hoses and carburettor after the motorcycle has been used. Before disconnecting any fuel hose, ensure the ignition is switched OFF, and have some absorbent rag handy to catch any fuel. It is vital that no dirt or debris is allowed to enter the fuel tank or the carburettor. Any foreign matter in the fuel system components could result in damage or malfunction.

Always perform service procedures in a well-ventilated area to prevent a build-up of fumes.

Never work in a building containing a gas appliance with a pilot light, or any other form of naked flame. Ensure that there are no naked light bulbs or any sources of flame or sparks nearby.

Do not smoke (or allow anyone else to smoke) while in the vicinity of petrol (gasoline)

or of components containing it. Remember the possible presence of vapour from these sources and move well clear before smoking.

Check all electrical equipment belonging to the house, garage or workshop where work is being undertaken (see the *Safety first!* section of this manual). Remember that certain electrical appliances such as drills, cutters etc, create sparks in the normal course of operation and must not be used near petrol (gasoline) or any component containing it. Again, remember the possible presence of fumes before using electrical equipment.

Always mop up any spilt fuel and safely dispose of the rag used.

Any stored fuel that is drained off during servicing work must be kept in sealed containers that are suitable for holding petrol (gasoline), and clearly marked as such; the containers themselves should be kept in a safe place. Note that this last point applies equally to the fuel tank if it is removed from the machine; also remember to keep its filler cap closed at all times.

Read the *Safety first!* section of this manual carefully before starting work.

2 Fuel tank and valve

⚠ **Warning: Refer to the precautions given in Section 1 before starting work.**

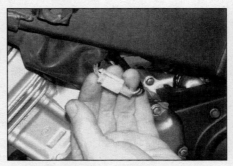

2.2 Disconnect the wiring connector

2.4 Release the seat cowling peg from the tank grommet on each side

Fuel tank

Removal

Note: *If the fuel tank is removed from the bike, it should not be placed in an area where sparks or open flames could ignite the fumes coming out of the tank. Be especially careful inside garages where a natural gas-type appliance is located, because the pilot light could cause an explosion.*

1 Make sure the fuel cap is secure. Remove the rider's seat and the left-hand fairing side panel (see Chapter 8).

2 Free the wiring loom from the clip on the inside of the frame above the sprocket cover, then draw the rubber boot off the connectors and disconnect the fuel level sensor off-white 3-pin wiring connector **(see illustration)**.

3 Unscrew the bolt and remove the collar securing the rear of the tank **(see illustration)**.

4 Carefully pull the front of the seat cowling away from the tank on each side to release the pegs from the grommets. Draw the tank back slightly, then lift and support it so there is a gap between it and the frame on each side **(see illustration)**.

5 Place a rag for catching any residual fuel under the fuel valve. Release the clamps and detach the fuel hose from the front of the valve and the vacuum hose from the base **(see illustration)**.

6 Release the clamps and detach the breather and overflow hoses from the underside

2.3 Unscrew the tank mounting bolt (arrowed)

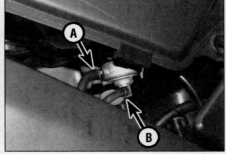

2.5 Detach the fuel hose (A) and the vacuum hose (B)

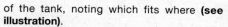

2.6 Pull the breather and overflow hoses (arrowed) off their unions

2.7 Carefully lift the tank away

2.13 Locate the tab in the rubber sleeve

of the tank, noting which fits where (**see illustration**).

7 Carefully lift the tank off the frame and remove it (**see illustration**). Note the rubber mounts and remove them for safekeeping if required.

8 Check all the tank rubbers for signs of damage or deterioration and replace them with new ones if necessary.

Installation

9 Depending on how the tank has been stood and how full it is there is the possibility of fuel having made its way into the breather pipe which could spurt out of the union on the base when it is moved – be prepared with some rag for this. Once the tank is upright the pipe will fill itself with air.

10 Make sure all mounting rubbers are in place (**see illustrations 2.6 and 2.5**). Position the tank on the frame and support it as before.

11 Fit the breather and overflow hoses onto their unions and secure them with the clamps (**see illustration 2.6**).

12 Fit the fuel and vacuum hoses onto their unions on the tap and secure them with the clamps (**see illustration 2.5**).

13 Manoeuvre the tank into position on the frame, locating the tab on the front in the slot in the rubber sleeve (**see illustration**). Align the mounting at the rear, again making sure the rubber pad is in place, then fit the collar and tighten the bolt (**see illustration 2.3**).

14 Connect the fuel pump wiring connector (**see illustration 2.2**). Secure the wiring in the boot.

15 Start the engine and check that there is no sign of fuel leakage.

Repair

16 All repairs to the fuel tank should be carried out by a professional who has experience in this critical and potentially dangerous work. Even after cleaning and flushing of the fuel system, explosive fumes can remain and ignite during repair of the tank.

Fuel valve

Check

17 Remove the tank (Steps 1 to 7), and for best access the air filter housing (Section 4).

18 Detach the fuel hose from the carburettor and the fuel valve vacuum hose from its union on the intake duct (**see illustrations**). Connect the hoses to the unions on the valve (**see illustration 2.5**).

19 Place the end of the fuel hose in a container suitable for holding fuel. Apply suction to the end of the vacuum hose, at which point fuel should flow freely from the valve into the container.

20 If it doesn't, remove the valve from the tank and check the strainer. If necessary remove the strainer and flush it through from the inside. Check the gauze for damage and replace it with a new one if necessary. Fit the strainer back onto the valve using a new O-ring.

21 If the fuel flow problem is not due to a blocked strainer, the valve has failed internally and should be replaced with a new one.

Removal and installation

22 Remove the tank (Steps 1 to 7).

23 Unscrew the nut and remove the valve (**see illustration**). Pull the strainer off and discard the O-ring.

24 Fit the strainer onto the valve using a new O-ring. Install the valve, taking care not to dislodge the strainer, and tighten the nut, to the torque setting specified at the beginning of the Chapter if you have the correct tools. Make sure there is no leakage before riding the bike.

25 Install the tank (Steps 9 to 15).

3 Fuel gauge and level sensor

Check

1 The circuit consists of the level sensor mounted in the fuel tank and the gauge mounted in the instrument cluster. If the instruments malfunction first check the instrument cluster fuse (see Chapter 9).

2 To check the gauge, remove the left-hand fairing side panel (see Chapter 8), then free the wiring loom from the clip on the inside of the frame above the sprocket cover, draw the rubber boot off the connectors and disconnect the fuel level sensor off-white 3-pin wiring connector (**see illustration 2.2**). Connect a jumper wire between the yellow/white and

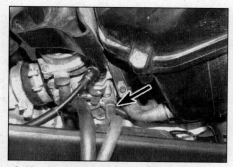

2.18a Detach the fuel hose (arrowed) . . .

2.18b . . . and the vacuum hose (arrowed)

2.23 Unscrew the nut (arrowed) to release the valve

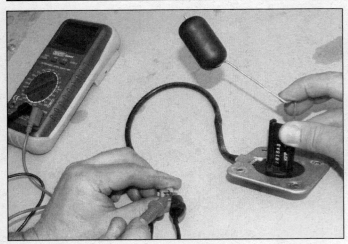
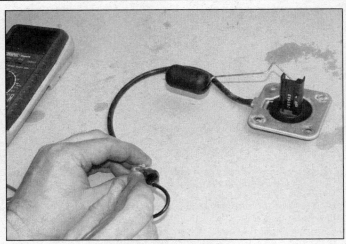

3.5a Check the resistances with the float in the FULL position . . .   3.5b . . . and the EMPTY position

3.9 Unscrew the mounting plate nuts and withdraw the sensor

3.10 Fit a new O-ring onto the tank

green wire terminals on the loom side of the connector, then turn the ignition on – the gauge needle should move the FULL position. Disconnect the jumper wire from the yellow/white terminal and connect it to the blue/white wire terminal – the needle should swing to E. Detach the jumper wire and turn the ignition off.

3 If the gauge does not respond as described check the wiring between the sensor connector and the gauge for continuity, and check for continuity to earth in the green wire, referring to Chapter 9 for access to the instrument cluster wiring and for the wiring diagram. If that is good check for voltage at the white/green wire to the gauge. If the wiring is good the gauge is faulty.

4 If the gauge and wiring are good, remove the level sensor from the tank (Steps 7 to 9). Check that no fuel has entered the float due to a leak, and check that the arm moves up and down smoothly.

5 Connect the probes of an ohmmeter to the specified terminals on the sensor connector as shown in the table and check the resistance of the sensor in both the FULL and EMPTY positions for each connection **(see illustrations)**. If the readings are widely different from those specified, replace the sensor with a new one.

	FULL POSITION	EMPTY POSITION
GREEN – BLUE/WHITE	566 ohms	33 ohms
GREEN – YELLOW/WHITE	33 ohms	566 ohms
BLUE/WHITE – YELLOW/WHITE	600 ohms	600 ohms

Replacement

 Warning: Refer to the precautions given in Section 1 before starting work.

6 The fuel gauge is part of the instrument cluster and is covered in Chapter 9.

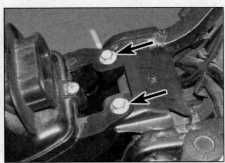

4.2 Unscrew the bolts (arrowed)

7 To replace the sensor, first remove the fuel tank (see Section 2).
8 Make sure the cap is secure, then turn the tank over and lay it on a cushion of rags to protect it and soak up any fuel that may leak.
9 Unscrew the nuts securing the sensor and carefully manoeuvre it out of the tank **(see illustration)**. Discard the O-ring as a new one must be used **(see illustration 3.10)**.
10 Fit a new O-ring onto the tank **(see illustration)**. Fit the sensor into the tank with the wiring to the back **(see illustration 3.9)**. Tighten the nuts evenly and a little at a time in a criss-cross pattern.
11 Install the tank (see Section 2), and check carefully that there are no leaks around the sensor before using the bike.

---

4   Air filter housing

Removal

1 Remove the fuel tank (see Section 2).
2 Unscrew the two bolts securing the air filter housing **(see illustration)**.
3 Draw the carburettor air vent hose from its holder on the left-hand side of the housing **(see illustration)**.

4.3 Draw the vent hose out

4.4 Release the clamp then remove the plug (arrowed) and the clamp

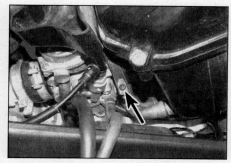

4.5 Slacken the clamp screw (arrowed) . . .

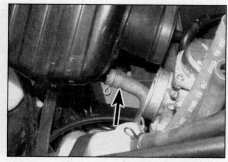

4.6a . . . then displace the housing and detach the breather hose (arrowed)

4.6b Note the routing of the drain hose as you remove the housing

4.8 The fuel tank hoses route through the hole in the tray

5.2a Detach the hoses from the water pump . . .

4 Release the clamp securing the plug in the bottom of the air filter housing drain hose, then remove the plug and slide the clamp off **(see illustration)**.

5 Slacken the clamp screw securing the air intake duct to the back of the carburettor **(see illustration)**.

6 Draw the air intake duct off the carburettor and lift the air filter housing slightly, and when accessible release the clamp and detach the crankcase breather tube **(see illustration)**. Remove the housing, noting the routing of the drain hose on the underside **(see illustration)**, and how the fuel tank drain and breather hoses route through the tray at the front **(see illustration 4.8)**.

7 Cover the carburettor intake with a clean rag.

Installation

8 Installation is the reverse of removal. Make sure the air intake duct is correctly fitted onto the back of the carburettor and does not get kinked, and tighten the clamp **(see illustration 4.5)**. Make sure the drain hose is correctly routed and the crankcase breather hose is securely connected. Make sure the fuel tank drain and breather hoses route through the tray at the front **(see illustration)**.

5 Carburettor removal and installation

> ⚠️ **Warning: Refer to the precautions given in Section 1 before starting work.**

Removal

1 Remove the fuel tank (see Section 2) and the air filter housing (Section 4). Drain the coolant (see Chapter 1).

2 Release the clamps securing the carburettor heater system coolant hoses to the water pump and the thermostat housing and pull them off their unions, being prepared with a rag to catch any residual coolant **(see illustrations)**.

3 Pull the carburettor drain hose off its union on the bottom of the float chamber **(see illustration)**.

4 Detach the throttle and choke cables from the carburettor (see Section 9).

5 Fully slacken the clamp screw securing the carburettor to the cylinder head intake duct, noting the orientation of the clamp **(see illustration)**. Ease the carburettor back

5.2b . . . and the thermostat housing

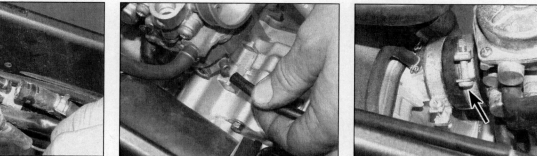

5.3 Detach the drain hose

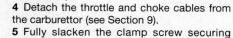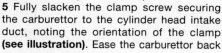

5.5a Slacken the clamp screw (arrowed) . . .

5.5b . . . and remove the carburettor

5.7a Check each duct for cracks and deterioration

5.7b Make sure the carburettor is fully engaged and correctly aligned with the tab

out of the duct and remove it, bringing the various hoses with it, noting their routing **(see illustration)**. *Note: Keep the carburettor level to prevent fuel spillage from the float chamber.*

Caution: Stuff clean rag into the cylinder head intake after removing the carburettor, to prevent anything from falling in.

6 Place a suitable container below the float chamber, then slacken the drain screw and drain all the fuel from the carburettor. Tighten the screw once all the fuel has been drained.

Installation

7 Installation is the reverse of removal, noting the following.
● Check for cracks or splits in the air intake duct on the front of the air filter housing and the cylinder head intake duct, and replace them with new ones if necessary **(see illustration)**.
● Make sure the carburettor is fully engaged with the cylinder head intake duct – a squirt of WD40 or a smear of oil will ease entry **(see illustration)**. Make sure the clamp is positioned correctly.
● Make sure all hoses are correctly routed and secured and not trapped or kinked.
● Refer to Section 9 for installation of the throttle and choke cables. Check the operation of the cables and adjust them as necessary (see Chapter 1).
● Check idle speed and adjust as necessary (see Chapter 1).

| 6 | Carburettor overhaul | |

General information

1 Poor engine performance, hesitation, hard starting, stalling, flooding and backfiring are all signs that carburettor overhaul may be required.
2 Keep in mind that many so-called carburettor problems are really not carburettor problems at all, but mechanical problems within the engine, ignition system malfunctions, an intake air leak or a fault with the PAIR system. Try to establish for certain that the carburettor is in need of maintenance before stripping it down.
3 Check the fuel valve and its strainer, the fuel and vacuum hoses, the intake duct on the cylinder head and its joint clamps, the air filter and air duct between the housing and the carburettor, the ignition system, the spark plug and the valve clearances and the PAIR system before assuming that a carburettor overhaul is required.
4 Most carburettor problems are caused by dirt particles, varnish and other deposits which build up in and block the fuel and air passages. Also, in time, gaskets and O-rings shrink or deteriorate and cause fuel and air leaks which lead to poor performance.
5 Before disassembling the carburettor, make

sure you have all the necessary O-rings and other parts, some carburettor cleaner, a supply of clean rags, some means of blowing out the carburettor passages and a clean place to work.
6 When overhauling the carburettor, disassemble it completely and clean the parts thoroughly with a carburettor cleaning solvent and dry them with filtered, unlubricated compressed air. Blow through the fuel and air passages with compressed air to force out any dirt that may have been loosened but not removed by the solvent. Once the cleaning process is complete, reassemble the carburettor using new gaskets and O-rings.

Disassembly

> ⚠ **Warning: Refer to the precautions given in Section 1 before starting work.**

7 Remove the carburettor (see Section 5).
8 Detach the fuel hose, the vent hose and the heater system hoses, noting which fits where **(see illustration)**. Check the condition of the hoses and replace them with new ones if they are damaged, deformed or deteriorated.
9 Undo the top cover retaining screws and remove the cover **(see illustration)**. Remove the spring from inside the piston **(see illustration)**.
10 Carefully peel the diaphragm away from its sealing groove in the carburettor and withdraw the diaphragm/piston assembly **(see illustration 6.39b)**. Turn the needle holder anti-clockwise to release it and remove the holder noting the spring fitted into its underside **(see**

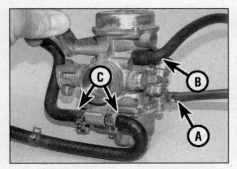

6.8 Fuel hose (A), vent hose (B), heater system hoses (C)

6.9a Undo the screws (arrowed) and remove the cover . . .

6.9b . . . and the spring

6.10a Release the needle holder . . .

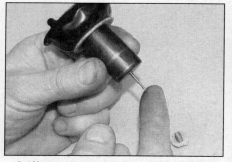

6.10b . . . then push the needle up and remove it

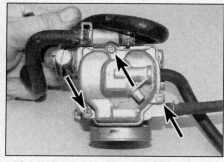

6.11a Undo the screws (arrowed) and remove the float chamber . . .

illustration). Push the jet needle up from the bottom of the piston and withdraw it from the top (see illustration).

Caution: Do not use a sharp instrument to displace the diaphragm, as it is easily damaged.

11 Undo the screws securing the float chamber to the base of the carburettor and remove it (see illustration). Remove the rubber seal and discard it, as a new one must be used (see illustration).

12 Displace and withdraw the float pivot pin and remove the float assembly, noting how it fits (see illustration). Unhook the needle valve from the tab on the float, noting how it fits (see illustration 6.35a).

13 Unscrew and remove the main jet (see illustration).

14 Push on the needle jet from inside the venturi and withdraw it from the bottom (see illustrations).

15 Unscrew and remove the pilot jet (see illustration).

16 The pilot screw can be removed from the carburettor, but note that its setting will be disturbed. To record the pilot screw's current setting, turn the screw in until it seats lightly,

counting the exact number of turns. Unscrew and remove the pilot screw along with its spring, washer and O-ring, which may need to coaxed out with a small screwdriver (see illustrations). Discard the O-ring, as a new one must be used.

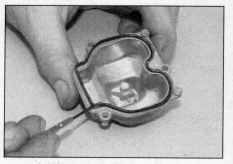

6.11b . . . and discard the seal

6.12 Displace the pin and remove the float

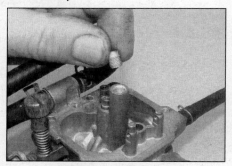

6.13 Unscrew the main jet . . .

6.14a . . . then push on the needle jet (arrowed) to displace it . . .

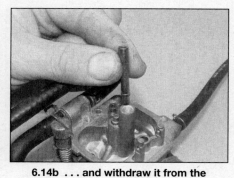

6.14b . . . and withdraw it from the carburettor

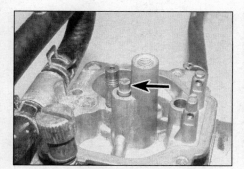

6.15 Unscrew the pilot jet (arrowed)

6.16a Remove the pilot screw and spring . . .

6.16b . . . and retrieve the washer and O-ring

6.17a Undo the screws . . .

6.17b . . . and remove the cover, spring and diaphragm . . .

6.17c . . . and the O-ring

17 Undo the air cut-off valve cover screws and remove the cover, spring and diaphragm, noting how they fit **(see illustrations)**. Remove the small O-ring from the air passage and discard it **(see illustration)**.

18 Undo the choke valve cover screws and remove the cover **(see illustration)**. Remove the rubber seal from the cover and discard it.

Cleaning

Caution: Use only a dedicated carburettor cleaner or petroleum-based solvent for carburettor cleaning. Do not use caustic cleaners.

19 Squirt carburettor cleaner through all of the fuel and air passages, and clean the float chamber, the choke valve cover, plunger and bore.

20 Use a jet of compressed air to blow out all passages.

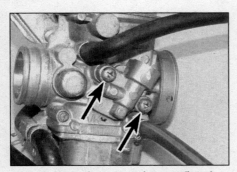

6.18 Undo the screws (arrowed) and remove the choke valve cover

6.27 Check the tip of the needle valve for wear (arrowed)

Caution: Never clean the jets or passages with a piece of wire or a drill bit, as they will be enlarged, causing the fuel and air metering rates to be upset.

Inspection

21 Make sure the choke plunger slides up and down easily in the valve cover bore. Check the plunger spring for distortion and fatigue. Replace worn parts with new ones.

22 If removed from the carburettor, check the tapered portion of the pilot screw and the spring and O-ring for wear or damage **(see illustration 6.31)**. Replace the assembly with a new one if necessary – individual parts are not available.

23 Check the carburettor body, float chamber and top cover for cracks, distorted sealing surfaces and other damage. If any defects are found, replace the faulty component with a new one, although replacement of the entire carburettor will be necessary if the body is damaged.

24 Check the piston diaphragm for splits, holes, creases and general deterioration. Holding it up to a light will help to reveal problems of this nature. Replace it with a new one if necessary – it is not available separately from the piston. Similarly check the air cut-off valve diaphragm. Check the spring for each diaphragm for distortion and fatigue.

25 Insert the piston in the carburettor body and check that it moves up and down smoothly. Check the surface of the piston for wear. If it is worn excessively or doesn't move smoothly, replace it with a new one.

26 Check the jet needle is straight by rolling it on

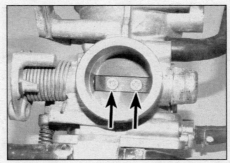

6.28 Make sure the screws (arrowed) are tight

a flat surface such as a piece of glass. Replace it with a new one if it is bent, or if the tip is worn.

27 Check the tip of the float needle valve and the valve seat **(see illustration)**. If the valve has grooves or scratches in it, or is in any way worn, it must be replaced with a new one.

28 Operate the throttle pulley to make sure the butterfly valve opens and closes smoothly. If it doesn't, clean the throttle linkage, and also check the butterfly for distortion, or for any debris caught between its edge and the carburettor. Also check that the butterfly is central on the shaft – if the screws securing it to the shaft have come loose it may be catching **(see illustration)**.

29 Check the float for damage. This will usually be apparent by the presence of fuel inside the float. If it is damaged, replace it with a new one.

30 Check the tip of the peg in the centre of the inner face of the air cut-off valve diaphragm for wear **(see illustration 6.40a)**.

Reassembly and float height check

Note: *When reassembling the carburettor, be sure to use the new O-rings, seals and other parts supplied in the rebuild kit. Do not overtighten the carburettor jets and screws, as they are easily damaged.*

31 Fit the spring, washer and O-ring onto the pilot screw (if removed), then thread the screw in until it seats lightly **(see illustration)**. Now, turn the screw out the number of turns previously recorded, or to the initial setting of 1 3/4 turns out.

6.31 Install the pilot screw and set it to the initial number of turns out

6.32 Thread the pilot jet into its bore

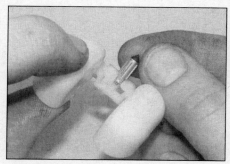

6.35a Fit the needle valve onto the float . . .

6.35b . . . then locate the float and insert the pin

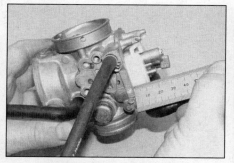

6.36 Measuring float height

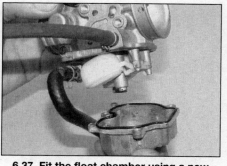

6.37 Fit the float chamber using a new seal

6.38a Make sure the spring is in the holder

32 Screw the pilot jet in **(see illustration)**.
33 Fit the needle jet up into its bore until it seats **(see illustration 6.14b and a)**.
34 Screw the main jet into the needle jet **(see illustration 6.13)**.
35 Slide the float needle valve onto the slot on the float assembly **(see illustration)**. Position the float assembly onto the carburettor, making sure the needle valve locates in the seat, then insert the pivot pin **(see illustration)**.
36 To check the float height, hold the carburettor so the float hangs down, then tilt it back until the needle valve is just seated, but not so far that the needle's spring-loaded tip is compressed. Measure the height of the float above the chamber mating surface with

an accurate ruler **(see illustration)**. The height should be as specified at the beginning of the Chapter. If not, replace the float assembly with a new one – it cannot be adjusted.
37 Fit a new rubber seal onto the float chamber, making sure it is seated properly in its groove **(see illustration 6.11b)**. Fit the chamber onto the carburettor and tighten its screws **(see illustration)**.
38 Check that the spring is fitted to the needle holder **(see illustration)**. Fit the needle into the piston, then fit the needle holder onto it, making sure the spring end locates against the head of the needle. Press it gently down and turn it clockwise to secure it **(see illustrations)**.

6.38b Fit the needle into the piston . . .

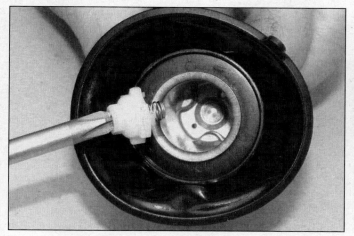

6.38c . . . then fit the holder . . .

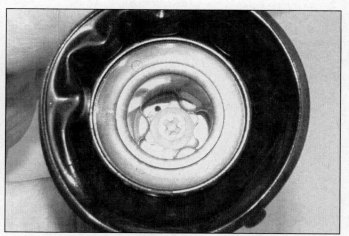

6.38d . . . and turn it to lock it under the tabs

6.39a Fold the diaphragm down . . .

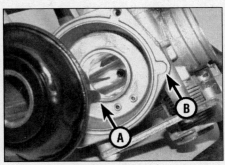

6.39b . . . then fit the piston, making sure the needle enters the jet and the tab (A) aligns with the cut-out (B)

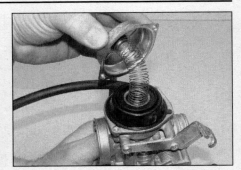

6.39c Fit the spring into the piston and the cover onto the spring . . .

6.39d . . . then locate the cover, making sure it is correctly aligned and seated

6.40a Fit the air cut-off diaphragm . . .

6.40b . . . the spring and the cover

39 Fold the diaphragm down over the piston **(see illustration)**. Fit the piston/diaphragm assembly into the carburettor, making sure the needle is correctly aligned with the needle jet, and the tab on the rim of the diaphragm is aligned with the cut-out in the carburettor, and hold the piston up with your finger **(see illustration)**. Press the rim of the diaphragm into its groove, making sure it is correctly seated. Keeping the piston held up, fit the spring into it, making sure it locates correctly onto the needle holder, then fit the cover, making sure it is correctly orientated for the diaphragm tab and locating the centre peg into the top of the spring and the outer pegs into the holes in the carburettor body **(see illustration)**. Make sure the diaphragm rim stays in place and the cover is seated on it, then tighten the cover screws **(see illustration)**. Release the piston and check

that it moves smoothly in the guide by pushing it up with your finger. Note that the piston should descend slowly and smoothly as the diaphragm draws air into the chamber – it should not drop sharply under spring pressure.

40 Fit the small O-ring onto the air cut-off valve air passage with its flat side facing in **(see illustration 6.17c)**. Fit the diaphragm so the tip on its inner face locates in the hole, then fit the spring into the cover, fit the cover, and tighten the screws **(see illustrations)**.

41 Fit the new seal into its groove in the choke valve cover, then fit the cover and tighten its screws **(see illustrations)**.

42 Fit the fuel hose, the vent hose and the heater system hoses onto their unions and secure them with their clamps **(see illustration 6.8)**.

43 Install the carburettor. Carry out pilot screw adjustment as described in the next

section if the pilot screw has been disturbed or if a new pilot screw has been fitted.

7 Air/fuel mixture adjustment

1 If the engine runs extremely rough at idle or continually stalls, and if a carburettor overhaul does not cure the problem, the pilot screw may require adjustment. It is worth noting at this point that unless you have the experience to carry this out it is best to entrust the task to a motorcycle dealer. The pilot screw is located on the left-hand side of the carburettor, between the float chamber and the intake duct on the cylinder head **(see illustration)**. Make sure the valve clearances are correct (see Chapter 1).

6.41a Locate the seal in the groove . . .

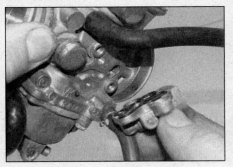

6.41b . . . then fit the cover

7.1 Adjust the pilot screw using a small screwdriver

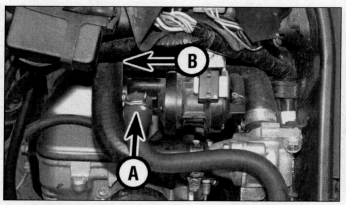

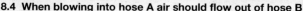

8.4 When blowing into hose A air should flow out of hose B

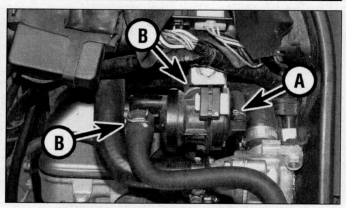

8.9 Detach the vacuum hose (A) and the air hoses (B)

2 Screw in the pilot screw until it seats lightly, then back it out to the initial setting of 1 3/4 turns. Warm the engine up to normal working temperature, then adjust the idle speed to its specified setting (see Chapter 1).

3 With the engine running, turn the pilot screw by a small amount either side of this position to find the point at which the highest consistent idle speed is obtained. Lightly open the throttle two or three times, then readjust the idle speed. Now turn the pilot screw in until the engine speed drops by 100 rpm (approx ¾ of a turn – the specified setting is for one turn out. When you've reached this position, reset the idle speed to the specified amount (see Chapter 1).

8 Pulse secondary air (PAIR) system

General information

1 To reduce the amount of unburned hydrocarbons released in the exhaust gases, a pulse secondary air (PAIR) system is fitted. The system consists of the control valve (mounted above the carburettor), the reed valve (fitted in the valve cover) and the hoses linking them. The air intake hose to the valve has an air filter fitted. The control valve is actuated by a vacuum taken off the intake duct via a hose.

2 Under certain operating conditions, the vacuum from the intake duct opens up the PAIR control valve which then allows filtered air to be drawn through the reed valve and cylinder head passage and into the exhaust port. The air mixes with the exhaust gases, causing any unburned particles of the fuel in the mixture to be burnt in the exhaust port/pipe. This process changes a considerable amount of hydrocarbons and carbon monoxide into relatively harmless carbon dioxide and water. The reed valve in the valve cover is fitted to prevent the flow of exhaust gases back up the cylinder head passage and into the control valve.

Testing

Control valve

3 Remove the valve from the motorcycle (see below).

4 Check the operation of the control valve by blowing through the air filter housing hose union; air should flow through the reed valve hose union **(see illustration)**. Now apply a vacuum of 360 mmHg to the control valve and repeat the check; no air should flow through the valve if it is functioning correctly. Replace the valve with a new one if faulty.

5 Make sure the air filter in the air intake hose is not blocked and clean and replace it with a new one if necessary.

Reed valves

6 Remove the fairing side panels (see Chapter 8). Disconnect the hose from the reed valve

housing **(see illustration 8.13)**. Attach a clean auxiliary hose of the correct bore and about 12 inches long to the union.

7 Check the valve by blowing and sucking on the auxiliary hose end. Air should flow through the hose only when blown down it and not when sucked back up. If this is not the case the reed valve is faulty, though it is worth removing it (see below) and cleaning off any carbon deposits.

Component renewal

Control valve

8 Remove the fuel tank (see Section 2).

9 Release the clamps and detach the vacuum hose and the air hoses from the control valve **(see illustration)**.

10 Remove the valve from its bracket. If required unscrew the bolt and remove the bracket.

11 Installation is the reverse of removal. Make sure the hoses are pushed fully onto their unions and secured by their clamps **(see illustration 8.9)**.

Reed valve

12 Remove the fairing side panels (see Chapter 8).

13 Release the clamp and detach the air hose from its union **(see illustration)**.

14 Unscrew the bolts securing the reed valve cover and remove the cover **(see illustration)**. Remove the reed valve, noting which way around it is fitted **(see illustration)**.

8.13 Release the clamp and detach the hose (arrowed)

8.14a Unscrew the bolts (arrowed) and remove the cover . . .

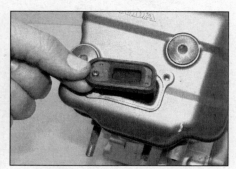

8.14b . . . and the reed valve

8.15 Make sure the valve is seated before fitting the cover

9.2a Slacken the locknut (arrowed) . . .

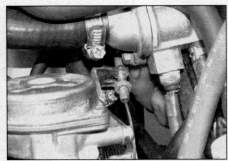

9.2b . . . free the cable from the bracket . . .

15 Installation is the reverse of removal. Make sure the reed valve and housing are clean and correctly fitted **(see illustration)**. Tighten the cover bolts to the torque setting specified at the beginning of the Chapter.

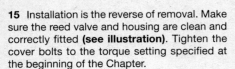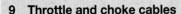

9 Throttle and choke cables

⚠ **Warning: Refer to the precautions given in Section 1 before proceeding.**

Throttle cable

Removal

1 Remove the air filter housing (see Section 4).

2 Slacken the locknut on the cable adjuster and free the cable from the bracket, noting how it locates **(see illustrations)**. Free the cable end from the pulley on the carburettor **(see illustration)**.

3 Draw the cable out, noting its routing.

4 Unscrew the cable elbow nut from the handlebar switch housing **(see illustration)**. Undo the switch housing screws and separate the halves of the handlebar switch **(see illustration)**. Detach the cable end from the pulley, then unscrew the cable elbow from the switch housing.

Installation

5 Thread the throttle cable elbow into the switch housing without it becoming tight

9.2c . . . and from the pulley

– the elbow must stay loose so that it aligns itself. Lubricate the cable end with multi-purpose grease and fit it into the throttle pulley. Assemble the switch housing onto the handlebar, making sure the pin locates in the hole, then fit the screws and tighten them **(see illustration 9.4b)**.

6 Feed the cable through to the carburettor, making sure it is correctly routed. The cable must not interfere with any other component and should not be kinked or bent sharply. Now tighten the cable elbow nut on the housing **(see illustration 9.4a)**.

7 Lubricate the cable end with multi-purpose grease and fit it into the pulley **(see illustration 9.2c)**. Locate the adjuster in the bracket **(see illustration 9.2b)**, then set the nuts so the cable freeplay is as specified (see Chapter 1).

8 Operate the throttle to check that it opens and closes freely.

9 Turn the handlebars back-and-forth to make

9.4a Slacken the locknut (arrowed)

sure the cable doesn't cause the steering to bind.

10 Install the air filter housing (see Section 4).

11 Start the engine and check that the idle speed does not rise as the handlebars are turned. If it does, the throttle cable is routed incorrectly. Correct the problem before riding the motorcycle.

Choke cable

Removal

12 Remove the air filter housing (see Section 4).

13 Unscrew the cable holder from the carburettor, then withdraw the choke valve plunger and remove the washer **(see illustrations)**. Draw the spring up and free the cable end from the plunger, then remove the

9.4b Undo the screws (arrowed) and split the switch housing

9.13a Unscrew the holder . . .

9.13b . . . then withdraw the plunger . . .

9.13c . . . and remove the washer

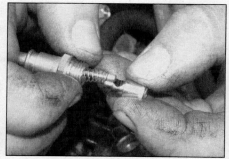

9.13d Free the plunger . . .

9.13e . . . and remove the spring . . .

9.13f . . . the holder . . .

9.13g . . . the elbow and the rubber boot

9.14a Unscrew the nut . . .

9.14b . . . then draw the cable up and out of the bracket

9.18 Make sure the cable and spring seat correctly

spring and the holder **(see illustrations)**. If required draw the elbow out of the boot and off the cable **(see illustration)**.

14 Unscrew the nut holding the cable in its bracket in the top yoke **(see illustration)**. Draw the cable up and slip it out of the bracket **(see illustration)**.

15 Draw the cable out, noting its routing.

Installation

16 Feed the cable through to the carburettor, making sure it is correctly routed. The cable must not interfere with any other component and should not be kinked or bent sharply.

17 Slip the cable into its bracket on the top yoke, then seat the cable on the bracket and tighten the nut to secure it **(see illustrations 8.14b and a)**.

18 Feed the cable through the rubber boot and the elbow, then fit the holder, slip the spring over the inner cable and fit the end into its socket in the plunger **(see illustrations 9.13g, f, e and d)**. Make sure the spring locates

correctly onto the plunger **(see illustration)**. Locate the washer against the nut, then fit the plunger into the carburettor and tighten the holder **(see illustrations 9.13c, b and a)**.

19 Operate the choke to check that it opens and closes freely.

20 Turn the handlebars back-and-forth

to make sure the cable doesn't cause the steering to bind.

21 Install the air filter housing (see Section 4).

---

10 Exhaust system

> ⚠ **Warning: If the engine has been running the exhaust system will be very hot. Allow the system to cool before carrying out any work.**

Removal

Silencer

1 Unscrew the three bolts securing the silencer to the pipe **(see illustration)**.

2 Unscrew the nut on the silencer mounting bolt, then withdraw the bolt and remove the silencer **(see illustrations)**.

10.1 Unscrew the bolts (arrowed)

10.2a Unscrew the nut (arrowed) . . .

10.2b . . . then withdraw the bolt and remove the silencer

10.6 Unscrew the nut and remove the bolt

10.8 Unscrew the header pipe nuts and draw the flange off

3 Remove the sealing ring between the silencer and pipe and discard it.

4 Check the condition of the mounting bolt, washers, collar and rubber and replace them with new ones if necessary.

 Exhaust system clamp bolts tend to become corroded and seized. It is advisable to spray them with WD40 or a similar product before attempting to slacken them.

Complete system

5 Remove the lower fairing (see Chapter 8).

6 Unscrew the nut on the exhaust pipe mounting bolt, then withdraw the bolt **(see illustration)**.

7 Unscrew the nut on the silencer mounting bolt **(see illustration 10.2a)**.

8 Unscrew the nuts securing the header pipe to the cylinder head and draw the flange off the studs **(see illustration)**.

9 Support the system, then withdraw the silencer bolt **(see illustration 10.2b)** and manoeuvre the system out from under the bike **(see illustration)**.

10 Remove the sealing ring from the port in the cylinder head and discard it **(see illustration)**.

11 If required separate the silencer from the pipe (Steps 1 and 3), and remove the heat shield and guard.

12 Check the condition of the mounting bolts, washers, collars and rubbers and replace them with new ones if necessary.

Installation

13 Installation is the reverse of removal, noting the following:

● Replace any damaged, deformed or deteriorated mounting rubbers with new ones.
● Use a new sealing ring in the cylinder head port, and dab it with grease to stick it in place **(see illustration)**.
● Use a new sealing ring between the pipe and the silencer.
● Apply a smear of copper grease to all nuts and bolts to prevent them from seizing up.
● Leave all fasteners loose until the entire system has been installed, making alignment easier.
● Tighten the downpipe nuts first, then the pipe and silencer mounting bolts/nuts.
● Run the engine and check the system for leaks.

11 Catalytic converter

General information

1 A catalytic converter is incorporated in the exhaust system to minimise the level of exhaust pollutants released into the atmosphere.

2 The catalytic converter consists of a heat tube impregnated with a catalyst material, over which the hot exhaust gases pass. The catalyst speeds up the oxidation of harmful carbon monoxide, unburned hydrocarbons and soot, effectively reducing the quantity of harmful products released into the atmosphere via the exhaust gases.

3 The catalytic converter is of the open-loop type, providing no feedback to the fuel and ignition systems.

Precautions

4 The catalytic converter is a reliable and simple device which needs no maintenance in itself, but there are some facts of which an owner should be aware if the converter is to function properly for its full service life.

● DO NOT use leaded or lead replacement petrol (gasoline) – the additives will coat the precious metals, reducing their converting efficiency and will eventually destroy the catalytic converter.
● Always keep the ignition and fuel systems well-maintained in accordance with the manufacturer's schedule – if the fuel/air mixture is suspected of being incorrect have it checked on an exhaust gas analyser.
● If the engine develops a misfire, do not ride the bike at all (or at least as little as possible) until the fault is cured.
● DO NOT use fuel or engine oil additives – these may contain substances harmful to the catalytic converter.
● DO NOT continue to use the bike if the engine burns oil to the extent of leaving a visible trail of blue smoke.
● Remember that the catalytic converter and oxygen sensor are FRAGILE – do not strike them with tools during servicing work.

10.9 Remove the system from the bike

10.10 Remove the old sealing ring and discard it

10.13 Always use a new sealing ring

Chapter 4B
Fuel system – fuel injection models

Contents

Degrees of difficulty

| **Easy,** suitable for novice with little experience 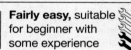 | **Fairly easy,** suitable for beginner with some experience 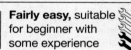 | **Fairly difficult,** suitable for competent DIY mechanic 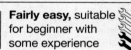 | **Difficult,** suitable for experienced DIY mechanic 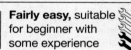 | **Very difficult,** suitable for expert DIY or professional |

Specifications

Fuel
Grade	Unleaded. Minimum 91 RON (Research Octane Number) for Europe.
Fuel tank capacity (including reserve)	10.0 litres
Reserve volume (gauge needle goes into red zone)	approx. 2.1 litres

Fuel injection system
Throttle body model	GQ16A
Idle speed	1450 ± 100 rpm
Fuel pressure at specified idle speed	43 psi (3.0 Bar)
Minimum fuel flow rate	13.9 cc every 10 seconds

Fuel injection system test data
Note: *All values given are only accurate at 20°C (68°F)*
Engine coolant temperature (ECT) sensor resistance	2.3 to 2.6 K-ohms
Fuel injector resistance	9.0 to 12.0 ohms
Ignition pulse generator minimum peak voltage output	0.7 volt
Idle air control valve (IACV) resistance	110 to 150 ohms @ 25°C (77°F)

Torque settings
Engine coolant temperature (ECT) sensor	23 Nm
Fuel injector holder bolts	5.4 Nm
Idle air control valve (IACV) screws	2.1 Nm
Throttle body sensor unit Torx screws	3.4 Nm
Fuel pump nuts	12 Nm
Oxygen sensor	25 Nm

1 General information and precautions

General information

The fuel supply system consists of the fuel tank with internal strainers and level sensor/ pump unit, the fuel hoses, the injector, the throttle body, the throttle cable, and idle speed adjuster. Note that the idle speed and fast idle speed for cold starting is set automatically by the ECU. The fuel pump is switched on and off with the engine via a relay. The injection system, known as PGM-FI, supplies fuel and air to the engine the throttle body. The injector is operated by the Engine Control Unit (ECU) using the information obtained from the various sensors it monitors – refer to Section 3 for more information on the operation of the fuel injection system.

Many of the fuel system service procedures are considered routine maintenance items and for that reason are covered in Chapter 1.

Note: *Individual engine management system components can be checked but not repaired. If system troubles occur, and the faulty component can be isolated, the only cure for the problem in most cases is to*

2.3 Disconnect the breather hose (arrowed) from the base of the air filter housing

replace the part with a new one. Keep in mind that most electronic parts, once purchased, cannot be returned. To avoid unnecessary expense, make very sure the faulty component has been positively identified before buying a new part.

Precautions

⚠️ **Warning: Petrol (gasoline) is extremely flammable, so take extra precautions when you work on any part of the fuel system. Always remove the battery (see Chapter 9). Donít smoke or allow open flames or bare light bulbs near the work area, and donít work in a garage where a natural gas-type appliance is present. If you spill any fuel on your skin, rinse it off immediately with soap and water. When you perform any kind of work on the fuel system, wear safety glasses and have a fire extinguisher suitable for a class B type fire (flammable liquids) on hand.**

Some residual pressure will remain in the fuel feed hose after the motorcycle has been used. Before disconnecting any fuel hose, ensure the ignition is switched OFF and make sure you have plenty of clean rag and a suitable container for catching and storing the fuel. It is vital that no dirt or debris is allowed to enter any part of the system while a fuel hose is disconnected. Any foreign matter in the fuel system components could result in injector damage or malfunction. Ensure the ignition is switched OFF before disconnecting or reconnecting any fuel injection system wiring connector. If a connector is disconnected or reconnected with the ignition switched ON, the engine control unit (ECU) may be damaged.

Always perform service procedures in a well-ventilated area to prevent a build-up of fumes.

Never work in a building containing a gas appliance with a pilot light, or any other form of naked flame. Ensure that there are no naked light bulbs or any sources of flame or sparks nearby.

Do not smoke (or allow anyone else to smoke) while in the vicinity of petrol (gasoline) or of components containing it. Remember the possible presence of vapour from these sources and move well clear before smoking.

Check all electrical equipment belonging to the house, garage or workshop where work is being undertaken (see the Safety first! section of this manual). Remember that certain electrical appliances such as drills, cutters etc, create sparks in the normal course of operation and must not be used near petrol (gasoline) or any component containing it. Again, remember the possible presence of fumes before using electrical equipment.

Always mop up any spilt fuel and safely dispose of the rag used.

Any stored fuel that is drained off during servicing work must be kept in sealed containers that are suitable for holding petrol (gasoline), and clearly marked as such; the containers themselves should be kept in a safe place. Note that this last point applies equally to the fuel tank if it is removed from the machine; also remember to keep its filler cap closed at all times.

Read the Safety first! section of this manual carefully before starting work.

2 Air filter housing

Removal

1 Remove the fuel tank as described in Section 7.
2 Remove the air filter (see Chapter 1).
3 Release the clamp and disconnect the crankcase breather hose from the base of the air filter housing **(see illustration)**.
4 Slacken the clamp securing the air intake duct to the rear of the throttle body **(see illustration)**.
5 Release the clamp and disconnect the fuel tank drain hose **(see illustration)**.

2.4 Slacken the intake duct clamp (arrowed)

2.5 Disconnect the fuel tank drain hose (arrowed)

6 Note their fitted positions, then release the fuel feed hose and fuel pump wiring loom from the guides on the air filter housing, then undo the bolts and manoeuvre the housing upwards from position. Disconnect the drain hose from the base of the housing as it's withdrawn **(see illustrations)**. Cover the throttle body with a clean rag.

Installation

7 Installation is the reversal of removal. Ensure all fasteners are securely tightened, and any wiring loom/hoses are correctly routed.

3 Fuel injection system description

1 The CBR125RW7-on models are equipped with Honda's programmed fuel injection (PGM-FI) system. It is controlled by a management system with an engine control unit (ECU) that operates both the injection and ignition systems.
2 The engine control unit (ECU) monitors signals from the following sensors.
● Throttle position (TP) sensor – informs the ECU of the throttle position, and the rate of throttle opening or closing.
● Engine coolant temperature (ECT) sensor – informs the ECU of engine temperature. It also actuates the temperature gauge (see Chapter 3).
● Manifold absolute pressure (MAP) sensor – informs the ECU of the engine load by monitoring the pressure in the throttle body inlet tract.
● Intake air temperature (IAT) sensor – informs the ECU of the temperature of the air entering the throttle body.
● Ignition pulse generator – informs the ECU of engine speed and crankshaft position (see Chapter 5).
● Lean angle sensor – stops the engine if the bike falls over.
● Oxygen sensor – informs the ECU of the oxygen content of the exhaust gases.
3 All the information from the sensors is analysed by the ECU, and from that it determines the appropriate ignition and fuelling requirements of the engine. The ECU controls the fuel injector by varying its pulse width – the length of time the injector is held open – to provide more or less fuel, as appropriate for cold starting, warm up, idle, cruising, and acceleration.
4 At all times, the engine idle speed is controlled by the ECU, and is not adjustable.
5 If there is an abnormality in any of the readings obtained from any sensor, the ECU enters its back-up mode. In this event, the ECU ignores the abnormal sensor signal, and assumes a pre-programmed value which will allow the engine to continue running (albeit at reduced efficiency). If the ECU enters this back-up mode, or when any faults occur, the fuel injection system (FI) warning light in

2.6a Unclip the fuel feed hose from the side of the housing (arrowed)

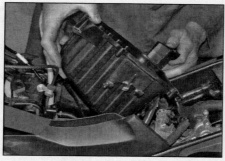

2.6c . . . lift the rear of the housing . . .

2.6b Undo the bolts (arrowed) at the rear of the air filter housing . . .

2.6d . . . and disconnect the drain hose (arrowed)

the instrument cluster will come on or flash (depending on the situation), and the relevant fault code will be stored in the ECU memory. The fault can be identified using the fault codes which can be accessed using the self-diagnosis function (see Section 4). However if there are certain faults detected in the injector or ignition pulse generator, the back-up mode becomes ineffective and the ECU will not allow the engine to run at all.

4 Fuel injection system fault diagnosis

1 If the fuel injection system (FI) warning light on the instrument cluster comes on when the motorcycle is running, a fault has occurred in the fuel injection/ignition system. The engine control unit (ECU) will store the relevant fault code in its memory and this code can be read as follows using the self-diagnostic mode of the ECU. While the engine is running above 5000 rpm and the motorcycle is being ridden, the light will come on and stay on. When the motorcycle is on its sidestand and the engine is off or running below 5000 rpm, the light will flash, the pattern of the flashes indicating the code for the fault the ECU has identified.
2 If the engine can be started, place the motorcycle on its sidestand then start the engine and allow it to idle. Whilst the engine is idling, observe the FI warning light on the instrument cluster.
3 If the engine cannot be started, place the motorcycle on its sidestand. With the kill

switch in the run position turn the engine over on the starter motor for more than ten seconds and observe the FI warning light on the instrument cluster.
4 Alternatively, and to check for any stored fault codes even though the warning lights have not illuminated, gain access to the fuel injection system data link connector (DLC), which is a capped 4-pin connector coming out of the wiring loom under the right-hand side of the upper fairing **(see illustration)**. Ensure the ignition is switched OFF then remove the cap and fit the Honda DLC short connector (Part No. 070PZ-ZY30100, available at reasonable cost from your dealer). Make sure the kill switch is in the RUN position then turn the ignition ON and observe the warning light. If there are no stored fault codes, the light will come on and stay on. If there are stored fault codes, the light will flash.

4.4 The fault diagnosis DLC (arrowed) has a red cap, and is located under the right-hand side of the upper fairing (fairing removed for clarity)

Fault code (No. of flashes)	Symptoms	Possible causes

0 – no code (warning light off)	Engine does not start	Blown fuse (main or circuit)
		Faulty power supply to engine control unit (ECU)
		Short circuit in ECU output voltage wire
		Faulty engine stop relay or wiring
		Faulty engine stop switch/open circuit on switch earth (ground) wire
		Faulty ignition switch
		Faulty lean angle sensor or wiring
		Faulty engine control unit (ECU)
		No fuel to injector:
		  Clogged fuel pipe
		  Blocked fuel filter
		  Faulty fuel pump

0 – no code (warning light off)	Engine runs normally	Open or short circuit in warning light wiring Faulty engine control unit (ECU)
0 – no code (warning light constantly on)	Engine runs normally	Short circuit in data link connector or wiring Faulty engine control unit (ECU)
1	Engine runs normally	Faulty manifold absolute pressure (MAP) sensor or wiring
7	Engine difficult to start at low temperatures	Faulty engine coolant temperature (ECT) sensor or wiring
8	Poor throttle response	Faulty throttle position (TP) sensor or wiring
9	Engine runs normally	Faulty intake air temperature (IAT) sensor or wiring
12	Engine does not start	Faulty injector or wiring
21	Engine operates normally	Faulty oxygen sensor (O2) or wiring
33	Engine operates normally	Faulty EPROM in ECU
54	Engine does not start	Faulty lean angle sensor or wiring

5 The light emits long (1.3 second) and short (0.5 second) flashes to give out the fault code. A long flash is used to indicate the first digit of a double digit fault code (i.e. 10 and above). If a single digit fault code is being displayed (i.e. 0 – 9), there will be a number of short flashes equivalent to the code being displayed. For example, two long (1.3 sec) flashes followed by three short (0.5 sec) flashes indicates the fault code number 23. If there is more than one fault code, there will be a gap before the other codes are revealed (the codes will be revealed in order, starting with the lowest and finishing with the highest). Once all codes have been revealed, the ECU will continuously run through the code(s) stored in its memory, revealing each one in turn with a short gap between them. The fault codes are shown in the accompanying table. Switch off the ignition and (where necessary) remove the tool from the data link connector. Identify the fault using the table above, then refer below for checking procedures.

6 Once the fault has been identified and corrected, it will be necessary to reset the system by removing the fault code from the ECU memory. To do this, ensure the ignition is switched OFF then fit the Honda DLC short connector (see Step 4). Make sure the kill switch is in the RUN position, then turn the ignition switch ON. Disconnect the tool from the DLC. When the tool is disconnected the light should come on for about five

seconds, during which time the tool must be reconnected. The light should start to flash when it is reconnected, indicating that all fault codes have been erased. Turn off the ignition then remove the tool. Check the FI warning light (in some cases it may be necessary to repeat the erasing procedure more than once) then refit the cap over the DLC.

7 While some of the sensors can be checked using home equipment, there are others which can only be tested using the Honda diagnostic system (HDS) tester which can be plugged into the system. If a fault appears, use the diagnostic function and fault code system described above to work out which component is faulty. First ensure that the relevant system wiring connectors are securely connected and free of corrosion – poor connections are the cause of the majority of problems. Also check the wiring itself for any obvious faults or breaks, and use a continuity tester to check the wiring between the component, its connectors and the ECU, referring to the wiring diagram and Electrical System Fault Finding section in Chapter 9. Next refer to Section 5 to see if there are any other specific checks that can be made on that particular component. If this fails to reveal the cause of the problem, the motorcycle should be taken to a suitably-equipped Honda dealer for testing. They will have the tester which should locate the fault quickly and simply.

8 Also ensure that the fault is not due to poor

maintenance – i.e. check that the air filter element is clean, that the spark plug is in good condition, that the valve clearances are correctly adjusted, the cylinder compression pressure is correct, and the ignition timing is correct (refer to Chapters 1, 2 and 5). It is also worth removing the sensor(s) in question (see Section 5) and checking that the sensing tip or head is clean and not obstructed by anything.

5 Fuel injection and engine management system components

Caution: Ensure the ignition is switched OFF before disconnecting/reconnecting any fuel injection system wiring connector. If a connector is disconnected/reconnected with the ignition switched ON the engine control unit (ECU) could be damaged.

Manifold absolute pressure (MAP) sensor

Check

1 The MAP sensor is mounted on the throttle body. The sensor can only be checked using the Honda diagnostic system tester, however, the sensor power supply can be checked as follows.

2 Remove the fuel tank (see Section 7). Disconnect the wiring connector from the

5.2 Throttle body sensor unit wiring plug (arrowed)

5.5a Undo the 3 Torx screws (arrowed) . . .

5.5b . . . and pull the sensor unit from the side of the throttle body

sensor unit **(see illustration)**. Connect the positive (+) lead of a voltmeter to the light green/yellow wire terminal of the sensor wiring connector, then connect the negative (–) lead to the green/orange terminal. Turn the ignition switch ON and set the kill switch to RUN and check that a voltage of 3.80 to 5.25 volts is present. If it is, the MAP sensor may be faulty. If there is no voltage, check for continuity in each wire to the ECU.

Removal and installation

3 The MAP sensor is part of the sensor unit attached to the throttle body. Honda stress that the sensor unit must not be dismantled. Consequently, if the MAP sensor is faulty, the complete sensor unit must be replaced as follows:

4 Remove the throttle body as described in Section 6.

5 Undo the 3 Torx screws, and remove the sensor unit, complete with sealing ring **(see illustrations)**.

6 If available, use compressed air to clean the various passages in the throttle body.

7 Using a new sealing ring, fit the sensor unit, aligning the slot of the throttle position sensor with the end of the spindle in the throttle body **(see illustrations)**. Tighten the Torx screws to the specified torque.

8 Refit the throttle body as described in Section 6.

9 It's now necessary to reset the throttle position sensor fully closed position as follows:

10 Remove any stored fault codes from the ECU memory as described in paragraph 6 of Section 4.

11 Turn the ignition switch off, and fit the Honda short connector to the DLC as described in Section 4, paragraph 4.

12 Disconnect the engine coolant temperature sensor (ECT) wiring plug **(see illustration 5.15)**, then use a length of wire to bridge the yellow/blue and green/orange terminals of the ECT wiring harness plug.

13 Turn the ignition switch on, and within 10 seconds (while the FI light is blinking), disconnect the bridging wire from the ECT harness plug. If the FI warning light now starts to rapidly blink (0.3 seconds duration and intervals) the throttle position sensor reset

5.7a Renew the sealing ring . . .

procedure has been successful. If the FI light doesn't blink as stated, repeat the procedure from paragraph 10 onwards.

Engine coolant temperature (ECT) sensor

Check

14 Raise the fuel tank (see Section 7) and support it securely.

15 Disconnect the wiring connector from the sensor **(see illustration)**. With the engine cold, connect an ohmmeter between the terminals on the sensor which connect to the yellow/blue and green/orange wires and measure its resistance **(see illustration)**. Compare the reading obtained to that given in the Specifications, noting that the specified value is valid at 20°C (68°F). If the resistance reading differs greatly from that specified, the sensor is probably faulty.

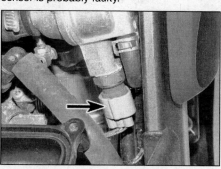

5.15a Disconnect the ECT sensor wiring plug (arrowed)

5.7b . . . and align the sensor slot with the end of the spindle (arrowed)

16 If the sensor appears to be functioning correctly, check its power supply. Connect the positive (+) lead of a voltmeter to the yellow/blue wire terminal in the sensor wiring connector, then connect the negative (–) lead to a good earth. Turn the ignition switch ON and check that a voltage of 4.75 to 5.25 volts is present. If it isn't, there is a fault in the yellow/blue wire or the ECU.

Removal and installation

17 Drain the cooling system (see Chapter 1), then raise the fuel tank (see Section 7).

18 Disconnect the sensor wiring connector **(see illustration 15.5a)**. Unscrew and remove the sensor. Discard the sealing washer.

19 Fit a new sealing washer onto the sensor. Install the sensor and tighten it to the torque setting specified at the beginning of the Chapter. Connect the wiring.

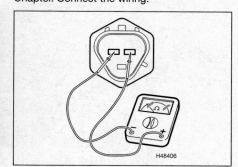

5.15b ECT sensor resistance test

5.23 Connect an ohmmeter between the middle and right-hand sensor terminals to measure the IAT resistance

5.26 Fuel injector wiring plug (arrowed)

20 Refill the cooling system (see Chapter 1), and refit the fuel tank.

Throttle position (TP) sensor

Check

21 The throttle sensor operation can only be checked using the Honda diagnostic system tester. Its power supply can be checked as follows. Disconnect the wiring connector from the sensor **(see illustration 5.2)**. Connect the positive (+) lead of a voltmeter to the green/orange terminal of the sensor wiring connector, then connect the negative (–) lead to a good earth. Turn the ignition switch ON and check that a voltage of 4.75 to 5.25 volts is present. If it isn't, there is a fault in the green/orange wire or the ECU.

Removal and installation

22 The TP sensor is part of the sensor unit attached to the throttle body. Honda stress that the sensor unit must not be dismantled. Consequently, if the TP sensor is faulty, the complete sensor unit must be replaced as described in paragraphs 4 to 13 of this Section.

Intake air temperature (IAT) sensor

Check

23 The IAT sensor is part of the sensor unit attached to the throttle body. Disconnect the sensor unit wiring plug, and connect an ohmmeter across the sensor terminals (middle and right-hand end) and measure its resistance **(see illustration)**. Compare the reading obtained to that given in the Specifications noting that the specified value is valid at 20°C (68°F). If the resistance reading differs greatly from that specified, the sensor is probably faulty.

24 If the sensor appears to be functioning correctly, check its power supply. Connect the positive (+) lead of a voltmeter to the grey/blue terminal of the sensor wiring connector, then connect the negative (–) lead to the green/orange terminal. Turn the ignition switch ON and check that a voltage of 4.75 to 5.25 volts is present. If it isn't, there is a fault in the grey/blue wire, green/orange wire, or the ECU.

Removal and installation

25 The IAT sensor is part of the sensor unit attached to the throttle body. Honda stress that the sensor unit must not be dismantled. Consequently, if the IAT sensor is faulty, the complete sensor unit must be replaced as described in paragraphs 4 to 13 of this Section.

Fuel injector

⚠️ *Warning: Refer to the precautions given in Section 1 before starting work.*

Check

26 Peel back the rubber boot, and disconnect the wiring connector from the injector. Connect an ohmmeter between the terminals and measure the resistance **(see illustration)**. Compare the reading to that given in the Specifications. Also check that there is no continuity to earth on the black/white wire terminal on the injector. If the resistance of the injector differs greatly from that specified, or there is a continuity to earth, a new injector should be installed. Also check for battery voltage at the black/white wire terminal in the wiring connector with the ignition ON and the kill switch set to RUN. If there is no voltage, check the wiring. Check for continuity in the pink/green wire in the connector – there should be no continuity to earth, and there should be continuity to the wire terminal in the ECU wiring connector.

Removal

27 Remove the air filter housing (Section 2). For best access remove the throttle body (see Section 6).

28 Disconnect the wiring connector from the injector **(see illustration 5.26)**.

29 Have some rag to hand to catch residual fuel. Pull up the locking clip, squeeze together the locking tabs and pull the quick/release connector from the fuel pipe above the injector **(see illustrations)**. Plug/cover the openings to prevent contamination.

30 Unscrew the injector holder bolts **(see**

5.29a Pull up the locking clip (arrowed) . . .

5.29b . . . then squeeze together the locking tabs and pull the connection from the injector pipe

5.30a Undo the injector holder bolts (arrowed) . . .

5.30b . . . and pull the holder and injector from the throttle body

5.30c Renew the seal in the throttle body . . .

illustrations). Carefully lift off the injector holder and injector. Remove the seal from the injector, and from the throttle body. Discard them as new ones must be used.

Installation

31 Lubricate the new injector/holder seals with clean engine oil, then fit them to the injector.

32 Align the injector with the holder as shown, then carefully press the assembly into the throttle body **(see illustration)**. Tighten the injector holder bolts to the specified torque.

33 Reconnect the fuel pipe and the injector wiring plug. Where applicable, refit the throttle body as described in Section 6, and the air filter housing as described in Section 2.

Ignition pulse generator coil

34 See Chapter 5.

Oxygen sensor

Check

35 Apart from the wiring checks that are outlined in Section 4, the operation of the oxygen sensor can only be checked using the Honda diagnostic system tester.

Removal and installation

Note: *The oxygen sensor is delicate and will not work if it is dropped or knocked, or if any cleaning materials are used on it. Ensure the exhaust system is cold before proceeding.*

36 Remove the fairing right-hand side panel as described in Chapter 8, and disconnect the sensor wiring plug **(see illustration)**.

37 Unclip the metal cover, and pull the wiring cord from the sensor **(see illustrations)**. Discard the wiring cord – Honda insist it must be renewed.

38 Unscrew the sensor from the cylinder head.

39 Fit the new sensor, and tighten it to the specified torque.

40 Position the new sensor wiring cord in line with the cylinder barrel, and press it squarely onto the sensor without rotating it.

41 With the wiring cord correctly fitted, refit the metal cover, and reconnect the wiring plug **(see illustration)**.

42 Refit the fairing panel as described in Chapter 8.

Lean angle sensor

Check

43 Remove the fairing (see Chapter 8).

44 With the ignition switch ON and the kill switch set to run, connect the negative (–) lead of a voltmeter to the green/orange wire

5.30d . . . and on the injector (arrowed)

5.32 Align the tab (arrowed) on the holder with the injector connector (arrowed) as shown

5.36 Oxygen sensor wiring plug (arrowed)

5.37a Unclip the metal cover . . .

5.37b . . . and pull the wiring cord from the sensor (arrowed)

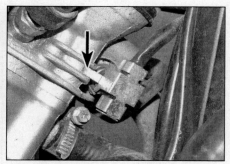

5.41 Note the tab (arrowed) on the metal cover engages with the fin on the cylinder head

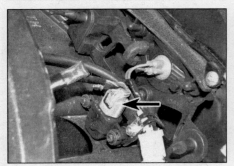

5.44 Lean angle sensor wiring plug (arrowed)

5.46 Undo the screws (arrowed) and remove the lead angle sensor

terminal of the lean angle sensor connector **(see illustration)**. Connect the voltmeter positive (+) lead to the white/red wire terminal of the connector and check that a voltage of 4.75 to 5.25 volts is present. If it isn't, there is a fault in the green/orange wire, white/red wire, or the ECU. No further testing of the lean angle sensor is possible without access to the Honda diagnostic system tester.

Removal and installation

45 Remove the fairing (see Chapter 8).
46 Disconnect the lean angle sensor wiring connector **(see illustration 5.44)**. Undo the screws and remove the sensor **(see illustration)**. Note the collars in the mounting grommets.
47 Installation is the reverse of removal. Make

sure the collars are in place and the sensor is fitted with its UP mark facing upwards and with the wiring to the front.

Idle air control valve (IACV)

Check

48 The idle air control valve (IACV) is fitted to the throttle body. Disconnect the valve wiring plug **(see illustration)** and connect an

ohmmeter across the valve's inner terminals and measure the resistance **(see illustration)**. Compare the reading obtained to that given in the Specifications noting that the specified value is valid at 25°C (77°F). Repeat this test across the valve's outer terminals. If the resistance reading differs greatly from that specified, the valve is probably faulty.
49 If the valve appears to be functioning correctly, check for continuity between each of the wiring loom connector terminals and earth. If continuity is present, there is a fault in the relevant wire, or the ECU.
50 The functionality of the valve can be checked by removing it (as described below), then reconnecting the wiring plug and turning the ignition (and KILL switch) to ON. The valve should briefly operate and emit a 'beep'.

Removal and installation

51 Disconnect the IACV wiring plug, undo the 2 security screws, then pull the valve and setting plate from the throttle body **(see illustrations)**. If greater access is required, remove the throttle body as described in Section 6.
52 Gently turn the sleeve of the valve clockwise until it rests against the stop.
53 Align the slot in the valve sleeve with the pin in the throttle body, and refit the valve **(see illustrations)**.
54 Refit the setting plate aligning the lug on the valve with the slot in the plate **(see**

5.48a Disconnect the IACV wiring plug (arrowed)

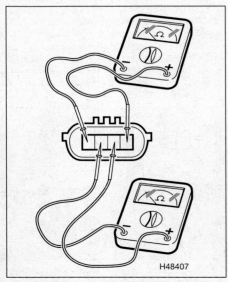

5.48b IACV resistance test connections

5.51a Undo the Torx security screws (arrowed) . . .

5.51b . . . and pull the valve and setting plate from the throttle body

5.53a Align the slot (arrowed) in the valve sleeve . . .

5.53b . . . with the pin (arrowed) in the throttle body

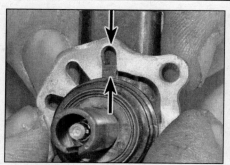

5.54 Align the lug (arrowed) on the valve with the right-hand slot (arrowed) in the setting plate

5.58a Press-in the centre pin, pull out the clip . . .

5.58b . . . and open the rubber sheet

illustration). Tighten the retaining screws to the specified torque, and reconnect the wiring plug.

Engine control unit (ECU)

Check

55 The engine control unit (ECU) itself cannot be checked, but a process of elimination of other possible faulty components can point to it being faulty. The best thing to do is to substitute it with one known to be good and see whether the problem is solved. Otherwise the only thing you can do is to check all the wiring and connectors between all components in the system and the ECU. Alternatively take the bike to a Honda dealer equipped with the test harness.

Removal and installation

56 Make sure the ignition is OFF.
57 Remove the fuel tank as described in Section 7.
58 Remove the clip and open the rubber sheet behind the frame headstock **(see illustrations)**.
59 Disconnect the ECU wiring plug **(see illustration)**.
60 Lift the rubber holder from its mounting, and remove the ECU from the holder.
61 Installation is the reverse of removal.

6 Throttle body

> **Warning: Refer to the precautions given in Section 1 before starting work.**

Removal

1 Remove the air filter housing (Section 2). Have some rag to hand to catch residual fuel.
2 Disconnect the wiring plugs from the throttle body.
3 Pull up the locking clip, squeeze together the locking tabs and pull the quick/release connector from the fuel pipe above the injector **(see illustration 5.29a and 5.29b)**. Plug/cover the openings to prevent contamination.
4 Slacken the clamp securing the throttle body to the intake duct, and pull the throttle body rearwards from the duct **(see illustrations)**.
5 Slacken the locknut, undo the adjusting nut and disengage the throttle cable end fitting from the throttle body quadrant **(see illustration)**.
6 Manoeuvre the throttle body from place. Tape over or stuff clean rag into the cylinder head intake after removing the throttle body assembly to prevent anything from falling in.
Caution: The throttle body assembly must be treated as a sealed unit. NEVER loosen any of the white-painted nuts/bolts/screws on the assembly as these are pre-set

5.59 Depress the catch and disconnect the ECU wiring plug

at the factory. The only components on the assembly which are serviceable are described in Section 5.
Caution: NEVER use a solvent-based cleaner to clean the throttle body components. The throttle bores are covered with a molybdenum coating which could be removed by the cleaner.

Installation

7 Remove the tape/plugs from the intake. Lubricate the inside of the rubbers with a light smear of engine oil to aid installation.
8 Reconnect the throttle cable end fitting to the quadrant on the throttle body and engage the adjustment nut with its lug. Do not tighten the locknut at this stage.
9 Align the lug on the throttle body with the cut-out in the intake rubber, and press

6.4a Slacken the throttle body-to-intake duct clamp (arrowed) . . .

6.4b . . . and pull the throttle body rearwards

6.5 Slacken the throttle cable locknut (arrowed)

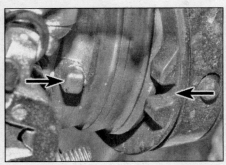

6.9 The lug (arrowed) must align with the cut-out (arrowed) in the intake duct

the throttle body fully into place **(see illustration)**.

10 Ensure the clamp is correctly located, then tighten the clamp screw until the gap between the ends of the clamp band is approximately 7.0 mm.

7.2a Remove the bolts (arrowed) at the front of the tank . . .

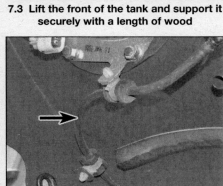

7.7a Unclip the fuel pipe (arrowed) . . .

7.1 Undo the screws (arrowed) and remove the fuel tank cover

11 Reconnect the fuel pipe and the wiring plugs.

12 Refit the air cleaner housing as described in Section 2, then adjust the throttle cable as described in Chapter 1.

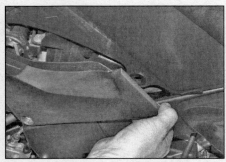

7.2b . . . and pull the side panel lugs from the grommets in the tank

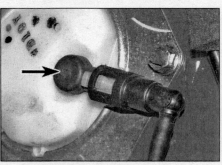

7.6a Peel back the rubber boot (arrowed) . . .

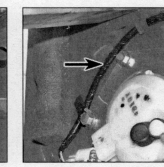

7.7b . . . and the pump wiring harness (arrowed)

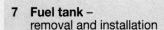

7 Fuel tank –
removal and installation

> **Warning: Refer to the precautions given in Section 1 before starting work.**

Removal

1 Remove the rider's seat as described in Chapter 8, then undo the screws and remove the cover from the front of the fuel tank **(see illustration)**.

2 Remove the 2 bolts at the front of the tank, then pull the side panel lugs from the grommets at the rear of the tank **(see illustrations)**.

3 Lift the front edge of the tank, and support it with a suitable length of wood etc. **(see illustration)**.

4 Disconnect the fuel pump wiring plug, then start the engine, and let it idle until it stalls. Turn the ignition off.

5 Disconnect the battery negative lead as described in Chapter 9.

6 Pull back the rubber boot, squeeze together the locking tabs and pull the fuel pipe from the port on the pump cover **(see illustrations)**. Be prepared for fuel spillage. Plug the openings to prevent contamination.

7 Note their routing, then unclip the fuel pipe and pump wiring harness from the clips on the underside of the fuel tank **(see illustrations)**.

8 Slacken the clamp and disconnect the tank breather hose **(see illustration)**.

9 Undo the mounting bolt at the rear,

7.6b . . . then squeeze together the locking tabs and pull the pipe from the port

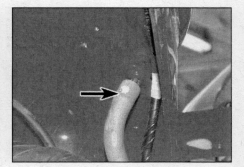

7.8 Disconnect the breather hose (arrowed)

7.9 Remove the rear mounting bolt (arrowed)

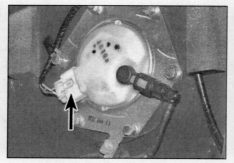

9.3 Disconnect the fuel pump wiring connector (arrowed)

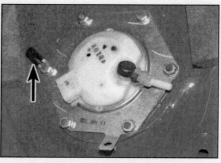

9.7 Undo the retaining nuts. Note the wiring clip (arrowed)

and manoeuvre the tank from place **(see illustration)**.

Installation

10 Refitting is a reversal of removal.

8 Fuel pressure check

> ⚠ **Warning: Refer to the precautions given in Section 1 before starting work.**

Note: *A pressure gauge is required for this check. Honda specify the use of their gauge (Pt. No. 07406-0040004) along with a pressure gauge manifold (Pt. No. 07ZAJ-S5A0111) and pipe/fittings (Pt. No. 07ZAJ-S5A0120, 0130, and 0150). If a different gauge is used suitable pipes and fitting will be needed to 'T' into the fuel supply pipe from the tank.*

1 Carry out the procedure described in paragraph 1 to 5 of the previous Section.

2 Disconnect the fuel pipe from the pump unit on the underside of the tank, then connect the pressure gauge and pipes between the pump outlet and the pipe to the injector.

3 Temporarily reconnect the pump wiring plug and the battery negative lead.

4 Start the engine, and allow it to idle. Note the pressure present in the fuel system by reading the gauge, then turn the engine off. Compare the reading obtained to that given in the Specifications.

5 If the fuel pressure is higher than specified, the fuel pump is faulty and must be replaced with a new one.

6 If the fuel pressure is lower than specified, likely causes are:
- Leaking fuel hose union.
- Blocked fuel strainer.
- Faulty fuel pump.

If necessary remove the fuel pump and clean the strainer. If the filter is blocked or the pressure regulator is faulty a new pump assembly must be installed (Section 9) – individual components are not available.

7 On completion, disconnect the battery negative (–) lead again. Remove the pressure gauge assembly, being prepared to catch the residual fuel.

8 Reverse the procedures described in paragraphs 1 to 5 of the previous section.

9 Fuel pump/level sensor

> ⚠ **Warning: Refer to the precautions given in Section 1 before starting work.**

Check

1 The fuel pump is located on the underside of the fuel tank, and incorporates the fuel level sensor. The fuel pump runs for a few seconds when the ignition is switched ON to pressurise the fuel system, and then cuts out until the engine is started. Check that it does this. If the pump is thought to be faulty, first check the main and fuel pump fuses (see Chapter 9). If they are OK proceed as follows.

2 Raise the fuel tank as described in paragraphs 1 to 3 of Section 7.

3 Ensure the ignition is switched OFF then disconnect the fuel pump wiring connector **(see illustration)**. Connect the positive (+) lead of a voltmeter to the black/white wire terminal on the loom side of the connector and the negative (–) lead to the brown/white wire terminal. Switch the ignition ON whilst noting the reading obtained on the meter.

4 If battery voltage is present for a few seconds, the fuel pump circuit is operating correctly and the fuel pump itself is faulty and must be replaced with a new one.

5 If no reading is obtained, check the fuel pump circuit wiring for continuity and make sure all the connectors are free from corrosion and are securely connected. Repair/replace the wiring as necessary and clean the connectors using electrical contact cleaner. If this fails to reveal the fault, check the following components.
- Engine stop switch (see Chapter 9).
- Lean angle sensor (see Section 5).
- Engine control unit (ECU) (see Section 5).

Removal

6 Remove the fuel tank as described in Section 7.

7 Clean the area around the pump, then gradually and evenly, working in a 'criss-cross' pattern, undo the pump retaining nuts. Note the retaining clip fitted under the nut(s) **(see illustration)**.

8 Remove the setting plate, then lift the pump/sensor unit and seal from the tank **(see illustrations)**. Take care not to damage the sensor float arm as it is withdrawn.

9 Examine the pump for any signs of damage, and check the filter in the base of the unit for debris **(see illustration)**.

9.8a Remove the setting plate . . .

9.8b . . . then carefully lift the pump/sensor unit from the tank

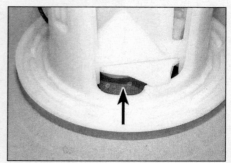

9.9 Check the filter (arrowed) in the base of the pump

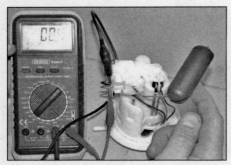

9.11 With an ohmmeter connected between the sensor terminals, raise the float to the full position

9.13a Renew the sealing ring (arrowed)

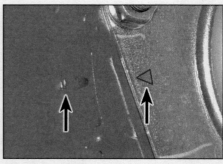

9.13b Align the triangular marks on the setting plate and tank underside (arrowed)

10 If required, the fuel level sensor can be checked as follows:

11 Connect an ohmmeter between the two terminals of the sensor **(see illustration)**. With the float arm in the 'full' position, the resistance should be 6 – 10 ohms, and with the float arm in the 'empty' position, the resistance should be 90 – 100 ohms.

12 Note parts are not available separately for the pump/level sensor unit. If faulty/damaged/worn, the complete unit must be renewed.

Installation

13 Renew the pump unit sealing ring, and position the unit in the tank. Align the slots on the setting plate with the tabs of the pump unit flange, and the triangular mark on the setting plate with the corresponding mark on the tank underside **(see illustrations)**.

14 Tighten the pump retaining nuts to the specified torque, gradually and evenly, working in a 'criss-cross' pattern.

15 The remainder of refitting is a reversal of removal. Make sure the hose clamps are secure. Check for leakage after starting the engine.

10 Catalytic converter

General information

1 A catalytic converter is incorporated in the exhaust system to minimise the level of exhaust pollutants released into the atmosphere.

2 The catalytic converter consists of a canister containing a fine mesh impregnated with a catalyst material, over which the hot exhaust gases pass. The catalyst speeds up the oxidation of harmful carbon monoxide, unburned hydrocarbons and soot, effectively reducing the quantity of harmful products released into the atmosphere via the exhaust gases.

3 The catalytic converter is of the closed-loop type with exhaust gas oxygen content information being fed back to the fuel injection system engine control unit (ECU) by the oxygen sensor.

4 Refer to Chapter 4A for exhaust system removal and installation, and Section 5 for oxygen sensor removal and installation information.

Precautions

5 The catalytic converter is a reliable and simple device which needs no maintenance in itself, but there are some facts of which an owner should be aware if the converter is to function properly for its full service life.

● DO NOT use leaded or lead replacement petrol (gasoline) – the additives will coat the precious metals, reducing their converting efficiency and will eventually destroy the catalytic converter.

● Always keep the ignition and fuel systems well-maintained in accordance with the manufacturer's schedule – if the fuel/air mixture is suspected of being incorrect have it checked on an exhaust gas analyser.

● If the engine develops a misfire, do not ride the bike at all (or at least as little as possible) until the fault is cured.

● DO NOT use fuel or engine oil additives – these may contain substances harmful to the catalytic converter.

● DO NOT continue to use the bike if the engine burns oil to the extent of leaving a visible trail of blue smoke.

● Remember that the catalytic converter and oxygen sensor are FRAGILE – do not strike them with tools during servicing work.

Chapter 5
Ignition system

Contents

Degrees of difficulty

Easy, suitable for novice with little experience	Fairly easy, suitable for beginner with some experience	Fairly difficult, suitable for competent DIY mechanic	Difficult, suitable for experienced DIY mechanic	Very difficult, suitable for expert DIY or professional

Specifications

General information
Spark plug .... see Chapter 1

Ignition timing
At idle
  R-4, R-5 and RW-6 models .... 12° BTDC
  RW-7, RW-8, RW-9 and RW-A models .... 8° BTDC

Pulse generator coil
Resistance .... approx. 112 ohms
Minimum peak voltage (see text) .... 0.7 volts

Ignition coil
Primary winding resistance .... approx. 1 ohm @ 20°C
Secondary winding resistance (without plug cap) .... approx 12 K-ohms @ 20°C
Initial voltage (see text)................................... Battery voltage (approximately 12 volts)
Minimum peak voltage (see text) .... 100 volts min
Spark plug cap resistance .... approx 5 K-ohms @ 20°C

Torque wrench settings
Timing inspection cap .... 6 Nm

1 General information

All models are fitted with a fully transistorised electronic ignition system which, due to its lack of mechanical parts, is totally maintenance-free. The system comprises a trigger, pulse generator coil, ignition control unit (ICU) on carburettor models or engine control unit (ECU) on fuel injected models, and ignition HT coil (refer to the Wiring diagrams at the end of Chapter 9).

The ignition trigger, which is on the alternator rotor on the left-hand end of the crankshaft, magnetically operates the pulse generator coil as the crankshaft rotates. The pulse generator coil sends a signal to the ignition control unit, which then supplies the ignition HT coil with the power necessary to produce a spark at the plug.

The ICU/ECU incorporates an electronic advance system controlled by signals from the ignition trigger and pulse generator coil.

The system incorporates a safety interlock circuit which will cut the ignition if the sidestand is extended whilst the engine is running and in gear, or if a gear is selected whilst the engine is running and the sidestand is extended. It also prevents the engine from being started if the engine is in gear unless the clutch lever is pulled in.

Because of their nature, the individual ignition system components can be checked but not repaired. If ignition system troubles occur, and the faulty component can be isolated, the only cure for the problem is to replace the part with a new one. Keep in mind that most electrical parts, once purchased, cannot be returned. To avoid unnecessary expense, make very sure the faulty component has been positively identified before buying a replacement part.

Note that there is no provision for adjusting the ignition timing.

2 Ignition system check

Warning: The energy levels in electronic systems can be very high. On no account should the ignition be switched on whilst the plug or plug cap is being held. Shocks from the HT circuit can be most unpleasant. Secondly, it is vital that the engine is not turned over or run with a plug cap removed, and that the plug is soundly earthed (grounded) when the system is checked for sparking. The ignition system components can be seriously damaged if the HT circuit becomes isolated.

1 As no means of adjustment is available, any failure of the system can be traced to failure of a system component or a simple wiring fault. Of the two possibilities, the latter is by far

2.2 Pull the cap off the spark plug

the most likely. In the event of failure, check the system in a logical fashion, as described below.

2 Remove the right-hand fairing side panel (see Chapter 8). Pull the cap off the spark plug **(see illustration)**. Fit a spare spark plug into the cap and lay the plug against the cylinder head with the threads contacting it. If necessary, hold the spark plug with an insulated tool.

 Warning: Do not remove the spark plug from the engine to perform this check – atomised fuel being pumped out of the open spark plug hole could ignite, causing severe injury! Make sure the plug is securely held against the engine – if it is not earthed when the engine is turned over, the ignition control unit could be damaged.

3 Check that the transmission is in neutral, then turn the ignition switch ON, and turn the engine over on the starter motor. If the system is in good condition a regular, fat blue spark should be evident at the plug electrodes. If the spark appears thin or yellowish, or is non-existent, further investigation will be necessary.

4 The ignition system must be able to produce a spark which is capable of jumping a particular size gap – Honda do not give a specification, but a healthy system should produce a spark capable of jumping at least 6 mm. Simple ignition spark gap testing tools are commercially available – follow the manufacturer's instructions, and check each spark plug **(see illustration)**.

5 If the test results are good the entire ignition system can be considered good. If the spark appears thin or yellowish, or is non-existent, further investigation is necessary.

6 Ignition faults can be divided into two categories, namely those where the ignition system has failed completely, and those which are due to a partial failure. The likely faults are listed below, starting with the most probable source of failure. Work through the list systematically, referring to the subsequent sections for full details of the necessary checks and tests, and to the Wiring Diagram at the end of Chapter 9. Before checking the following items ensure that the battery is fully charged and that all fuses are in good condition.

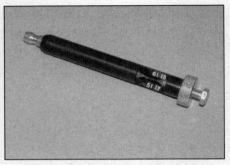

2.4 A typical spark gap testing tool

- Loose, corroded or damaged wiring connections, broken or shorted wiring between any of the component parts of the ignition system (see Chapter 9).
- Faulty HT lead or spark plug cap, faulty spark plug, dirty, worn or corroded plug electrodes, or incorrect gap between electrodes.
- Faulty ignition (main) switch (see Chapter 9).
- Faulty neutral, clutch or sidestand switch, or safety circuit diodes (see Chapter 9).
- Faulty pulse generator coil or damaged trigger.
- Faulty ignition HT coil.
- Faulty ignition control unit (ICU).

7 If the above checks don't reveal the cause of the problem, have the ignition system tested by a Honda dealer.

3 Ignition HT coil

Check

1 Remove the right-hand fairing side panel (see Chapter 8). Remove the fuel tank (see Chapter 4A or 4B). Draw the front of the rubber wiring connector holder cover back to expose the coil **(see illustration)**. Check the coil visually for loose or damaged connectors and terminals, cracks and other damage.

2 Make sure the ignition is off.

3 Disconnect the primary wiring connector

3.1 Draw the rubber cover back to access the coil (A). Coil mounting bolts (B)

3.3 Disconnect the coil primary wiring connector

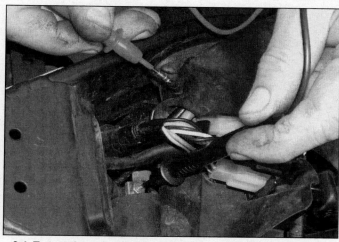

3.4 To test the coil primary resistance, connect the multimeter leads between the primary circuit terminal and a mounting bolt

(see illustration). Pull the cap off the spark plug (see illustration 2.2).

4 Set an ohmmeter or multimeter to the ohms x 1 scale and measure the resistance between the primary terminal on the coil side of the connector and one of the coil mounting bolts (see illustration). This will give a resistance reading of the primary windings of the coil and should be consistent with the value given in the Specifications at the beginning of the Chapter.

5 To check the condition of the secondary windings, set the meter to the K ohm scale. Unscrew the plug cap from the end of the HT lead (see illustration). Connect one meter probe to the primary terminal on the coil side of the connector, and insert the other in the end of the HT lead (see illustration). If the reading obtained is not within the range shown in the Specifications, it is possible that the coil is defective. To confirm this, it must be tested as described below using the specified equipment, or by a Honda dealer.

6 If the reading is as specified, measure the resistance of the spark plug cap by connecting the meter probes between the HT lead socket and the spark plug contact (see illustration). If the reading obtained is not as specified, replace the spark plug cap with a new one.

7 Honda specify their own Imrie diagnostic tester (model 625), or the peak voltage adapter (Pt. No. 07HGJ-0020100) with an aftermarket digital multimeter having an impedance of 10 M-ohm/DCV minimum, for a complete test. If this equipment is available, reconnect the wiring connector to the coil. Connect the cap to a new spark plug and lay the plug on the engine with the threads contacting it. If necessary, hold the spark plug with an insulated tool. Connect the positive (+) lead of the voltmeter and peak voltage adapter arrangement to the black/yellow primary wire terminal on the coil, with the wiring connector still connected, and connect the negative (–) lead to a suitable earth (ground) point.

8 Check that the transmission is in neutral, then turn the ignition switch ON. Note the initial voltage reading on the meter, then turn the engine over on the starter motor and note the ignition coil peak voltage reading on the meter. Once both readings have been noted, turn the ignition switch off and disconnect the meter.

9 If the initial voltage reading is not as expected or the peak voltage readings are lower than the specified minimum then a fault is present somewhere else in the ignition system circuit (see Section 2).

10 If the initial and peak voltage readings are as specified and the plug does not spark, then the coil is faulty and must be replaced with a new one; the coil is a sealed unit and cannot therefore be repaired.

Removal and installation

11 Remove the right-hand fairing side panel (see Chapter 8). Remove the fuel tank (see Chapter 4A or 4B). Draw the front of the rubber wiring connector holder cover back to expose the coil (see illustration 3.1).

12 Disconnect the primary wiring connector from the coil (see illustration 3.3). Pull the cap off the spark plug (see illustration 2.2).

13 Unscrew the two bolts and remove the coil (see illustration 3.1).

14 Installation is the reverse of removal.

---

4 Pulse generator coil

Check

1 Remove the left-hand fairing side panel (see Chapter 8).

2 Free the wiring loom from the clip on

3.5a To test the coil secondary resistance unscrew the cap from the lead . . .

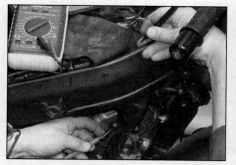

3.5b . . . and connect the multimeter leads between the primary circuit terminal and the spark plug lead end

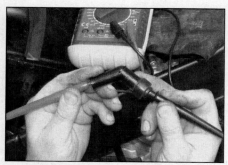

3.6 Measuring the resistance of the spark plug cap

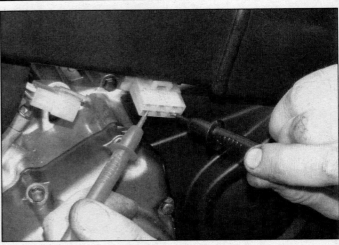

4.2a Disconnect the wiring connector (arrowed) . . .

4.2b . . . and measure the resistance of the coil

the inside of the frame above the sprocket cover, then draw the rubber boot off the connectors and disconnect the white 6-pin wiring connector **(see illustration)**. Using a multimeter set to the ohms x 100 scale, measure the resistance between the blue/yellow and green wire terminals on the alternator side of the connector **(see illustration)**. If the reading obtained is not within the range shown in the Specifications, it is possible that the coil is defective. To confirm this, it must be tested as described below using the specified equipment, or by a Honda dealer. Reconnect the 6-pin wiring connector.

3 Honda specify their own Imrie diagnostic tester (model 625), or the peak voltage adapter (Pt. No. 07HGJ-0020100) with an aftermarket digital multimeter having an impedance of 10 M-ohm/DCV minimum, for a complete test. If this equipment is available, disconnect the 6-pin connector from the ignition control unit **(see illustration 5.5c)**, connect the positive (+) lead of the voltmeter and peak voltage adapter arrangement to the blue/yellow wire terminal on the wiring harness side of the wiring connector, and connect the negative (–) lead to earth on the frame.

4 Check that the transmission is in neutral, then turn the ignition switch ON, turn the engine over on the starter motor and note the peak voltage reading on the meter. If the peak voltage reading is lower than the specified minimum, the pulse generator coil is faulty.

5 If the ignition pulse generator coil functions correctly then the fault must be in the wiring harness to the ignition control unit. Check the wiring for continuity, referring to the wiring diagram at the end of Chapter 9. If the wiring is good, the ICU could be faulty.

Removal and installation

6 Remove the alternator stator and replace it with a new one (see Chapter 9) – the pulse generator coil and stator only come as a complete unit. The sensor is mounted inside it.

---

5   Ignition control unit

Check

1 If the tests shown in the preceding or following Sections have failed to isolate the cause of an ignition fault, it is possible that the ignition control unit itself is faulty. No test details are available with which the unit can be tested. The best way to determine whether it

is faulty is to substitute it with a known good one, if available. Otherwise, take the unit to a Honda dealer for assessment.

2 Before condemning the ICU make sure the wiring connector terminals are clean and none of the wires have broken – remove the fuel tank to access the ICU, then fold back the rubber cover and lift the ICU off its stay – the connector is on the underside **(see illustrations 5.5a, b and c)**. Make sure the ignition is off before disconnecting the wiring connector.

3 Also make sure the power supply and earth wires are good – with the ignition off disconnect the wiring connector, then check for battery voltage at the black wire terminal of the connector using a voltmeter, with the ignition on. Also check for continuity to earth in the green wire.

Removal and installation

4 Remove the fuel tank (see Chapter 4A). Make sure the ignition is off.

5 Fold the rubber cover aside, then lift the ignition control unit off its stay and disconnect the wiring connector from the underside **(see illustrations)**.

6 Remove the unit from its rubber sleeve.

7 Installation is the reverse of removal. Make sure the wiring connector is securely connected.

5.5a Fold the cover aside . . .

5.5b . . . then displace the ICU . . .

5.5c . . . and disconnect its wiring connector

6.4 Timing inspection cap (arrowed)

6.5 Timing mark aligned with notch (arrowed) at idle speed

6 Ignition timing

General information

1 Since no provision exists for adjusting the ignition timing and since no component is subject to mechanical wear, there is no need for regular checks: only if investigating a fault such as a loss of power or a misfire, should the ignition timing be checked.

2 The ignition timing is checked dynamically (engine running) using a stroboscopic lamp. The inexpensive neon lamps should be adequate in theory, but in practice may produce a pulse of such low intensity that the timing mark remains indistinct. If possible, one of the more precise xenon tube lamps should be used, powered by an external source of the appropriate voltage. **Note:** *Do not use the machine's own battery, as an incorrect reading* may result from stray impulses within the machine's electrical system.

Check

3 Warm the engine up to normal operating temperature, then stop it.

4 Unscrew the timing inspection cap from the top of the alternator cover on the left-hand side of the engine **(see illustration)**.

5 The mark on the timing rotor which indicates the firing point at idle speed is a scribed line next to the 'F' mark **(see illustration)**. The static timing mark with which this should align is the notch in the inspection hole.

> **HAYNES HINT** *The timing marks can be highlighted with white paint to make them more visible under the stroboscope light.*

6 Connect the timing light to the HT lead as described in the manufacturer's instructions.

7 Start the engine and aim the light at the inspection hole.

8 With the machine idling at the specified speed, the line next to the 'F' mark should align with the static timing mark.

9 Slowly increase the engine speed whilst observing the 'F' mark. The mark should appear to move anti-clockwise, increasing in relation to the engine speed until it reaches full advance (no identification mark).

10 As already stated, there is no means of adjustment of the ignition timing on these machines. If the ignition timing is incorrect, or suspected of being incorrect, one of the ignition system components is at fault, and the system must be tested as described in the preceding Sections of this Chapter.

11 Install the timing inspection cap using a new O-ring if required, and smear the O-ring and the cap threads with clean oil. Tighten the cap to the torque setting specified at the beginning of the Chapter.

Chapter 6
Frame and suspension

Contents

Degrees of difficulty

Easy, suitable for novice with little experience	Fairly easy, suitable for beginner with some experience	Fairly difficult, suitable for competent DIY mechanic	Difficult, suitable for experienced DIY mechanic	Very difficult, suitable for expert DIY or professional

Specifications

Front forks

Fork oil type	Honda Ultra Cushion 10W oil or equivalent 10W fork oil
Fork oil capacity	206 ± 2.5 cc
Fork oil level*	131 mm
Fork spring free length (min)	
Standard	412.4 mm
Service limit	404.1 mm
Fork tube runout limit	0.2 mm

*Oil level is measured from the top of the tube with the fork spring removed and the leg fully compressed.

Torque settings

Clutch lever pivot bolt and nut	6 Nm
Drive chain slider screw	6 Nm
Footrest bracket mounting bolts	27 Nm
Fork damper rod bolt	20 Nm
Fork top bolt	23 Nm
Fork yoke clamp bolts	
Top yoke bolts	23 Nm
Bottom yoke bolts	27 Nm
Front brake lever pivot bolt and nut	6 Nm
Handlebar clamp bolts	27 Nm
Handlebar end-weight screws	9 Nm
Shock absorber bolts/nut	
Top bolt	39 Nm
Bottom bolt/nut	44 Nm
Sidestand pivot bolt	18 Nm
Sidestand pivot bolt nut	44 Nm
Steering head bearing adjuster nut	
Initial setting	27 Nm
Final setting	1 Nm
Steering stem nut	88 Nm
Swingarm pivot bolt nut	88 Nm

1 General information

All models have a box-section twin-spar steel frame which uses the engine as a stressed member.

Front suspension is by a pair of conventional oil-damped telescopic forks.

At the rear, a box-section steel swingarm acts on a single shock absorber. The swingarm pivots through the frame.

2 Frame inspection and repair

1 The frame should not require attention unless accident damage has occurred. In most cases, fitting a new frame is the only satisfactory remedy for such damage. Frame specialists have the jigs and other equipment necessary for straightening a frame to the required standard of accuracy, but even then there is no simple way of assessing to what extent it may have been over-stressed.

2 After a high mileage, the frame should be examined closely for signs of cracking or splitting at the welded joints. Loose engine mounting bolts can cause ovaling or fracturing of the mounting points. Minor damage can often be repaired by specialised welding, depending on the extent and nature of the damage.

3 Remember that a frame that is out of alignment will cause handling problems. If, as the result of an accident, misalignment is suspected, it will be necessary to strip the machine completely so the frame can be thoroughly checked.

3.1a Remove the split pin (arrowed) and washer . . .

3.2a Remove the split pin (arrowed) and washer . . .

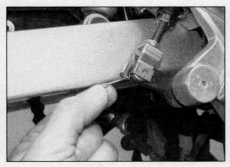

3.4a Remove the split pin . . .

3.1b . . . and withdraw the pivot pin (arrowed) from the top

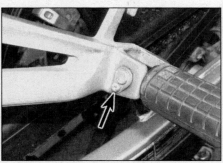

3.2b . . . then undo the screw (arrowed) and withdraw the pivot pin

3.4b . . . then withdraw the clevis pin

3 Footrests, brake pedal and gearchange lever

Footrests

Removal

1 To remove a rider's footrest, straighten and remove the split pin from the bottom of the footrest pivot pin, collecting the washer, then withdraw the pivot pin and remove the footrest, noting the washer (see illustrations). Discard the split pin. If required unscrew the bolt on the underside and remove the bottom plate, then draw the rubber off the peg. All components are available individually.

2 To remove a passenger footrest, straighten and remove the split pin from the bottom of the footrest pivot pin, then undo the pin retaining screw, withdraw the pin and remove the footrest, noting the washer (see illustrations). Discard the split pin. If required draw the rubber off the peg. All components are available individually.

Installation

3 Installation is the reverse of removal. Apply a small amount of multi-purpose grease to the pivot pin. Use new split pins on the pivot pins, and bend the ends round the pivot pin.

Brake pedal

Removal

4 Straighten and remove the split pin from the clevis pin securing the brake pedal to the master cylinder pushrod, then withdraw the pin and detach the pushrod from the pedal (see illustrations). Discard the split pin as a new one should be used.

5 Unhook the brake pedal return spring and the brake light switch spring from the hook on the pedal (see illustration).

6 Straighten and remove the split pin securing the brake pedal on its pivot and remove the pedal and the thrust washer (see illustration 3.5). Discard the split pin.

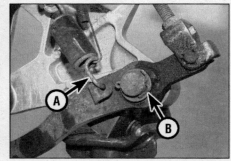

3.5 Unhook the springs (A), then release the split pin (B)

Installation

7 Installation is the reverse of removal, noting the following:

- Apply grease to the pedal pivot on the footrest bracket – clean off any old grease first.
- Slide the thrust washer onto the pivot, then the pedal, then fit a new split pin and bend its ends round the pedal boss **(see illustration 3.5).**
- Use a new split pin on the clevis pin securing the brake pedal to the master cylinder pushrod and bend its ends round the pin **(see illustration 3.4a).**
- Check the operation of the rear brake light switch (see Chapter 1).

Gearchange lever and linkage

Removal

8 Remove the lower fairing (see Chapter 8).

9 Pull back the rubber boot from each end of the gearchange lever linkage rod, then straighten and remove the split pins, remove the washers, and detach the rod from the lever and the arm **(see illustration)**. Discard the split pins as new ones should be used.

10 Remove the circlip, washer and wave washer securing the lever in the footrest bracket, then slide the lever out of the bracket **(see illustration)**.

Installation

11 Installation is the reverse of removal, noting the following:

- Make sure the rubber boots for each end of the linkage are in good condition and replace them with new ones if necessary.
- Apply grease to the pivot section on the lever.
- Slide the lever into the bracket, then slide the wave washer onto the end of the pivot section, then the thrust washer, then fit the circlip, making sure it locates in the its groove **(see illustration 3.10).**
- Use new split pins to secure the linkage to the lever and arm and bend their ends round **(see illustration 3.9).**

4 Sidestand

Removal

1 The sidestand is attached to the frame. Springs anchored between them ensure the stand is held in the retracted or extended position. Support the bike on an auxiliary stand.

2 First displace the sidestand switch (see Chapter 9). There is no need to disconnect its wiring connector or remove it completely, just let it hang from its wiring.

3 Unhook the stand springs, then unscrew the nut from the pivot bolt **(see illustrations)**. Unscrew the pivot bolt and remove the stand.

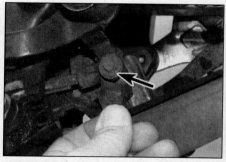

3.9 Pull the boot back to expose the split pin (arrowed) securing each end of the rod

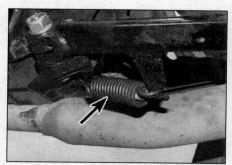

4.3a Unhook the springs (arrowed) . . .

Installation

4 Apply grease to the pivot bolt shank, then position the stand and tighten the bolt to the torque setting specified at the beginning of the Chapter. Fit the nut and tighten it to the specified torque **(see illustration 4.3b)**.

5 Install the sidestand switch (see Chapter 9). Reconnect the springs and check that they hold the stand securely up when not in use – an accident is almost certain to occur if the stand extends while the machine is in motion **(see illustration 4.3a)**. Check the operation of the switch (see Chapter 1).

5 Handlebars and levers

1 As a precaution, remove the fuel tank (see Chapter 4A or 4B) and the fairing (see Chap-

5.3a Disconnect the wiring connectors (arrowed)

3.10 Release the circlip (arrowed) and remove the lever

4.3b . . . then unscrew the nut (arrowed) from the pivot bolt

ter 8). Though not actually necessary, this will prevent the possibility of damage should a tool slip. **Note:** *If the top yoke is being removed to access the steering head bearings, the handlebars can be displaced from the tops of the forks without detaching the assemblies from them – see Steps 6 and 11 only.*

Right handlebar removal

2 Remove the mirror (see Chapter 8).

3 Disconnect the wires from the brake light switch **(see illustration)**. Unscrew the two master cylinder assembly clamp bolts and position the assembly clear of the handlebar, wrapping it in some rag, and making sure no strain is placed on the hydraulic hose **(see illustration)**. Keep the master cylinder reservoir upright to prevent possible fluid leakage.

4 Unscrew the two handlebar switch/throttle

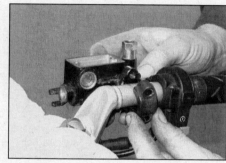

5.3b Unscrew the master cylinder clamp bolts and displace the assembly

5.4 Undo the screws (arrowed) and split the housing

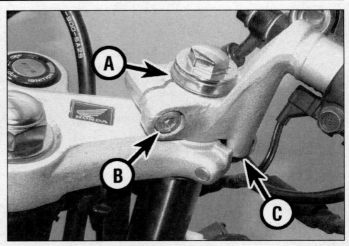

5.6a Remove the stopper ring (A), then slacken the clamp bolt (B). Note how the lug (C) locates

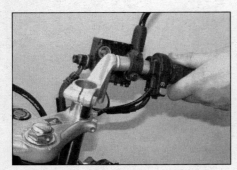

5.6b Lift the handlebar up off the fork

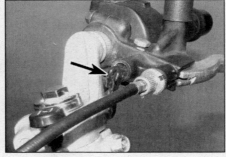

5.8a Disconnect the wiring connectors (arrowed)

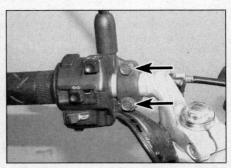

5.8b Unscrew the clamp bolts (arrowed) and displace the assembly

housing screws and separate the halves **(see illustration)**. The throttle pulley can be slid off the end of the handlebar with the cable still attached to it and the housing after the handlebar has been lifted off the fork.

5 Unscrew the handlebar end-weight retaining screw, then remove the weight from the end of the handlebar **(see illustration 5.10)**.

6 Remove the handlebar stopper ring from the groove in the top of the fork, using a small screwdriver to ease it out **(see illustration 5.11a)**. Slacken the handlebar clamp bolt, then

ease the handlebar up and off the fork **(see illustrations)**. Slide the throttle twistgrip and switch housing assembly off the handlebar.

Left handlebar removal

7 Remove the mirror (see Chapter 8).

8 Disconnect the wires from the clutch switch **(see illustration)**. Unscrew the two clutch lever bracket clamp bolts and position the assembly clear of the handlebar, wrapping it in some rag **(see illustration)**.

9 Unscrew the two handlebar switch

housing screws and separate the halves **(see illustration)**.

10 If required, unscrew the handlebar end-weight retaining screw, then remove the weight from the end of the handlebar and slide off the grip **(see illustration)**. If the grip has been glued on, you will probably have to slit it with a knife to remove it.

11 Remove the handlebar stopper ring from the groove in the top of the fork, using a small screwdriver to ease it out **(see illustration)**. Slacken the handlebar clamp bolt, then

5.9 Undo the screws (arrowed) and split the housing

5.10 Handlebar end-weight screw (arrowed)

5.11a Remove the stopper ring . . .

ease the handlebar up and off the fork (see illustrations).

Handlebar weights

12 If a new handlebar is being installed, you need to transfer the inner weight to the new bar – to do this, reinstall the end-weight and tighten its screw. Squirt some lubricant (such as WD40) into the inner weight retainer tab hole, then press down on the tab using a screwdriver and twist and pull the end-weight, drawing the inner weight assembly out. Remove the end-weight and discard the retainer as a new one should be used. Check the condition of the rubbers on the inner weight and fit new ones if they are damaged, deformed or deteriorated.

Installation

13 Installation is the reverse of removal, noting the following.

● Slide the throttle twistgrip and cable housing assembly onto the handlebar before fitting the handlebar onto the fork, and smear some grease onto the handlebar.

● When fitting the handlebar onto the fork, slide it down and seat it on the top yoke, locating the lug on the underside in the gap between the clamping sections of the top yoke (see illustration 5.13a) – the lug is not a close fit, so pull the bar back so the rear face of the lug butts against the rear section of the yoke, ensuring each side is positioned exactly the same. Tighten the handlebar clamp bolts to the torque setting specified at the beginning of the Chapter. Fit the stopper rings into their grooves (see illustration 6.10).

5.14a Undo the nut . . .

5.15a Slacken the lockring and thread the adjuster in

5.11b . . . then slacken the clamp bolt (arrowed) . . .

5.13a Locate the lug (arrowed) in the gap in the top yoke clamp

● When installing the handlebar inner weights, locate the tab on the retainer in the hole in the handlebar.

● When installing the handlebar end-weights, align the boss with the cut-out on the inner

5.14b . . . then undo the pivot screw and remove the lever

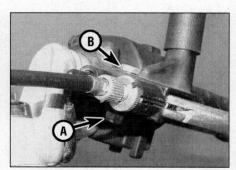

5.15b Unscrew the locknut (A) then undo the pivot screw (B) and remove the lever

5.11c . . . and lift the handlebar off the fork

5.13b Align the clamp mating surfaces with the punch mark (arrowed)

weight inside the handlebar. Clean the threads of the end-weight retaining screws and apply a suitable non-permanent thread locking compound. Tighten them to the specified torque setting. If new grips are being fitted, secure them using a suitable adhesive.

● Make sure the front brake master cylinder and clutch lever bracket clamps are installed with the UP mark facing up (see illustration 5.3b and 5.8b), and with the clamp mating surfaces aligned with the punch mark on the top of the handlebar (see illustration 5.13b). Tighten the top clamp bolt first.

● Make sure the pin in the top half of the right-hand switch housing and the bottom half of the left-hand switch housing locates in its hole in the handlebar. Tighten the front housing screw first, then the rear (see illustration 5.4 or 5.9).

● Do not forget to reconnect the front brake light switch and clutch switch wiring connectors (see illustrations 5.3a and 5.8a).

Levers

14 To remove the front brake lever, undo the lever pivot screw locknut, then undo the pivot screw and remove the lever (see illustrations).

15 To remove the clutch lever loosen the adjuster lockring then thread the adjuster into the bracket to provide freeplay in the cable (see illustration). Undo the lever pivot screw locknut, then undo the pivot screw and remove the lever, detaching the cable nipple as you do (see illustration).

6.4 There are two cable-ties securing wiring to each fork

6.5a Slacken the fork clamp bolt (arrowed) in the top yoke

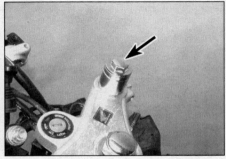

6.5b Slacken the fork top bolt (arrowed) now if the fork is to be disassembled

16 Installation is the reverse of removal, noting the following.
● Apply silicone grease to the contact area between the front brake master cylinder pushrod tip and the brake lever.
● Apply lithium or molybdenum grease to the pivot screw shafts and the contact areas between the lever and its bracket.
● Tighten the pivot bolts and nuts to the torque setting specified at the beginning of the Chapter.
● Adjust clutch cable freeplay (see Chapter 1).

6 Fork removal and installation

Removal

1 For best access and to prevent the possibility of damage, remove the fairing (see Chapter 8). Remove the front mudguard (see Chapter 8).
2 Remove the front wheel (see Chapter 7). Tie the front brake caliper back so that it is out of the way.
3 Displace the handlebars, then wrap them in some rag and support them to one side (see Section 5, Steps 6 and 11).
4 Note the routing of the cables, hose and wiring around the forks. Release the cable-ties securing the wiring to each fork (see illustration).
5 Working on one fork at a time, slacken the fork clamp bolt in the top yoke (see

illustration). If the fork is to be disassembled, or if the fork oil is being changed, slacken the fork top bolt now (see illustration).
6 Slacken the fork clamp bolt in the bottom yoke, and remove the fork by twisting it and pulling it down (see illustrations).

> **HAYNES HINT**
> *If the fork legs are seized in the yokes, spray the area with penetrating oil and allow time for it to soak in before trying again.*

Installation

7 Remove all traces of corrosion from the fork tube and the yokes. Make sure you install the forks the correct way round – the right-hand fork slider has the lugs to carry the brake caliper.
8 Slide the fork up through the bottom yoke and into the top yoke, making sure all cables, hoses and wiring are routed on the correct side of the fork, and making sure the fork protrudes enough from the top yoke to accommodate the handlebar (see illustrations 6.6b and 6.5b). Temporarily tighten the clamp bolt in the bottom yoke to hold the fork (see illustration 6.6a).
9 If the fork has been dismantled or if the fork oil was changed, tighten the fork top bolt to the specified torque setting (see illustration 6.5b).
10 Fit the handlebar onto the fork and seat it on the top yoke, locating the lug on the underside in the gap between the clamping

sections of the top yoke (see illustration 5.13a). Fit the stopper ring into its groove (see illustration), then slacken the fork clamp bolt in the bottom yoke and draw the fork down so the stopper ring seats against the top of the handlebar clamp, then tighten the clamp bolt in the bottom yoke, this time to the torque setting specified at the beginning of the Chapter. Now tighten the fork clamp bolt in the top yoke to its specified torque setting (see illustration 6.5a).
11 Pull the handlebar back so the rear face of the lug butts against the rear section of the yoke, ensuring each side is positioned exactly the same, and tighten the handlebar clamp bolt to its specified torque setting (see illustration 5.11b).
12 Install the front wheel (see Chapter 7) and the front mudguard (see Chapter 8).
13 Check the operation of the front forks and brake before taking the machine out on the road.

7 Fork oil change

1 After a high mileage the fork oil will deteriorate and its damping and lubrication qualities will be impaired. Always change the oil in both fork legs.
2 Remove the fork; ensure that the top bolt is loosened while the fork is still clamped in the bottom yoke (see Section 6).
3 Support the fork leg in an upright position and

6.6a Bottom yoke fork clamp bolts (arrowed)

6.6b Draw the fork down and out of the yokes

6.10 Fit the stopper ring into its groove (arrowed)

7.3 Unscrew the fork top bolt . . .

7.4a . . . and remove the spacer . . .

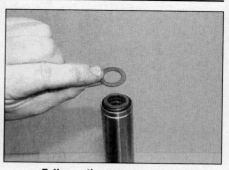

7.4b . . . the spacer seat . . .

unscrew the fork top bolt from the top of the fork tube – the bolt is under pressure from the fork spring, so use a ratchet tool so it does not need to be removed from the bolt as you unscrew it, and maintain some downward pressure on it, particularly as you come to the end of the threads **(see illustration)**. If the top bolt O-ring is damaged or deteriorated fit a new one.

4 Slide the fork tube down into the slider and remove the spacer, the spacer seat and the spring as they become exposed **(see illustrations)**. Wipe any excess oil off the spring and spacer.

5 Invert the fork leg over a suitable container and pump the fork to expel as much oil as possible **(see illustration)**. Support the fork upside down in the container and allow it to drain for a few minutes. If the fork oil contains metal particles inspect the fork bush for wear (see Section 8).

6 Slowly pour in the specified quantity of the specified grade of fork oil, then pump the fork several times to distribute it evenly **(see illustration)**. Slide the fork tube into the slider until it seats then measure the oil level from the top of the tube **(see illustration)**. Add or subtract oil until it is at the level specified at the beginning of this Chapter.

7 Fit the spring into the fork with its closer-wound coils at the bottom **(see illustration)**. Lift the tube out of the slider until it is flush with the top of the spring, then fit the spacer seat **(see illustration 7.4b)**. Lift the tube some more and fit the spacer **(see illustration 7.4a)**.

8 Smear some fork oil onto the top bolt O-ring. Fit the top bolt into the fork tube, compressing the spring as you do, and thread it in (making sure it does not cross-thread), keeping downward pressure on the spring **(see**

illustration). The top bolt can be tightened to the specified torque setting at this stage if the tube is held between the padded jaws of a vice, but do not risk distorting the tube by doing so. A better method is to tighten the top bolt when the fork leg is being installed and is securely held in the bottom yoke.

9 Install the fork (see Section 6).

8 Fork overhaul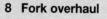

Disassembly

1 Remove the fork; ensure that the top bolt is loosened while the leg is still clamped in the bottom yoke (see Section 6). Always dismantle the fork legs separately to avoid interchanging

7.4c . . . and the spring

7.5 Invert the fork over a container and tip the oil out

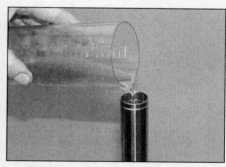

7.6a Pour the oil into the top of the tube . . .

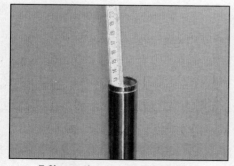

7.6b . . . then measure the level

7.7 Fit the spring with its closer-wound coils at the bottom

7.8 Thread the top bolt into the tube

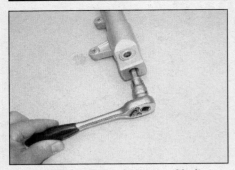

8.2 Slacken the damper rod bolt

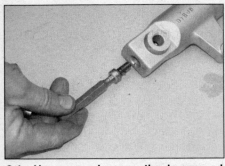

8.4a Unscrew and remove the damper rod bolt . . .

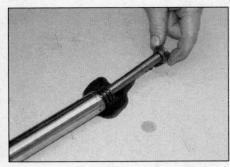

8.4b . . . then tip the damper rod out

parts and thus causing an accelerated rate of wear. Store all components in separate, clearly marked containers.

2 Lay the fork flat on the bench, on the right-hand fork with the caliper mounting lugs to the left, then hold the fork down and slacken the damper rod bolt in the base of the fork slider **(see illustration)**. If the bolt does not slacken but instead the rod turns with the bolt inside the fork, try compressing the fork so that more pressure is exerted on the damper rod head, or if available use an air-ratchet. Otherwise, follow Step 3, then use a length of wood doweling, tapered on the end to engage the head of the damper rod, passed down through the fork tube and pressed into the top of the damper rod to hold it.

3 Refer to Section 7, Steps 3 to 5 and drain the oil from the fork.

4 Remove the damper rod bolt and its copper

sealing washer from the bottom of the slider **(see illustration)**. Discard the sealing washer as a new one must be used on reassembly. Tip the damper rod out of the fork tube **(see illustration)**.

5 Carefully prise out the dust seal from the top of the slider. Withdraw the tube from the slider, then tip the damper rod seat out of the slider **(see illustrations)**. Discard the dust seal as a new one must be used – it comes with the oil seal as a set.

6 Remove the retaining clip **(see illustration)**.

7 Prise the oil seal from the slider using either a seal hook or an internal puller with slide-hammer attachment **(see illustrations)**. If a seal hook is used take great care not to damage the rim of the slider.

8 If necessary (see Step 12), remove the fork bush using an internal puller with slide-hammer attachment – only remove the bush

if it or the slider needs to be replaced with a new one.

Inspection

9 Clean all parts in solvent and blow them dry with compressed air, if available. Check the fork tube for score marks, scratches, flaking of the chrome finish and excessive or abnormal wear. Look for dents in the tube and replace the tube in both forks if any are found. Check the fork seal seat for nicks, gouges and scratches. If damage is evident, leaks will occur.

10 Check the fork tube for runout using V-blocks and a dial gauge. If the amount of runout exceeds the service limit specified, the tube should be replaced with a new one.

⚠️ **Warning: If the tube is bent or exceeds the runout limit, it should not be straightened; replace it with a new one.**

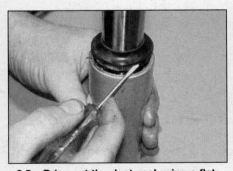

8.5a Prise out the dust seal using a flat-bladed screwdriver

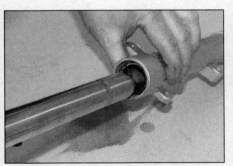

8.5b Draw the tube out of the slider . . .

8.5c . . . then tip the damper rod seat out

8.6 Prise out the retaining clip using a flat-bladed screwdriver

8.7a Locate the puller under the oil seal then expand the puller . . .

8.7b . . . and jar the seal out using the slide-hammer attachment

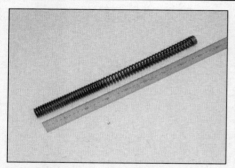

8.11 Measure the free length of the spring

8.12 Check the bush (arrowed) for wear

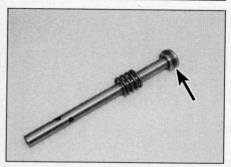

8.13 Check the damper rod for damage and the ring (arrowed) for wear

8.14a Drive the bush into place . . .

8.14b . . . until it seats

8.15a Fit the oil seal . . .

11 Check the spring (both the main spring and the rebound spring on the damper rod) for cracks and other damage. Measure the main spring free length and compare the measurement to the specifications at the beginning of the Chapter **(see illustration)**. If it is defective or sagged below the service limit, replace the main springs in both forks with new ones. Never replace only one spring.

12 Examine the working surface of the bush **(see illustration)**; if the grey Teflon outer surface has been worn away to reveal the copper inner surface over more than 75% of the surface area, or if the bush is scored or badly scuffed, it must be replaced with a new one (Step 8).

13 Check the damper rod, and in particular the ring in its head, for damage and wear, and replace it with a new one if necessary (the ring is available separately) **(see illustration)**.

Reassembly

14 If removed, smear the bush with clean fork oil and press it squarely into its recess in the top of the slider as far as possible, then use a seal driver or a suitable socket and drive it in until it seats **(see illustrations)**.

15 Smear the lips of the **new** oil seal with fork oil and press it squarely into its recess in the top of the slider, with its markings face upwards, then use a seal driver or a suitable socket and drive it in until it seats and the retaining clip groove is visible above it **(see illustrations)**.

HAYNES HiNT *Place the old oil seal on top of the new one to protect it when driving the seal into place.*

16 Once the seal is correctly seated, fit the retaining clip, making sure it is correctly located in its groove **(see illustration)**.

8.15b . . . and drive it into place . . .

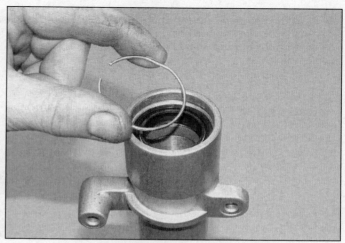

8.16 Fit the seal retaining clip into its groove

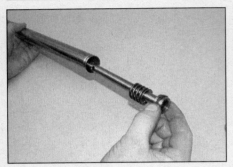

8.17a Fit the damper rod into the tube . . .

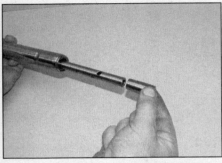

8.17b . . . so it protrudes from the bottom, then fit the seat . . .

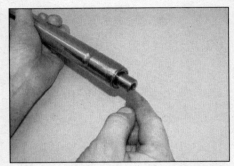

8.17c . . . and locate it in the bottom of the tube

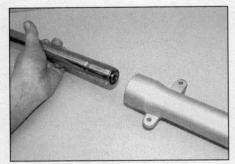

8.18 Fit the tube into the slider

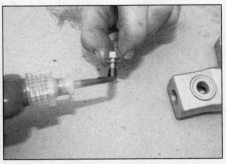

8.19a Fit the bolt using threadlock and a new sealing washer . . .

method (Step 2), or wait until the fork is fully reassembled and can be compressed to exert spring pressure on the damper rod head.

20 Lubricate the lips of the new dust seal then slide it down the fork tube and press it into position **(see illustration)**.

21 Refer to Section 7, Steps 6 to 8 and fill the fork with oil and finish reassembly.

22 If the damper rod bolt requires tightening (see Step 19), have an assistant compress the fork so that maximum spring pressure is placed on the damper rod head while the bolt is tightened to the specified torque setting.

23 Install the fork (see Section 6).

9 Steering stem

Removal

Note: *Uncaged ball bearings are fitted, which means that those in the bottom of the steering head are likely to drop free and be lost when the steering stem is lowered out of the head. Prepare for this by holding a container below the lower yoke to catch the balls as you lower the stem.*

1 Remove the fairing (see Chapter 8) and the fuel tank (see Chapter 4A or 4B). Remove the front forks (see Section 6).

2 Disconnect the horn wiring connectors **(see illustration)**. Unscrew the bolts securing the front brake hose/horn holder to the bottom yoke and displace it, noting how the handlebar and ignition switch wiring routes between it and the yoke **(see illustration)**.

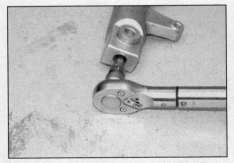

8.19b . . . and tighten it to the specified torque

8.20 Fit the dust seal into the top of the slider

17 If removed, fit the rebound spring onto the damper rod, and fit the ring into its groove in the head **(see illustration 8.13)**. Slide the damper rod into the top of the fork tube and all the way down so it protrudes from the bottom of the tube **(see illustrations)**. Fit the seat onto the bottom of the rod, then push the rod back into the tube so the seat fits into the bottom of the tube **(see illustrations)**.

18 Oil the fork tube and bush with the specified fork oil. Insert the tube into the slider, twisting it as you do and making sure the lips of the seal do not turn inside, and push it fully down until it contacts the bottom **(see illustration)**.

19 Lay the fork flat on the bench, on the right-hand fork with the caliper mounting lugs to the right. Fit a new copper sealing washer onto the damper bolt and apply a few drops of a suitable non-permanent thread locking

compound **(see illustration)**. Fit the bolt into the bottom of the slider and tighten it to the specified torque setting **(see illustration)**. If the damper rod rotates inside the tube as you tighten the bolt, either use the wood doweling

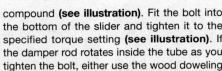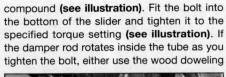

9.2a Disconnect the wiring connectors (arrowed) . . .

9.2b . . . then unscrew the bolts (arrowed) securing the holder

9.3 Unscrew the cable holder bolt (arrowed)

9.4a Fold the cover aside . . .

9.4b . . . and disconnect the wiring connector (arrowed)

3 Unscrew the bolt securing the choke cable holder to the underside of the top yoke **(see illustration)**.

4 If the top yoke is being removed from the bike rather than just being displaced, fold the rubber cover aside and disconnect the ignition switch wiring connector **(see illustrations)**. Release the wiring from any clips or ties and feed it through to the yoke, noting its routing. Release the brake hose and throttle and clutch cables from the guides **(see illustration)**.

5 Unscrew and remove the steering stem nut, and remove the washer **(see illustration)**. Lift the top yoke up off the steering stem and position it clear, using a rag to protect other components if it is only being displaced **(see illustration)**.

6 Support the bottom yoke and unscrew the bearing adjuster nut using your fingers (it shouldn't be tight), or a C-spanner **(see illustration)**.

7 Hold a container below the lower yoke (see **Note** above), then gently lower the steering stem out of the frame, hopefully catching all 18 balls as they drop out **(see illustration)**. Remove any balls that have stuck in place on the stem or in the steering head.

8 Remove the inner race from the top of the steering head and collect the bearing 18 balls – it is wise to again hold the container below the head as you remove the race in case the balls drop down through the frame **(see illustration)**.

9 Wash all traces of old grease from the bearing balls and races using solvent or paraffin, then check them for wear or damage as described in Section 10. **Note:** *Do not*

9.4c Release the hose and cables from the guides (arrowed)

9.5b . . . the lift the top yoke up off the stem

9.5a Unscrew the nut and remove the washer . . .

9.6 Unscrew the adjuster nut . . .

attempt to remove the races from the steering head or the steering stem unless they are to be replaced with new ones (see Section 10).

Installation

10 Smear a liberal quantity of multi-purpose grease onto the bearing races, then stick the lower bearing balls to the grease on the steering stem inner race and the upper bearing balls to the grease on the outer race set in the steering head **(see illustration)**. There should be 18 balls for each race.

9.7 . . . then draw the bottom yoke/ steering stem out of the steering head

9.8 Remove the inner race then pick the balls out

9.10 Fit the bearing balls as described using plenty of grease

11 Carefully lift the steering stem/bottom yoke up through the steering head, making sure all balls stay in place, and when it has located turn it a few times to spread and seat the lower bearing balls, then support it. Fit the inner race into the top of the steering head, taking care not dislodge the balls, and turn it to spread and seat the balls **(see illustration 9.8)**. Apply some clean engine oil to the adjuster nut and thread the nut on the steering stem **(see illustration 9.6)**.

12 If the Honda service tool (Part No. 07916-3710101) or a suitable peg spanner (which can be made by cutting castellations into an old socket **(see illustration)** and a torque wrench are available, tighten the adjuster nut to the initial torque setting specified at the beginning of the Chapter, then turn the steering stem through its full lock at least five times, then slacken the nut so that it is loose, and then tighten it to the final torque setting specified. Ensure that the steering stem is able to move freely from lock-to-lock following adjustment. Now install the top yoke, forks, wheel and all remaining components so that their leverage and inertia can be taken into account (Steps 14 and 15), then refer to the check and adjustment procedures in Chapter 1 to set the bearings.

13 If the correct tools are not available, tighten the nut fairly tight using a C-spanner so that bearing play is eliminated, but the steering stem is able to move freely from lock-to-lock, then slacken the nut so that it is loose, and then tighten it finger-tight only – the nut must be literally on the point of being loose, do not put effort into tightening it finger-tight (when the top yoke is fitted and the steering stem nut is tightened these act to lock the adjuster nut in place). Now install the top yoke, forks, wheel and all remaining components so that their leverage and inertia can be taken into account (Steps 14 and 15), then refer to the check and adjustment procedures in Chapter 1 to set the bearings.

Caution: Take great care not to apply excessive pressure because this will cause premature failure of the bearings.

14 Fit the top yoke onto the steering stem **(see illustration 9.5b)**. Fit the steering stem nut with its washer and tighten it finger-tight **(see illustration 9.5a)**. Temporarily install one

10.3 Check the races for wear and damage

9.12 A peg spanner can be made by cutting castellations into an old socket

of the forks to align the top and bottom yokes, and secure it by tightening the bottom yoke clamp bolts only (see Section 6). Now tighten the steering stem nut to the torque setting specified at the beginning of the Chapter **(see illustration)**.

15 Install the remaining components in a reverse of the removal procedure, referring to the relevant Sections or Chapters, and to the torque settings specified at the beginning of the Chapter. Make sure the wiring, cables and hose are correctly routed **(see illustrations 9.2b and 9.4c)**.

16 Recheck the steering head bearing adjustment as described in Chapter 1.

10 Steering head bearings

Inspection

1 Remove the steering stem (see Section 9).

2 Wash all traces of old grease from the bearing balls and races using paraffin or solvent, and check them for wear or damage.

3 The races should be polished and free from indentations **(see illustration)**. Inspect the bearing balls for signs of wear, damage or discoloration. If there are any signs of wear on any of the above components both upper and lower bearing assemblies must be replaced with a new set. Only remove the outer races in the steering head and the lower bearing inner

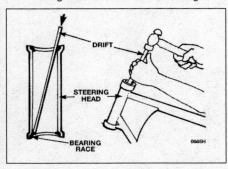

10.4 Drive the bearing races out with a brass drift locating it as shown

9.14 Tighten the stem nut to the specified torque

race on the steering stem if they need to be replaced with new ones – do not reuse them once they have been removed.

Replacement

4 The outer races are an interference fit in the steering head – tap them from position using a suitable drift located on the exposed inner lip of the race **(see illustration)**. Tap firmly and evenly around each race to ensure that it is driven out squarely. Curve the end of the drift slightly to improve access if necessary.

5 Alternatively, remove the races using a slide-hammer type bearing extractor; these can often be hired from tool shops.

6 Press the new outer races into the head using a drawbolt arrangement **(see illustration)**, or drive them in using a large diameter tubular drift (to do this the bike must be solidly supported as all the force needs to be transmitted to the race). Ensure that the drawbolt washer or drift (as applicable) bears only on the outer edge of the race and does not contact the working surface. Alternatively, have the races installed by a Honda dealer equipped with the bearing race installation tools.

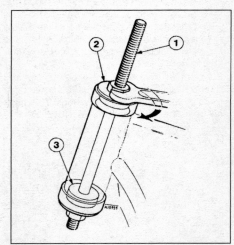

10.6 Drawbolt arrangement for fitting steering stem bearing outer races

1 Long bolt or threaded bar
2 Thick washer
3 Guide for lower race

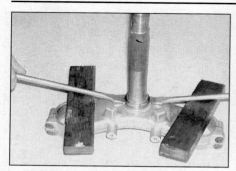

10.7a Remove the lower bearing race using screwdrivers . . .

10.7b . . . a cold chisel . . .

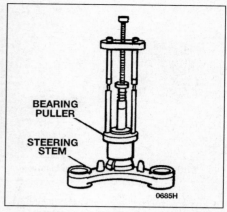

10.7c . . . or a puller if necessary

 Installation of new bearing outer races is made much easier if the races are left overnight in the freezer. This causes them to contract slightly making them a looser fit. Alternatively (but much less effective), use a freeze spray.

7 Only remove the lower bearing inner race from the steering stem if a new one is being fitted. To remove the race, use two screwdrivers placed on opposite sides to work it free, using blocks of wood to improve leverage and protect the yoke, or tap under it using a cold chisel **(see illustration)**. If you use the cold chisel method, first thread the steering stem nut onto the top then position the yoke on its front for stability – the nut will protect the threads from the transmitted force of the impact of the chisel **(see illustration)**. If the race is firmly in place it will be necessary to use a puller **(see illustration)**. Take the steering stem to a Honda dealer if required.
8 Remove the dust seal from the bottom of the stem and replace it with a new one. Smear the new one with grease.
9 Fit the new lower race onto the steering stem. Tap the new race into position using a length of tubing with an internal diameter slightly larger than the steering stem **(see illustration)**.
10 Install the steering stem (see Section 9).

11 Rear shock absorber

⚠ *Warning: Do not attempt to disassemble the shock absorber. Improper disassembly could result in serious injury. No individual components are available for it.*

Removal

1 Support the motorcycle so that no weight is transmitted through any part of the rear suspension (axle stands under the rider's footrest brackets work well) – tie the front brake lever to the handlebar to ensure the bike can't roll forward. Position a support under

the rear wheel or swingarm so that it does not drop when the shock absorber is removed, but also making sure that the weight of the machine is off the rear suspension so that the shock is not compressed.
2 Remove the seat cowling (see Chapter 8).
3 Unscrew the nut and withdraw the bolt securing the bottom of the shock absorber to the swingarm **(see illustration)**.
4 Unscrew the bolt securing the top of the shock absorber, accessing it via the hole in the frame **(see illustration)**. Support the shock absorber, then withdraw the bolt and remove the shock absorber from the bottom **(see illustration)**.

Inspection

5 Inspect the shock absorber for obvious physical damage and oil leakage, and the coil spring for looseness, cracks or signs of fatigue **(see illustration)**.

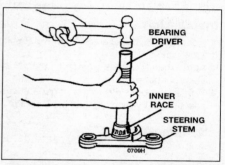

10.9 Drive the new bearing on using a suitable bearing driver or a length of pipe, taking care that it doesn't contact the working surface of the race

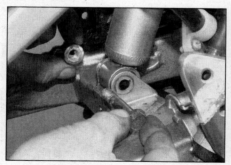

11.3 Unscrew the nut and withdraw the bottom bolt . . .

11.4a . . . then unscrew the top bolt . . .

11.4b . . . and remove the shock absorber

11.5 Check around the rod for signs of oil (arrowed)

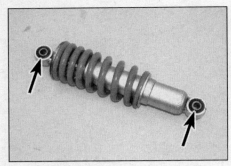

11.6 Check for wear in the bushes (arrowed)

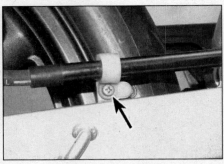

12.3a Undo the screw (arrowed) to free the brake hose . . .

12.3b . . . then release it from the front guide

6 Inspect the bushes in the shock absorber mounts and the mounts themselves for wear or damage **(see illustration)**. If necessary replace the shock absorber with a new one.

Installation

7 Installation is the reverse of removal, noting the following:
● Apply multi-purpose grease to the shock absorber bolts.
● Tighten the bolts/nut to the torque settings specified at the beginning of the Chapter.

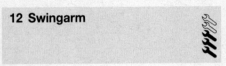

12 Swingarm

Removal

1 Support the motorcycle so that no weight

is transmitted through any part of the rear suspension (axle stands under the rider's footrest brackets work well) – tie the front brake lever to the handlebar to ensure the bike can't roll forward.

2 Remove the rear wheel (see Chapter 7). Remove the drive chain adjusters.

3 Undo the screw securing the rear brake hose guide to the swingarm **(see illustration)**. Free the hose from the front guide **(see illustration)**. Displace the rear brake caliper assembly from the swingarm, noting how it locates, and tie it to the passenger footrest bracket, making sure no strain is placed on the hose **(see illustration)**. Retrieve the rubber damper from the lug for safekeeping.

4 Unscrew the bolts securing the chainguard and remove it, noting how it fits – if required unscrew the footrest bracket bolts and displace the bracket to access the front bolt **(see illustration)**.

5 Unscrew the nut and withdraw the bolt securing the bottom of the shock absorber to the swingarm **(see illustration 11.3)**.

6 Lever the swingarm pivot blanking caps out of the frame using a small screwdriver **(see illustration)**. Unscrew the nut on the right-hand end of the swingarm pivot bolt **(see illustration)**.

7 Withdraw the pivot bolt then manoeuvre the swingarm out of the frame **(see illustrations)**.

8 Remove the chain slider from the swingarm if necessary, noting the collar with the screw **(see illustration)**. If it is badly worn or damaged, it should be replaced with a new one.

Inspection

9 Thoroughly clean the swingarm, removing all traces of dirt, corrosion and grease.

10 Inspect the swingarm closely, looking for obvious signs of wear such as heavy scoring,

12.3c Displace the caliper assembly and remove the rubber damper (arrowed)

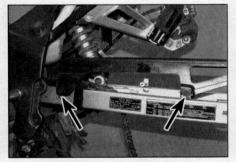

12.4 Unscrew the bolts (arrowed) and remove the chainguard

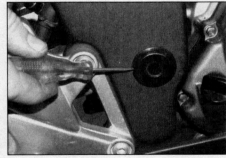

12.6a Remove the blanking caps . . .

12.6b . . . then unscrew the nut

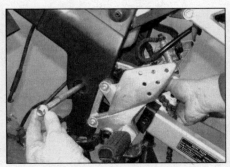

12.7a Withdraw the pivot bolt . . .

12.7b . . . and remove the swingarm

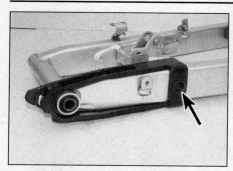

12.8 Undo the screw (arrowed) and remove the slider

12.11 Check the bush in each pivot

12.14 Make sure the slider locates over the lug (arrowed)

and cracks or distortion due to accident damage.

11 Inspect the bushes in the swingarm pivots for wear or damage **(see illustration)**. If necessary replace the swingarm with a new one – the bushes are not available separately.

12 Check the swingarm pivot bolt for straightness by rolling it on a flat surface such as a piece of plate glass (first wipe off all old grease and remove any corrosion using wire wool). Replace the pivot bolt with a new one if it is bent.

Installation

13 Clean off all old grease, then lubricate the bushes and the pivot bolt with multi-purpose grease.

14 If removed, install the chain slider, making sure it locates correctly over the lug at the front **(see illustration)**. Do not forget to fit the collar with the screw.

15 Offer up the swingarm and have an assistant hold it in place **(see illustration 12.7b)**. Make sure the drive chain is looped

over the front of the swingarm. Slide the pivot bolt through from the left-hand side **(see illustration 12.7a)**.

16 Thread the nut onto the pivot bolt and tighten it lightly **(see illustration 12.6b)**.

17 Align the shock absorber then install the bolt and tighten the nut to the specified torque setting **(see illustration 11.3)**.

18 Install the chainguard **(see illustration 12.4)**. If removed fit the footrest bracket to the frame and tighten the bolts to the torque setting specified at the beginning of the Chapter.

19 Fit the rubber damper for the caliper bracket onto the lug on the swingarm, then locate the brake calliper assembly **(see illustration 12.3c)**. Fit the brake hose into its front guide, and fit the rear guide onto the swingarm **(see illustrations 12.3b and a)**.

20 Fit the drive chain adjusters into the swingarm. Install the rear wheel (see Chapter 7).

21 Take the bike off its auxiliary stand(s) and

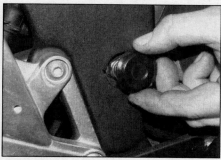

12.21 Fit the blanking cap on each side

rest it on the sidestand. Tighten the swingarm pivot bolt nut to the specified torque setting. Fit the swingarm pivot blanking caps into the frame **(see illustration)**.

22 Check and adjust the drive chain slack (see Chapter 1). Check the operation of the rear suspension and brake before taking the machine on the road.

Chapter 7
Brakes, wheels and final drive

Contents

Degrees of difficulty

| **Easy,** suitable for novice with little experience | 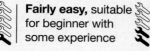 | **Fairly easy,** suitable for beginner with some experience | | **Fairly difficult,** suitable for competent DIY mechanic | | **Difficult,** suitable for experienced DIY mechanic | | **Very difficult,** suitable for expert DIY or professional | |

Specifications

Front brake

Brake fluid type	DOT 4
Caliper bore ID	
Standard.	25.400 to 25.450 mm
Service limit	25.460 mm
Caliper piston OD	
Standard.	25.318 to 25.368 mm
Service limit	25.310 mm
Master cylinder bore ID	
Standard.	11.000 to 11.043 mm
Service limit	11.055 mm
Master cylinder piston OD	
Standard.	10.957 to 10.984 mm
Service limit	10.945 mm
Disc thickness	
Standard.	3.8 to 4.2 mm
Service limit	3.5 mm
Disc maximum runout	0.25 mm

Rear brake

Brake fluid type	DOT 4
Caliper bore ID	
Standard	32.030 to 32.080 mm
Service limit	32.090 mm
Caliper piston OD	
Standard	31.948 to 31.998 mm
Service limit	31.94 mm
Master cylinder bore ID	
Standard	12.700 to 12.743 mm
Service limit	12.755 mm
Master cylinder piston OD	
Standard	15.827 to 15.854 mm
Service limit	15.815 mm
Disc thickness	
Standard	3.8 to 4.2 mm
Service limit	3.5 mm
Disc maximum runout	0.25 mm

Wheels

Maximum wheel runout (front and rear)	
Axial (side-to-side)	2.0 mm
Radial (out-of-round)	2.0 mm
Maximum axle runout (front and rear)	0.20 mm

Tyres

Tyre pressures	see *Pre-ride checks*
Tyre sizes*	
Front	80/90-17MC (44P)
Rear	100/80-17MC (52P)

Refer to the owners handbook or the tyre information label on the swingarm for approved tyre brands.

Final drive

Drive chain slack and lubricant	see Chapter 1
Drive chain type	DID 428V13-124LE (124 links)
Sprocket sizes	
Front (engine) sprocket	15T
Rear (wheel) sprocket	42T

Torque settings

Brake caliper bleed valves	5.5 Nm
Brake disc bolts	42 Nm
Brake hose banjo bolts	34 Nm
Engine sprocket (front sprocket) retainer plate bolts	10 Nm
Front axle nut	59 Nm
Front brake caliper mounting bolts	30 Nm
Front brake pad retaining pin	17 Nm
Rear axle nut	59 Nm
Rear brake pad retaining pin	17 Nm
Rear sprocket nuts	64 Nm

---

1 General information

All models have a single hydraulically operated disc brake front and rear. The sliding type calipers are of Nissin manufacturer, the front having two pistons and the rear caliper having a single piston.

The drive to the rear wheel is by chain and sprockets.

All models are fitted with cast alloy wheels designed for tubeless tyres only.

Caution: Disc brake components rarely require disassembly. Do not disassemble components unless absolutely necessary. If a hydraulic brake hose is loosened or disconnected, the union sealing washers must be renewed and the system bled upon reassembly. Do not use solvents on internal brake components. Solvents will cause the seals to swell and distort. Use only clean brake fluid of the correct type for cleaning. Use care when working with brake fluid as it can injure your eyes and it will damage painted surfaces and plastic parts.

2 Front brake pads

Warning: The dust created by the brake system is harmful to your health. Never blow it out with compressed air and don't inhale

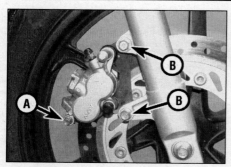

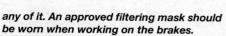

2.1 Slacken the pin (A), then unscrew the bolts (B) . . .

2.2 . . . and slide the front caliper off the disc

2.3a Unscrew the pin . . .

any of it. An approved filtering mask should be worn when working on the brakes.

1 Slacken the pad retaining pin **(see illustration)**.

2 Unscrew the caliper mounting bolts and slide the caliper off the disc **(see illustration)**. Free the brake hose from the mudguard to give more freedom of movement if required **(see illustration 3.2)**.

3 Unscrew and remove the pad pin, then remove the pads, noting how they fit **(see illustrations)**. **Note:** *Do not operate the brake lever while the pads are out of the caliper.*

4 Inspect the surface of each pad for contamination and check that the friction material has not worn beyond its service limit (see Chapter 1, Section 6). If either pad is worn down to, or beyond, the service limit wear indicator (i.e. the wear indicator is no longer visible), is fouled with oil or grease, or heavily scored or damaged, fit a set of new pads. **Note:** *It is not possible to degrease the friction material; if the pads are contaminated in any way they must be replaced with new ones.*

5 If the pads are in good condition clean them carefully, using a fine wire brush which is completely free of oil and grease to remove all traces of road dirt and corrosion. Using a pointed instrument, dig out any embedded particles of foreign matter. If required, spray with a dedicated brake cleaner to remove any dust.

6 Check the condition of the brake disc (see Section 4).

7 Remove all traces of corrosion from the pad pin and check it for wear and damage. Check the condition of the O-ring on its inner end and replace it with a new one if necessary.

8 Slide the caliper off the bracket **(see illustration)**. Clean around the exposed section of each piston to remove any dirt or debris that could cause the seals to be damaged. If new pads are being fitted, now push the pistons all the way back into the caliper to create room for them; if the old pads are still serviceable push the pistons in a little way. To push the pistons back use finger pressure or a piece of wood as leverage, or place the old pads back in the caliper and use a metal bar or a screwdriver inserted between them, or use grips and a piece of

wood, with rag or card to protect the caliper body. Alternatively obtain a proper piston-pushing tool from a good tool supplier. If there is too much brake fluid in the reservoir It may be necessary to remove the master cylinder reservoir cover, plate and diaphragm and siphon some out (see *Pre-ride checks*). If the pistons are difficult to push back, remove the bleed valve cap, then attach a length of clear hose to the bleed valve and place the open end in a suitable container, then open the valve and try again (see Section 11). Take great care not to draw any air into the system. If in doubt, bleed the brake afterwards.

9 If either piston appears seized, first block or hold the other piston using wood or cable-ties, then apply the brake lever and check whether the piston in question moves at all. If it moves out but can't be pushed back in the chances are there is some hidden corrosion stopping it. If it doesn't move at all, or to fully clean and

inspect the pistons, overhaul the caliper (see Section 3).

10 Clean off all traces of corrosion and hardened grease from the slider pins on the bracket and from the boots in the caliper. Replace the rubber boots with new ones if they are damaged, deformed or deteriorated **(see illustration 3.6)**. Make sure the lower slider pin is tight. Apply a smear of silicone-based grease to the boots and slider pins, and to the O-ring on the retaining pin **(see illustration)**.

11 Make sure the pad spring is correctly located in the caliper **(see illustration)**. Slide the caliper onto the bracket **(see illustration 2.8)**.

12 Lightly smear the back and the front edge of the backing material with copper-based grease, making sure that none gets on the friction material. Also smear the pad pin.

13 Fit the outer pad into the caliper, making sure its upper end locates correctly against the

2.3b . . . and remove the pads

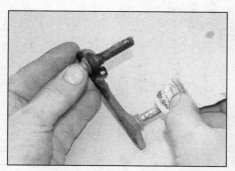

2.10 Smear the pins and boots with suitable grease

2.8 Slide the caliper off the bracket

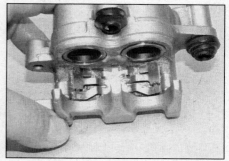

2.11 Make sure the spring is correctly fitted

2.13a Make sure the pad locates correctly

2.13b Smear the post with copper grease

Removal

Note: *If the caliper is being overhauled (usually due to sticking pistons or fluid leaks) read through the entire procedure first and make sure that you have obtained all the new parts required, including some new DOT 4 brake fluid.*

1 If the caliper is being overhauled, slacken the brake pad retaining pin **(see illustration 2.1)**. If the caliper is just being displaced from the forks as part of the wheel removal procedure, the brake pads can be left in place.

2 Free the brake hose from the mudguard to give more freedom of movement if required **(see illustration)**.

3 If the caliper is being completely removed or overhauled, unscrew the brake hose banjo bolt and detach the banjo union, noting its alignment with the caliper **(see illustration 3.22)**. Wrap clingfilm around the banjo union and secure the hose in an upright position to minimise fluid loss. Discard the sealing washers, as new ones must be fitted on reassembly.

4 Unscrew the caliper mounting bolts and slide the caliper off the disc **(see illustrations 2.1 and 2.2)**. If the caliper is just being displaced, secure it to the motorcycle with a cable-tie to avoid straining the brake hose. **Note:** *Do not operate the brake lever while the caliper is off the disc.*

5 If the caliper is being overhauled, remove the brake pads (see Section 2).

Overhaul

6 Slide the caliper off the bracket **(see illustration 2.8)**. Clean the exterior of the caliper and bracket with denatured alcohol or brake system cleaner. Have some clean rag ready to catch any spilled brake fluid. Clean off all traces of corrosion and hardened grease from the slider pins on the bracket and from the boots in the caliper. Replace the rubber boots with new ones if they are damaged, deformed or deteriorated **(see illustration)**. Make sure the lower slider pin is tight.

7 Find a piece of wood that fits between the pistons and the arms on the inner side of the caliper. Make sure the bleed valve is tight. Use the

2.14 Slide the caliper onto the disc and fit the bolts

caliper bracket **(see illustration)**. Smear some copper grease over the inner pad locating post and the pad retaining pin **(see illustration)**. Fit the inner pad, locating its curved end over the post **(see illustration 2.3b)**. Press the lower end of each pad up against the spring so the holes for the pad pin align, then insert the pin and tighten it finger-tight **(see illustration 2.3a)**.

14 Slide the caliper onto the disc making sure the pads locate correctly on each side **(see illustration)**. Install the caliper mounting bolts and tighten them to the torque setting specified at the beginning of the Chapter. Fit the brake hose onto the mudguard if displaced.

15 Tighten the pad pin to the torque setting specified at the beginning of this Chapter **(see illustration 2.1)**.

16 Operate the brake lever until the pads contact with the disc. Check the level of fluid in the hydraulic reservoir and top-up if necessary (see *Pre-ride checks*).

17 Check the operation of the front brake before riding the motorcycle.

3 Front brake caliper

⚠ **Warning: If a caliper is in need of an overhaul all old brake fluid should be flushed from the system. Also, the dust created by the brake system may contain asbestos, which is harmful to your health. Never blow it out with compressed air and do not inhale any of it. An approved filtering mask should be worn when working on the brakes. Overhaul of the brake caliper must be done in a spotlessly clean work area to avoid contamination and possible failure of the brake hydraulic system components. Do not, under any circumstances, use petroleum-based solvents to clean brake parts. Use clean DOT 4 brake fluid, dedicated brake cleaner or denatured alcohol only. To prevent damage from spilled brake fluid, always cover paintwork when working on the braking system.**

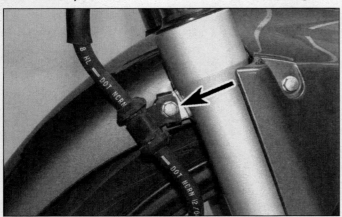

3.2 Unscrew the bolt (arrowed) to free the hose from the mudguard

3.6 Check the condition of the boots (arrowed) and fit new ones if necessary

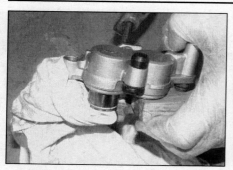

3.8a Apply compressed air to the fluid passage . . .

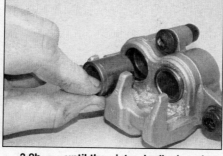

3.8b . . . until the piston is displaced

3.10 Remove the seals and discard them

wood to block one piston and prevent it moving, and place some rag over the other piston. Place the caliper piston-down on the bench.

8 Apply compressed air gradually and progressively, starting with a fairly low pressure, to the fluid inlet in the caliper and allow the unblocked piston to ease out of its bore, controlling it with hand pressure and the rag **(see illustrations)**.

9 If the piston is stuck in its bore due to corrosion, find a suitable bolt to block the fluid inlet banjo bolt bore and thread it in, then unscrew the bleed valve and apply the air to this in the same way – the narrower bore will allow more air pressure to be applied to the piston as less can escape. Do not try to remove a piston by levering it out or by using pliers or other grips. If the piston has completely seized you may have to replace the caliper with a new one.

10 Remove the dust seal and the piston seal from the piston bore using a soft wooden or plastic tool to avoid scratching the bore **(see illustration)**. Discard the seals as new ones must be fitted.

11 Clean the piston and bore with clean DOT 4 brake fluid. If compressed air is available, blow it through the fluid galleries in the caliper to ensure they are clear (make sure it is filtered and unlubricated).

Caution: Do not, under any circumstances, use a petroleum-based solvent to clean brake parts.

12 Inspect each caliper bore and piston for signs of corrosion, nicks and burrs and loss of plating. If surface defects are present, the pistons and/or

the caliper assembly must be replaced with new ones. If the necessary measuring equipment is available, compare the dimensions of the caliper bores and pistons to those specified at the beginning of this Chapter, and obtain new pistons or a new caliper if necessary.

13 Lubricate the new piston seal with clean brake fluid and fit it into the inner (large) groove in the caliper bore **(see illustrations)**.

14 Lubricate the new dust seal with silicone grease and fit it into the outer groove in the caliper bore **(see illustration)**.

15 Lubricate the piston with clean brake fluid and fit it, closed-end first, into the caliper bore, taking care not to displace the seals **(see illustration)**. Using your thumbs, push the piston all the way in, making sure it enters the bore squarely.

16 Repeat for the other piston.

17 Apply a smear of silicone-based grease to the boots and slider pins **(see**

3.13a Lubricate the new piston seal with brake fluid . . .

illustration 2.10). Slide the caliper onto the bracket **(see illustration 2.8)**.

Installation

18 If the caliper has not been overhauled, refer to Steps 6 and 17 and clean, check and re-grease the slider pins and boots.

19 If removed, install the brake pads (see Section 2).

20 Slide the caliper onto the brake disc, making sure the pads locate correctly on each side **(see illustration 2.14)**.

21 Install the caliper mounting bolts and tighten them to the torque setting specified at the beginning of the Chapter. If necessary tighten the pad pin to the torque setting specified at the beginning of this Chapter **(see illustration 2.1)**.

22 Connect the brake hose to the caliper, using new sealing washers on each side of the banjo fitting **(see illustration)**. Locate the hose

3.13b . . . then fit it into its groove . . .

3.14 . . . followed by the new dust seal

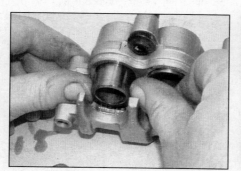

3.15 Fit the piston and push it all the way in

3.22 Always use new sealing washers and align the hose between the lugs

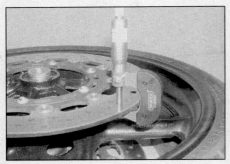

4.2 Measure the thickness of the disc

4.3 Checking disc runout with a dial gauge

4.5 The disc is secured by six bolts

elbow between the lugs on the caliper. Tighten the banjo bolt to the specified torque setting.
23 Fit the brake hose onto the mudguard if displaced **(see illustration 3.2)**.
24 Top up the hydraulic reservoir with DOT 4 brake fluid (see *Pre-ride checks*) and bleed the system as described in Section 11. Check that there are no fluid leaks and test the operation of the brake before riding the motorcycle.

4 Front brake disc

Inspection

1 Inspect the surface of the disc for score marks and other damage. Light scratches are normal after use and won't affect brake operation, but deep grooves and heavy score marks will reduce braking efficiency and accelerate pad wear. If the disc is badly grooved it must be replaced with a new one.
2 The disc must not be machined or allowed to wear down to a thickness less than the service limit as listed in this Chapter's Specifications. The minimum thickness is also stamped on the disc **(see illustration)**. Check the thickness of the disc with a micrometer and replace it with a new one if necessary.
3 To check if the disc is warped, position the bike on an auxiliary stand with the front wheel raised off the ground. Mount a dial gauge to the fork leg, with the gauge plunger touching the surface of the disc about 10 mm from the outer edge **(see illustration)**.

Rotate the wheel and watch the gauge needle, comparing the reading with the limit listed in the Specifications at the beginning of this Chapter. If the runout is greater than the service limit, check the wheel bearings for play (see Chapter 1). If the bearings are worn, install new ones (see Section 16) and repeat this check. If the disc runout is still excessive, a new disc will have to be fitted.

Removal

4 Remove the wheel (see Section 14).
5 If you are not replacing the disc with a new one, mark the relationship of the disc to the wheel, so it can be installed in the same position. Unscrew the disc retaining bolts, loosening them evenly and a little at a time in a criss-cross pattern to avoid distorting the disc, then remove the disc **(see illustration)**.

Installation

6 Before installing the disc, make sure there is no dirt or corrosion where the disc seats on the hub. If the disc does not sit flat when it is bolted down, it will appear to be warped when checked or when the front brake is applied.
7 Install the disc on the wheel with its marked side facing out, aligning the previously applied matchmarks (if you're reinstalling the original disc), and making sure the arrow points in the direction of normal wheel rotation.
8 Clean the threads of the disc mounting bolts, then apply a suitable non-permanent thread locking compound. Install the bolts and tighten them evenly and a little at a time in a criss-cross pattern to the torque setting specified at the beginning of this Chapter.

Clean the disc using acetone or brake system cleaner. If a new disc has been installed remove any protective coating from its working surfaces. **Note:** *Always fit new brake pads when installing a new disc.*
9 Install the front wheel (see Section 14).
10 Operate the brake lever several times to bring the pads into contact with the disc. Check the operation of the brake before riding the motorcycle.

5 Front brake master cylinder

⚠️ *Warning: If the brake master cylinder is in need of an overhaul all old brake fluid should be flushed from the system. Overhaul must be done in a spotlessly clean work area to avoid contamination and possible failure of the brake hydraulic system components. Do not, under any circumstances, use petroleum-based solvents to clean brake parts; use clean DOT 4 brake fluid, dedicated brake cleaner or denatured alcohol only. To prevent damage from spilled brake fluid, always cover paintwork when working on the braking system.*

Removal

Note: *If the master cylinder is being overhauled (usually due to sticking or poor action, or fluid leaks) read through the entire procedure first and make sure that you have obtained all the new parts required, including some new DOT 4 brake fluid.*
1 Disconnect the wiring connectors from the brake light switch **(see illustration)**.
2 If the master cylinder is being overhauled, follow Steps 3 to 8. If the master cylinder is just being displaced, follow this Step only: unscrew the master cylinder clamp bolts and remove the back of the clamp, noting how it fits, then position the master cylinder assembly clear of the handlebar **(see illustration 5.6)**. Ensure no strain is placed on the hydraulic hose. Keep the reservoir upright.
3 Remove the brake lever (see Chapter 6). Remove the mirror (see Chapter 8).
4 Slacken the reservoir cover screws **(see illustration)**.

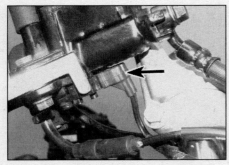

5.1 Disconnect the brake light switch wires (arrowed)

5.4 Slacken the cover screws

5.5 Brake hose banjo bolt – note its alignment

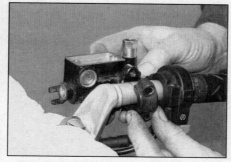

5.6 Unscrew the bolts and remove the master cylinder and its clamp

5.9 Remove the boot

5 Unscrew the brake hose banjo bolt and detach the banjo union, noting its alignment with the master cylinder **(see illustration)**. Wrap clingfilm around the banjo union and secure the hose in an upright position to minimise fluid loss. Discard the sealing washers as new ones must be fitted on reassembly.

6 Unscrew the master cylinder clamp bolts and remove the back of the clamp, noting how it fits, then lift the master cylinder and reservoir away from the handlebar **(see illustration)**.

7 Remove the reservoir cover, diaphragm plate and diaphragm. Drain the brake fluid from the master cylinder and reservoir into a suitable container. Wipe any remaining fluid out of the reservoir with a clean rag.

8 If required, undo the screw securing the brake light switch to the bottom of the master cylinder and remove the switch **(see illustration 5.19)**.

Overhaul

9 Remove the rubber boot from the master cylinder **(see illustration)**.

10 Depress the piston and use circlip pliers to remove the circlip, then slide out the piston assembly and the spring, noting how they fit **(see illustrations)**. If they are difficult to remove, apply low pressure compressed air to the brake fluid outlet. Lay the parts out in

the proper order to prevent confusion during reassembly.

11 Clean the master cylinder bore with clean brake fluid. If compressed air is available, blow it through the fluid galleries to ensure they are clear (make sure the air is filtered and unlubricated).

12 Check the master cylinder bore for corrosion, scratches, nicks and score marks. If the necessary measuring equipment is available, compare the dimensions of the piston and bore to those given in the Specifications at the beginning of this Chapter. If damage or wear is evident, the master cylinder must be replaced with a new one. If

5.10a Release the circlip . . .

the master cylinder is in poor condition, then the caliper should be checked as well.

13 The dust boot, circlip, washer, piston, seal, cup and spring are all included in the master cylinder rebuild kit. Use all of the new parts, regardless of the apparent condition of the old ones.

14 Smear the cup and seal with new brake fluid. Fit them into their grooves in the piston so their flared ends will fit into the master cylinder first – the seal is bigger than the cup and fits into the shallower groove in the piston **(see illustration)**.

15 Fit the spring onto the end of the piston, twisting it slightly clockwise to spread the coils if necessary **(see illustration)**.

5.10b . . . then draw out the piston assembly and the spring

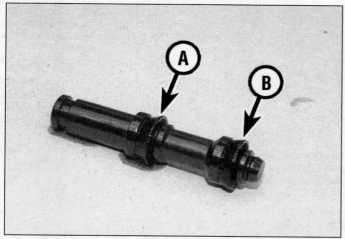

5.14 Fit the seal (A) and the cup (B) onto the piston as shown

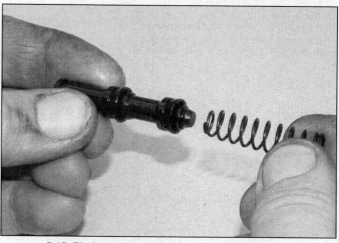

5.15 Fit the spring onto the end of the piston . . .

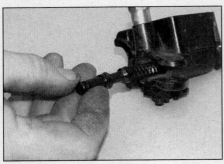

5.16a . . . then fit them into the cylinder

5.16b Fit the washer and circlip onto the piston

5.17 Fit the rubber boot and press it into place

5.19 Front brake light switch and its mounting screw (arrowed)

5.20 Align the clamp mating surface with the punch mark (arrowed)

5.21 Always use new sealing washers

16 Lubricate the piston and the master cylinder bore with new brake fluid and slide the assembly into the master cylinder **(see illustration)**. Make sure the lips on the cup and seal do not turn inside out. Fit the washer and circlip over the end of the piston **(see illustration)**. Push the piston in to compress the spring and fit the circlip into its groove, making sure it locates correctly **(see illustration 5.10a)**.

17 Smear some silicone grease onto the lips and inside of the rubber boot. Fit the rubber boot onto the piston so its outer end lips locate in the groove and press the boot into place in the end of the cylinder **(see illustration)**.

18 Inspect the reservoir diaphragm and fit a new one it if it is damaged or deteriorated.

Installation

19 If removed, fit the brake light switch onto the bottom of the master cylinder, making sure the pin locates in the hole, and tighten the screw **(see illustration)**.

20 Attach the master cylinder to the handlebar **(see illustration 5.6)**, aligning the clamp joint with the punch mark on the top of the handlebar, then fit the back of the clamp with its UP mark facing up **(see illustration)**. Tighten the upper bolt first, then the lower bolt.

21 Connect the brake hose to the master cylinder, using new sealing washers on each side of the banjo fitting **(see illustration)**.

Locate the hose elbow against the rear face of the lower of the lugs, not between the lugs as may seem logical **(see illustration 5.5)**. Tighten the banjo bolt to the torque setting specified at the beginning of this Chapter.

22 Install the brake lever (see Chapter 6). Install the mirror (see Chapter 8).

23 Connect the brake light switch wiring **(see illustration 5.1)**.

24 Fill the fluid reservoir to the correct level with new DOT 4 brake fluid (see *Pre-ride checks*). Refer to Section 11 and bleed the air from the system.

25 Check the operation of the front brake before riding the motorcycle.

6 Rear brake pads

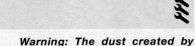

> ⚠ *Warning: The dust created by the brake system may contain asbestos, which is harmful to your health. Never blow it out with compressed air and don't inhale any of it. An approved filtering mask should be worn when working on the brake.*

1 Push the caliper against the disc to force the piston in – this creates room for the new pads **(see illustration)**. If there is too much brake fluid in the reservoir it may be necessary to remove the master cylinder reservoir cover,

plate and diaphragm and siphon some out (see *Pre-ride checks*). If the piston is difficult to push back, remove the bleed valve cap, then attach a length of clear hose to the bleed valve and place the open end in a suitable container, then open the valve and try again (see Section 11). Take great care not to draw any air into the system. If in doubt, bleed the brake afterwards.

2 If the piston appears seized, apply the brake pedal and check whether the piston moves at all. If it moves out but can't be pushed back in the chances are there is some hidden corrosion stopping it. If it doesn't move at all, or to fully clean and inspect the piston, remove the caliper and overhaul it (see Section 7).

3 Remove the pad retaining pin plug, then

6.1 Push on the caliper to force the piston in

6.3a Remove the plug . . .

6.3b . . . then unscrew the pin . . .

6.3c . . . and remove the pads

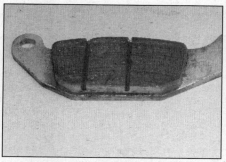

6.4 Check the pads as described

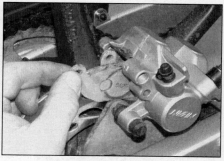

6.9a Install the pads . . .

6.9b . . . locating the inner pad end over the post (arrowed)

unscrew the retaining pin **(see illustrations)**. Remove the pads, noting how they fit **(see illustration)**. Note: *Do not operate the brake pedal while the pads are out of the caliper.*

4 Inspect the surface of each pad for contamination and check that the friction material has not worn beyond its service limit (see Chapter 1, Section 6) **(see illustration)**. If either pad is worn down to, or beyond, the service limit wear indicator, is fouled with oil or grease, or heavily scored or damaged, fit a new set of pads. It is not possible to degrease the friction material; if the pads are contaminated in any way they must be replaced with new ones.

5 If the pads are in good condition clean them carefully, using a fine wire brush which is completely free of oil and grease to remove

6.10 Push the pads up to align the holes and insert the pin

all traces of road dirt and corrosion. Using a pointed instrument, dig out any embedded particles of foreign matter. If required, spray with a dedicated brake cleaner to remove any dust.

6 Check the condition of the brake disc (see Section 8).

7 Remove all traces of corrosion from the pad pin and check it for wear and damage. Check the condition of the O-ring on its inner end and replace it with a new one if necessary.

8 Lightly smear the back and the front edges of the backing material with copper-based grease, making sure that none gets on the friction material. Also smear the pad pin and the post on the bracket for the inner pad.

9 Slide the pads into the caliper so that the friction material of each pad faces the disc **(see illustration)** – the pad with the curved end is the inner pad, and this locates over the post on the bracket **(see illustration)**. Make sure the leading edge of the outer pad locates correctly against the guide on the bracket.

10 Apply a smear of silicone grease to the O-ring on the inner end of the pad pin. Push up on the end of each pad so the pads compress the spring and insert the pad pin when the holes are aligned **(see illustration)**. Tighten the pad pin to the specified torque setting. Fit the plug.

11 Operate the brake pedal until the pads contact with the disc. Check the level of fluid in the rear hydraulic reservoir and top-up if necessary (see *Pre-ride checks*).

12 Check the operation of the rear brake before riding the motorcycle.

7 Rear brake caliper

> **Warning: If the caliper is in need of overhaul all old brake fluid should be flushed from the system. Also, the dust created by the brake system may contain asbestos, which is harmful to your health. Never blow it out with compressed air and do not inhale any of it. An approved filtering mask should be worn when working on the brakes. Overhaul must be done in a spotlessly clean work area to avoid contamination and possible failure of the brake hydraulic system components. Do not, under any circumstances, use petroleum-based solvents to clean brake parts; use clean DOT 4 brake fluid, dedicated brake cleaner or denatured alcohol only, as described. To prevent damage from spilled brake fluid, always cover paintwork when working on the braking system.**

Removal

Note: *If the caliper is being overhauled (usually due to a sticking piston or fluid leaks) read through the entire procedure first and make sure that you have obtained all the new parts*

7.2 Brake hose banjo bolt (arrowed) – note its alignment

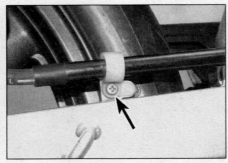

7.3 Undo the screw (arrowed) to free the hose

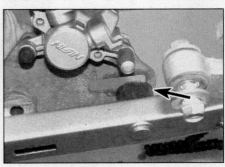

7.4 Displace the caliper assembly and remove the rubber damper (arrowed)

required, including some new DOT 4 brake fluid.

1 If the caliper is being overhauled, remove the brake pads (see Section 6).

2 If the caliper is being completely removed or overhauled, unscrew the brake hose banjo bolt and detach the banjo union, noting its alignment with the caliper **(see illustration)**. Wrap clingfilm around the banjo union and secure the hose in an upright position to minimise fluid loss. Discard the sealing washers as new ones must be fitted on reassembly.

3 If the caliper is just being displaced, undo the screw securing the brake hose guide to the swingarm **(see illustration)**.

4 Remove the rear wheel (see Section 15). Remove the rear brake caliper assembly from the swingarm, noting how it locates. Retrieve the rubber damper from the lug for safekeeping **(see illustration)**. If the caliper

has just been displaced tie it to the passenger footrest bracket, making sure no strain is placed on the hose. **Note:** *Do not operate the brake pedal while the caliper is off the disc.*

Overhaul

5 Slide the caliper off the bracket **(see illustration)**. Clean the exterior of the caliper and bracket with denatured alcohol or brake system cleaner. Have some clean rag ready to catch any spilled brake fluid. Clean off all traces of corrosion and hardened grease from the slider pins on the bracket and from the boots in the caliper. Replace the rubber boots with new ones if they are damaged, deformed or deteriorated **(see illustration)**. Make sure the rear slider pin is tight.

6 Place a piece of wood between the piston and the caliper body – it should be just thick enough to stop the piston leaving the bore entirely **(see illustration)**. Apply compressed

air gradually and progressively, starting with a fairly low pressure, to the fluid inlet on the caliper body and allow the piston to ease out of its bore, controlling it with the wood **(see illustration)**.

7 If the piston is stuck in its bore due to corrosion, find a suitable bolt to block the fluid inlet banjo bolt bore and thread it in, then unscrew the bleed valve and apply the air to this in the same way – the narrower bore will allow more air pressure to be applied to the piston as less can escape. Do not try to remove the piston by levering it out or by using pliers or other grips. If the piston has completely seized you may have to replace the caliper with a new one.

8 Remove the dust seal and the piston seal from the piston bore using a soft wooden or plastic tool to avoid scratching the bore **(see illustration)**. Discard the seals as new ones must be fitted.

9 Clean the piston and bore with clean brake fluid. If compressed air is available, blow it through the fluid galleries in the caliper to ensure they are clear (make sure it is filtered and unlubricated).

Caution: Do not, under any circumstances, use a petroleum-based solvent to clean brake parts.

10 Inspect the caliper bore and piston for signs of corrosion, nicks and burrs and loss of plating. If surface defects are present, the piston and/or the caliper assembly must be replaced with new ones. If the necessary measuring equipment is available, compare the dimensions of the caliper bore and piston

7.5a Slide the caliper off the bracket

7.5b Check the condition of the boots (arrowed) and fit new ones if necessary

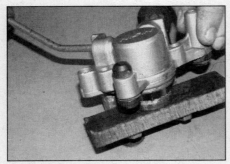

7.6a Fit the wood, then apply the compressed air as described . . .

7.6b . . . until the piston is displaced

7.8 Remove the seals and discard them

7.11a Lubricate the new piston seal with brake fluid . . .

7.11b . . . then fit it into its groove . . .

7.12 . . . followed by the new dust seal

7.13 Fit the piston and push it all the way in

7.16 Make sure the spring (arrowed) is correctly fitted

7.18 Always use new sealing washers

to those specified at the beginning of this Chapter, and obtain a new piston or a new caliper if necessary.

11 Lubricate the new piston seal with clean brake fluid and fit it into the inner (large) groove in the caliper bore **(see illustrations)**.

12 Lubricate the new dust seal with silicone grease and fit it into the outer groove in the caliper bore **(see illustration)**.

13 Lubricate the piston with clean brake fluid and fit it, closed-end first, into the caliper bore, taking care not to displace the seals **(see illustration)**. Using your thumbs, push the piston all the way in, making sure it enters the bore squarely.

14 Apply a smear of silicone-based grease to the boots and slider pins **(see illustration 2.10)**. Slide the caliper onto the bracket **(see illustration 7.5a)**.

Installation

15 If the caliper has not been overhauled, refer to Steps 5 and 14 and clean, check and re-grease the slider pins and boots.

16 Make sure that the pad spring is correctly fitted **(see illustration)**.

17 Fit the rubber damper for the caliper bracket onto the lug on the swingarm, then locate the brake caliper assembly **(see illustration 7.4)**. If detached fit the rear brake hose guide onto the swingarm **(see illustration 7.3)**. Install the rear wheel (see Section 15).

18 If detached, connect the brake hose to the caliper, using new sealing washers on each side of the fitting **(see illustration)**. Locate the

hose elbow between the lugs on the caliper **(see illustration 7.2)**. Tighten the banjo bolt to the torque setting specified at the beginning of the Chapter.

19 Install the brake pads (see Section 6).

20 Top up the hydraulic reservoir with DOT 4 brake fluid (see *Pre-ride checks*) and bleed the system as described in Section 11. Check that there are no fluid leaks and test the operation of the brake before riding the motorcycle.

8 Rear brake disc

Inspection

1 Refer to Section 4 of this Chapter, noting that the dial gauge should be attached to the swingarm.

Removal

2 Remove the rear wheel (see Section 15).

Caution: Don't lay the wheel down and allow it to rest on the disc or sprocket – they could become warped. Set the wheel on wood blocks so the wheel rim supports the weight of the wheel.

3 If you are not replacing the disc with a new one, mark the relationship of the disc to the wheel so it can be installed in the same position. Unscrew the disc retaining bolts, loosening them evenly and a little at a time in a criss-cross pattern to avoid distorting the disc, then remove the disc **(see illustration)**.

Installation

4 Before installing the disc, make sure there is no dirt or corrosion where the disc seats on the hub. If the disc does not sit flat when it is bolted down, it will appear to be warped when checked or when the rear brake is used.

5 Install the disc on the wheel with its marked side facing out, aligning the previously applied matchmarks (if you're reinstalling the original disc).

6 Clean the threads of the disc mounting bolts, then apply a suitable non-permanent thread locking compound. Install the bolts and tighten them evenly and a little at a time in a criss-cross pattern to the torque setting specified at the beginning of this Chapter. Clean the disc using acetone or brake system cleaner. If a new disc has been installed, remove any protective coating from its

8.3 The disc is secured by four bolts

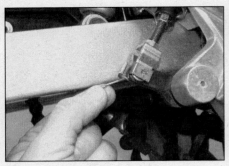

9.1a Remove the split pin . . .

9.1b . . . then withdraw the clevis pin

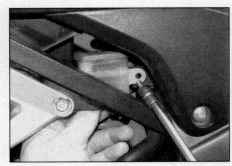

9.2a Detach the fluid reservoir . . .

working surfaces. Always fit new brake pads with a new disc.

7 Install the rear wheel (see Section 15).

8 Operate the brake pedal several times to bring the pads into contact with the disc. Check the operation of the rear brake before riding the motorcycle.

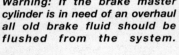

9 Rear brake master cylinder

 Warning: If the brake master cylinder is in need of an overhaul all old brake fluid should be flushed from the system.

Overhaul must be done in a spotlessly clean work area to avoid contamination and possible failure of the brake hydraulic system components. Do not, under any circumstances, use petroleum-based solvents to clean brake parts; use clean DOT 4 brake fluid, dedicated brake cleaner or denatured alcohol only, as described. To prevent damage from spilled brake fluid, always cover paintwork when working on the braking system.

Removal

Note: If the master cylinder is being overhauled (usually due to sticking or poor action, or fluid leaks) read through the entire procedure first and make sure that you have obtained all the new parts required, including some new DOT 4 brake fluid.

1 Straighten and remove the split pin from the clevis pin securing the brake pedal to the master cylinder pushrod, then withdraw the pin and detach the pushrod from the pedal **(see illustrations)**. Discard the split pin as a new one should be used.

2 Undo the bolt securing the fluid reservoir to the frame and draw the reservoir out, then undo the reservoir cover screws and remove the reservoir cover and diaphragm **(see illustrations)**. Pour the brake fluid into a suitable container. Wipe any remaining fluid out of the reservoir with a clean rag.

3 Undo the brake hose banjo bolt and detach the banjo union, noting its alignment with the master cylinder **(see illustration)**. Once disconnected, wrap clingfilm around the banjo union and secure the hose in an upright position to minimise fluid loss. Discard the sealing washers as new ones must be fitted on reassembly.

4 Undo the bolts securing the master cylinder to the footrest bracket and remove the master cylinder along with the reservoir **(see illustrations)**.

Overhaul

5 Release the clip securing the reservoir hose to the union on the master cylinder and detach the hose, being prepared to catch any residual fluid **(see illustration)**.

6 If required, undo the screw securing the fluid reservoir hose union and detach it from

9.2b . . . then remove the cover assembly and drain it

9.3 Brake hose banjo bolt (arrowed) – note its alignment

9.4a Unscrew the bolts (arrowed) . . .

9.4b . . . and remove the master cylinder and reservoir

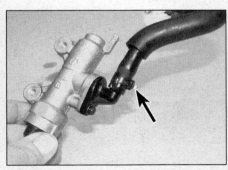

9.5 Release the clip (arrowed) and pull the hose off its union

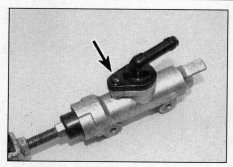

9.6 Undo the screw (arrowed) and remove the union

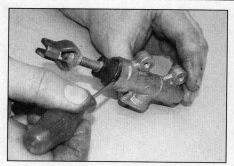

9.7a Remove the rubber boot . . .

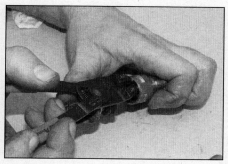

9.7b . . . then release the circlip . . .

the master cylinder **(see illustration)**. Discard the O-ring as a new one must be used. Inspect the reservoir hose for cracks or splits and replace it with a new one if necessary.

7 Dislodge the rubber dust boot from the base of the master cylinder and from around the pushrod, noting how it locates **(see illustration)**. Push the pushrod in and, using circlip pliers, remove the circlip from its groove in the master cylinder and slide out the pushrod assembly, the piston assembly and the spring, noting how they fit **(see illustrations)**. Lay the parts out in order as you remove them to prevent confusion during reassembly.

8 Slacken the locknut holding the clevis on the bottom of the pushrod, then dislodge and remove the roll pin from under the clevis using a suitable drift **(see illustration)**. Note how far the clevis is threaded up the pushrod, then thread it off, followed by the locknut **(see illustration)**. Remove the rubber boot and the circlip.

9 Clean the master cylinder bore with clean brake fluid. If compressed air is available, blow it through the fluid galleries to ensure

9.7c . . . and remove the pushrod, piston and spring

they are clear (make sure the air is filtered and unlubricated).

10 Check the master cylinder bore for corrosion, scratches, nicks and score marks. If the necessary measuring equipment is available, compare the dimensions of the piston and bore to those given in the Specifications at the beginning of this Chapter. If damage or wear is evident, the master cylinder must be replaced with a new one. If

9.8a Slacken the locknut . . .

the master cylinder is in poor condition, then the caliper should be checked as well.

11 The dust boot, circlip, piston, seal, cup and spring are all included in the master cylinder rebuild kit. Use all of the new parts, regardless of the apparent condition of the old ones.

12 Smear some silicone grease onto the lips and inside of the rubber boot. Fit the new circlip and rubber boot onto the pushrod,

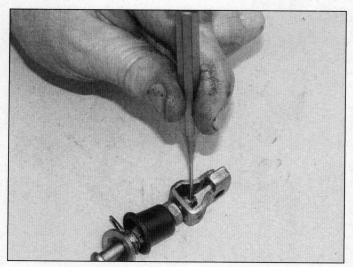

9.8b . . . then remove the roll pin

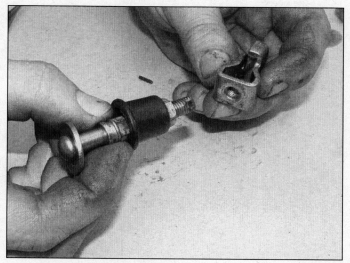

9.8c Thread the clevis and locknut off then remove the boot and circlip

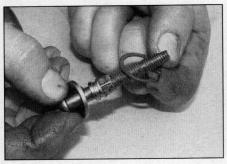

9.12a Fit the circlip . . .

9.12b . . . boot . . .

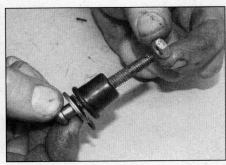

9.12c . . . locknut . . .

9.12d . . . and clevis . . .

9.12e . . . then drive the roll pin into the hole

9.12f Set the clevis position then tighten the locknut against it

then thread the locknut and clevis on **(see illustrations)**. Drive a new roll pin into the pushrod, then set the position of the clevis as noted on removal **(see illustration)** – Honda specify the distance between the centre of the pedal joint eye and the lower mounting bolt hole should be 85 mm (measured parallel to the pushrod). Tighten the locknut securely against the pedal joint, counter-holding the pushrod using a spanner on the hex **(see illustration)**.

13 Smear the cup and seal with new brake fluid. Fit them into their grooves in the piston so their flared ends will fit into the master cylinder first – the cup is smaller than the seal and fits into the deeper groove in the piston **(see illustrations)**.

14 Fit the spring onto the end of the piston, twisting it slightly clockwise to spread the coils if necessary **(see illustration)**.

15 Lubricate the piston and master cylinder bore with new brake fluid and slide the assembly into the master cylinder **(see illustration)**. Make sure the lips on the seal do not turn inside out.

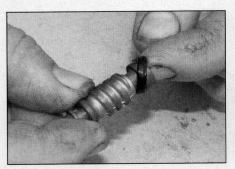

9.13a Fit the seal into the groove on the outer end of the piston . . .

9.13b . . . and the cup into the groove on the inner end . . .

9.13c . . . as shown

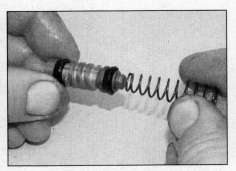

9.14 Fit the spring onto the end of the piston . . .

9.15 . . . then fit them into the cylinder

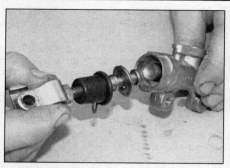

9.16a Locate the pushrod against the piston and push them in . . .

9.16b . . . then fit the circlip into the groove

9.17a Fit the new boot into the cylinder . . .

9.17b . . . and locate it in its groove

9.18a Fit a new O-ring . . .

9.18b . . . then press the union into place

16 Smear some silicone grease onto the rounded end of the pushrod and locate it against the end of the piston **(see illustration)**. Push the piston in using the pushrod until the washer is beyond the circlip groove, then locate the circlip in the groove **(see illustration)**.

17 Press the rubber boot into place in the end of the cylinder and fit the outer end lips into the groove in the pushrod **(see illustrations)**.

18 If removed, fit a new fluid reservoir hose union O-ring into the master cylinder, then press the union in and secure it with the screw **(see illustrations)**.

19 Connect the hose to the union on the master cylinder and secure it with the clip **(see illustration)**. Check that the hose is secured with a clip at the reservoir end as well. If the clips have weakened, use new ones.

Installation

20 Locate the master cylinder on the inside of the footrest bracket, then fit the mounting bolts and tighten them **(see illustration)**.

21 Align the clevis with the brake pedal, then insert the pin and secure it with a new split pin, bending its ends round the clevis pin to lock it **(see illustrations 9.1b and a)**.

22 Connect the brake hose to the master cylinder, using new sealing washers on each side of the banjo fitting **(see illustration)**. Locate the hose elbow against the outer face of the lug **(see illustration 9.3)**. Tighten the banjo bolt to the torque setting specified at the beginning of this Chapter.

23 Fill the fluid reservoir to the correct level with new DOT 4 brake fluid (see *Pre-ride checks*). Refer to Section 11 and bleed the air from the system.

24 Fit the fluid reservoir onto its mount and tighten the bolt **(see illustration 9.2a)**.

25 Check the operation of the rear brake before riding the motorcycle.

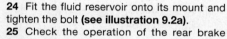

10 Brake hoses and fittings

Inspection

1 Brake hose condition should be checked regularly and the hoses replaced with new ones at the specified interval (see Chapter 1).

2 Twist and flex the hoses while looking for cracks, bulges and seeping hydraulic fluid. Check extra carefully around the areas where the hoses connect with the banjo fittings, as these are common areas for hose failure.

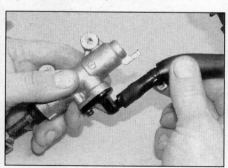

9.19 Fit the reservoir hose onto its union

9.20 Fit the master cylinder and tighten the bolts

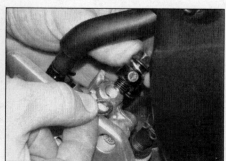

9.22 Always use new sealing washers

3 Inspect the banjo fittings connected to the brake hoses. If the fittings are rusted, scratched or cracked, fit new hoses.

Removal and installation

4 The brake hoses have banjo fittings on each end. Cover the surrounding area with plenty of rags and unscrew the banjo bolt at each end of the hose, noting the alignment of the fitting with the master cylinder or brake caliper (see illustrations 3.22, 5.5, 7.2 and 9.3). Free the hose from any clips or guides and remove it, noting its routing. Discard the sealing washers. **Note:** *Do not operate the brake lever or pedal while a brake hose is disconnected.*

5 Position the new hose, making sure it isn't twisted or otherwise strained, and ensure that it is correctly routed through any clips or guides and is clear of all moving components. Make sure the elbow locates correctly.

6 Check that the fittings align correctly, then install the banjo bolts, using new sealing washers on both sides of the fittings (see illustrations 3.22, 5.21, 7.18 and 9.22). Tighten the banjo bolts to the torque setting specified at the beginning of this Chapter.

7 Flush the old brake fluid from the system, refill with new DOT 4 brake fluid (see *Pre-ride checks*) and bleed the air from the system (see Section 11).

8 Check the operation of the brakes before riding the motorcycle.

11 Brake system bleeding and fluid change

Bleeding

1 Bleeding the brakes is simply the process of removing air from the brake fluid reservoir, master cylinder, the hose and the brake caliper. Bleeding is necessary whenever a brake system hydraulic connection is loosened, after a component or hose is replaced with a new one, or when the master cylinder or caliper is overhauled. Leaks in the system may also allow air to enter, but leaking brake fluid will reveal their presence and warn you of the need for repair.

2 To bleed the brakes, you will need some new DOT 4 brake fluid, a length of clear flexible hose, a small container partially filled with clean brake fluid, some rags, a spanner to fit the brake caliper bleed valve, and help from an assistant (see illustration). Bleeding kits that include the hose, a one-way valve and a container are available and greatly simplify the task.

3 Cover painted components to prevent damage in the event that brake fluid is spilled.

4 Refer to 'Pre-ride checks' and remove the reservoir cover, diaphragm plate and diaphragm and slowly pump the brake lever (front brake) or pedal (rear brake) a few times, until no air bubbles can be seen floating up from the holes in the bottom of the reservoir. This bleeds the air from the master cylinder end of the line. Temporarily refit the reservoir cover.

5 Pull the dust cap off the bleed valve (see illustrations). If using a ring spanner fit it onto the valve (see illustration). Attach one end of the hose to the bleed valve and, unless you're using a one-man kit, submerge the other end in the clean brake fluid in the container (see illustration 11.2).

> **HAYNES HINT** *To avoid damaging the bleed valve during the procedure, loosen it and then tighten it temporarily with a ring spanner before attaching the hose. With the hose attached, the valve can then be opened and closed either with an open-ended spanner, or by leaving the ring spanner located on the valve and fitting the hose above it.*

6 Check the fluid level in the reservoir. Do not allow the fluid level to drop below the lower mark during the procedure.

7 Carefully pump the brake lever or pedal three or four times and hold it in (front) or down (rear) while opening the bleed valve (see illustration). When the valve is opened, brake fluid will flow out of the caliper into the clear tubing, and the lever will move toward the handlebar, or the pedal will move down. If there is air in the system there will be air bubbles in the brake fluid coming out of the caliper.

8 Tighten the bleed valve, then release the brake lever or pedal gradually. Repeat the process until no air bubbles are visible in the brake fluid leaving the caliper, and the lever or pedal is firm when applied, topping the reservoir up when necessary. On completion, disconnect the hose, then tighten the bleed valve to the torque setting specified at the beginning of this Chapter and install the dust cap.

> **HAYNES HINT** *If it is not possible to produce a firm feel to the lever or pedal, the fluid may be aerated. Let the brake fluid in the system stabilise for a few hours and then repeat the procedure when the tiny bubbles in the system have settled out.*

9 Top-up the reservoir, then install the diaphragm, diaphragm plate, and cover (see *Pre-ride checks*). Wipe up any spilled brake fluid. Check the entire system for fluid leaks.

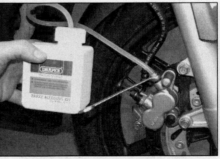

11.2 Set-up for bleeding the brakes

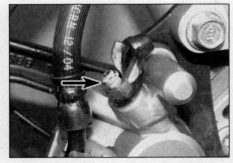

11.5a Front brake caliper bleed valve (arrowed)

11.5b Rear brake caliper bleed valve (arrowed)

11.5c Fit the ring spanner before connecting the hose

11.7 Bleeding the rear brake caliper

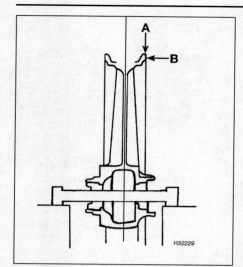

12.2 Check the wheel for radial (out-of-round) runout (A) and axial (side-to-side) runout (B)

10 Check the operation of the brakes before riding the motorcycle.

Fluid change

11 Changing the brake fluid is a similar process to bleeding the brakes and requires the same materials plus a suitable tool (such as a syringe) for siphoning the fluid out of the reservoir. Also ensure that the container is large enough to take all the old fluid when it is flushed out of the system.

12 Follow Steps 3 and 5, then remove the reservoir cap, diaphragm plate and diaphragm and siphon the old fluid out of the reservoir. Wipe the reservoir clean. Fill the reservoir with new brake fluid, then carefully pump the brake lever or pedal three or four times and hold it in (front) or down (rear) while opening the caliper bleed valve. When the valve is opened, brake fluid will flow out of the caliper into the clear tubing, and the lever will move toward the handlebar, or the pedal will move down.

13 Tighten the bleed valve, then release the brake lever or pedal gradually. Keep the reservoir topped-up with new fluid to above the LOWER level at all times or air may enter the system and greatly increase the length of the task. Repeat the process until new fluid can be seen emerging from the caliper bleed valve.

 Old brake fluid is invariably much darker in colour than new fluid, making it easy to see when all old fluid has been expelled from the system.

14 Disconnect the hose, then tighten the bleed valve to the specified torque setting and install the dust cap.

15 Top-up the reservoir, then install the

diaphragm, diaphragm plate, and cover (see *Pre-ride checks*). Wipe up any spilled brake fluid. Check the entire system for fluid leaks.

16 Check the operation of the brakes before riding the motorcycle.

Draining the system for overhaul

17 Draining the brake fluid is again a similar process to bleeding the brakes. Follow the procedure described above for changing the fluid, but quite simply do not put any new fluid into the reservoir – the system fills itself with air instead.

12 Wheel inspection and repair

1 In order to carry out a proper inspection of the wheels, it is necessary to support the bike upright so that the wheel being inspected is raised off the ground. Position the motorcycle on an auxiliary stand. Clean the wheels thoroughly to remove mud and dirt that may interfere with the inspection procedure or mask defects. Make a general check of the wheels (see Chapter 1) and tyres (see *Pre-ride checks*).

2 Attach a dial gauge to the fork or the swingarm and position its tip against the side of the wheel rim. Spin the wheel slowly and check the axial (side-to-side) runout of the rim **(see illustration)**.

3 In order to accurately check radial (out of round) runout with the dial gauge, remove the wheel from the machine, and the tyre from the wheel. With the axle clamped in a vice and the dial gauge positioned on the top of the rim, the wheel can be rotated to check the runout **(see illustration 12.2)**.

4 An easier, though slightly less accurate, method is to attach a stiff wire pointer to the fork or the swingarm and position the end a fraction of an inch from the wheel rim where the wheel and tyre join. If the wheel is true, the distance from the pointer to the rim will be constant as the wheel is rotated. **Note:** *If wheel runout is excessive, check the wheel bearings very carefully before renewing the wheel.*

5 The wheels should also be inspected for cracks, flat spots on the rim and other damage.

Look very closely for dents in the area where the tyre bead contacts the rim. Dents in this area may prevent complete sealing of the tyre against the rim, which leads to deflation of the tyre over a period of time. If damage is evident, or if runout in either direction is excessive, the wheel will have to be renewed. Never attempt to repair a damaged cast alloy wheel.

13 Wheel alignment check

1 Misalignment of the wheels due to a bent frame or forks can cause strange and possibly serious handling problems. If the frame or forks are at fault, repair by a frame specialist or renewal are the only options.

2 To check wheel alignment you will need an assistant, a length of string or a perfectly straight piece of wood and a ruler. A plumb bob or spirit level for checking that the wheels are vertical will also be required.

3 In order to make a proper check of the wheels it is necessary to support the bike in an upright position, using an auxiliary stand. First ensure that the chain adjuster markings coincide on each side of the swingarm (see Chapter 1, Section 1). Next, measure the width of both tyres at their widest points. Subtract the smaller measurement from the larger measurement, then divide the difference by two. The result is the amount of offset that should exist between the front and rear tyres on both sides of the machine.

4 If a string is used, have your assistant hold one end of it about halfway between the floor and the rear axle, with the string touching the back edge of the rear tyre sidewall.

5 Run the other end of the string forward and pull it tight so that it is roughly parallel to the floor **(see illustration)**. Slowly bring the string into contact with the front edge of the rear tyre sidewall, then turn the front wheel until it is parallel with the string. Measure the distance from the front tyre sidewall to the string.

6 Repeat the procedure on the other side of the motorcycle. The distance from the front tyre sidewall to the string should be equal on both sides.

7 As previously mentioned, a perfectly

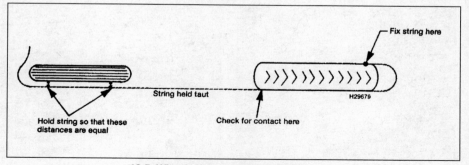

13.5 Wheel alignment check using string

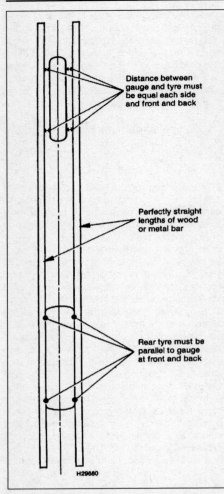

13.7 Wheel alignment check using a straight-edge

Distance between gauge and tyre must be equal each side and front and back

Perfectly straight lengths of wood or metal bar

Rear tyre must be parallel to gauge at front and back

straight length of wood or metal bar may be substituted for the string **(see illustration)**.

8 If the distance between the string and tyre is greater on one side, or if the rear wheel appears to be out of alignment, have your machine checked by a Honda dealer or frame specialist.

9 If the front-to-back alignment is correct, the wheels still may be out of alignment vertically.

14.4 **Detach the speedometer cable if required**

10 Using a plumb bob or spirit level, check the rear wheel to make sure it is vertical. To do this, hold the string of the plumb bob against the tyre upper sidewall and allow the weight to settle just off the floor. If the string touches both the upper and lower tyre sidewalls and is perfectly straight, the wheel is vertical. If it is not, adjust the stand until it is.

11 Once the rear wheel is vertical, check the front wheel in the same manner. If both wheels are not perfectly vertical, the frame and/or major suspension components are bent.

14 Front wheel

Removal

1 Position the motorcycle on an auxiliary stand so that the front wheel is off the ground. Always make sure the motorcycle is properly supported. If a support is being placed under the engine, remove the lower fairing (see Chapter 8).

2 Displace the front brake caliper (see Section 3). Support the caliper with a cable-tie or a bungee cord so that no strain is placed on the hydraulic hose. There is no need to disconnect the hose from the caliper. **Note:** *Do not operate the front brake lever with the caliper removed.*

3 If required, remove the front mudguard (see Chapter 8).

4 If required push in the tab securing the

14.5 **Unscrew the axle nut . . .**

speedometer cable in the drive housing and draw the cable out **(see illustration)**. Alternatively leave the cable connected and displace the drive housing from the wheel as it is removed.

5 Unscrew the nut from the left-hand end of the axle **(see illustration)**.

6 Take the weight of the wheel, then withdraw the axle from the right-hand side **(see illustration)**. Carefully lower the wheel and draw it forwards.

7 Remove the spacer from the right-hand side of the wheel and the speedometer drive housing from the left-hand side, noting how it fits **(see illustrations)**. Clean all old grease off the spacer, drive housing, axle and bearing seals.

Caution: Don't lay the wheel down and allow it to rest on the disc – it could become warped. Set the wheel on wood blocks so the disc doesn't support the weight of the wheel.

8 Check the axle is straight by rolling it on a flat surface such as a piece of plate glass (first remove any corrosion using wire wool). If the equipment is available, place the axle in V-blocks and measure the runout using a dial gauge. If the axle is bent or the runout exceeds the limit specified, replace it with a new one.

9 Check the condition of the grease seals and wheel bearings (see Section 16).

Installation

10 Make sure the gear and washer behind it are correctly located in the speedometer drive

14.6 **. . . then withdraw the axle and remove the wheel**

14.7a **Remove the spacer . . .**

14.7b **. . . and the drive housing**

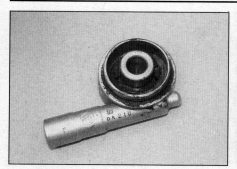

14.10 Check and lubricate the drive housing

14.11 Locate the tabs (arrowed) in the cut-outs

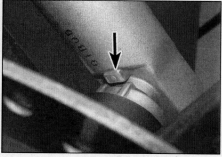

14.13 Locate the lug (arrowed) between the raised tabs

14.14 Tighten the axle nut to the specified torque

14.16 Push the cable into the housing so the tab locates

16 If detached, make sure the O-ring on the end of the speedometer cable is fitted and smear it with grease. Push the inner cable up and make sure it is engaged in the speedometer. Push the cable into the drive housing, making sure the inner cable locates in the shaft, setting the retaining tab in the cut-out **(see illustration)**.

17 Apply the front brake a few times to bring the pads back into contact with the disc.

18 Check for correct operation of the front brake before riding the motorcycle.

15 Rear wheel

housing **(see illustration)**. Make sure the flat tabs on the speedometer drive plate are correctly located in the cut-outs in the wheel hub **(see illustration 16.10a)**.

11 Apply a smear of grease to the inside of the wheel spacer and to the speedometer drive housing, and also to the outside where they fit into the wheel. Fit the spacer into the right-hand side of the wheel **(see illustration 14.7a)**. Fit the drive housing into the left-hand side, locating the raised tabs on the drive plate in the cut-outs in the housing **(see illustration)**.

12 Manoeuvre the wheel into position between the forks, making sure the brake disc is on the right-hand side. Apply a thin coat of grease to the axle.

13 Lift the wheel into place, making sure the spacer and speedometer drive housing remain in position, and that the lug on the bottom of the left-hand fork locates between the raised tabs on the top of the speedometer drive housing **(see illustration)**. Slide the axle in from the right-hand side **(see illustration 14.6)**.

14 Fit the axle nut and tighten it to the torque setting specified at the beginning of the Chapter **(see illustration)**. Counter-hold the axle head if necessary.

15 Lower the front wheel to the ground, then install the brake caliper (see Section 3). If removed, install the front mudguard (see Chapter 8).

Removal

1 Position the motorcycle on an auxiliary stand so that the rear wheel is off the ground. Always make sure the motorcycle is properly supported. Create some slack in the chain (see Chapter 1, Section 1).

2 Unscrew the axle nut and remove the washer **(see illustration)**.

3 Take the weight of the wheel, then withdraw the axle from the left-hand side and lower the wheel to the ground **(see illustration)**. If the axle is difficult to withdraw, drive it through with a drift, making sure you don't damage the threads.

15.2 Unscrew the axle nut and remove the washer

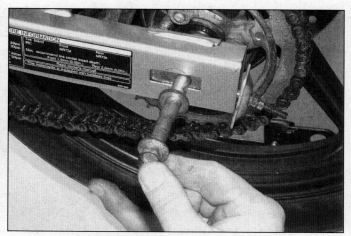

15.3 Withdraw the axle and lower the wheel

15.4a Remove the chain adjusters . . .

15.4b . . . then disengage the chain and draw the wheel out

15.6a Remove the large spacer from the left-hand side . . .

4 Remove the chain adjuster from each end of the swingarm **(see illustration)**. Disengage the chain from the sprocket and remove the wheel from the swingarm **(see illustration)**. *Caution: Do not lay the wheel down and allow it to rest on the disc or the sprocket – they could become warped. Set the wheel on wood blocks so the disc or the sprocket doesn't support the weight of the wheel. Do not operate the brake pedal with the wheel removed.*

5 With the wheel removed take care not to dislodge the rear brake caliper assembly from the swingarm. If required undo the screw securing the rear brake hose guide to the swingarm, then displace the bracket, noting how it locates, and tie it to the passenger footrest bracket, making sure no strain is placed on the hose **(see illustrations 7.3 and 7.4)**. Retrieve the rubber damper from the lug for safekeeping.

6 Remove the spacer from each side of the wheel **(see illustrations)**. Clean all old grease of the spacers, axle and seals.

7 Check the axle is straight by rolling it on a flat surface such as a piece of plate glass (if the axle is corroded, first remove any corrosion with wire wool). If the equipment is available, place the axle in V-blocks and check the runout using a dial gauge. If the axle is bent or the runout exceeds the limit specified at the beginning of the Chapter, replace it with a new one.

8 Check the condition of the grease seals and wheel bearings (see Section 16).

Installation

9 Apply a smear of grease to the inside of the wheel spacers, and also to the outside where they fit into the wheel. Fit the large spacer into the left-hand side of the wheel and the small one into the right. Apply a thin coat of grease to the axle.

10 If removed fit the rubber damper for the caliper bracket onto the lug on the swingarm, then locate the brake caliper assembly **(see illustration 7.4)**. Fit the rear brake hose guide onto the swingarm **(see illustration 7.3)**.

11 Manoeuvre the wheel into position between the ends of the swingarm with the sprocket to the left, making sure the disc locates between the brake pads **(see illustration)**. Engage the drive chain with the sprocket **(see illustration 15.4b)**. Slide the chain adjusters into the ends of the swingarm **(see illustration 15.4a)**.

12 Lift the wheel into position and slide the axle in from the left **(see illustration 15.3)**, making sure it passes through the chain adjusters, and the spacers and caliper bracket remain correctly installed. Check that everything is correctly aligned, then fit the washer and axle nut but leave it loose **(see illustration 15.2)**.

13 Position the machine on its sidestand, then check and adjust the drive chain slack (see Chapter 1). On completion tighten the axle nut to the torque setting specified at the beginning of the Chapter.

14 Operate the brake pedal several times to bring the pads into contact with the disc. Check the operation of the rear brake before riding the bike.

16 Wheel bearings

Caution: Don't lay the wheel down and allow it to rest on the disc – it could become warped. Set the wheel on wood blocks so the wheel rim supports the weight of the wheel, or keep the wheel upright. Don't operate the brake lever/pedal with the wheel removed.

Note: *Always renew the wheel bearings in pairs, never individually. Never reuse bearings once they have been disturbed – removal will destroy them.*

Front wheel bearings

1 Remove the wheel (see Section 14).

2 Lever out the bearing seal from each side of the hub using a flat-bladed screwdriver or a seal hook **(see illustration)**. Take care not to damage the hub. Discard the seals as new ones must be fitted on reassembly. Remove the speedometer drive plate from the left-hand side, noting how it locates **(see illustration 16.10a)**.

3 Inspect the bearings – check that the inner race turns smoothly, quietly and freely and that the outer race is a tight fit in the hub.

4 If the bearings are worn, remove them using a metal rod (preferably a brass punch) inserted through the centre of the opposite bearing and locating it on the inner race, pushing the bearing spacer aside to expose it **(see illustration)**.

15.6b . . . and the small spacer from the right side

15.11 Make sure the disc sits between the pads

16.2 Lever out the bearing seals

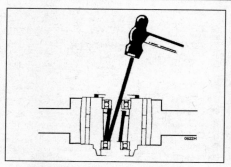

16.4a Locate the drift as shown . . .

16.4b . . . and drive the bearing out

16.7 Using a socket to drive the bearing in

16.10a Fit the drive plate locating the tabs in the cut-outs . . .

16.10b . . . then press the seal into place

16.12 Lift the sprocket coupling off the wheel

Curve the end of the drift to obtain better purchase if necessary. Strike the drift with a hammer, working evenly around the bearing, to drive it from the hub **(see illustration)**. Remove the spacer which fits between the bearings.

5 Turn the wheel over and remove the other bearing using the same procedure.

6 Thoroughly clean the hub area of the wheel with a suitable solvent and inspect the bearing seats for scoring and wear. If the seats are damaged, consult a Honda dealer before reassembling the wheel.

7 The new bearings can be installed in the hub using a drawbolt arrangement or by using a bearing driver or suitable socket **(see illustration)**. Ensure that the drawbolt washer or driver (as applicable) bears only on the bearing's outer race, not the balls, and does not contact the bearing housing walls.

8 Install the **new** right-hand bearing first, with the

marked side facing outwards. Ensure the bearing is fitted squarely and all the way into its seat.

9 Turn the wheel over then install the bearing spacer and the other **new** bearing, driving it in until it contacts the spacer.

10 Fit the speedometer drive plate into the left-hand side, locating the flat tabs in the cut-outs in the hub **(see illustration)**. Apply a smear of grease to the new seals, then press them into the hub **(see illustration)**. Level the seals with the rim of the hub with a small block of wood **(see illustration 16.21b)**.

11 Clean the brake disc using acetone or brake system cleaner, then install the front wheel (see Section 14).

Rear wheel bearings

12 Remove the wheel (see Section 15) and lift the sprocket coupling out of the hub, noting the spacer inside it **(see illustration)**.

13 Lever out the bearing seal from the right-hand side of the hub using a flat-bladed screwdriver or a seal hook **(see illustration)**. Take care not to damage the hub. Discard the seal as a new one should be fitted on reassembly.

14 Inspect the bearings in both sides of the hub – check that the inner race turns smoothly, quietly and freely and that the outer race is a tight fit in the hub.

15 If the bearings are worn, remove them using an internal expanding puller with slide-hammer attachment, which can be obtained commercially **(see illustrations)**. Draw the bearing out on one side, then remove the spacer which fits between the bearings.

16 Turn the wheel over and remove the remaining bearing using the same procedure.

17 Thoroughly clean the hub area of the wheel with a suitable solvent and inspect the bearing seats for scoring and wear. If the

16.13 Lever out the bearing seal

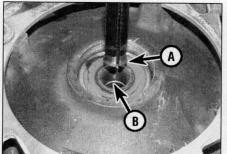

16.15a Locate the knife edges (A) under the lower edge of the bearing (B) and tighten the tool so they expand into the groove . . .

16.15b . . . and pull the bearing out

16.18 Using a socket to drive the bearing in

16.21a Press the seal into place . . .

16.21b . . . and set it flush as shown

seats are damaged, consult a Honda dealer before reassembling the wheel.

18 The new bearings can be installed in the hub using a drawbolt arrangement or by using a bearing driver or suitable socket **(see illustration)**. Ensure that the drawbolt washer or driver (as applicable) bears only on the bearing's outer race and does not contact the balls or score the bearing housing walls.

19 Install the **new** right-hand bearing first, with the marked or sealed side facing outwards. Ensure the bearing is fitted squarely and all the way into its seat.

20 Turn the wheel over then install the bearing spacer and the other **new** bearing.

21 Apply a smear of grease to the new seal, then press it into the right-hand side of the hub **(see illustration)**. Level the seal with the rim of the hub with a small block of wood **(see illustration)**.

22 Check the sprocket coupling/rubber

dampers (see Section 20). Check the condition of the hub O-ring and clean it or replace it with a new one if necessary **(see illustration)**. Smear the O-ring with oil. Fit the sprocket coupling into the wheel, making sure the spacer is fitted **(see illustration 16.12)**. Clean the brake disc using acetone or brake system cleaner, then install the rear wheel (see Section 15).

Sprocket coupling bearing

23 Remove the rear wheel (see Section 15) and lift the sprocket coupling out of the hub **(see illustration 16.12)**.

24 Remove the spacer from inside the coupling **(see illustration)**.

25 Lever out the bearing seal on the outside of the coupling using a flat-bladed screwdriver or a seal hook **(see illustration)**. Take care not to damage the rim of the coupling. Discard the seal as a new one should be fitted on reassembly.

26 Inspect the bearing – check that the inner races turn smoothly, quietly and freely, and that the outer race is a tight fit in the coupling.

27 Support the coupling on blocks of wood, sprocket side down, and drive the bearing out from the inside using a bearing driver or socket **(see illustration)**.

28 Thoroughly clean the bearing seat with a suitable solvent and inspect it for scoring and wear. If the seat is damaged, consult a Honda dealer before reassembling the wheel.

29 Use a bearing driver or suitable socket to install the **new** bearing **(see illustration)**. Ensure that the driver bears only on the bearing's outer race and does not contact the balls or bearing housing walls. Ensure the bearing is fitted squarely and all the way onto the seat.

30 Apply a smear of grease to the new seal, then press it into the coupling, using a bearing driver or suitable socket **(see illustration)**.

16.22 Fit a new O-ring if necessary

16.24 Remove the spacer from inside the coupling

16.25 Lever out the bearing seal

16.27 Drive the bearing out from the inside

16.29 Using a socket to drive the bearing in

16.30 Fit the grease seal and press or tap it into place

Level the seal with the rim of the coupling with a small block of wood **(see illustration 16.21b)**.

31 Fit the spacer **(see illustration 16.24)**.

32 Check the sprocket coupling/rubber dampers (see Section 20). Check the condition of the hub O-ring and clean it or replace it with a new one if necessary. Smear the O-ring with oil. Fit the sprocket coupling into the wheel and install the rear wheel (see Section 15).

17 Tyres

General information

1 The wheels are designed to take tubeless tyres only. Tyre sizes are given in the Specifications at the beginning of this Chapter and are also stated on the tyre information label stuck to the swingarm.

2 Refer to the *Pre-ride checks* listed at the beginning of this manual for tyre maintenance.

Fitting new tyres

3 When selecting new tyres, refer to the tyre information in the Owner's Handbook. Ensure that front and rear tyre types are compatible, the correct size and correct speed rating; if necessary seek advice from a Honda dealer or tyre fitting specialist **(see illustration)**.

4 It is recommended that tyres are fitted by a motorcycle tyre specialist rather than attempted in the home workshop. This is particularly relevant in the case of tubeless tyres because the force required to break the seal between the wheel rim and tyre bead is substantial, and is usually beyond the capabilities of an individual working with normal tyre levers. Additionally, the specialist will be able to balance the wheels after tyre fitting and renew the tyre valve.

5 Note that punctured tubeless tyres can in some cases be repaired. Repairs must be carried out by a motorcycle tyre fitting specialist. Honda advise that a repaired tyre should not be used at speeds above 50 mph (80 kmh) for the first 24 hours, and not above 75 mph (120 kmh) thereafter.

18 Drive chain

Cleaning

1 Refer to Chapter 1, Section 1, for details of routine cleaning with the chain installed on the sprockets.

2 If the chain is extremely dirty remove it from the motorcycle and soak it in paraffin (kerosene) for approximately five or six minutes, then clean it using a soft brush. *Caution: Don't use gasoline (petrol), solvent or other cleaning fluids which might damage its internal sealing properties. Don't use high-pressure water. Remove the chain, wipe it off, then blow dry it with compressed air immediately. The entire process shouldn't take longer than ten minutes – if it does, the O-rings in the chain rollers could be damaged.*

Removal and installation

3 Remove the front sprocket cover (see Section 19).

4 Remove the swingarm (see Chapter 6).

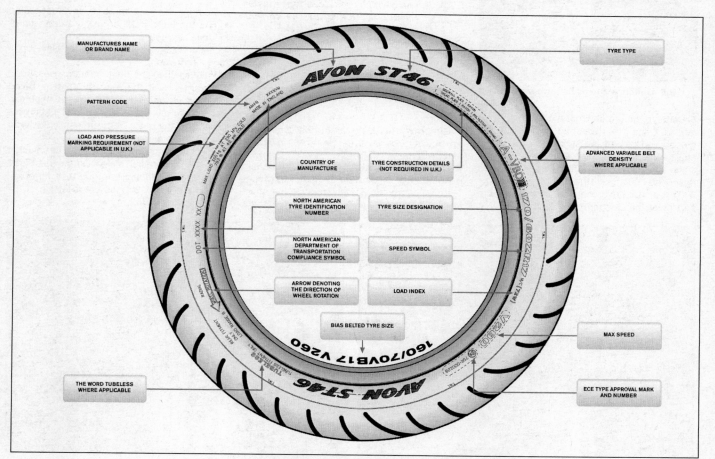

17.3 Common tyre sidewall markings

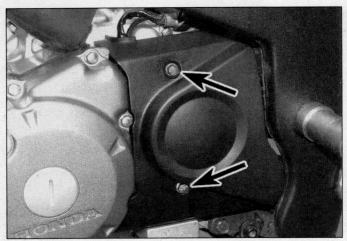

19.1a Unscrew the bolts (arrowed) . . .

19.1b . . . and remove the cover

19.5 Unscrew the bolts (arrowed) . . .

5 Remove the old chain. If the chain is to be reused, clean it as described and wipe all old grease and dirt off the sprockets, swingarm chain slider and front sprocket housing. If the chain is to be renewed, fit new sprockets as described in Section 19.

6 Fit the new drive chain over the swingarm and install the swingarm (see Chapter 6).

7 Install the front sprocket cover (see Section 19).

8 On completion, adjust and lubricate the chain following the procedures described in Chapter 1, Section 1.

> ⚠ **Warning: NEVER install a drive chain which uses a clip-type master (split) link. Use ONLY the correct specification endless chain.**

19 Sprockets

Check

1 Unscrew the bolts securing the front sprocket cover and remove it **(see illustrations)**.

2 Check the wear pattern on both sprockets (see Chapter 1, Section 1). If the sprocket teeth are worn excessively, replace the chain and both sprockets as a set – worn sprockets can ruin a new drive chain and vice versa.

3 Adjust and lubricate the chain following the procedures described in Chapter 1.

Removal and installation

Front sprocket

4 Remove the front sprocket cover (see Step 1). Tie the front brake on using a cable-tie or suitable alternative.

5 Unscrew the sprocket retainer plate bolts **(see illustration)**.

6 Fully slacken the drive chain as described in Chapter 1. If the rear sprocket is being removed as well, remove the rear wheel now to create full slack (see Section 15). Otherwise disengage the chain from the rear sprocket if required to provide more slack.

7 Turn the sprocket retainer plate to unlock it from the splines then slide it off the shaft **(see illustration)**. Slide the chain and sprocket off the shaft then slip the sprocket out of the chain **(see illustration)**.

19.7a . . . and remove the retainer plate as described

19.7b Draw the sprocket off the shaft and disengage the chain

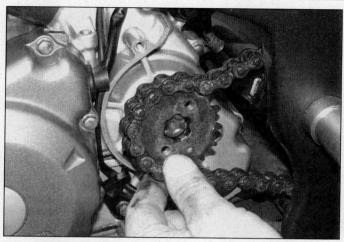

19.8 Fit the sprocket into the chain and onto the shaft

19.10 Tighten the bolts to the specified torque

8 Engage the new sprocket with the chain, making sure the marked side is facing out, and slide it on the shaft **(see illustration)**. Fit the retainer plate, then turn it in the groove so it is locked in the splines **(see illustration 19.7a)**.

9 If the rear wheel was removed, change the sprocket now and install the wheel (see Section 15). If the chain was merely disengaged, fit it back onto the rear sprocket. Take up the slack in the chain.

10 Install the front sprocket retainer plate bolts and tighten them to the torque setting specified at the beginning of the Chapter **(see illustration)**.

11 Fit the sprocket cover (see Step 1). Adjust and lubricate the chain following the procedures described in Chapter 1.

Rear sprocket

12 Remove the rear wheel (see Section 15).

13 Unscrew the nuts securing the sprocket to the hub assembly. Remove the sprocket, noting which way round it fits. Check the condition of the sprocket studs and replace them all with new ones if any are damaged. Make sure they are tight.

14 Fit the sprocket onto the hub with the stamped mark facing out. Install the nuts and tighten them evenly and in a criss-cross sequence to the torque setting specified at the beginning of the Chapter.

15 Install the rear wheel (see Section 15).

20 Rear sprocket coupling/ rubber dampers

1 Remove the rear wheel (see Section 15). Grasp the sprocket and feel for play between the sprocket coupling and the wheel hub by attempting to twist the sprocket in each direction. Any play indicates worn rubber damper segments.

Caution: Do not lay the wheel down on the disc as it could become warped. Lay the wheel on wooden blocks so that the disc is off the ground.

2 Lift the sprocket coupling away from the wheel leaving the rubber dampers in position **(see illustration 16.12)**. Note the spacer inside the coupling and remove it if it is likely to drop out **(see illustration 16.24)**. Check the coupling for cracks or any obvious signs of damage.

3 Lift the rubber damper segments from the wheel and check them for cracks, hardening and general deterioration **(see illustration)**. Renew them as a set if necessary.

4 Check the condition of the hub O-ring – if it is damaged, deformed or deteriorated replace it with a new one and smear it with oil **(see illustration 16.22)**. Otherwise clean it and smear it with oil.

5 Checking and replacement procedures for the sprocket coupling bearing are in Section 16.

6 Installation is the reverse of removal. Make sure the spacer is still correctly installed in the coupling, or install it if it was removed **(see illustration 16.24)**.

7 Install the rear wheel (see Section 15).

20.3 Check the rubber dampers as described

Notes

Chapter 8
Bodywork

Contents

Degrees of difficulty

Easy, suitable for novice with little experience	**Fairly easy,** suitable for beginner with some experience	**Fairly difficult,** suitable for competent DIY mechanic	**Difficult,** suitable for experienced DIY mechanic	**Very difficult,** suitable for expert DIY or professional

1 General information

This Chapter covers the procedures necessary to remove and install the bodywork. Since many service and repair operations on these motorcycles require the removal of the body panels, the procedures are grouped here and referred to from other Chapters.

In the case of damage to the bodywork, it is usually necessary to remove the broken component and replace it with a new (or used) one. The material that the body panels are composed of doesn't lend itself to conventional repair techniques. Note that there are however some companies that specialize in 'plastic welding' and there are a number of DIY bodywork repair kits now available for motorcycles.

When attempting to remove any body panel, first study it closely, noting any fasteners and associated fittings, to be sure of returning everything to its correct place on installation. In some cases the aid of an assistant will be required when removing panels, to help avoid the risk of damage to paintwork. Once the evident fasteners have been removed, try to withdraw the panel as described but DO NOT FORCE IT – if it will not release, check that all fasteners have been removed and try again.

When installing a body panel, first study it closely, noting any fasteners and associated fittings removed with it, to be sure of returning everything to its correct place. Check that all fasteners are in good condition, including the rubber mounts; replace any faulty fasteners with new ones before the panel is reassembled. Check also that all mounting brackets are straight and repair them or replace them with new ones if necessary before attempting to install the panel.

Tighten the fasteners securely, but be careful not to overtighten any of them or the panel may break (not always immediately) due to the uneven stress.

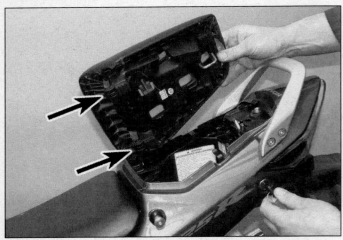

2.1 Unlock and remove the seat – note how the tabs (arrowed) locate

2.3a Unscrew the bolt (arrowed) . . .

2 Seats

Passenger seat

1 Insert the ignition key into the seat lock (located on the left-hand side of the seat cowling) and turn it clockwise to unlock the seat **(see illustration)**. Lift the back of the seat and draw it back to disengage the tabs.
2 On installation, make sure the two tabs at the front of the seat and the lock bar at the rear locate correctly, then push down on the back of the seat to engage the latch.

Rider's seat

3 Remove the passenger seat. Unscrew the bolt securing the back of the seat (see

illustration). Note the collar fitted in the rubber grommet. Draw the seat back and up to remove it, noting how it locates **(see illustration)**.
4 Remove the collar from the mount and check the condition of the grommet, and replace it with a new one if necessary.
5 On installation, make sure the grommet and collar are correctly fitted in the seat mount, and that the hooks on the underside of the seat locate correctly.

3 Seat cowling

1 Remove both seats (see Section 2).
2 Unscrew the four passenger grab-rail bolts and remove the grab-rail **(see illustration)**.

2.3b . . . then remove the seat, noting how its hooks (arrowed) locate

3 Undo the screw at the front on each side and the bungee hook in the middle on each side **(see illustration)**.

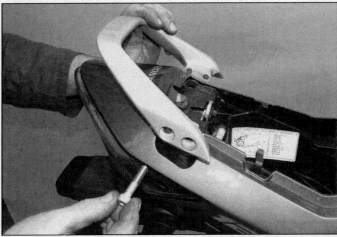

3.2 Unscrew the four bolts and remove the grab-rail

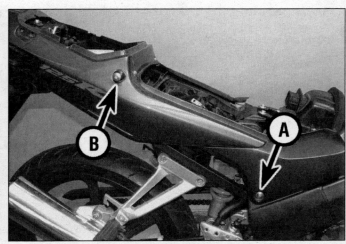

3.3 Undo the screw (A) and bungee hook (B) on each side

3.4 Remove the mid-section

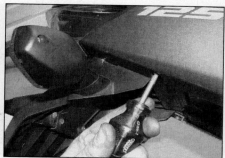

3.5 Undo the screw on each side

3.6 Release the peg on each side from the fuel tank . . .

4 Undo the two screws securing the mid-section and remove it **(see illustration)**.
5 Undo the screw at the rear on each underside **(see illustration)**.
6 Carefully pull the front away from the fuel tank on each side to release the peg from the grommet **(see illustration)**.
7 Carefully remove the cowling by pulling the sides away and drawing it back and off the bike **(see illustration)**.

8 Installation is the reverse of removal. Tighten the passenger grab-rail bolts to 27 Nm.

4 Mirrors

1 Lift the rubber boot off the mirror base **(see illustration)**.

2 Counter-hold the hex on the mirror base and slacken the locknut, noting that it has a left-hand thread and so must be turned clockwise to slacken it **(see illustration)**. Now unscrew the mirror stem from the base, again turning it clockwise and remove the mirror **(see illustration)**.
3 If required unscrew the base from the master cylinder or clutch lever bracket, according to side.

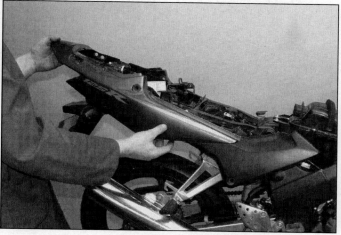

3.7 . . . and remove the cowling as described

4.1 Lift the boot to expose the nuts

4.2a Counter-hold the base and slacken the locknut . . .

4.2b . . . then unscrew the stem and remove the mirror

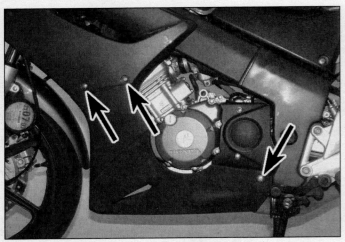

6.1a Undo the screws (arrowed) on each side . . .

6.1b . . . and remove the lower fairing

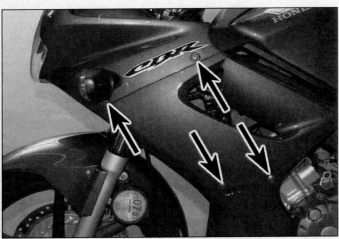

6.3 Undo the screws (arrowed) . . .

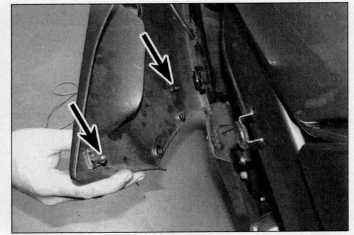

6.4a . . . then release the pegs (arrowed) and remove the panel . . .

4 Installation is the reverse of removal. Set the position of the mirror as required, then tighten the locknut to secure it.

5 Fuel tank cover

1 Undo the two screws and detach the front cover from the fuel tank.
2 Installation is the reverse of removal.

6 Fairing panels

Lower fairing

1 Undo the three screws on each side, then manoeuvre the lower fairing out from under the bike **(see illustrations)**. If required, the three elements of the lower fairing can be separated by removing the three screws.

2 Installation is the reverse of removal. Make sure the lower fairing engages correctly with the fairing side panels.

Fairing side panels
R-4, R-5 and RW-6 models

3 Undo the four screws securing the fairing side panel to the fairing and lower fairing **(see illustration)**.

6.4b . . . noting how it engages with the fairing

4 Carefully pull the panel away to release the pegs from the grommets on the radiator and frame **(see illustration)**. Note how the slot in the top of the side panel engages with the tab on the fairing **(see illustration)**.
5 When removing the left-hand panel free the speedometer cable from its guides on the inside **(see illustration)**.
6 Installation is the reverse of removal.

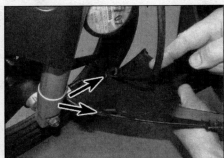

6.5 Free the cable from its guides (arrowed) on the left-hand panel

6.8a Undo the screws at the top edge (arrowed) . . .

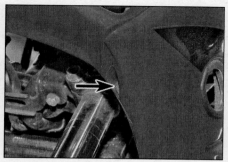

6.8b . . . the screw (arrowed) at the front edge . . .

6.8c . . . pull the rear edge outwards to release the lug from the grommet . . .

6.8d . . . and unclip the front edge

6.10a Undo the screws (arrowed) . . .

6.10b . . . and remove the panel

RW-7, RW-8, RW-9 and RW-A models

7 Remove the lower fairing and cockpit trim as described in this Section, then remove the relevant front turn signal as described in Chapter 9.

8 Undo the screws, pull the lugs at the rear edge from the rubber grommets, and unclip the front edge of the panel **(see illustrations)**.

9 Installation is the reversal of removal.

Cockpit trim panels

R-4, R-5 and RW-6 models

10 Undo the two screws securing the panel and remove it, noting how it locates **(see illustrations)**. Note the washers with the windshield screw.

11 Installation is the reverse of removal.

RW-7, RW-8, RW-9 and RW-A models

12 Undo the four screws securing the panel, and manoeuvre it from place **(see illustrations)**.

13 Installation is the reversal of removal.

Fairing

R-4, R-5 and RW-6 models

14 Remove the fairing side panels (see Steps 3 to 5).

15 Remove the cockpit trim panels (see Step 7).

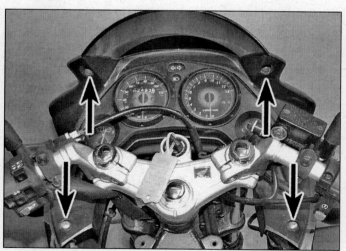

6.12a Undo the screws (arrowed) . . .

6.12b . . . and manoeuvre the cockpit trim panel from place

6.16a Pull back the boot to expose the wiring connectors

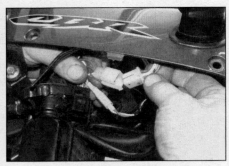

6.16b Disconnect the headlight wiring connector

6.18a Unscrew the bolt (arrowed) on each side . . .

6.18b . . . and the two at the front . . .

6.19 . . . and remove the fairing, noting how it locates

6.20 Undo the screw (arrowed) on each side to free the panel

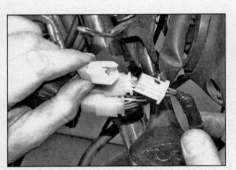

6.24 Disconnect the headlight/sidelight wiring plug

16 Release the rubber boot and wiring from the two ties on the right-hand inner side of the fairing **(see illustration)**. Pull the boot back and disconnect the headlight wiring connector **(see illustration)**.

17 Remove the front turn signals (see Chapter 9).

18 Unscrew the bolt on each side at the back and the two under the windshield **(see illustrations)**.

19 Carefully lift the fairing off its mounts and draw it forwards **(see illustration)**. Note how the pegs locate in the grommets in the stay as the fairing is removed.

20 If required undo the two screws and remove the trim section from the underside of the fairing at the front, noting how its tabs locate **(see illustration)**.

21 If required remove the headlight assembly (see Chapter 9).

22 Installation is the reverse of removal.

RW-7, RW-8, RW-9 and RW-A models

23 Remove the fairing side panels and cockpit trim as described in this Section.

24 Disconnect the headlight/sidelight wiring plug **(see illustration)**.

25 Undo the two retaining bolts and manoeuvre the fairing from position **(see illustrations)**.

6.25a Remove the bolts (arrowed) . . .

6.25b . . . and remove the fairing

26 If required, remove the headlight assembly (see Chapter 9).
27 Installation is the reversal of removal.

7 Front mudguard

1 Unscrew the two bolts on each side of the mudguard, noting how the rear bolt on the right-hand side also secures the brake hose **(see illustration)**.
2 Draw the mudguard up and then forwards, noting how it fits, and remove it **(see illustration)**. Note the brace on the underside as it could drop out **(see illustration)**. Also note the collar fitted in each bolt hole in the mudguard – they should stay in place, but take care not to lose them.
3 Installation is the reverse of removal. It is advisable to locate the brace by itself between the forks, then fit the mudguard onto the brace **(see illustration)**.

8 Windshield

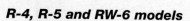

R-4, R-5 and RW-6 models

1 Remove the fairing (Section 6).
2 Undo the two remaining outer screws securing the windshield, noting the washers **(see illustration)**. Undo the centre screw at

7.1 Unscrew the bolts on each side (arrowed) . . .

7.2a . . . and remove the mudguard

7.2b Remove the brace (arrowed)

7.3 Fit the brace between the forks first, then fit the mudguard

the bottom on the inside of the fairing **(see illustration)**.
3 Carefully remove the windshield, noting how it engages with the fairing. Note the rubber-bodied wellnuts for the lower outer screws – they are a push-fit into in the windshield.
4 Installation is the reverse of removal.

RW-7, RW-8, RW-9 and RW-A models

5 Remove the cockpit trim as described in Section 6.
6 Undo the two screws and remove the windshield **(see illustration)**.
7 Refitting is a reversal of removal.

8.2a Undo the screw (arrowed) on each side . . .

8.2b . . . and the screw (arrowed) on the inside

8.6 Windshield retaining screws (arrowed)

Chapter 9
Electrical system

Contents

Degrees of difficulty

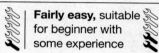

Easy, suitable for novice with little experience	**Fairly easy,** suitable for beginner with some experience	**Fairly difficult,** suitable for competent DIY mechanic	**Difficult,** suitable for experienced DIY mechanic	**Very difficult,** suitable for expert DIY or professional

Specifications

Battery
Capacity
R-4, R-5 and RW-6 models	12V, 5 Ah
RW-7, RW-8, RW-9 and RW-A models	12V, 6 Ah

Voltage
Fully-charged	13.0 to 13.2 V
Uncharged	below 12.3 V

Charging rate
Normal	0.5 A for 5 to 10 hrs
Quick	2.5 A for 1 hr

Charging system
Current leakage	0.1 mA (max)
Alternator stator coil resistance	0.2 to 0.6 ohms

Alternator output
R-4, R-5 and RW-6 models	230 W @ 5000 rpm
RW-7, RW-8, RW-9 and RW-A models	290 W @ 5000 rpm
Regulated voltage output.	14.0 to 15.5 V @ 5000 rpm

Starter motor
Brush length
Standard.	10 to 10.5 mm
Service limit (min)	3.5 mm

Fuses
Main fuse	30 A

Circuit fuses:
R-4, R-5 and RW-6 models	10 A x 3
RW-7, RW-8, RW-9 and RW-A models	10 A x 4

Bulbs

Headlight
   R-4, R-5 and RW-6 model . . . . 35/35W x 2
   RW-7, RW-8, RW-9 and RW-A models . . . . 55 W x 2
Sidelight . . . . 5 W
Brake/tail light . . . . 21/5 W
Licence plate light . . . . 5 W
Turn signal lights. . . . . 21 W x 4 (amber from RW-7 onward)
Instrument lights and warning lights . . . . 1.7 W x 7
Fl warning light – RW-7, RW-8, RW-9 and RW-A models . . . . LED

Torque settings

Alternator rotor bolt . . . . 64 Nm
Alternator stator and pick-up coil bolts . . . . 10 Nm
Footrest bracket mounting bolts . . . . 27 Nm

1 General information

All models have a 12 volt electrical system charged by a three-phase alternator with a separate regulator/rectifier.

The regulator maintains the charging system output within the specified range to prevent overcharging, and the rectifier converts the ac (alternating current) output of the alternator to dc (direct current) to power the lights and other components and to charge the battery. The alternator rotor is mounted on the left-hand end of the crankshaft.

The starter motor is mounted on the front of the crankcase. The starting system includes the motor, the battery, the relay and the various wires and switches. Some of the switches are part of a starter interlock system which prevents the engine from being started if the sidestand is down and the engine is in gear. The engine can be started with the sidestand up when it is in gear as long as the clutch lever is pulled in. The system will also cut the engine should the sidestand extend while the engine is running and in gear – see Chapter 1 for further information and checks on the system.

Note: *Keep in mind that electrical parts, once purchased, often cannot be returned. To avoid unnecessary expense, make very sure the faulty component has been positively identified before buying a replacement part.*

2 Electrical system fault finding

1 A typical electrical circuit consists of an electrical component, the switches, relays, etc, related to that component and the wiring and connectors that link the component to the battery and the frame.

2 Before tackling any troublesome electrical circuit, first study the wiring diagram thoroughly to get a complete picture of what makes up that individual circuit. Trouble spots, for instance, can often be narrowed down by noting if other components related to that circuit are operating properly or not. If several components or circuits fail at one time, chances are the fault lies either in the fuse or in the common earth (ground) connection, as several circuits are often routed through the same fuse and earth (ground) connections.

3 Electrical problems often stem from simple causes, such as loose or corroded connections or a blown fuse. Prior to any electrical fault finding, always visually check the condition of the fuse, wires and connections in the problem circuit. Intermittent failures can be especially frustrating, since you can't always duplicate the failure when it's convenient to test. In such situations, a good practice is to clean all connections in the affected circuit, whether or not they appear to be good. All of the connections and wires should also be wiggled to check for looseness which can cause intermittent failure.

4 A multimeter will enable a full range of electrical tests to be made, although a continuity tester or test light are also useful for certain electrical checks **(see illustrations)**.

Continuity checks

5 The term continuity describes the uninterrupted flow of electricity through an electrical circuit. Continuity can be checked with a multimeter set to the ohms (Ω) function or a dedicated continuity tester. Both instruments are powered by an internal battery, therefore the checks are made with the ignition OFF. As a safety precaution, always disconnect the battery negative (-) lead before making continuity checks, particularly if ignition switch checks are being made.

6 If using a multimeter, select the appropriate ohms scale. On analogue meters touch the meter probes together and check that meter reads zero; where necessary adjust the meter so that it reads zero. After using the meter, always switch it OFF to conserve its battery.

Switch continuity checks

7 If a switch is at fault, trace its wiring up to the wiring connectors. Separate the wire connectors and inspect them for security and condition. A build-up of dirt or corrosion here will most likely be the cause of the problem – clean up and apply a water dispersant such as WD40.

8 If using a test meter, set the meter to the

2.4a Digital multimeter

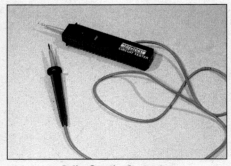
2.4b Continuity tester

2.4c Test light

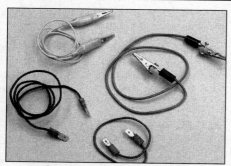

2.21 A selection of jumper wires

ohms x 10 scale and connect its probes across the wires from the switch. Simple ON/OFF type switches, such as brake light switches, only have two wires whereas combination switches, like the ignition switch, have many internal links. Study the wiring diagram to ensure that you are connecting across the correct pair of wires. Continuity should be indicated with the switch ON and no continuity with it OFF.

9 Note that the polarity of the test probes doesn't matter for continuity checks, although care should be taken to follow specific test procedures if a diode or solid-state component is being checked. A continuity tester can be used in the same way. The light should come on to indicate continuity in the ON switch position, but should extinguish in the OFF position.

Wiring continuity checks

10 Many electrical faults are caused by damaged wiring, often due to incorrect routing or chaffing on frame components. Loose, wet or corroded wire connectors can also be the cause of electrical problems.

11 A continuity check can be made on a single length of wire by disconnecting it at each end and connecting a meter or continuity tester across both ends of the wire. Continuity (low or no resistance – 0 ohms) should be indicated if the wire is good. If no continuity (high resistance) is shown, suspect a broken wire.

Voltage checks

12 A voltage check can determine whether current is reaching a component. Use a multimeter set to the dc voltage scale or a test light. The test light is the cheaper component, but the meter has the advantage of being able to give a voltage reading.

13 Connect the meter or test light in parallel (across the load).

14 First identify the relevant wiring circuit by referring to the wiring diagram at the end of this manual. If other electrical components share the same power supply (i.e. are fed from the same fuse), take note whether they are working correctly – this is useful information in deciding where to start checking the circuit.

15 If using a meter, check first that the meter leads are plugged into the correct terminals on the meter (red to positive (+), black to negative

(-). Set the meter to the dc volts function, at a range suitable for the battery voltage – 0 to 20 vdc. Connect the meter red probe (+) to the power supply wire and the black probe to a good metal earth (ground) on the motorcycle's frame or directly to the battery negative terminal. Battery voltage should be shown on the meter with the ignition switched ON.

16 If using a test light, connect its positive (+) probe to the power supply terminal and its negative (-) probe to a good earth (ground) on the motorcycle's frame. With the ignition ON, the test light should illuminate.

17 If no voltage is indicated, work back towards the fuse continuing to check for voltage. When you reach a point where there is voltage, you know the problem lies between that point and your last check point.

Earth (ground) checks

18 Earth connections are made either directly to the engine or frame (such as sensors, neutral switch etc. which only have a positive feed) or by a separate wire into the earth circuit of the wiring harness. Alternatively a short earth wire is sometimes run from the component directly to the motorcycle's frame.

19 Corrosion is often the cause of a poor earth connection.

20 If total failure is experienced, check the security of the main earth lead from the negative (-) terminal of the battery and also the main earth point on the wiring harness. If corroded, dismantle the connection and clean all surfaces back to bare metal. Remake the connection and prevent further corrosion from forming by smearing battery terminal grease over the connection.

21 To check the earth on a component, use an insulated jumper wire to temporarily bypass its earth connection **(see illustration)**. Connect one end of the jumper wire between the earth terminal or metal body of the component and the other end to the motorcycle's frame. If the circuit works with the jumper wire installed, the earth circuit is faulty. Check the wiring for open-circuits or poor connections. Clean up direct earth connections, removing all traces of corrosion and remake the joint.

---

3 Battery removal, installation and inspection

Caution: Be extremely careful when handling or working around the battery. The electrolyte is very caustic and an explosive gas (hydrogen) is given off when the battery is charging.

Removal and installation

1 Make sure the ignition is switched OFF. Remove the rider's seat (see Chapter 8).

2 Release and remove the battery cover clip by unscrewing the centre of the clip then drawing the body out of the cover **(see illustration)**. Lift the cover to expose the battery **(see illustration)**.

3 Unscrew the negative (–) terminal bolt first and disconnect the lead from the battery **(see illustration)**. Lift up the red insulating cover to access the positive (+) terminal, then unscrew the bolt and disconnect the lead.

4 Lift the battery from the bike **(see illustration)**.

3.2a Release the trim clip as described . . .

3.2b . . . then lift the cover

3.3 Disconnect the negative lead first, then disconnect the positive lead (arrowed)

3.4 Lift the battery out

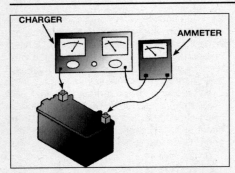

4.2 If the charger doesn't have ammeter built in, connect one in series as shown. DO NOT connect the ammeter between the battery terminals or it will be ruined

5 On installation, clean the battery terminals and lead ends with a wire brush, fine sandpaper or steel wool. Reconnect the leads, connecting the positive (+) terminal first.

> **HAYNES HiNT**
>
> *Battery corrosion can be kept to a minimum by applying a layer of battery terminal grease or petroleum jelly (Vaseline) to the terminals after the leads have been connected. DO NOT use a mineral based grease.*

6 Fit the battery cover and secure it by inserting the body of the clip into the hole, then pushing the centre of the clip into the body **(see illustration 3.2a)**. Install the seat (see Chapter 8).

Inspection

7 The battery fitted to all models covered in this manual is of the maintenance-free (sealed) type, therefore requiring no regular maintenance. However, the following checks should still be performed.
8 Check the battery terminals and leads are tight and free of corrosion. If corrosion is evident, clean the terminals as described above, then protect them from further corrosion (see *Haynes Hint*).

9 Keep the battery case clean to prevent current leakage, which can discharge the battery over a period of time (especially when it sits unused). Wash the outside of the case with a solution of baking soda and water. Rinse the battery thoroughly, then dry it.
10 Look for cracks in the case and replace the battery with a new one if any are found. If acid has been spilled on the frame or battery box, neutralise it with a baking soda and water solution, dry it thoroughly, then touch up any damaged paint.
11 If the motorcycle sits unused for long periods of time, disconnect the leads from the battery terminals, negative (−) terminal first. Refer to Section 4 and charge the battery once every month to six weeks.
12 Check the condition of the battery by measuring the voltage present at the battery terminals. Connect the voltmeter positive (+) probe to the battery positive (+) terminal, and the negative (−) probe to the battery negative (−) terminal. When fully-charged there should be 13.0 to 13.2 volts present. If the voltage falls below 12.3 volts remove the battery (see above), and recharge it as described below in Section 4.

4 Battery charging

Caution: Be extremely careful when handling or working around the battery. The electrolyte is very caustic and an explosive gas (hydrogen) is given off when the battery is charging.

1 Remove the battery (see Section 3). Connect the charger to the battery, making sure that the positive (+) lead on the charger is connected to the positive (+) terminal on the battery, and the negative (−) lead is connected to the negative (−) terminal.
2 Honda recommend that the battery is charged at the normal rate specified at the beginning of the Chapter. Exceeding this figure can cause the battery to overheat, buckling the

plates and rendering it useless. Few owners will have access to an expensive current controlled charger, so if a normal domestic charger is used check that after a possible initial peak, the charge rate falls to a safe level **(see illustration)**. If the battery becomes hot during charging **stop**. Further charging will cause damage. **Note:** *In emergencies the battery can be charged at the quick rate specified. However, this is not recommended and the normal charging rate is by far the safer method of charging the battery.*
3 If the recharged battery discharges rapidly if left disconnected it is likely that an internal short caused by physical damage or sulphation has occurred. A new battery will be required. A sound item will tend to lose its charge at about 1% per day.
4 Install the battery (see Section 3).
5 If the motorcycle sits unused for long periods of time, charge the battery once every month to six weeks and leave it disconnected or use a trickle charger.

5 Fuses and main relay

Fuses

1 The electrical system is protected by fuses of different ratings. The main fuse is integral with the starter relay, which is located under the rider's seat on the left-hand side of the battery. The circuit fuses, each in its own holder, are just behind the starter relay, and under an extension of the battery cover (labelled FUSE).
2 Remove the rider's seat (see Chapter 8).
3 To access the main fuse disconnect the starter relay wiring connector **(see illustration)**.
4 To access the circuit fuses release and remove the battery cover clip by unscrewing the centre of the clip then drawing the body out of the cover, then lift the cover to expose the fuses **(see illustrations 3.2a and b)**. Unclip the lid of the relevant fuseholder **(see illustration)**.

5.3 Disconnect the starter relay wiring connector to access the main fuse (arrowed)

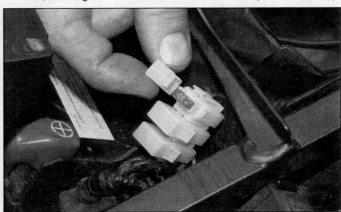

5.4 Unclip the lid to access the fuse

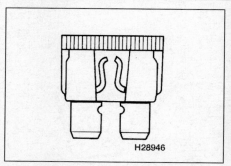

5.5a A blown fuse can be identified by a break in its element

5.5b Spare fuses (arrowed)

5.8a Main relay (arrowed) – R-4, R-5, RW-6

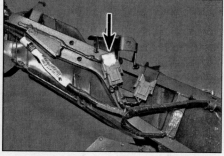

5.8b Main relay (arrowed) – RW-7, RW-8, RW-9, RW-A

5 The fuses can be removed and checked visually. If you can't pull the fuse out with your fingertips, use a pair of long-nose pliers. A blown fuse is easily identified by a break in the element (see illustration). Each fuse is clearly marked with its rating and must only be replaced by a fuse of the correct rating. A spare fuse of each rating is housed in the battery cover (see illustration). If a spare fuse is used, always replace it with a new one so that a spare of each rating is carried on the bike at all times.

⚠ *Warning: Never put in a fuse of a higher rating or bridge the terminals with any other substitute, however temporary it may be. Serious damage may be done to the circuit, or a fire may start.*

6 If the new fuse blows immediately check the wiring circuit very carefully for evidence of a short-circuit. Look for bare wires and chafed, melted or burned insulation.

7 Occasionally a fuse will blow or cause an open-circuit for no obvious reason. Corrosion of the fuse ends and fusebox terminals may occur and cause poor fuse contact. If this happens, remove the corrosion with a wire brush or emery paper, then spray the fuse end and terminals with electrical contact cleaner.

Main relay

8 The relay controls power from the ignition switch to the fuses (except the main fuse), thereby controlling all lighting, signalling and instrumentation functions. If the relay is suspected of being faulty, test it as follows.

Remove the seat cowling (see Chapter 8), then displace the relay from its mount and disconnect the wiring connector (see illustrations).

9 Set a multimeter to the ohms x 1 scale and connect it across the relay's A and B terminals (see illustration). There should be no continuity (infinite resistance). Using a fully-charged 12 volt battery and two insulated jumper wires, connect the positive (+) terminal of the battery to the D terminal on the relay, and the negative (–) terminal to the C terminal. At this point the relay should be heard to click and the meter read 0 ohms (continuity). If this is the case the relay is good. If the relay does not click when battery voltage is applied and indicates no continuity (infinite resistance) across its terminals, it is faulty and must be replaced with a new one.

10 If the relay is good, check for battery voltage at the black wire terminal in the connector with the ignition ON. Also check for continuity to earth in the green wire. If necessary check all the wiring in the circuit for continuity, referring to the wiring diagram at the end of the Chapter. Also make sure that all the terminals in the connectors are clean and secure. Repair or renew the wiring or connectors as necessary.

6 Lighting system check

1 The battery provides power for operation of the lights. If a light fails first check the bulb (see relevant Section), and the bulb terminals in the holder. If none of the lights work, always check battery voltage before proceeding. Low battery voltage indicates either a faulty battery or a defective charging system. Refer to Section 3 for battery checks and Section 29 for charging system tests. Also, check the fuses and main relay (Section 5) – if there is more than one problem at the same time, it is likely to be a fault relating to a multi-function component, such as one of the fuses governing more than one circuit, or the main relay or the ignition switch. When checking for a blown filament in a bulb, it is advisable to back up a visual check with a continuity test of the filament as it is not always apparent that a bulb has blown. When testing for continuity, remember that on single terminal bulbs it is the metal body of the bulb that is the earth (ground).

Headlight

2 All models have two twin filament bulbs. If one headlight beam fails to work, first check the bulb (see Section 7). If both headlight beams fail to work, first check the fuse (see Section 5), and then the bulb(s) (see Section 7). If they are good, the problem lies in the wiring or connectors, the lighting relay or the dimmer switch. Refer to Section 20 for the switch testing procedures, and also to the wiring diagram at the end of this Chapter.

3 The relay controls the headlights, and

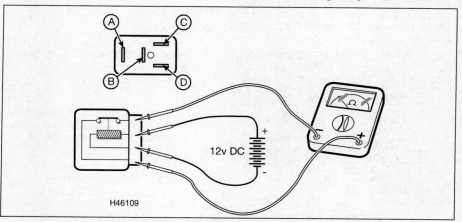

5.9 Main relay test and terminal identification (see text)

6.3 Headlight relay (arrowed)

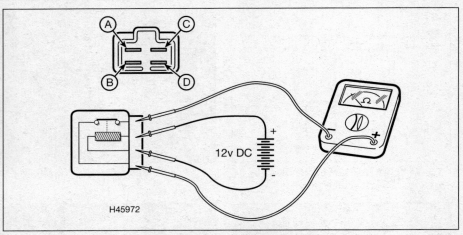

6.4 Headlight relay test and terminal identification

cuts power to them when the starter button is pushed. If the relay is suspected of being faulty, test it as follows. Remove the instrument cluster (Section 15), then displace the relay from its mount and disconnect the wiring connector **(see illustration)**.

4 If a substitute is not available, remove the suspect one and test it as follows: set a multimeter to the ohms x 1 scale and connect it across the relay's A and B terminals **(see illustration)**. There should be no continuity (infinite resistance). Using a fully-charged 12 volt battery and two insulated jumper wires, connect the positive (+) terminal of the battery to the D terminal on the relay, and the negative (–) terminal to the C terminal. At this point the relay should be heard to click and the meter read 0 ohms (continuity). If this is the case the relay is good. If the relay does not click when battery voltage is applied and indicates no continuity (infinite resistance) across its terminals, it is faulty and must be replaced with a new one.

5 If the relay is good, check for battery voltage at the brown wire terminal in the connector with the ignition ON. If there is no voltage check the wiring between the connector and the fuse. If necessary check all the wiring in the headlight circuit for continuity, referring to the wiring diagram at the end of the Chapter. Also make sure that all the terminals in the connectors are clean and secure. Repair or renew the wiring or connectors as necessary.

6 If a LO beam does not work, and the bulb is good, check for battery voltage at the white wire terminal on the headlight wiring connector with the ignition ON. If a HI beam

does not work, and the bulb is good, check for battery voltage at the blue wire terminal on the headlight wiring connector with the ignition ON. If voltage is present, check for continuity to earth (ground) in the green wire from the wiring connector. Repair or renew the wiring or connectors as necessary.

Tail light

7 If the tail light fails to work, first check the bulb (Section 9), then the fuse (Section 5). If they are good, remove the tail light unit (see Section 10), disconnecting the tail light wiring connector, and check for battery voltage at the brown wire terminal on the loom side of the connector with the ignition switch ON. If voltage is present, check for continuity to earth (ground) in the green wire from the wiring connector. If no voltage is indicated, check the wiring and connectors in the tail light circuit, referring to the wiring diagram at the end of this Chapter.

Brake light

8 If the brake light fails to work, first check the bulb (Section 9), then the fuse (Section 5). If they are good remove the tail light unit (see Section 10), disconnecting the tail light wiring connector, and check for battery voltage at the green/yellow wire terminal on the loom side of the connector, first with the front brake lever pulled in, then with the rear brake pedal

pressed down. If voltage is present with one brake on but not the other, then the switch or its wiring is faulty. If voltage is present in both cases, check for continuity to earth (ground) in the green wire from the wiring connector. If no voltage is indicated, check the wiring and connectors between the brake light and the brake switches, the fuse, and the ignition switch, then check the switches themselves. Refer to Section 14 for the switch testing procedures, and also to the wiring diagram at the end of this Chapter.

Licence plate light

9 If the licence plate light bulb fails to work, first check the bulb (Section 9), then the fuse (Section 5). If they are good remove the tail light unit (see Section 10), then disconnect the license plate light wiring connectors **(see illustration)** and check for battery voltage at the brown wire terminal on the loom side of the wiring connector with the ignition switch ON. If voltage is present, check for continuity to earth (ground) in the green wire from the wiring connector. If no voltage is indicated, check the wiring and connectors in the license plate light circuit, referring to the wiring diagram at the end of this Chapter.

Turn signals

10 See Section 11.

7 Headlight bulbs and sidelight bulb

Note: *It is a good idea to use a paper towel or dry cloth when handling the new bulb to prevent injury if it breaks, and to increase bulb life.*

Headlight

R-4, R-5 and RW-6 models

1 Turn the handlebars to the left or right to access the back of the headlight on the side required. Remove the rubber dust cover, noting how it fits **(see illustration)**.

6.9 Licence plate light wiring connectors (arrowed)

7.1 Remove the dust cover

7.2a Release the clip . . .

7.2b . . . and remove the bulb

7.3 Release the bulb from its holder and fit
a new one

7.7a Disconnect the wiring plug . . .

7.7b . . . and pull the dust cover from the
rear of the headlight

7.8a Push the retaining clip across to
release it . . .

2 Release the bulbholder retaining clip, noting how it fits, then withdraw the holder and bulb **(see illustrations)**.

3 Carefully push the bulb in and turn it anti-clockwise to release it from the holder **(see illustration)**.

4 Line up the pins on the new bulb with the slots in the holder, then push the bulb in and turn it clockwise, making sure it locates correctly. Fit the bulbholder into the headlight and secure it in position with the retaining clip.

5 Fit the dust cover, making sure it is correctly seated and with the TOP mark at the top.

6 Check the operation of the headlight.

RW-7, RW-8, RW-9, RW-A models

7 Pull the wiring connector from the rear of the headlight bulb, and remove the rubber dust cover from the headlight, noting how it fits **(see illustrations)**.

8 Release the bulb retaining clip, noting how it fits, then withdraw the bulb from the headlight, and pull the bulb from the holder **(see illustrations)**.

9 Align the tabs of the new bulb with the slots in the headlight, refit the bulb holder, then push it into place and secure the retaining clip.

10 Refit the rubber dust cover with the 'arrow' mark at the top **(see illustration)**, then refit the wiring connector.

7.8b . . . withdraw the bulb from the
headlight . . .

7.8c . . . and pull it from the holder

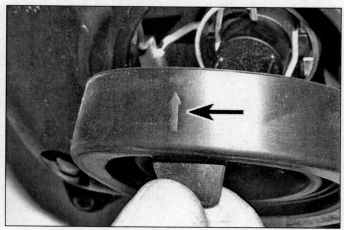

7.10 The arrow mark on the dust cover must be uppermost
(arrowed)

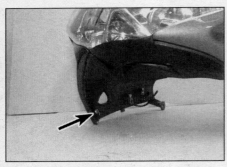

7.11 Undo the screw (arrowed) on each side and remove the panel

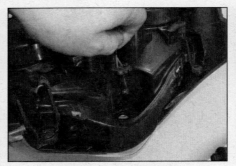

7.12a Withdraw the bulb holder . . .

7.12b . . . and pull the bulb out

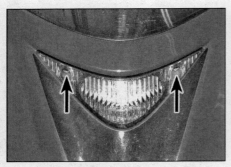

7.15 Undo the sidelight lens screws (arrowed)

7.16 Pull the capless bulb from place

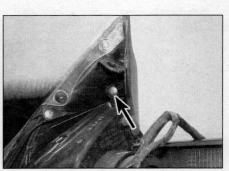

8.2a Undo the screw (arrowed) on each side . . .

Sidelight

R-4, R-5 and RW-6 models

11 Undo the two screws securing the trim panel on the underside of the fairing and remove the panel **(see illustration)**.

12 Carefully pull the bulbholder out of the headlight, then pull the bulb out of the holder **(see illustrations)**.

13 Fit the new bulb in the bulbholder, then fit the holder into the headlight.

14 Fit the trim panel. Check the operation of the sidelight.

RW-7, RW-8, RW-9, RW-A models

15 Undo the two screws and remove the lens from the front of the upper fairing **(see illustration)**.

16 Pull the capless bulb from the holder **(see illustration)**.

17 Press the new bulb into the holder, then refit the lens. Tighten the retaining screws securely.

8 Headlight

Removal and installation

1 Remove the fairing (see Chapter 8).

2 Undo the screws securing the headlight assembly to the fairing and lift it out **(see illustrations)**.

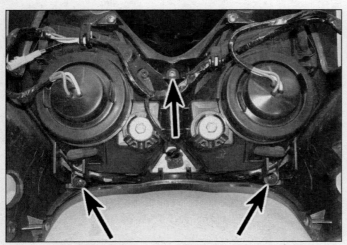

8.2b . . . and the screws (arrowed) and remove the headlight from the fairing on R-4, R-5 and RW-6 models

8.2c Headlight retaining screws (arrowed) – RW-7, RW-8, RW-9, RW-A models

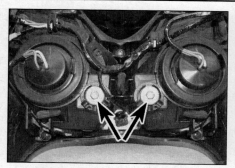

8.6a Vertical alignment adjusters (arrowed) – R-4, R-5 and RW-6 models

8.6b Insert a crosshead screwdriver through the aperture in the cockpit trim panel to access the headlight vertical alignment adjusters – RW-7, RW-8, RW-9, RW-A models

9.2a Release the bulbholder from the tail light . . .

3 If required remove the headlight bulbs and the sidelight bulbholder (see Section 7), then release the headlight loom from its clips and remove it.

4 Installation is the reverse of removal. Make sure all the wiring is correctly routed, connected and secured. Check the operation of the headlight and sidelight. Check the headlight aim.

Headlight aim

Note: *An improperly adjusted headlight may cause problems for oncoming traffic or provide poor, unsafe illumination of the road ahead. Before adjusting the headlight aim, be sure to consult with local traffic laws and regulations – for UK models refer to MOT Test Checks in the Reference section.*

5 The headlight beams can adjusted vertically. Before making any adjustment, check that the tyre pressures are correct and the suspension is adjusted as required. Make any adjustments to the headlight aim with the machine on level ground, with the fuel tank half full and with an assistant sitting on the seat.

6 Adjustment is made by turning the adjuster screw on the bottom inner corner of the relevant beam unit (R-4, R-5, RW-6 models), or by rotating the adjustment screws at the

outer edges of the cockpit (RW-7, RW-8, RW-9, RW-A models) **(see illustrations)**.

---

9 Brake/tail light bulb and licence plate bulb

Note: *It is a good idea to use a paper towel or dry cloth when handling the new bulb to prevent injury if it breaks, and to increase bulb life.*

Brake/tail light bulb

1 Displace the tail light unit (Section 10).
2 Turn the bulbholder anti-clockwise to release it and withdraw it from the light unit **(see illustration)**. Carefully push the bulb in and turn it anti-clockwise to release it from the holder **(see illustration)**.
3 Line up the pins on the new bulb with the slots in the holder (the pins heights are different so that it can only be fitted one way), then push the bulb in and turn it clockwise, making sure it locates correctly. Fit the bulbholder into the light unit and turn it clockwise.
4 Install the tail light unit (Section 10).

Licence plate light bulb

5 Undo the two screws and remove the lens **(see illustrations)**.

9.2b . . . and the bulb from the holder

6 Carefully pull the bulb out of its socket and replace it with a new one **(see illustration)**.
7 Make sure the rubber seal is in place and in good condition. Fit the lens – do not over-tighten the screws as the lens and threads are easily damaged.

---

10 Tail light unit

1 Remove the passenger seat (see Chapter 8).
2 Undo the screw and remove the collar, then draw the tail light out, noting how the

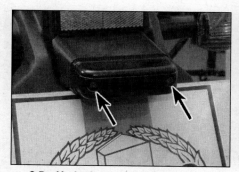

9.5a Undo the screws (arrowed) . . .

9.5b . . . and remove the lens

9.6 Pull the bulb out of the socket

10.2a Undo the screw . . .

10.2b . . . remove the collar . . .

10.2c . . . and withdraw the tail light

10.3 Tail light wiring connector (arrowed)

10.4 Locate the pegs in the grommets

4 If voltage was present, short between the white/green and grey wire terminals on the connector using a jumper wire. Turn the ignition ON and operate the turn signal switch. If the turn signals come on (but don't flash), the relay is confirmed faulty.

5 If the turn signals do not come on, check the grey wire for continuity to the left-hand switch housing, and repair or renew the wiring or connectors as required.

6 If all is good so far, or if the turn signals work on one side but not the other, check the wiring between the left-hand switch housing and the turn signals themselves. Repair or renew the wiring or connectors as necessary.

pegs locate in the grommets **(see illustrations)**.

3 Either turn the bulbholder anti-clockwise to release it from the light unit **(see illustration 9.2a)**, or disconnect the wiring connector and remove the unit with the bulbholder in place **(see illustration)**.

4 Installation is the reverse of removal **(see illustration)**. Check the operation of the tail and brake lights.

11 Turn signal circuit check

1 Most turn signal problems are the result of a burned out bulb or corroded socket. This is especially true when the turn signals function

on one side (although possibly too quickly), but fail to work on the other side. If this is the case, first check the bulbs, the sockets and the wiring connectors. If all the turn signals fail to work, first check the fuse (see Section 5), and then the relay (see below). If they are good, the problem lies in the wiring or connectors, or the switch. Refer to Section 20 for the switch testing procedures, and also to the wiring diagram at the end of this Chapter.

2 To check the relay remove the seat cowling (see Chapter 8). Disconnect the relay wiring connector **(see illustration)**.

3 Check for battery voltage at the white/green wire terminal on the loom side of the connector with the ignition ON. If no voltage is present, check the wiring from the relay to the ignition (main) switch (via the fuse) for continuity.

12 Turn signal bulbs

Note: *It is a good idea to use a paper towel or dry cloth when handling the new bulb to prevent injury if the bulb should break and to increase bulb life.*

1 Remove the screw securing the lens and detach the lens from the housing, noting how it fits **(see illustration)**. Remove the rubber seal if it is loose, and discard it if it is damaged, deformed or deteriorated.

2 Push the bulb into the holder and twist it anti-clockwise to remove it **(see illustration)**. Check the socket terminals for corrosion and clean them if necessary.

11.2 Turn signal relay (arrowed)

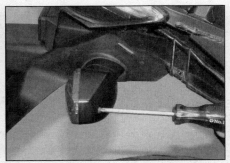

12.1 Undo the screw and remove the lens

12.2 Release the bulb and replace it with a new one

12.4 Make sure the tab locates correctly

3 Line up the pins of the new bulb with the slots in the socket, then push the bulb in and turn it clockwise until it locks into place.

4 Fit a new rubber seal if required, and make sure it is properly seated and does not get pinched. Fit the lens onto the housing, locating the tab on the inner end into the cut-out in the housing, and install the screw **(see illustration)**. Do not over-tighten the screw as it is easy to strip the threads or crack the lens.

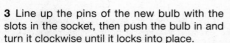

13 Turn signal assemblies

Front turn signals

1 On R-4, R-5 and RW-6 models, remove the fairing side panel (see Chapter 8).

13.2c The left-hand signal connector (arrowed) is under the trim panel

13.6 Rear turn signal wiring connectors (arrowed)

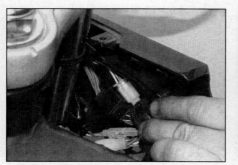

13.2a Pull back the boot to expose the connectors . . .

2 Disconnect the turn signal wiring connector – on the right-hand side it is inside a rubber boot which will have to be released and pulled back **(see illustrations)**. On the left-hand side remove the cockpit trim panel to access the connector (see Chapter 8) **(see illustration)**.

3 Unscrew the nut securing the stem to the inside of the fairing stay and remove the turn signal, taking care as you draw the wiring through **(see illustrations)**.

4 Installation is the reverse of removal. Check the operation of the turn signals.

Rear turn signals

5 Remove the tail light unit (see Section 10).
6 Disconnect the turn signal wiring connector **(see illustration)**.
7 Unscrew the nut securing the turn signal stem to the inside of the rear mudguard and remove the turn signal, taking care as you draw the wiring through **(see illustration)**.

13.3a Unscrew the nut (arrowed) . . .

13.7 Unscrew the nut (arrowed) and remove the turn signal

13.2b . . . and disconnect the turn signal connector

8 Installation is the reverse of removal. Check the operation of the turn signals.

14 Brake light switches

Circuit check

1 Before checking the switches, and if not already done, check the brake light circuit (see Section 6).

2 The front brake light switch is mounted on the underside of the brake master cylinder. Disconnect the wiring connectors from the switch **(see illustration)**. Using a continuity tester, connect the probes to the terminals of the switch. With the brake lever at rest, there should be no continuity. With the brake lever applied, there should be continuity. If the

13.3b . . . and remove the turn signal

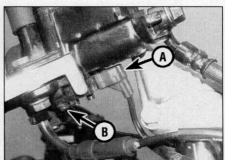

14.2 Front brake switch wiring connectors (A) and mounting screw (B)

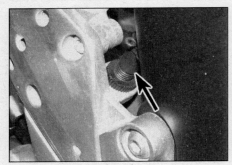

14.3a Rear brake light switch (arrowed)

14.3b Disconnect the wiring connector (arrowed)

14.10 Detach the spring (A) and remove the boot (B). Adjustment nut (C)

switch does not behave as described, replace it with a new one.

3 The rear brake light switch is mounted on the inside of the rider's right-hand footrest bracket, above the brake pedal **(see illustration)**. Remove the seat cowling (Chapter 8) to access the wiring connector and disconnect it **(see illustration)**. Using a continuity tester, connect the probes to the terminals on the switch side of the wiring connector. With the brake pedal at rest, there should be no continuity. With the brake pedal applied, there should be continuity. If the switch does not behave as described, replace it with a new one, although check first that switch is adjusted correctly (see Step 11).

4 If the switches are good, check for voltage at one of the wiring connectors for the front switch (lever pulled in), and at the white/green wire terminal for the rear switch connector (loom side) with the ignition switch ON – there should be battery voltage. If there's no voltage present, check the wiring between the connector and the ignition switch via the fusebox (see the wiring diagram at the end of this Chapter). If voltage is present, check the other wire (front) or green/yellow (rear) wire for continuity to the brake light wiring connector, referring to the relevant wiring diagram. Repair or renew the wiring as necessary.

Switch replacement

Front brake lever switch

5 The switch is mounted on the underside

of the brake master cylinder. Disconnect the wiring connectors from the switch **(see illustration 14.2)**.

6 Remove the single screw securing the switch to the master cylinder and remove the switch **(see illustration 14.2)**.

7 Installation is the reverse of removal. Make sure the peg on the switch is correctly located in its hole before tightening the screw. The switch isn't adjustable.

Rear brake pedal switch

8 The rear brake light switch is mounted on the inside of the right-hand rider's footrest bracket, above the brake pedal **(see illustration 14.3a)**. Remove the fuel tank (see Chapter 4A or 4B), and if required for better access the seat cowling (Chapter 8) to access the wiring connector and disconnect it. Feed the wiring down to the switch, noting its routing and releasing it from any ties.

9 Unscrew the footrest bracket mounting bolts and displace the bracket so that you can access the back of it.

10 Unhook the switch spring, then slip the rubber boot off the bottom of the switch **(see illustration)**. Thread the switch out of its adjustment nut, then remove the nut from the mounting.

11 Installation is the reverse of removal. Tighten the footrest bracket bolts to the torque setting specified at the beginning of the Chapter. Make sure the brake light is activated just before the rear brake pedal takes effect. If

adjustment is necessary, hold the switch body and turn the adjustment nut as required until the brake light is activated correctly – if the brake light comes on too late or not at all, turn the ring clockwise (when looked at from the top) so the switch threads out of the bracket. If the brake light comes on too soon or is permanently on, turn the ring anti-clockwise so the switch threads into the bracket.

15 Instrument cluster

Removal

1 Remove the cockpit trim panels (see Chapter 8).

2 Release the rubber boot from the clip on the right-hand inner side of the fairing **(see illustration)**. Pull the boot back and disconnect the instrument cluster wiring connectors.

3 Unscrew the two bolts, then lift the instrument cluster off the bracket, noting how the peg on the underside locates in the grommet **(see illustration)**.

4 Unscrew the knurled ring and detach the speedometer cable **(see illustration)**.

Installation

5 Installation is the reverse of removal. Check the condition of the rubber grommet and

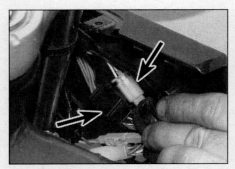

15.2 Pull back the boot and disconnect the instrument wiring connectors (arrowed)

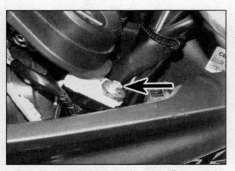

15.3 Unscrew the bolt (arrowed) on each side . . .

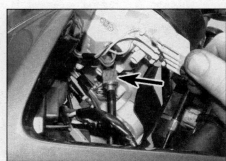

15.4 . . . then displace the instrument cluster and detach the speedometer cable (arrowed)

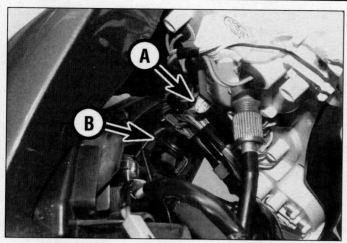

15.5 The peg (A) locates in the grommet (B)

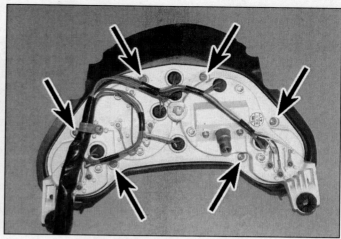

16.8a Undo the screws (arrowed) . . .

replace it with a new one if necessary. Make sure the peg locates fully in the grommet **(see illustration)**. Make sure that the wiring connectors are secure.

16 Instruments check

Instrument cluster power check

1 If none of the instruments or displays are working, first check the fuse (see Section 5).
2 If the fuse is good, remove the right-hand cockpit trim panel (see Chapter 8). Release the rubber boot and wiring from the clip on the right-hand inner side of the fairing **(see illustration 15.2)**. Pull the boot back and check the instrument cluster wiring connectors for loose or broken connections.
3 To check the power input wire, check for battery voltage at the white/green wire terminal on the wiring loom side of the connector and

a good earth (ground) with the ignition switch ON. There should be battery voltage. If there is no voltage, refer to the wiring diagram and check the wire between the connector and the fuse for loose or broken connections or a damaged wire.
4 If the power input is good, but there is no instrument function, remove the instrument cluster (Section 15) and check the wiring terminals on the back are secure.

Speedometer

Check

5 If the speedometer does not work, first check the cable (Section 18), then remove the front wheel and check the drive gear and plate (see Chapter 7).
6 If they are good the speedometer itself is probably faulty, in which case it must be replaced with a new one.

Replacement

7 Remove the instrument cluster (Section 15).

8 Undo the large screws and lift the front cover off **(see illustrations)**.
9 Carefully pull the speedometer bulbholder out **(see illustration)**.
10 Undo the two screws securing the speedometer and lift it out **(see illustration 16.9)**.
11 Installation is the reverse of removal.

Tachometer

Check

12 First check for power to the instruments (Steps 1 to 4). Reconnect the instrument wiring connectors, then check for continuity to earth in the green wire on the back of the tachometer.
13 Start the engine and check the voltage between the yellow/green (+) wire and the green (-) wire on the back of the tachometer **(see illustration 16.16)**. A pulsing voltage of 6 volts should be present. If not check for continuity in the yellow/green wire to the ignition control unit (ICU) – remove the fuel tank to access it (see Chapter 4A or 4B),

16.8b . . . and remove the cover

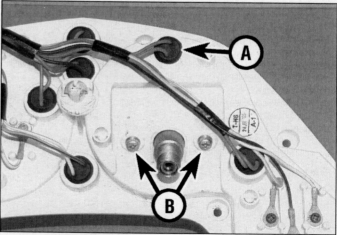

16.9 Speedometer bulb (A) and screws (B)

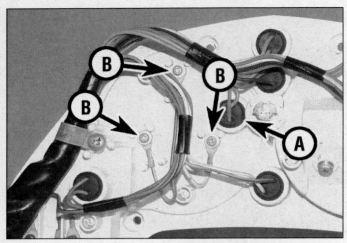

16.16 Tachometer bulb (A) and screws (B)

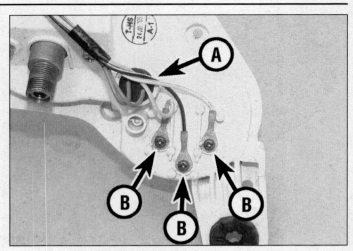

16.22 Fuel gauge bulb (A) and screws (B)

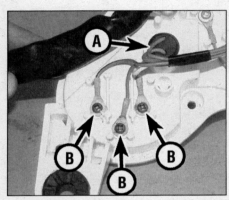

16.28 Temperature gauge bulb (A) and screws (B)

then displace the unit to access the wiring connector on its underside. If the wiring is good, the fault lies in either the ICU or the tachometer itself.

Replacement

14 Remove the instrument cluster (Section 15).
15 Undo the large screws and lift the front cover off **(see illustrations 16.8a and b)**.
16 Carefully pull the tachometer bulbholder out **(see illustration)**.
17 Undo the three screws securing the wiring connectors, then lift the tachometer out **(see illustration 16.16)**.
18 Installation is the reverse of removal. Make sure each wire is connected to its correct terminal – they are marked according to the colour coding of the wires (i.e. the white/green wire connects to the terminal marked W/G).

Fuel gauge

Check

19 The fuel gauge and level sensor are covered in Chapter 4A or 4B.

Replacement

20 Remove the instrument cluster (Section 15).

21 Undo the large screws and lift the front cover off **(see illustrations 16.8a and b)**.
22 Carefully pull the fuel gauge bulbholder out **(see illustration)**.
23 Undo the three screws securing the wiring connectors, then lift the fuel gauge out **(see illustration 16.22)**.
24 Installation is the reverse of removal. Make sure each wire is connected to its correct terminal – they are marked according to the colour coding of the wires (i.e. the white/green wire connects to the terminal marked W/G).

Temperature gauge

Check

25 The temperature gauge and sensor are covered in Chapter 3.

Replacement

26 Remove the instrument cluster (Section 15).
27 Undo the large screws and lift the front cover off **(see illustrations 16.8a and b)**.
28 Carefully pull the temperature gauge bulbholder out **(see illustration)**.
29 Undo the three screws securing the wiring connectors, then lift the temperature gauge out.

30 Installation is the reverse of removal. Make sure each wire is connected to its correct terminal – they are marked according to the colour coding of the wires (i.e. the white/green wire connects to the terminal marked W/G).

17 Instrument and warning light bulbs

1 Remove the instrument cluster (Section 15).
2 Carefully pull the relevant bulbholder out of the back of the instrument cluster, then pull the bulb out of the holder and replace it with a new one **(see illustrations)**.

18 Speedometer cable

1 Remove the left-hand fairing side panel (see Chapter 8).
2 Remove the instrument cluster (Section 15).
3 Push in the tab securing the speedometer

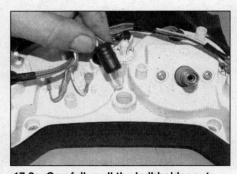

17.2a Carefully pull the bulbholder out . . .

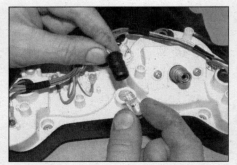

17.2b . . . then remove the bulb

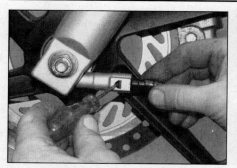

18.3 Release the tab by pushing it in and pull the cable out

19.1a Fold the rubber cover aside . . .

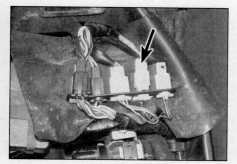

19.1b . . . and disconnect the ignition switch wiring connector (arrowed)

cable in the drive housing and draw the cable out **(see illustration)**.

4 Remove the cable, noting its routing.

5 Installation is the reverse of removal. Make sure the O-ring on the end of the speedometer cable is fitted and smear it with grease. Push the cable into the drive housing, making sure the inner cable locates in the shaft, setting the retaining tab in the cut-out.

19 Ignition switch

 Warning: To prevent the risk of short circuits, disconnect the battery negative (–) lead before making any ignition switch checks.

Check

1 Remove the fuel tank (see Chapter 4A or 4B). Release the rubber wiring connector holder cover from its clip and fold it aside **(see illustration)**. Disconnect the ignition switch connector **(see illustration)**.

2 Using an ohmmeter or a continuity tester, check the continuity of the connector terminal pair. Continuity should exist with the ignition switch in the ON position, and there should be no continuity with it OFF.

3 If the switch fails the test, check for continuity in the wiring between the connector and the switch, and check the terminals on the switch. If it is good, check for battery voltage at the red wire terminal on the loom side of the connector. If there is none, check for continuity in the wire to the starter relay (Section 26), and check the main fuse (Section 5). If there is voltage, check the black wire between the connector and the main relay for continuity, then check the relay itself (Section 5).

Removal and installation

4 Remove the fuel tank (see Chapter 4A or 4B).

5 Release the rubber wiring connector holder cover from its clip and fold it aside **(see illustration 19.1a)**. Disconnect the ignition switch connector **(see illustration 19.1b)**. Feed the wiring back to the switch, freeing it from any clips and ties and noting its routing.

6 Remove the top yoke (see Chapter 6, Section 9 and follow the relevant steps). Undo the screws and remove the switch from the top yoke **(see illustration)**.

7 Installation is the reverse of removal. Make sure the wiring connector is correctly routed and securely connected.

20 Handlebar switches

Check

1 Generally speaking, the switches are reliable and trouble-free. Most troubles, when they do occur, are caused by dirty or corroded contacts, but wear and breakage of internal parts is a possibility that should not be overlooked. If breakage does occur, the entire switch and related wiring harness will have to be replaced with a new one, as individual parts are not available.

2 The switches can be checked for continuity using an ohmmeter or a continuity test light. Always disconnect the battery negative (–) lead, which will prevent the possibility of a short circuit, before making the checks.

3 Remove the fuel tank (see Chapter 4A or 4B). Release the rubber cover from its clip and fold it aside **(see illustration 19.1a)**. Disconnect the relevant switch wiring connector(s) **(see illustration)**.

4 Check for continuity between the terminals of the switch connector with the switch in the various positions (i.e. switch off – no

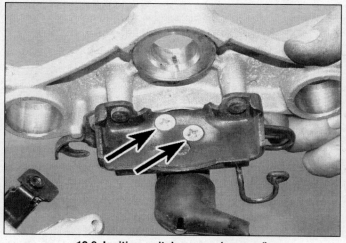

19.6 Ignition switch screws (arrowed)

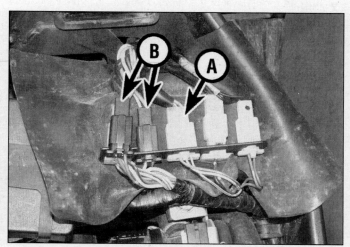

20.3 Right-hand switch wiring connector (A), left-hand switch wiring connectors (B)

20.9 Left-hand switch housing screws (arrowed)

21.3 Neutral switch wiring connector (arrowed)

continuity, switch on – continuity) – see the wiring diagram at the end of this Chapter. Continuity should exist between the terminals connected by a solid line on the diagram when the switch is in the indicated position.

5 If the continuity check indicates a problem exists, displace the switch housing and spray the switch contacts with electrical contact cleaner (there is no need to remove the switch completely). If they are accessible, the contacts can be scraped clean with a knife or polished with crocus cloth. If switch components are damaged or broken, it will be obvious when the switch is disassembled.

Removal and installation

6 Remove the fuel tank (see Chapter 4A or 4B). Release the rubber wiring connector holder cover from its clip and fold it aside **(see illustration 19.1a)**. Disconnect the relevant switch wiring connector(s) **(see illustration 20.3)**. Feed the wiring back to the switch, freeing it from any clips and ties and noting its routing.

7 If removing the right-hand switch disconnect the wires from the brake light switch **(see illustration 14.2)**. If removing the left-hand switch disconnect the wires from the clutch switch **(see illustration 23.2)**.

8 To remove the right-hand switch, refer to Chapter 4A for removal of the throttle cable, which involves detaching the switch housing from the handlebars. Free the throttle cable from the twistgrip and remove it from the housing.

9 To remove the left-hand switch, unscrew

the two handlebar switch screws and free the switch from the handlebar by separating the halves **(see illustration)**.

10 Installation is the reverse of removal. Make sure the locating pin in the switch housing locates in the hole in the handlebar. Refer to Chapter 4A for installation of the throttle cable and right-hand switch housing.

21 Neutral switch

1 The neutral switch is part of the starter safety circuit which prevents or stops the engine running if the transmission is in gear whilst the sidestand is down, and prevents the engine from starting if the transmission is in gear unless the sidestand is up and the clutch lever is pulled in.

Check

2 Before checking the electrical circuit, check the neutral bulb (Section 17) and the fuse (see Section 5).

3 The switch is located in the left-hand side of the crankcase below the front sprocket cover. Free the wiring loom from the clip on the inside of the frame above the sprocket cover, then draw the rubber boot off the connectors and disconnect the neutral switch single wire bullet connector **(see illustration)** – it should be accessible with the fairing left-hand side panel in place, but remove it if necessary (see Chapter 8).

4 Make sure the transmission is in neutral. With the connector disconnected and the ignition switch ON, the neutral light should be out. If not, the wire between the connector, clutch switch diode and instrument cluster must be earthed (grounded) at some point.

5 Check for continuity between the switch terminal and the crankcase. With the transmission in neutral, there should be continuity. With the transmission in gear, there should be no continuity. If the tests prove otherwise, then remove the switch (see below) and check whether the plunger or its spring is bent or damaged, or just stuck **(see illustration)**. Replace the switch with a new one if necessary.

6 If the continuity tests prove the switch is good, check for voltage at the wire terminal. If there's no voltage present, check the wire between the switch, clutch switch diode, instrument cluster and fusebox (see the wiring diagram at the end of this Chapter).

7 If the switch is good, check the other components (sidestand switch, clutch switch and neutral switch diode) and their wiring and connectors in the starter circuit as described in the relevant sections of this Chapter. If all components are good, check the wiring between the various components (see the wiring diagram at the end of this Chapter). Repair or renew the wiring as required.

Removal

8 The switch is located in the left-hand side of the crankcase below the front sprocket cover. Remove the front sprocket cover **(see illustration)**.

9 Free the wiring loom from the clip on the inside of the frame above the sprocket cover, then draw the rubber boot off the connectors and disconnect the neutral switch single wire bullet connector **(see illustration 21.3)** – it should be accessible with the fairing left-hand side panel in place, but remove it if necessary (see Chapter 8). Feed the wiring down to the switch, noting its routing.

10 Clean the area around the switch. Unscrew the bolt and pull the switch from the crankcase **(see illustration)**. Note that there is a plunger with a spring behind a bore in the end of the selector drum that bears against the switch contacts – take care that it

21.5 Make sure the plunger moves in and out smoothly and freely and the spring is not deformed

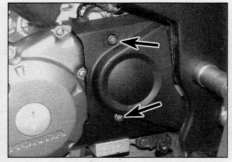

21.8 Unscrew the bolts (arrowed) and remove the cover

21.10 Unscrew the bolt (arrowed) and remove the switch

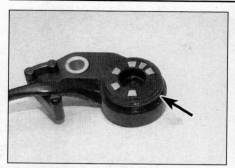

21.11 Check the contacts for wear. Note the O-ring (arrowed)

does not drop out as you remove the switch, and remove them for safekeeping **(see illustration 21.5)**.

11 Check the contacts on the inner face of the switch for wear and damage and replace the switch with a new one if necessary **(see illustration)**. Check the tip of the plunger for wear and the spring for fatigue and distortion.

Installation

12 Check the condition of the O-ring on the switch and replace it with a new one if necessary **(see illustration 21.11)**.
13 Fit the spring and plunger into the offset hole in the end of the selector drum **(see illustration 21.5)**.
14 Smear the O-ring with oil, then install the switch and tighten the bolt **(see illustration)**.
15 Feed the wiring up to the connector, making sure it is correctly routed, and connect it. Check the operation of the neutral light **(see illustration 21.3)**.
16 Install the front sprocket cover.

22 Sidestand switch

1 The sidestand switch is part of the starter safety circuit which prevents or stops the engine running if the transmission is in gear whilst the sidestand is down, and prevents the engine from starting if the transmission is in gear unless the sidestand is up and the clutch lever is pulled in.

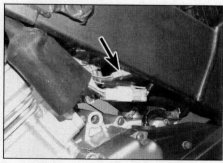

22.2 Sidestand switch wiring connector (arrowed)

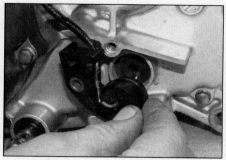

21.14 Make sure the plunger stays in place and the O-ring does not distort

Check

2 The sidestand switch is mounted on the stand pivot. Free the wiring loom from the clip on the inside of the frame above the sprocket cover, then draw the rubber boot off the connectors and disconnect the green 2-pin wiring connector **(see illustration)** – it should be accessible with the fairing left-hand side panel in place, but remove it if necessary (see Chapter 8).
3 Check the operation of the switch using an ohmmeter or continuity test light. Connect the meter between the terminals on the switch side of the connector. With the sidestand up there should be continuity (zero resistance) between the terminals, and with the stand down there should be no continuity (infinite resistance).
4 Check for voltage at the green/white wire terminal on the loom side of the connector with the ignition ON – there should be battery voltage.
5 If the switch does not perform as expected, it is faulty and must be replaced with a new one. If the switch is good, check the other components (clutch switch, neutral switch and diodes) and their wiring and connectors in the starter circuit as described in the relevant sections of this Chapter. If all components are good, check the wiring between the various components (see the wiring diagram at the end of this Chapter). Repair or renew the wiring as required.

Replacement

6 The sidestand switch is mounted on the

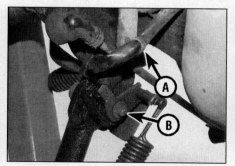

22.7 Free the wiring from the tie (A). Sidestand switch mounting bolt (B)

stand pivot. Free the wiring loom from the clip on the inside of the frame above the sprocket cover, then draw the rubber boot off the connectors and disconnect the green 2-pin wiring connector **(see illustration 22.2)** – it should be accessible with the fairing left-hand side panel in place, but remove it if necessary (see Chapter 8). Feed the wiring back to the switch, freeing it from any clips and ties and noting its routing.
7 Unscrew the switch bolt and remove the retainer plate, the washer and the switch, noting how they locate **(see illustration)**.
8 Fit the new switch onto the sidestand, making sure the pin locates in the hole, and the lug on the stand bracket locates into the cut-out in the switch body. Fit the washer and retainer plate and secure the switch with the bolt **(see illustration 22.7)**.
9 Feed the wiring up to its connector, making sure it is correctly routed and secured by any clips and ties.
10 Reconnect the wiring connector and check the operation of the sidestand switch **(see illustration 22.2)**.

23 Clutch switch

1 The clutch switch is part of the starter safety circuit which prevents or stops the engine running if the transmission is in gear whilst the sidestand is down, and prevents the engine from starting if the transmission is in gear unless the sidestand is up and the clutch lever is pulled in. The switch isn't adjustable.

Check

2 The clutch switch is mounted under the clutch lever bracket. To check the switch, disconnect the wiring connectors from it **(see illustration)**. Connect the probes of an ohmmeter or a continuity tester to the two switch terminals. With the clutch lever pulled in, continuity should be indicated. With the clutch lever out, no continuity (infinite resistance) should be indicated.
3 If the switch is good, check the other components (sidestand switch, neutral switch

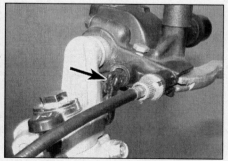

23.2 Clutch switch wiring connectors (arrowed)

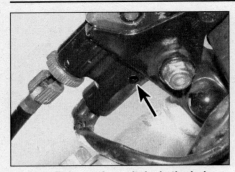

23.6 Release the switch via the hole (arrowed)

24.2 The diode blocks (arrowed)

and diodes) and their wiring and connectors in the starter circuit as described in the relevant sections of this Chapter. If all components are good, check the wiring between the various components (see the wiring diagram at the end of this Chapter).

Replacement

4 The clutch switch is mounted under the clutch lever bracket.
5 Disconnect the wiring connectors from the switch **(see illustration 23.2)**.
6 Release the switch from its housing and withdraw it, noting how it fits **(see illustration)**.
7 Installation is the reverse of removal. Make sure the switch is correctly located before tightening its screw.

24 Diodes

1 The diodes for the starter safety circuit are housed in two blocks which are plugged into the wiring loom between the seat cowling and the rear sub-frame on the right-hand side – remove the seat cowling to access them (see Chapter 8).
2 Pull the diode blocks out of their sockets **(see illustration)**. The neutral switch block has two terminals and houses a single diode, whereas the clutch switch block has three terminals and contains two diodes.

3 Test the diodes using an multimeter or continuity tester.
4 To test the neutral switch diode, connect the positive (+) probe to the B terminal of the diode block and the negative (–) probe to the A terminal of the block **(see illustration)**. The diode should show continuity. Now reverse the probes. The diode should show no continuity. If it doesn't behave as stated, replace the diode block with a new one.
5 To test the clutch switch diodes, connect the positive (+) probe to the A terminal of the diode block and the negative (–) probe to the C terminal of the block **(see illustration)**. The diode should show continuity. Now reverse the probes. The diode should show no continuity. Repeat the tests between the B and C terminals. The same results should be achieved. If it doesn't behave as stated, replace the diode block with a new one.
6 If each diode block is good, push it back into its socket, then check the other components in the starter circuit as described in the relevant sections of this Chapter. If all components are good, check the wiring between the various

components (see the wiring diagram at the end of this Chapter).

25 Horn

Check

1 The horn is mounted under the bottom yoke **(see illustration)**. On R-4, R-5 and RW-6 models, remove the left-hand fairing side panel (see Chapter 8). Turn the handlebars as required for best access.
2 Disconnect the wiring connectors from the horn. Using two jumper wires, apply voltage from a fully-charged 12V battery directly to the terminals on the horn. If the horn doesn't sound, replace it with a new one.
3 If the horn works check the fuse (Section 5), then check for voltage at the black wire connector with the ignition ON and the horn button pressed. If voltage is present, check the black/grey wire for continuity to earth.
4 If no voltage was present, check the black wire for continuity between the horn and the switch, and the brown wire from the switch to the fuse (see the wiring diagram at the end of this Chapter). With the ignition switch ON, check that there is voltage at the brown wire to the horn button in the left-hand switch gear. If there is, the problem lies between the switch and the horn. If there isn't, the problem lies between the ignition switch and the horn switch via the fuse.
5 If all the wiring and connectors are good, check the button contacts in the switch housing (see Section 20).

Replacement

6 The horn is mounted under the bottom yoke **(see illustration 25.1)**. On R-4, R-5 and RW-6 models, remove the left-hand fairing side panel (see Chapter 8). Turn the handlebars as required for best access.
7 Disconnect the wiring connectors from the horn. Unscrew the bolt securing the horn, noting the collar and rubber washers.
8 Install the horn, aligning the tab with the hole, fit the rubber washers and collar and tighten the bolt. Connect the wiring to the horn. Check that it works.

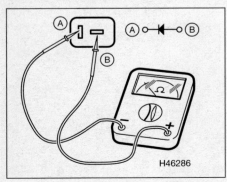

24.4 Neutral switch diode test

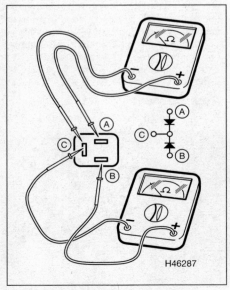

24.5 Clutch switch diode test

25.1 Horn wiring connectors (A) and mounting bolt (B)

26.2 Starter relay (arrowed)

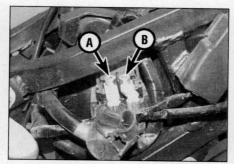

26.3 Starter motor lead (A), battery lead (B)

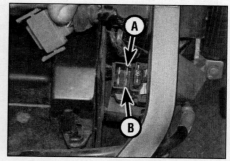

26.5 Connect the battery to the terminals – yellow/red (A), green/red(B)

26 Starter relay

Check

1 If the starter circuit is faulty, first check the fuses (see Section 5).

2 The starter relay is located under the rider's seat on the left-hand side of the battery **(see illustration)** – remove the rider's seat and for best access the seat cowling (see Chapter 8).

3 Lift the rubber terminal cover and unscrew the bolt securing the starter motor lead **(see illustration)**; position the lead away from the relay terminal. With the ignition switch ON, the engine kill switch in the RUN position, and the transmission in neutral, press the starter switch. The relay should be heard to click.

4 If the relay doesn't click, switch off the ignition and remove the relay as described below; test it as follows.

5 Set a multimeter to the ohms x 1 scale and connect it across the relay's starter motor and battery lead terminals **(see illustration 26.3)**. There should be no continuity. Using a fully-charged 12 volt battery and two insulated jumper wires, connect the positive (+) terminal of the battery to the yellow/red wire terminal of the relay, and the negative (–) terminal to the green/red wire terminal of the relay **(see illustration)**. At this point the relay should be heard to click and the multimeter read 0 ohms (continuity). If this is the case the relay

is proved good. If the relay does not click when battery voltage is applied and indicates no continuity (infinite resistance) across its terminals, it is faulty and must be replaced with a new one.

6 If the relay is good, check for continuity in the main lead from the battery to the relay. Also check that the terminals and connectors at each end of the lead are tight and corrosion-free.

7 Next check for battery voltage at the yellow/red wire terminal on the relay wiring connector with the ignition ON, the kill switch in the RUN position and the starter button pressed. If there is no voltage, check the wiring between the relay wiring connector and the starter button.

8 If voltage is present, check that there is continuity to earth in the green/red wire with the transmission in neutral (note that there will be a very slight resistance due to the neutral switch diode). If not check the wiring and connectors between the relay, the fusebox and the neutral switch, then if that is good check the switch itself and the diode.

9 Now put the transmission in gear, raise the sidestand and pull the clutch lever in and check for continuity to earth again. If there is no continuity, check the clutch switch and diodes and the sidestand switch as described in the relevant sections of this Chapter. If all components are good, check the wiring between the various components (see the wiring diagram at the end of this Chapter).

Replacement

10 The starter relay is located under the rider's seat on the left-hand side of the battery **(see illustration 26.2)** – remove the rider's seat and for best access the seat cowling (see Chapter 8).

11 Disconnect the battery terminals, remembering to disconnect the negative (–) terminal first (see Section 3).

12 Disconnect the relay wiring connector **(see illustration)**. Lift the insulating cover and unscrew the bolts securing the starter motor and battery leads to the relay and detach the leads **(see illustration 26.3)**. Remove the relay from its rubber sleeve. If the relay is being replaced with a new one, remove the main fuse from the relay.

13 Installation is the reverse of removal. Make sure the terminal bolts are securely tightened. Do not forget to fit the main fuse into the relay, if removed. Connect the negative (–) lead last when reconnecting the battery.

27 Starter motor removal and installation

Removal

1 Remove the rider's seat (see Chapter 8). Disconnect the battery negative (–) lead (see Section 3). The starter motor is mounted on the front of the engine.

2 Remove the lower fairing (see Chapter 8).

3 Peel back the rubber terminal cover on the starter motor **(see illustration)**. Unscrew the nut securing the starter lead to the motor and detach the lead – if the terminal is corroded, which is likely due to its position, spray it with some penetrating fluid and leave it awhile before attempting to undo it.

4 Unscrew the two bolts securing the starter motor to the crankcase, noting the earth lead secured by the top bolt **(see illustration)**. Slide the starter motor out and remove it **(see illustration)**.

5 Remove the O-ring on the end of the starter motor and discard it as a new one must be used.

26.12 Disconnect the relay wiring connector

27.3 Pull back the terminal cover then unscrew the nut and detach the lead

27.4a Unscrew the two bolts (arrowed), noting the earth lead . . .

27.4b . . . and remove the starter motor

27.6 Fit a new O-ring and lubricate it

Installation

6 Fit a new O-ring onto the end of the starter motor, making sure it is seated in its groove **(see illustration)**. Apply a smear of engine oil to the O-ring.

7 Manoeuvre the motor into position and slide it into the crankcase **(see illustration 27.4b)**. Ensure that the starter motor teeth mesh correctly with those of the starter idle/reduction gear. Install the mounting bolts, not forgetting to secure the earth lead with the top bolt, and tighten them **(see illustration)**.

8 Connect the starter lead to the motor and secure it with the nut **(see illustration 27.3)**. Fit the rubber cover over the terminal.

9 Install the lower fairing (see Chapter 8).

10 Connect the battery negative (–) lead and install the rider's seat (see Chapter 8).

28 Starter motor overhaul

Check

1 Remove the starter motor (see Section 27). Cover the body in some rag and clamp the motor in a soft-jawed vice – do not over-tighten it.

2 Using a fully-charged 12 volt battery and two insulated jumper wires, connect the positive (+) terminal of the battery to the protruding terminal on the starter motor, and the negative (–) terminal to one of the motor's mounting lugs. At this point the starter motor should spin. If this is the case the motor is proved good, though it is worth overhauling it if you suspect it of not working properly under load. If the motor does not spin, disassemble it for inspection.

Disassembly

3 Remove the starter motor (see Section 27).

4 Note any alignment marks between the main housing and the front and rear covers, or make your own if they aren't clear **(see illustration)**.

5 Unscrew the two long bolts, noting the O-rings, then remove the front cover from the motor along with its sealing ring **(see illustrations)**. Discard the sealing ring as a new one must be used. Remove the tabbed washer from the cover and slide the insulating washer and shim(s) from the front end of the armature (though they could be stuck to the tabbed washer), noting the number of shims and their correct fitted order **(see illustrations)**.

27.7 Do not forget to secure the earth lead with the top bolt

28.4 Note the alignment marks between the housing and the covers

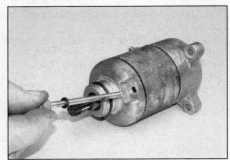

28.5a Unscrew and remove the two bolts . . .

28.5b . . . then remove the front cover and sealing ring (arrowed)

28.5c Remove the tabbed washer . . .

28.5d . . . and the insulating washer and shim(s)

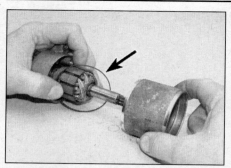

28.6 Remove the housing and the sealing ring (arrowed)

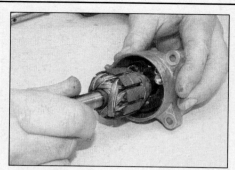

28.7 Draw the armature out of the rear cover

28.9a Slide the brushes out and remove the springs, then undo the screws (arrowed) . . .

28.9b . . . and remove the brush plate . . .

28.9c . . . and the insulators

28.10a Unscrew the nut (arrowed) and remove the plain washer and the large and small insulating washers

6 Hold the rear cover and armature and draw the main housing off **(see illustration)** – note that there will be some resistance due to the attraction of the magnets. Remove the sealing ring. Discard the sealing ring as a new one must be used.

7 Withdraw the armature from the rear cover **(see illustration)**. Remove the shim(s) from the rear end of the armature or from in the rear cover noting their correct fitted positions **(see illustration 28.21a)**.

8 At this stage check for continuity between the terminal bolt and its brush – there should be continuity (zero resistance). Check for continuity between the terminal bolt and the cover – there

should be no continuity (infinite resistance). Also check for continuity between the other brush and the rear cover – there should be continuity (zero resistance). If there is no continuity when there should be or vice versa, identify the faulty component and replace it with a new one.

9 Slide the brushes out of their housings and remove the springs **(see illustration)**. Undo the two screws securing the brushplate, noting how one secures a brush, and remove the washers. Lift the brushplate out of the cover **(see illustration)**. Remove the two insulators **(see illustration)**.

10 Noting the correct fitted location of each component, unscrew the nut from the terminal

bolt and remove the plain washer, the one large and two small insulating washers **(see illustration)**. Withdraw the terminal bolt from the cover, noting how it locates **(see illustration)**. Remove the O-ring from the bolt and the insulator piece from the cover.

Inspection

11 The parts of the starter motor that are most likely to require attention are the brushes. Measure the length of each brush and compare the results to the length listed in this Chapter's Specifications **(see illustration)**. If either of the brushes are worn beyond the service limit, fit a new set. If the brushes are

28.10b Remove the terminal bolt and its O-ring, and the insulator (arrowed)

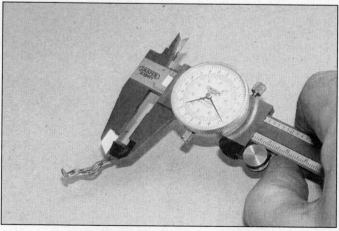

28.11 Measure the length of each brush

28.13a There should be continuity between the bars . . .

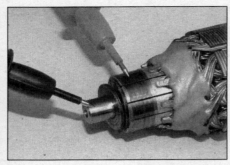

28.13b . . . and no continuity between the bars and the shaft

28.15a Check the bearing and seal in the front cover . . .

28.15b . . . and the bush (arrowed) in the rear cover

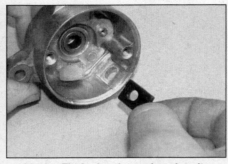

28.18a Fit the insulator piece into its cut-out

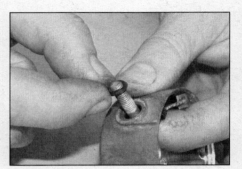

28.18b Fit the O-ring over the bolt . . .

not worn excessively, nor cracked, chipped, or otherwise damaged, they may be reused. Check the brush springs for distortion and fatigue. Check the brushplate and insulators for damage.

12 Inspect the commutator bars on the armature for scoring, scratches and discoloration. The commutator can be cleaned and polished with crocus cloth, but do not use sandpaper or emery paper. After cleaning, wipe away any residue with a cloth soaked in electrical system cleaner or denatured alcohol.

13 Using an ohmmeter or a continuity test light, check for continuity between the commutator bars **(see illustration)**. Continuity should exist between each bar and all of the others. Also, check for continuity between the commutator bars and the armature shaft **(see illustration)**. There should be no continuity (infinite resistance) between the commutator

and the shaft. If the checks indicate otherwise, the armature is defective and a new starter motor bust be obtained – the armature is not available separately.

14 Check the front end of the armature shaft for worn, cracked, chipped and broken teeth. If the shaft is damaged or worn, a new starter motor must be obtained – the armature is not available separately.

15 Inspect the front and rear covers for signs of cracks or wear. Check the oil seal and the needle bearing in the front cover and the bush in the rear cover for wear and damage – the seal, bearing, bush and covers are not listed as being available separately so if necessary a new starter motor must be fitted **(see illustrations)**.

16 Inspect the magnets in the main housing and the housing itself for cracks.

17 Inspect the insulating washers, O-ring and

sealing rings, replacing them with new ones if necessary.

Reassembly

18 Fit the insulator piece into the rear cover **(see illustration)**. Insert the terminal bolt through its hole **(see illustration 28.10b)**. Fit the O-ring down over the bolt and press it into place between the bolt and the cover **(see illustrations)**. Slide the small insulating washers onto the terminal bolt, followed by the large insulating washer and the plain washer **(see illustration 28.10a)**. Fit the nut onto the terminal bolt and tighten it securely.

19 Fit the brush insulators into the rear cover **(see illustration 28.9c)**. Fit the brushplate, making sure it locates correctly, then fit the washers and the screws, not forgetting to secure the brush **(see illustrations)**. Slide the springs and brushes

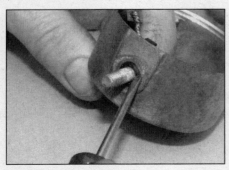

28.18c . . . then slide it down and press it into place

28.19a Locate the brushplate . . .

28.19b . . . then fit the washers . . .

28.19c . . . and the screws, not forgetting the brush

28.19d Fit the springs . . .

28.19e . . . then slide each brush into its housing

28.21a Fit the shim(s) onto the shaft . . .

28.21b . . . then push the brushes back as shown . . .

28.21c . . . and fit the armature into the rear cover making sure the brushes locate correctly onto the commutator

back into position in their housings (see illustrations).

20 At this stage check for continuity between the terminal bolt and the cover – there should be no continuity (infinite resistance). Also check for continuity between the uninsulated brush and the rear cover – there should be continuity (zero resistance). If there is no continuity when there should be or vice versa, identify the faulty component and replace it with a new one.

21 Fit the shim(s) onto the rear of the armature shaft (see illustration). Apply a smear of grease to the end of the shaft. Using a pair of external circlip pliers or something similar, push the brushes into the housing and hold them there (see illustration). Insert the armature into the rear cover so that the shaft end locates in its bush, then release the brushes so they locate against the commutator (see illustration).

22 Fit the sealing ring onto the rear of the main housing, which has a cut-out in its rim (see illustration). Grasp both the armature and the rear cover in one hand and hold them together – this will prevent the armature being drawn out by the magnets in the housing. Note however that you should take care not to let the housing be drawn forcibly onto the armature by the magnets. Carefully allow the housing to be drawn onto the armature, making sure the end with the cut-out faces the rear cover, that the cut-out locates over the tab on the insulator piece, and the marks between the cover and housing align (Step 4) (see illustrations).

23 Apply a smear of grease to the front cover oil seal lip. Fit the tabbed washer into the cover so that its teeth are correctly located with the cover ribs (see illustration 28.5c).

28.22a Fit a new sealing ring onto the rear of the housing . . .

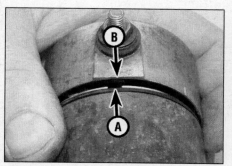

28.22c . . . locating the cut-out (A) over the tab (B)

24 Fit the sealing ring onto the front of the housing (see illustration). Slide the shim(s) onto the front end of the armature shaft then fit the insulating washer (see illustration 28.5d).

28.22b . . . then fit the housing onto the armature . . .

28.24 Fit a new sealing ring onto the front of the housing

Slide the front cover into position, aligning the marks **(see illustration 28.5b)**.

25 Check the marks made on removal are correctly aligned then fit the long bolts, not forgetting the O-rings (using new ones if necessary) and tighten them **(see illustration 28.5a)**.

26 Install the starter motor (see Section 27).

29 Charging system testing

1 If the performance of the charging system is suspect, the system as a whole should be checked first, followed by testing of the individual components. **Note:** *Before beginning the checks, make sure the battery is fully charged and that all system connections are clean and tight.*

2 Checking the output of the charging system and the performance of the various components within the charging system requires the use of a multimeter (with voltage, current, resistance checking facilities). If a multimeter is not available, the job of checking the charging system should be left to a Honda dealer.

3 When making the checks, follow the procedures carefully to prevent incorrect connections or short circuits resulting in irreparable damage to electrical system components.

Leakage test

Caution: Always connect an ammeter in series, never in parallel with the battery, otherwise it will be damaged. Do not turn the ignition ON or operate the starter motor when the ammeter is connected – a sudden surge in current will blow the meter's fuse.

4 Ensure the ignition is OFF, then remove the rider's seat (see Chapter 8) and disconnect the battery negative (-) lead (see Section 3).

5 Set the multimeter to the Amps function and connect its negative (-) probe to the battery negative (-) terminal, and positive (+) probe to the disconnected negative (-) lead **(see illustration)**. Always set the meter to a high amps range initially and then bring it

down to the mA (milli Amps) range; if there is a high current flow in the circuit it may blow the meter's fuse.

6 Battery current leakage should not exceed the maximum limit (see Specifications). If a higher leakage rate is shown there is a short circuit in the wiring, although if an after-market immobiliser or alarm is fitted, its current draw should be taken into account. Disconnect the meter and reconnect the battery negative (-) lead.

7 If leakage is indicated, refer to Wiring Diagram at the end of this Chapter to systematically disconnect individual electrical components and repeat the test until the source is identified.

Regulated output test

8 Remove the rider's seat (see Chapter 8), then start the engine and warm it up.

9 To check the regulated (DC) voltage output, allow the engine to idle with the headlight main beam (HI) turned ON. Connect a multimeter set to the 0-20 volts DC scale across the terminals of the battery with the positive (+) meter probe to battery positive (+) terminal and the negative (-) meter probe to battery negative (-) terminal (see Section 3).

10 Slowly increase the engine speed to 5000 rpm and note the reading obtained. Compare the result with the Specification at the beginning of this Chapter. If the regulated voltage output is outside the specification, check the alternator and the regulator (see Sections 30 and 31).

> **HAYNES HINT** *Clues to a faulty regulator are constantly blowing bulbs, with brightness varying considerably with engine speed, and battery overheating.*

30 Alternator

Special tool: A rotor puller is necessary to draw the alternator rotor off the crankshaft end (see Step 9).

Check

1 Free the wiring loom from the clip on

the inside of the frame above the sprocket cover, then draw the rubber boot off the connectors and disconnect the white 6-pin wiring connector **(see illustration)** – it should be accessible with the left-hand fairing side panel in place, but remove it if necessary (see Chapter 8).

2 Check the connector terminals for corrosion and security.

3 Using a multimeter set to the ohms x 1 (ohmmeter) scale measure the resistance between each of the yellow wires on the alternator side of the connector, taking a total of three readings, then check for continuity between each terminal and ground (earth). If the stator coil windings are in good condition the three readings should be within the range shown in the Specifications at the start of this Chapter, and there should be no continuity (infinite resistance) between any of the terminals and ground (earth). If not, the alternator stator coil assembly is at fault and should be replaced with a new one. **Note:** *Before condemning the stator coils, check the fault is not due to damaged wiring between the connector and the coils.*

Removal

4 Remove the lower fairing (see Chapter 8). Remove the front sprocket cover **(see illustration 21.8)**.

5 Drain the engine oil (see Chapter 1).

6 Free the wiring loom from the clip on the inside of the frame above the sprocket cover, then draw the rubber boot off the connectors and disconnect the white 6-pin wiring connector **(see illustration 30.1)** – it should be accessible with the left-hand fairing side panel in place, but remove it if necessary (see Chapter 8).

7 Working in a criss-cross pattern, evenly slacken the alternator cover bolts **(see illustration)**. Discard the sealing washer fitted with the centre top bolt and obtain a new one. Draw the cover off the engine, noting that it will be restrained by the force of the rotor magnets, and be prepared to catch any residual oil. Remove and discard the gasket. Remove the dowels from either the cover or the crankcase if loose.

8 To remove the rotor nut it is necessary to stop the rotor from turning. The best way is

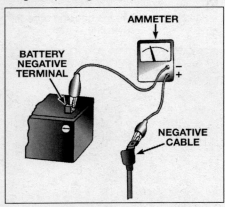

29.5 Checking the charging system leakage rate – connect the meter as shown

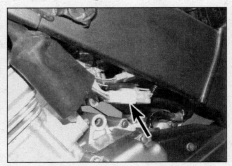

30.1 Disconnect the alternator wiring connector (arrowed)

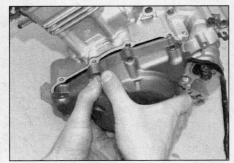

30.7 Unscrew the bolts and remove the cover

30.8 Using a rotor strap to hold the rotor while unscrewing the nut

30.9a Thread the puller onto the rotor . . .

30.9b . . . then hold the puller and turn the bolt

30.9c Remove the Woodruff key (arrowed) if it is loose

30.10 Unscrew the stator bolts (A) and the pulse generator bolts (B) and free the grommet (C)

30.13 Slide the rotor onto the shaft, aligning the cut-out with the Woodruff key

to use a commercially available rotor strap **(see illustration)**. If one is not available, try placing the transmission in gear and having an assistant apply the rear brake hard. Unscrew the nut and remove the washer.

9 To remove the rotor from the shaft it is necessary to use a rotor puller (Honda part No. 07KMC-HE00100, or a commercially available equivalent). Thread the rotor puller onto the centre of the rotor, then counter-hold it using a spanner on the flats and tighten the bolt in its centre until the rotor is displaced from the shaft **(see illustrations)**. Remove the Woodruff key from its slot in the crankcase if it is loose **(see illustration)**. If required detach the starter clutch from the rotor (see Chapter 2).

10 To remove the stator from the cover, unscrew its bolts and the bolts securing the pulse generator coil and the wiring clamp,

then remove the assembly, noting how the clamp and the rubber wiring grommet fit **(see illustration)**.

Installation

11 Fit the stator into the cover, aligning the rubber wiring grommet with the groove **(see illustration 30.10)**. Apply a suitable thread locking compound to the stator and pick-up coil bolts and tighten them to the torque setting specified at the beginning of the Chapter, not forgetting the wiring clamp. Apply a suitable sealant to the wiring grommet, then press it into the cut-out in the cover.

12 Clean the tapered end of the crankshaft and the corresponding mating surface on the inside of the rotor with a suitable solvent. Fit the Woodruff key into its slot in the crankshaft if removed **(see illustration 30.9c)**.

13 If removed fit the starter clutch onto the rotor (see Chapter 2). Make sure that no metal objects have attached themselves to the magnet on the inside of the rotor. Slide the rotor onto the shaft, making sure the groove on the inside of the rotor is aligned with and fits over the Woodruff key **(see illustration)**. Make sure the Woodruff key does not become dislodged when installing the rotor.

14 Apply some clean oil to the rotor nut threads and the underside of the head. Fit the nut with its washer and tighten it to the torque setting specified at the beginning of the Chapter, using the method employed on removal to prevent the rotor from turning **(see illustrations)**.

15 Fit the dowels into the crankcase if removed, then locate a new gasket onto the dowels **(see illustration)**. Smear a suitable

30.14a Lubricate the nut then install it with its washer . . .

30.14b . . . and tighten it to the specified torque

30.15a Make sure the dowels (arrowed) are in place, then fit the new gasket

30.15b Smear sealant onto the grommet

30.15c Use a new sealing washer on the centre top bolt

sealant onto the wiring grommet **(see illustration)**. Install the alternator cover, noting that the rotor magnets will forcibly draw the cover/stator on, making sure it locates onto the dowels **(see illustration 30.7)**. Tighten the cover bolts evenly in a criss-cross sequence, not forgetting to fit a new sealing washer with the centre top bolt **(see illustration)**.

16 Reconnect the wiring at the connector, then fit the boot and secure the wiring in the clip **(see illustration 30.1)**.

17 Fill the engine with oil to the correct level (see Chapter 1). Install the lower fairing panel and side panel if removed (see Chapter 8).

31 Regulator/rectifier

Check

1 On R-4, R-5 and RW-6 models, remove the seat cowling; on RW-7, RW-8, RW-9, RW-A models, remove the fairing left-hand sidepanel (see Chapter 8).

2 Disconnect the regulator/rectifier wiring connector **(see illustrations)**. Check the connector terminals for corrosion and security.

3 Set the multimeter to the 0-20 DC volts setting. Connect the meter positive (+) probe

to the red wire terminal on the loom side of the connector and the negative (–) probe to a suitable ground (earth) and check for voltage. Full battery voltage should be present at all times.

4 Switch the multimeter to the resistance (ohms) scale. Check for continuity between the green wire terminals on the loom side of the connector and ground (earth). There should be continuity in each terminal.

5 Set the multimeter to the ohms x 1 (ohmmeter) scale and measure the resistance between each of the yellow wires on the loom side of the connector, taking a total of three readings, then check for continuity between each terminal and ground (earth). The three

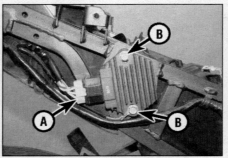

31.2a Regulator/rectifier wiring connector (A) and mounting bolts (B) – R-4, R-5, RW-6 models

readings should be within the range shown in the Specifications for the alternator stator coil at the start of this Chapter, and there should be no continuity (infinite resistance) between any of the terminals and ground (earth).

6 If the above checks do not provide the expected results check the wiring and connectors between the battery, regulator/rectifier and alternator for shorts, breaks, and loose or corroded terminals (see the wiring diagram at the end of this chapter).

7 If the wiring checks out, the regulator/rectifier unit is probably faulty. Honda provide no test data for the unit itself. Take it to a Honda dealer for confirmation of its condition before replacing it with a new one.

Removal and installation

8 On R-4, R-5 and RW-6 models, remove the seat cowling; on RW-7, RW-8, RW-9, RW-A models, remove the fairing left-hand sidepanel (see Chapter 8).

9 Disconnect the regulator/rectifier wiring connector **(see illustration 31.2a or b)**.

10 Unscrew the two bolts securing the regulator/rectifier to the rear sub-frame, noting the earth wire secured by the lower bolt, and remove it **(see illustration 31.2a or b)**.

11 Fit the new unit and tighten its bolts, not forgetting the earth wire with the lower bolt. Connect the wiring connector.

12 Install the seat cowling (see Chapter 8).

31.2b Regulator/rectifier mounting bolts (arrowed) – RW-7, RW-8, RW-9, RW-A models

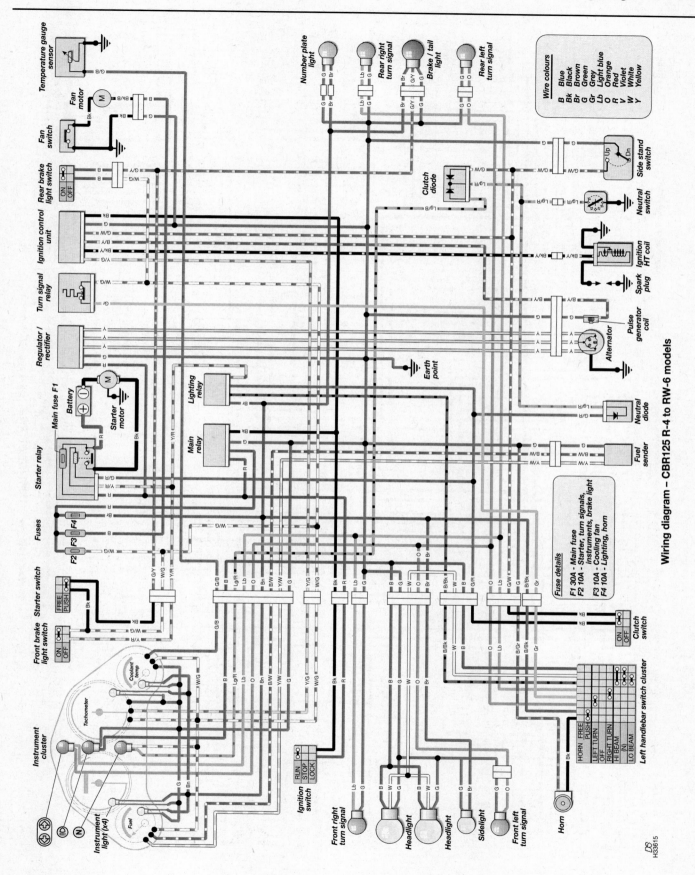

Wiring diagram – CBR125 R-4 to RW-6 models

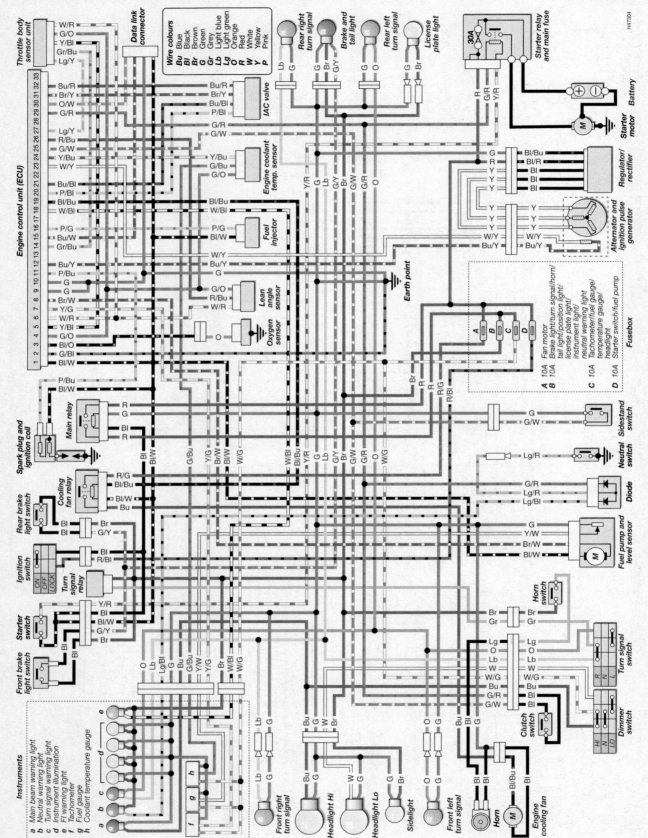

Wiring diagram - CBR125RW-7, RW-8, RW-9 and RW-A models

Length (distance)

Inches (in)	x 25.4	= Millimetres (mm)	x 0.0394	= Inches (in)
Feet (ft)	x 0.305	= Metres (m)	x 3.281	= Feet (ft)
Miles	x 1.609	= Kilometres (km)	x 0.621	= Miles

Volume (capacity)

Cubic inches (cu in; in^3)	x 16.387	= Cubic centimetres (cc; cm^3)	x 0.061	= Cubic inches (cu in; in^3)
Imperial pints (Imp pt)	x 0.568	= Litres (l)	x 1.76	= Imperial pints (Imp pt)
Imperial quarts (Imp qt)	x 1.137	= Litres (l)	x 0.88	= Imperial quarts (Imp qt)
Imperial quarts (Imp qt)	x 1.201	= US quarts (US qt)	x 0.833	= Imperial quarts (Imp qt)
US quarts (US qt)	x 0.946	= Litres (l)	x 1.057	= US quarts (US qt)
Imperial gallons (Imp gal)	x 4.546	= Litres (l)	x 0.22	= Imperial gallons (Imp gal)
Imperial gallons (Imp gal)	x 1.201	= US gallons (US gal)	x 0.833	= Imperial gallons (Imp gal)
US gallons (US gal)	x 3.785	= Litres (l)	x 0.264	= US gallons (US gal)

Mass (weight)

Ounces (oz)	x 28.35	= Grams (g)	x 0.035	= Ounces (oz)
Pounds (lb)	x 0.454	= Kilograms (kg)	x 2.205	= Pounds (lb)

Force

Ounces-force (ozf; oz)	x 0.278	= Newtons (N)	x 3.6	= Ounces-force (ozf; oz)
Pounds-force (lbf; lb)	x 4.448	= Newtons (N)	x 0.225	= Pounds-force (lbf; lb)
Newtons (N)	x 0.1	= Kilograms-force (kgf; kg)	x 9.81	= Newtons (N)

Pressure

Pounds-force per square inch (psi; lbf/in^2; lb/in^2)	x 0.070	= Kilograms-force per square centimetre (kgf/cm^2; kg/cm^2)	x 14.223	= Pounds-force per square inch (psi; lbf/in^2; lb/in^2)
Pounds-force per square inch (psi; lbf/in^2; lb/in^2)	x 0.068	= Atmospheres (atm)	x 14.696	= Pounds-force per square inch (psi; lbf/in^2; lb/in^2)
Pounds-force per square inch (psi; lbf/in^2; lb/in^2)	x 0.069	= Bars	x 14.5	= Pounds-force per square inch (psi; lbf/in^2; lb/in^2)
Pounds-force per square inch (psi; lbf/in^2; lb/in^2)	x 6.895	= Kilopascals (kPa)	x 0.145	= Pounds-force per square inch (psi; lbf/in^2; lb/in^2)
Kilopascals (kPa)	x 0.01	= Kilograms-force per square centimetre (kgf/cm^2; kg/cm^2)	x 98.1	= Kilopascals (kPa)
Millibar (mbar)	x 100	= Pascals (Pa)	x 0.01	= Millibar (mbar)
Millibar (mbar)	x 0.0145	= Pounds-force per square inch (psi; lbf/in^2; lb/in^2)	x 68.947	= Millibar (mbar)
Millibar (mbar)	x 0.75	= Millimetres of mercury (mmHg)	x 1.333	= Millibar (mbar)
Millibar (mbar)	x 0.401	= Inches of water (inH$_2$O)	x 2.491	= Millibar (mbar)
Millimetres of mercury (mmHg)	x 0.535	= Inches of water (inH$_2$O)	x 1.868	= Millimetres of mercury (mmHg)
Inches of water (inH$_2$O)	x 0.036	= Pounds-force per square inch (psi; lbf/in^2; lb/in^2)	x 27.68	= Inches of water (inH$_2$O)

Torque (moment of force)

Pounds-force inches (lbf in; lb in)	x 1.152	= Kilograms-force centimetre (kgf cm; kg cm)	x 0.868	= Pounds-force inches (lbf in; lb in)
Pounds-force inches (lbf in; lb in)	x 0.113	= Newton metres (Nm)	x 8.85	= Pounds-force inches (lbf in; lb in)
Pounds-force inches (lbf in; lb in)	x 0.083	= Pounds-force feet (lbf ft; lb ft)	x 12	= Pounds-force inches (lbf in; lb in)
Pounds-force feet (lbf ft; lb ft)	x 0.138	= Kilograms-force metres (kgf m; kg m)	x 7.233	= Pounds-force feet (lbf ft; lb ft)
Pounds-force feet (lbf ft; lb ft)	x 1.356	= Newton metres (Nm)	x 0.738	= Pounds-force feet (lbf ft; lb ft)
Newton metres (Nm)	x 0.102	= Kilograms-force metres (kgf m; kg m)	x 9.804	= Newton metres (Nm)

Power

Horsepower (hp)	x 745.7	= Watts (W)	x 0.0013	= Horsepower (hp)

Velocity (speed)

Miles per hour (miles/hr; mph)	x 1.609	= Kilometres per hour (km/hr; kph)	x 0.621	= Miles per hour (miles/hr; mph)

Fuel consumption*

Miles per gallon (mpg)	x 0.354	= Kilometres per litre (km/l)	x 2.825	= Miles per gallon (mpg)

Temperature

Degrees Fahrenheit = (°C x 1.8) + 32   Degrees Celsius (Degrees Centigrade; °C) = (°F - 32) x 0.56

It is common practice to convert from miles per gallon (mpg) to litres/100 kilometres (l/100km), where mpg x l/100 km = 282

This Section provides an easy reference-guide to the more common faults that are likely to afflict your machine. Obviously, the opportunities are almost limitless for faults to occur as a result of obscure failures, and to try and cover all eventualities would require a book. Indeed, a number have been written on the subject.

Successful troubleshooting is not a mysterious 'black art' but the application of a bit of knowledge combined with a systematic and logical approach to the problem. Approach any troubleshooting by first accurately identifying the symptom and then checking through the list of possible causes, starting with the simplest or most obvious and progressing in stages to the most complex.

Take nothing for granted, but above all apply liberal quantities of common sense.

The main symptom of a fault is given in the text as a major heading below which are listed the various systems or areas which may contain the fault. Details of each possible cause for a fault and the remedial action to be taken are given, in brief, in the paragraphs below each heading. Further information should be sought in the relevant Chapter.

1 Engine doesn't start or is difficult to start

- [ ] Starter motor doesn't rotate
- [ ] Starter motor rotates but engine does not turn over
- [ ] Starter works but engine won't turn over (seized)
- [ ] No fuel flow
- [ ] Engine flooded
- [ ] No spark or weak spark
- [ ] Compression low
- [ ] Stalls after starting
- [ ] Rough idle

2 Poor running at low speed

- [ ] Spark weak
- [ ] Fuel/air mixture incorrect
- [ ] Compression low
- [ ] Poor acceleration

3 Poor running or no power at high speed

- [ ] Firing incorrect
- [ ] Fuel/air mixture incorrect
- [ ] Compression low
- [ ] Knocking or pinking
- [ ] Miscellaneous causes

4 Overheating

- [ ] Engine overheats
- [ ] Firing incorrect
- [ ] Fuel/air mixture incorrect
- [ ] Compression too high
- [ ] Engine load excessive
- [ ] Lubrication inadequate
- [ ] Miscellaneous causes

5 Gearchanging problems

- [ ] Doesn't go into gear, or lever doesn't return
- [ ] Jumps out of gear
- [ ] Overselects

6 Clutch problems

- [ ] Clutch slipping
- [ ] Clutch not disengaging completely

7 Abnormal engine noise

- [ ] Knocking or pinking
- [ ] Piston slap or rattling
- [ ] Valve noise
- [ ] Other noise

8 Abnormal driveline noise

- [ ] Clutch noise
- [ ] Transmission noise
- [ ] Final drive noise

9 Abnormal frame and suspension noise

- [ ] Front end noise
- [ ] Shock absorber noise
- [ ] Brake noise

10 Excessive exhaust smoke

- [ ] White smoke
- [ ] Black smoke
- [ ] Brown smoke

11 Poor handling or stability

- [ ] Handlebars hard to turn
- [ ] Handlebars shake or vibrate excessively
- [ ] Handlebars pull to one side
- [ ] Poor shock absorbing qualities

12 Braking problems

- [ ] Brakes are spongy or don't hold
- [ ] Brake lever or pedal pulsates
- [ ] Brakes drag

13 Electrical problems

- [ ] Battery dead or weak
- [ ] Battery overcharged

1 Engine doesn't start or is difficult to start

Starter motor doesn't rotate

- [ ] Fuse blown. Check fuse (Chapter 9).
- [ ] Battery voltage low. Check and recharge battery (Chapter 9).
- [ ] Starter motor defective. Make sure the wiring to the starter is secure. Make sure the starter relay clicks when the start button is pushed. If the relay clicks, then the fault is probably in the wiring or motor.
- [ ] Starter relay faulty. Check it according to the procedure in Chapter 9.
- [ ] Starter button not contacting. The contacts could be wet, corroded or dirty. Disassemble and clean the switch (Chapter 9).
- [ ] Wiring open or shorted. Check all wiring connections and harnesses to make sure that they are dry, tight and not corroded.

Also check for broken or frayed wires that can cause a short to ground (earth) (see wiring diagram, Chapter 9).
- [ ] Ignition switch defective. Check the switch according to the procedure in Chapter 9. Replace the switch with a new one if it is defective.
- [ ] Faulty neutral/sidestand/clutch switch(es) or diodes. Check the wiring to each switch and the switch itself, and check the diodes, according to the procedures in Chapter 9.
- [ ] Fuel injection system shutdown due to system fault (Chapter 4B).

Starter motor rotates but engine does not turn over

- [ ] Starter clutch defective. Inspect and repair or replace (Chapter 2).
- [ ] Damaged idle/reduction or starter gears. Inspect and replace the damaged parts (Chapter 2).

1 Engine doesn't start or is difficult to start (continued)

Starter works but engine won't turn over (seized)

☐ Seized engine caused by one or more internally damaged components. Failure due to wear, abuse or lack of lubrication. Damage can include seized valves, rockers, camshaft, piston, crankshaft, bearings, or transmission gears or bearings. Refer to Chapter 2 for engine disassembly.

No fuel flow – carburettor models

☐ No fuel in tank.
☐ Fuel valve vacuum hose broken or disconnected.
☐ Tank cap air vent obstructed. Usually caused by dirt or water. Remove it and clean the cap vent hole.
☐ Fuel valve strainer clogged. Remove the valve and clean the strainer (Chapters 1 and 4A).
☐ Fuel hose clogged. Detach the fuel hose and carefully blow through it.
☐ Fuel passage clogged. For a passage to be clogged, either a very bad batch of fuel with an unusual additive has been used, or some other foreign material has entered the system. Many times after a machine has been stored for many months without running, the fuel turns to a varnish-like liquid and forms deposits on the inlet needle valve and jets. The carburettor should be removed and overhauled if draining the float bowl doesn't solve the problem.

No fuel flow – fuel injected models

☐ No fuel in tank.
☐ Fuel tank breather hose obstructed.
☐ Fuel pump faulty (see Chapter 4B).
☐ Fuel hose clogged. Remove the fuel hose and carefully blow through it.
☐ Fuel injector clogged. For the injector to be clogged, either a very bad batch of fuel with an unusual additive has been used, or some other foreign material has entered the tank. In some cases, if a machine has been unused for several months, the fuel turns to a varnish-like liquid which can cause an injector needle to stick to its seat. Drain the tank and clean the fuel system (Chapter 4B).

Engine flooded – carburettor models

☐ Float height too high. Check as described in Chapter 4A.
☐ Inlet needle valve worn or stuck open. A piece of dirt, rust or other debris can cause the inlet needle to seat improperly, causing excess fuel to be admitted to the float bowl. In this case, the float chamber should be cleaned and the needle and seat inspected. If the needle and seat are worn, then the leaking will persist and the parts should be replaced with new ones (Chapter 4A).
☐ Starting technique incorrect. Under normal circumstances (e.g., if all the carburettor functions are sound) the machine should start with little or no throttle. When the engine is cold, the choke should be operated and the engine started without opening the throttle. When the engine is at operating temperature, only a very slight amount of throttle should be necessary. If the engine is flooded, hold the throttle fully open while cranking the engine. This will allow additional air to reach the cylinder.

Engine flooded – fuel injected models

☐ Injector needle valve worn or stuck open, causing excess fuel to be admitted to the throttle body. In this case, the injector should be replaced with a new one.
☐ Starting technique incorrect. Under normal circumstances (i.e. if all the components of the fuel injection system are good) the machine should start with the throttle closed.

No spark or weak spark

☐ Ignition switch OFF.
☐ Battery voltage low. Check and recharge battery as necessary (Chapter 9).
☐ Spark plug dirty, defective or worn out. Locate reason for fouled plug using spark plug condition chart on the inside rear cover and follow the plug maintenance procedures in Chapter 1.
☐ Spark plug cap or lead faulty. Check condition. Replace either or both components if cracks or deterioration are evident (Chapter 5).

☐ Spark plug cap not making good contact. Make sure that the plug cap fits snugly over the plug end.
☐ Ignition control unit (carburettor models) defective (see Chapter 5). Engine control unit (fuel injected models) defective (see Chapter 4B).
☐ Pulse generator coil defective. Check the coil, referring to Chapter 5 for details.
☐ Ignition HT coil defective. Check the coil, referring to Chapter 5.
☐ Ignition switch shorted. This is usually caused by water, corrosion, damage or excessive wear. The switch can be disassembled and cleaned with electrical contact cleaner. If cleaning does not help, replace the switch (Chapter 9).
☐ Wiring shorted or broken. Make sure that all wiring connections are clean, dry and tight. Look for chafed and broken wires (Chapters 5 and 9).
☐ Fuel injection system shutdown due to system fault (Chapter 4B).

Compression low

☐ Spark plug loose. Remove the plug and inspect the threads. Reinstall and tighten to the specified torque (Chapter 1).
☐ Cylinder head not sufficiently tightened down. If the cylinder head is suspected of being loose, then there's a chance that the gasket or head is damaged if the problem has persisted for any length of time. The camshaft holder nuts should be tightened to the proper torque in the correct sequence (Chapter 2).
☐ Improper valve clearance. This means that the valve is not closing completely and compression pressure is leaking past the valve. Check and adjust the valve clearances (Chapter 1).
☐ Cylinder and/or piston worn. Excessive wear will cause compression pressure to leak past the rings. This is usually accompanied by worn rings as well. A top-end overhaul and rebore will be necessary (Chapter 2).
☐ Piston rings worn, weak, broken, or sticking. Broken or sticking piston rings usually indicate a lubrication or carburetion problem that causes excess carbon deposits or seizures to form on the pistons and rings. Top-end overhaul is necessary (Chapter 2).
☐ Piston ring-to-groove clearance excessive. This is caused by excessive wear of the piston ring lands. Piston replacement is necessary (Chapter 2).
☐ Cylinder head gasket damaged. If the head is allowed to become loose, or if excessive carbon build-up on the piston crown and combustion chamber causes extremely high compression, the head gasket may leak. Retorquing the head is not always sufficient to restore the seal, so gasket replacement is necessary (Chapter 2).
☐ Cylinder head warped. This is caused by overheating or improperly tightened camshaft holder nuts. Machine shop resurfacing or head replacement is necessary (Chapter 2).
☐ Valve spring broken or weak. Caused by component failure or wear; the springs must be replaced (Chapter 2).
☐ Valve not seating properly. This is caused by a bent valve (from over-revving or improper valve adjustment), burned valve or seat (improper fuelling) or an accumulation of carbon deposits on the seat (from fuelling or lubrication problems). The valves must be cleaned and/or replaced and the seats serviced if possible (Chapter 2).

Stalls after starting – carburettor models

☐ Improper choke action. Make sure the choke rod is getting a full stroke and staying in the out position.
☐ Ignition malfunction. See Chapter 5.
☐ Carburettor malfunction. See Chapter 4A.
☐ Fuel contaminated. The fuel can be contaminated with either dirt or water, or can change chemically if the machine is allowed to sit for several months or more. Drain the tank and check the fuel valve strainer (Chapters 4A and 1).
☐ Intake air leak. Check for a loose carburettor-to-intake connection, loose or missing vacuum hoses, or a loose carburettor top (Chapter 4A).
☐ Engine idle speed incorrect. Turn throttle stop screw until the engine idles at the specified rpm (Chapter 1).

1 Engine doesn't start or is difficult to start (continued)

Stalls after starting – fuel injected models

☐ Engine idle speed incorrect. Check the operation of the IACV (see Chapter 4B).
☐ Ignition malfunction (see Chapter 4B).
☐ Fuel injection system malfunction (see Chapter 4B).
☐ Fuel contaminated. The fuel can be contaminated with either dirt or water, or can change chemically if the machine has been unused for several months. Drain the tank and fuel system (Chapter 4B).
☐ Intake air leak. Check for loose throttle body-to-intake duct joints (Chapter 4B).

Rough idle – carburettor models

☐ Ignition malfunction. See Chapter 5.
☐ Idle speed incorrect. See Chapter 1.
☐ Carburettor malfunction. See Chapter 4A.
☐ Fuel contaminated. The fuel can be contaminated with either dirt or water, or can change chemically if the machine is allowed to sit for several months or more. Drain the tank and check the fuel valve strainer (Chapters 4A and 1).

Intake air leak

☐ Intake air leak. Check for a loose carburettor-to-intake connection, loose or missing vacuum hoses, or a loose carburettor top (Chapter 4A).
☐ Air filter clogged. Service or replace air filter element (Chapter 1).
☐ PAIR system hose detached or faulty reed valve or control valve. Check the system (Chapters 1 and 4A).

Rough idle – fuel injected models

☐ Idle speed incorrect (see Chapter 1). Check the operation of the IACV (see Chapter 4B).
☐ Fuel injection system malfunction (see Chapter 4B).
☐ Fuel contaminated. The fuel can be contaminated with either dirt or water, or can change chemically if the machine has been unused for several months. Drain the tank and the fuel system (Chapter 4B).
☐ Intake air leak. Check for loose throttle body-to-intake manifold connections (Chapter 4B).
☐ Air filter clogged. Clean the air filter element or replace it with a new one (Chapter 1).

2 Poor running at low speed

Spark weak

☐ Battery voltage low. Check and recharge battery (Chapter 9).
☐ Spark plug fouled, defective or worn out. Refer to Chapter 1 for spark plug maintenance.
☐ Spark plug cap or lead defective. Refer to Chapters 1 and 5 for details on the ignition system.
☐ Spark plug cap not making contact.
☐ Incorrect spark plug. Wrong type, heat range or cap configuration. Check and install correct plug listed in Chapter 1.
☐ Ignition control unit (carburettor models) defective (see Chapter 5). Engine control unit (fuel injected models) defective (see Chapter 4B).
☐ Pulse generator coil defective. See Chapter 5.
☐ Ignition HT coil defective. See Chapter 5.

Fuel/air mixture incorrect – carburettor models

☐ Pilot screw out of adjustment (Chapter 4A).
☐ Pilot jet or air passage clogged. Remove and overhaul the carburettor (Chapter 4A).
☐ Air bleed holes clogged. Remove carburettor and blow out all passages (Chapter 4A).
☐ Air filter clogged, poorly sealed or missing (Chapter 1).
☐ Air filter housing poorly sealed. Look for cracks, holes or loose clamps and replace or repair defective parts.
☐ Fuel level too high or too low. Check the float height (Chapter 4A).
☐ Fuel tank air vent obstructed. Make sure that the air vent passage in the filler cap is open.
☐ Carburettor intake duct loose. Check for cracks, breaks, tears or loose clamps. Replace the rubber intake.

Fuel/air mixture incorrect – fuel injected models

☐ Fuel tank breather hose obstructed.
☐ Fuel pump faulty (see Chapter 4B).
☐ Fuel hose clogged. Remove the fuel hose and carefully blow through it.
☐ Fuel injector clogged. In some cases, if a machine has been unused for several months, the fuel turns to a varnish-like liquid which can cause the injector needle to stick to its seat. Drain the tank and fuel system (Chapter 4B).
☐ Intake air leak. Check for loose throttle body-to-intake duct joints (Chapter 4B).
☐ Air filter clogged. Clean the air filter element or replace it with a new one (Chapter 1).

Compression low

☐ Spark plug loose. Remove the plug and inspect the threads. Reinstall and tighten to the specified torque (Chapter 1).
☐ Cylinder head not sufficiently tightened down. If the cylinder head is suspected of being loose, then there's a chance that the gasket and head are damaged if the problem has persisted for any length of time. The camshaft holder nuts should be tightened to the proper torque in the correct sequence (Chapter 2).
☐ Improper valve clearance. This means that the valve is not closing completely and compression pressure is leaking past the valve. Check and adjust the valve clearances (Chapter 1).
☐ Cylinder and/or piston worn. Excessive wear will cause compression pressure to leak past the rings. This is usually accompanied by worn rings as well. A top-end overhaul and rebore will be necessary (Chapter 2).
☐ Piston rings worn, weak, broken, or sticking. Broken or sticking piston rings usually indicate a lubrication or carburetion problem that causes excess carbon deposits or seizures to form on the pistons and rings. Top-end overhaul is necessary (Chapter 2).
☐ Piston ring-to-groove clearance excessive. This is caused by excessive wear of the piston ring lands. Piston replacement is necessary (Chapter 2).
☐ Cylinder head gasket damaged. If the head is allowed to become loose, or if excessive carbon build-up on the piston crown and combustion chamber causes extremely high compression, the head gasket may leak. Retorquing the head is not always sufficient to restore the seal, so gasket replacement is necessary (Chapter 2).
☐ Cylinder head warped. This is caused by overheating or improperly tightened camshaft holder nuts. Machine shop resurfacing or head replacement is necessary (Chapter 2).
☐ Valve spring broken or weak. Caused by component failure or wear; the springs must be replaced (Chapter 2).
☐ Valve not seating properly. This is caused by a bent valve (from over-revving or improper valve adjustment), burned valve or seat (improper fuelling) or an accumulation of carbon deposits on the seat (from fuelling, lubrication problems). The valves must be cleaned and/or replaced and the seats serviced if possible (Chapter 2).

Poor acceleration

☐ Timing not advancing. The pulse generator coil or the ignition control unit/engine control unit may be defective. If so, they must be replaced with new ones, as they can't be repaired.
☐ Engine oil viscosity too high. Using a heavier oil than that recommended in 'Pre-ride checks' can damage the oil pump or lubrication system and cause drag on the engine.
☐ Brakes dragging. Usually caused by debris which has entered the brake piston seals, or from a warped disc or bent axle. Repair as necessary (Chapter 7).

3 Poor running or no power at high speed

Firing incorrect

☐ Air filter restricted. Clean or replace filter (Chapter 1).

☐ Spark plug fouled, defective or worn out. See Chapter 1 for spark plug maintenance.

☐ Spark plug cap or lead wiring defective. See Chapters 1 and 5 for details of the ignition system.

☐ Spark plug cap not in good contact. See Chapter 5.

☐ Incorrect spark plug. Wrong type, heat range or cap configuration. Check and install correct plug listed in Chapter 1. A cold plug or one with a recessed firing electrode will not operate at low speeds without fouling.

☐ Ignition control unit (carburettor models) defective (see Chapter 5). Engine control unit (fuel injected models) defective (see Chapter 4B).

☐ Ignition HT coil defective. See Chapter 5.

Fuel/air mixture incorrect – carburettor models

☐ Main jet clogged. Dirt, water or other contaminants can clog the main jet. Clean the fuel valve strainer, the float chamber area, and the jets and carburettor passages (Chapter 4A).

☐ Main jet wrong size. The standard jetting is for sea level atmospheric pressure and oxygen content.

☐ Air filter clogged, poorly sealed, or missing (Chapter 1).

☐ Air filter housing poorly sealed. Look for cracks, holes or loose clamps, and replace or repair defective parts.

☐ Fuel level too high or too low. Check the float height (Chapter 4A).

☐ Fuel tank air vent obstructed. Make sure the air vent passage in the filler cap is open.

☐ Carburettor intake duct loose. Check for cracks, breaks, tears or loose clamps. Replace the rubber intake (Chapter 4A).

☐ Fuel valve strainer clogged. Remove the valve and clean it and the strainer (Chapters 1 and 4A).

☐ Fuel hose clogged. Detach the fuel hose and carefully blow through it.

Fuel/air mixture incorrect – fuel injected models

☐ Fuel tank breather hose obstructed.

☐ Fuel pump faulty (see Chapter 4B).

☐ Fuel hose clogged. Remove the fuel hose and carefully blow through it.

☐ Fuel injector clogged. In some cases, if a machine has been unused for several months, the fuel turns to a varnish-like liquid which can cause the injector needle to stick to its seat. Drain the tank and fuel system (Chapter 4B).

☐ Intake air leak. Check for loose throttle body-to-intake duct joints (Chapter 4B).

☐ Air filter clogged. Clean the air filter element or replace it with a new one (Chapter 1).

Compression low

☐ Spark plug loose. Remove the plug and inspect the threads. Reinstall and tighten to the specified torque (Chapter 1).

☐ Cylinder head not sufficiently tightened down. If the cylinder head is suspected of being loose, then there's a chance that the gasket and head are damaged if the problem has persisted for any length of time. The camshaft holder nuts should be tightened to the proper torque in the correct sequence (Chapter 2).

☐ Improper valve clearance. This means that the valve is not closing completely and compression pressure is leaking past the valve. Check and adjust the valve clearances (Chapter 1).

☐ Cylinder and/or piston worn. Excessive wear will cause compression pressure to leak past the rings. This is usually accompanied by worn rings as well. A top-end overhaul and rebore will be necessary (Chapter 2).

☐ Piston rings worn, weak, broken, or sticking. Broken or sticking piston rings usually indicate a lubrication or carburetion problem that causes excess carbon deposits or seizures to form on the pistons and rings. Top-end overhaul is necessary (Chapter 2).

☐ Piston ring-to-groove clearance excessive. This is caused by excessive wear of the piston ring lands. Piston replacement is necessary (Chapter 2).

☐ Cylinder head gasket damaged. If the head is allowed to become loose, or if excessive carbon build-up on the piston crown and combustion chamber causes extremely high compression, the head gasket may leak. Retorquing the head is not always sufficient to restore the seal, so gasket replacement is necessary (Chapter 2).

☐ Cylinder head warped. This is caused by overheating or improperly tightened camshaft holder nuts. Machine shop resurfacing or head replacement is necessary (Chapter 2).

☐ Valve spring broken or weak. Caused by component failure or wear; the springs must be replaced (Chapter 2).

☐ Valve not seating properly. This is caused by a bent valve (from over-revving or improper valve adjustment), burned valve or seat (improper fuelling) or an accumulation of carbon deposits on the seat (from fuelling, lubrication problems). The valves must be cleaned and/or replaced and the seats serviced if possible (Chapter 2).

Knocking or pinking

☐ Carbon build-up in combustion chamber. Use of a fuel additive that will dissolve the adhesive bonding the carbon particles to the crown and chamber is the easiest way to remove the build-up. Otherwise, the cylinder head will have to be removed and decarbonised (Chapter 2).

☐ Incorrect or poor quality fuel. Old or improper grades of fuel can cause detonation. This causes the piston to rattle, thus the knocking or pinking sound. Drain old fuel and always use the recommended unleaded fuel grade.

☐ Spark plug heat range incorrect. Uncontrolled detonation indicates the plug heat range is too hot. The plug in effect becomes a glow plug, raising cylinder temperatures. Install the proper heat range plug (Chapter 1).

☐ Improper air/fuel mixture. This will cause the cylinder to run hot, which leads to detonation. A blockage in the fuel system or an air leak can cause this imbalance. See Chapter 4A or 4B.

Miscellaneous causes

☐ Throttle valve doesn't open fully. Adjust the throttle cable slack (Chapter 1).

☐ Clutch slipping. May be caused by loose or worn clutch components. Refer to Chapter 2 for clutch overhaul procedures.

☐ Timing not advancing.

☐ Engine oil viscosity too high. Using a heavier oil than the one recommended in 'Pre-ride checks' can damage the oil pump or lubrication system and cause drag on the engine.

☐ Brakes dragging. Usually caused by debris which has entered the brake piston seals, or from a warped disc or bent axle. Repair as necessary.

4 Overheating

Engine overheats

- [ ] Coolant level low. Check and add coolant (*Pre-ride checks*).
- [ ] Leak in cooling system. Check cooling system hoses and radiator for leaks and other damage. Repair or replace parts as necessary (Chapter 3).
- [ ] Thermostat sticking open or closed. Check and replace as described in Chapter 3.
- [ ] Faulty radiator cap. Remove the cap and have it checked by a Honda dealer.
- [ ] Coolant passages clogged. Drain, flush and refill with fresh coolant (Chapter 1).
- [ ] Water pump defective. Remove the pump and check the components (Chapter 3).
- [ ] Clogged radiator fins. Clean them by blowing compressed air through the fins from the rear face of the radiator.
- [ ] Faulty cooling fan or fan switch (see Chapter 3).

Firing incorrect

- [ ] Spark plug fouled, defective or worn out. See Chapter 1 for spark plug maintenance.
- [ ] Incorrect spark plug.
- [ ] Faulty ignition system (Chapter 5).

Fuel/air mixture incorrect – carburettor models

- [ ] Main jet clogged. Dirt, water and other contaminants can clog the main jet. Clean the fuel valve strainer, the float chamber area and the jets and carburettor passages (Chapter 4A).
- [ ] Main jet wrong size. The standard jetting is for sea level atmospheric pressure and oxygen content.
- [ ] Air filter clogged, poorly sealed or missing (Chapter 1).
- [ ] Air filter housing poorly sealed. Look for cracks, holes or loose clamps and replace or repair.
- [ ] Fuel level too low. Check float height (Chapter 4A).
- [ ] Fuel tank air vent obstructed. Make sure that the air vent passage in the filler cap is open.
- [ ] Carburettor intake duct loose. Check for cracks, breaks, tears or loose clamps. Replace the rubber intake (Chapter 4A).

Fuel/air mixture incorrect – fuel injected models

- [ ] Fuel tank breather hose obstructed.
- [ ] Fuel pump faulty (see Chapter 4B).
- [ ] Fuel hose clogged. Remove the fuel hose and carefully blow through it.
- [ ] Fuel injector clogged. In some cases, if a machine has been unused for several months, the fuel turns to a varnish-like liquid which can cause the injector needle to stick to its seat. Drain the tank and fuel system (Chapter 4B).
- [ ] Intake air leak. Check for loose throttle body-to-intake manifold joints (Chapter 4B).
- [ ] Air filter clogged. Clean the air filter element or replace it with a new one (Chapter 1).

Compression too high

- [ ] Carbon build-up in combustion chamber. Use of a fuel additive that will dissolve the adhesive bonding the carbon particles to the piston crown and chamber is the easiest way to remove the build-up. Otherwise, the cylinder head will have to be removed and decarbonised (Chapter 2).
- [ ] Improperly machined head surface or installation of incorrect gasket during engine assembly.

Engine load excessive

- [ ] Clutch slipping. Can be caused by damaged, loose or worn clutch components. Refer to Chapter 2 for overhaul procedures.
- [ ] Engine oil level too high. The addition of too much oil will cause pressurization of the crankcase and inefficient engine operation. Check Specifications and drain to proper level (Chapter 1 and *Pre-ride checks*).
- [ ] Engine oil viscosity too high. Using a heavier oil than the one recommended in Chapter 1 can damage the oil pump or lubrication system as well as cause drag on the engine.
- [ ] Brakes dragging. Usually caused by debris which has entered the brake piston seals, or from a warped disc or bent axle. Repair as necessary.

Lubrication inadequate

- [ ] Engine oil level too low. Friction caused by intermittent lack of lubrication or from oil that is overworked can cause overheating. The oil provides a definite cooling function in the engine. Check the oil level (*Pre-ride checks*).
- [ ] Poor quality engine oil or incorrect viscosity or type. Oil is rated not only according to viscosity but also according to type. Some oils are not rated high enough for use in this engine. Check the Specifications section and change to the correct oil (Chapter 1 and Pre-ride checks).

Miscellaneous causes

- [ ] Modification to exhaust system. Most aftermarket exhaust systems cause the engine to run leaner, which make them run hotter. When installing an accessory exhaust system, always check with the manufacturer/supplier as to whether the fuel system requires adjustment.

5 Gearchanging problems

Doesn't go into gear or lever doesn't return

- [ ] Clutch not disengaging. See Section 5.
- [ ] Selector fork(s) bent or seized. Often caused by dropping the machine or from lack of lubrication. Overhaul the transmission (Chapter 2).
- [ ] Gear(s) stuck on shaft. Most often caused by a lack of lubrication or excessive wear in transmission bearings and bushes. Overhaul the transmission (Chapter 2).
- [ ] Selector drum binding. Caused by lubrication failure or excessive wear. Replace the drum and bearing (Chapter 2).
- [ ] Gearchange lever return spring weak or broken (Chapter 2).
- [ ] Gearchange lever broken. Splines stripped out of lever or shaft, caused by allowing the lever to get loose or from dropping the machine. Replace necessary parts (Chapter 2).
- [ ] Gearchange mechanism stopper arm broken or worn. Full engagement and rotary movement of selector drum results. Replace the arm (Chapter 2).
- [ ] Stopper arm spring broken. Allows arm to float, causing sporadic gearchange operation. Replace spring (Chapter 2).

Jumps out of gear

- [ ] Selector fork(s) worn. Overhaul the transmission (Chapter 2).
- [ ] Gear groove(s) worn. Overhaul the transmission (Chapter 2).
- [ ] Gear dogs or dog slots worn or damaged. The gears should be inspected and replaced. No attempt should be made to service the worn parts.

Overselects

- [ ] Stopper arm spring weak or broken (Chapter 2).
- [ ] Gearchange shaft return spring post broken or distorted (Chapter 2).

6 Clutch problems

Clutch slipping

- [ ] Cable freeplay insufficient. Check and adjust cable (Chapter 1).
- [ ] Friction plates worn or warped. Overhaul the clutch assembly (Chapter 2).
- [ ] Steel plates warped (Chapter 2).
- [ ] Clutch spring(s) broken or weak. Old or heat-damaged (from slipping clutch) springs should be replaced with new ones (Chapter 2).
- [ ] Clutch release mechanism defective. Replace any defective parts (Chapter 2).
- [ ] Clutch centre or housing unevenly worn. This causes improper engagement of the plates. Replace the damaged or worn parts (Chapter 2).

Clutch not disengaging completely

- [ ] Cable freeplay excessive. Check and adjust cable (Chapter 1).
- [ ] Clutch plates warped or damaged. This will cause clutch drag, which in turn will cause the machine to creep. Overhaul the clutch assembly (Chapter 2).

- [ ] Clutch spring tension uneven. Usually caused by a sagged or broken spring. Check and replace the springs as a set (Chapter 2).
- [ ] Engine oil deteriorated. Old, thin, worn out oil will not provide proper lubrication for the discs, causing the clutch to drag. Replace the oil and filter (Chapter 1).
- [ ] Engine oil viscosity too high. Using a heavier oil than recommended can cause the plates to stick together, putting a drag on the engine. Change to the correct weight oil (Chapter 1 and Pre-ride checks).
- [ ] Clutch housing seized on shaft. Lack of lubrication, severe wear or damage can cause the housing to seize on the shaft. Overhaul of the clutch, and perhaps transmission, may be necessary to repair the damage (Chapter 2).
- [ ] Clutch release mechanism defective. Worn or damaged release mechanism parts can stick and fail to apply force to the pressure plate. Overhaul the clutch cover components (Chapter 2).
- [ ] Loose clutch centre nut. Causes drum and centre misalignment putting a drag on the engine. Engagement adjustment continually varies. Overhaul the clutch assembly (Chapter 2).

7 Abnormal engine noise

Knocking or pinking

- [ ] Carbon build-up in combustion chamber. Use of a fuel additive that will dissolve the adhesive bonding the carbon particles to the piston crown and chamber is the easiest way to remove the build-up. Otherwise, the cylinder head will have to be removed and decarbonised (Chapter 2).
- [ ] Incorrect or poor quality fuel. Old or improper fuel can cause detonation. This causes the piston to rattle, thus the knocking or pinking sound. Drain the old fuel and always use the recommended grade fuel (Chapter 4A or 4B).
- [ ] Spark plug heat range incorrect. Uncontrolled detonation indicates that the plug heat range is too hot. The plug in effect becomes a glow plug, raising cylinder temperatures. Install the proper heat range plug (Chapter 1).
- [ ] Improper air/fuel mixture. This will cause the cylinder to run hot and lead to detonation. A blockage in the fuel system or an air leak can cause this imbalance. See Chapter 4A or 4B.

Piston slap or rattling

- [ ] Cylinder-to-piston clearance excessive. Caused by improper assembly. Inspect and rebore (Chapter 2).
- [ ] Connecting rod bent. Caused by over-revving, trying to start a badly flooded engine or from ingesting a foreign object into the combustion chamber. Replace the damaged parts (Chapter 2).
- [ ] Piston pin or piston pin bore worn or seized from wear or lack of lubrication. Replace damaged parts (Chapter 2).
- [ ] Piston ring(s) worn, broken or sticking. Overhaul the top-end (Chapter 2).
- [ ] Piston seizure damage. Usually from lack of lubrication or

overheating. Replace the piston and rebore the cylinder, as necessary (Chapter 2).
- [ ] Connecting rod upper or lower end clearance excessive. Caused by excessive wear or lack of lubrication. Replace worn parts.

Valve noise

- [ ] Incorrect valve clearances. Adjust the clearances by referring to Chapter 1.
- [ ] Valve spring broken or weak. Check and replace weak valve springs (Chapter 2).
- [ ] Camshaft or cylinder head worn or damaged. Lack of lubrication at high rpm is usually the cause of damage. Insufficient oil or failure to change the oil at the recommended intervals are the chief causes (Chapter 2).

Other noise

- [ ] Cylinder head gasket leaking.
- [ ] Exhaust pipe leaking at cylinder head connection. Caused by improper fit of pipe or loose exhaust flange. All exhaust fasteners should be tightened evenly and carefully. Failure to do this will lead to a leak.
- [ ] Crankshaft runout excessive. Caused by a bent crankshaft (from over-revving) or damage from an upper cylinder component failure. Can also be attributed to dropping the machine on either of the crankshaft ends.
- [ ] Engine mounting bolts loose. Tighten all engine mount bolts (Chapter 2).
- [ ] Crankshaft bearings worn (Chapter 2).
- [ ] Cam chain tensioner defective. Replace according to the procedure in Chapter 2.
- [ ] Cam chain, sprockets or guides worn (Chapter 2).

8 Abnormal driveline noise

Clutch noise

☐ Clutch housing/friction plate clearance excessive (Chapter 2).
☐ Loose or damaged clutch lifter plate and/or bolts (Chapter 2).
☐ Worn lifter plate bearing (Chapter 2).

Transmission noise

☐ Bearings worn. Also includes the possibility that the shafts are worn. Overhaul the transmission (Chapter 2).
☐ Gears worn or chipped (Chapter 2).
☐ Metal chips jammed in gear teeth. Probably pieces from a broken clutch, gear or selector mechanism that were picked up by the gears. This will cause early bearing failure (Chapter 2).

☐ Engine oil level too low. Causes a howl from transmission. Also affects engine power and clutch operation (*Pre-ride checks*).

Final drive noise

☐ Chain not adjusted properly (Chapter 1).
☐ Engine sprocket or rear sprocket loose. Tighten fasteners (Chapter 7).
☐ Sprocket(s) worn. Replace sprockets and chain (Chapter 7).
☐ Rear sprocket warped. Replace (Chapter 7).
☐ Sprocket coupling worn. Check coupling, dampers and bearing (Chapter 7).

9 Abnormal frame and suspension noise

Front end noise

☐ Low fluid level or improper viscosity oil in forks. This can sound like spurting and is usually accompanied by irregular fork action (Chapter 6).
☐ Spring weak or broken. Makes a clicking or scraping sound. Fork oil, when drained, will have a lot of metal particles in it (Chapter 6).
☐ Steering head bearings loose or damaged. Clicks when braking. Check and adjust or replace as necessary (Chapters 1 and 6).
☐ Fork clamp bolts loose. Make sure all fork clamp bolts are tight (Chapter 6).
☐ Fork tube bent. Good possibility if machine has been dropped. Replace tube with a new one (Chapter 6).
☐ Front axle nut loose. Tighten it to the specified torque (Chapter 6).

Shock absorber noise

☐ Fluid level incorrect. Indicates a leak caused by defective seal. Shock will be covered with oil. Replace shock (Chapter 6).
☐ Defective shock absorber with internal damage. This is in the body of the shock and can't be remedied. The shock must be replaced with a new one (Chapter 6).

☐ Bent or damaged shock body. Replace the shock with a new one (Chapter 6).

Brake noise

☐ Squeal caused by dust on brake pads. Usually found in combination with glazed pads. Renew pads (Chapter 7).
☐ Contamination of brake pads. Oil, brake fluid or dirt causing brake to chatter or squeal. Renew pads (Chapter 7).
☐ Pads glazed. Caused by excessive heat from prolonged use or from contamination. Do not use sandpaper, emery cloth, carborundum cloth or any other abrasive to roughen the pad surfaces as abrasives will stay in the pad material and damage the disc. A very fine flat file can be used, but pad replacement is suggested as a cure (Chapter 7).
☐ Disc warped. Can cause a chattering, clicking or intermittent squeal. Usually accompanied by a pulsating lever and uneven braking. Replace the disc (Chapter 7).
☐ Loose or worn wheel bearings. Check and replace as needed (Chapter 7).

10 Excessive exhaust smoke

White smoke

☐ Piston oil ring worn. The ring may be broken or damaged, causing oil from the crankcase to be pulled past the piston into the combustion chamber. Replace the rings with new ones (Chapter 2).
☐ Cylinder worn, cracked, or scored. Caused by overheating or oil starvation. The cylinder will have to be rebored and a new piston and rings installed.
☐ Valve oil seal damaged or worn. Replace oil seals with new ones (Chapter 2).
☐ Valve guide worn. Perform a complete valve job (Chapter 2).
☐ Engine oil level too high, which causes the oil to be forced past the rings. Drain oil to the proper level (Chapter 1 and *Pre-ride checks*).
☐ Head gasket broken between oil return and cylinder. Causes oil to be pulled into the combustion chamber. Replace the head gasket and check the head for warpage (Chapter 2).
☐ Abnormal crankcase pressurisation, which forces oil past the rings. Clogged breather or hose usually the cause (Chapter 3).

Black smoke – carburettor models

☐ Air filter clogged. Clean or replace the element (Chapter 1).
☐ Main jet too large or loose. Compare the jet size to the Specifications (Chapter 4A).
☐ Choke stuck, causing fuel to be pulled through choke circuit

(Chapter 4A).
☐ Fuel level too high. Check and adjust the float height as necessary (Chapter 4A).
☐ Float needle valve held off needle seat. Clean the float chamber and fuel line and replace the needle and seat if necessary (Chapter 4A).

Black smoke – fuel injected models

☐ Air filter clogged. Clean the air filter element or replace it with a new one (Chapter 1).
☐ Fuel injection system malfunction (Chapter 4B).

Brown smoke – carburettor models

☐ Main jet too small or clogged. Lean condition caused by wrong size main jet or by a restricted orifice. Clean float chamber and jets and compare jet size to Specifications (Chapter 4A).
☐ Fuel flow insufficient. Fuel inlet needle valve stuck closed due to chemical reaction with old fuel. Float height incorrect. Restricted fuel line. Clean line and float chamber.
☐ Carburettor intake duct loose (Chapter 4A).
☐ Air filter poorly sealed or not installed (Chapter 1).

Brown smoke – fuel injected models

☐ Air filter poorly sealed or not installed (Chapter 1).
☐ Fuel injection system malfunction (Chapter 4B).

11 Poor handling or stability

Handlebars hard to turn

- [ ] Steering stem nut too tight (Chapter 6).
- [ ] Bearings damaged. Roughness can be felt as the bars are turned from side-to-side. Replace bearings and races (Chapter 6).
- [ ] Races dented or worn. Denting results from a collision or hitting a pothole or from dropping the machine. Replace races and bearings (Chapter 6).
- [ ] Steering stem lubrication inadequate. Causes are grease getting hard from age or being washed out by high pressure washers. Disassemble steering head and repack bearings (Chapter 6).
- [ ] Steering stem bent. Caused by a collision, hitting a pothole or by dropping the machine. Replace damaged part. Don't try to straighten the steering stem (Chapter 6).
- [ ] Front tyre air pressure too low (*Pre-ride checks*).

Handlebars shake or vibrate excessively

- [ ] Tyres worn or out of balance (Chapter 7).
- [ ] Swingarm bearings worn. Check as described in Chapter 6.
- [ ] Rim(s) warped or damaged. Inspect wheels for runout (Chapter 7).
- [ ] Wheel bearings worn. Worn front or rear wheel bearings can cause poor tracking. Worn front bearings will cause wobble (Chapter 7).
- [ ] Handlebar clamp bolts loose (Chapter 6).
- [ ] Steering stem or fork clamp bolts loose. Tighten them to the specified torque (Chapter 6).
- [ ] Engine mounting bolts loose. Will cause excessive vibration with increased engine rpm (Chapter 2).

Handlebars pull to one side

- [ ] Frame bent. Definitely suspect this if the machine has been dropped. May or may not be accompanied by cracking near the bend. Replace the frame (Chapter 6).
- [ ] Wheel out of alignment. Caused by improper location of axle spacers (Chapter 7) or from bent steering stem or frame (Chapter 6).
- [ ] Swingarm bent or twisted. Caused by age (metal fatigue) or impact damage. Replace the swingarm (Chapter 6).
- [ ] Steering stem bent. Caused by impact damage or by dropping the motorcycle. Replace the steering stem (Chapter 6).
- [ ] Fork tube bent. Disassemble the forks and replace the damaged parts (Chapter 6).
- [ ] Fork oil level uneven. Check and add or drain as necessary (Chapter 6). Level must be the same in each fork.

Poor shock absorbing qualities

- [ ] Too hard:
  - a) Fork oil level excessive (Chapter 6).
  - b) Fork oil viscosity too high. Use a lighter oil (see the Specifications in Chapter 6).
  - c) Fork tube bent. Causes a harsh, sticking feeling (Chapter 6).
  - d) Shock shaft or body bent or damaged (Chapter 6).
  - e) Fork internal damage (Chapter 6).
  - f) Shock internal damage.
  - g) Tyre pressure too high (Pre-ride checks).
- [ ] Too soft:
  - a) Fork or shock oil insufficient and/or leaking (Chapter 6).
  - b) Fork oil level too low (Chapter 6).
  - c) Fork oil viscosity too light (Chapter 6).
  - d) Fork spring weak or broken (Chapter 6).
  - e) Shock internal damage or leakage (Chapter 6).

12 Braking problems

Brakes are spongy or don't hold

- [ ] Air in brake line. Caused by low fluid level in master cylinder or by leakage. Locate problem and bleed brakes (Chapter 7).
- [ ] Pads or disc worn (Chapters 1 and 7).
- [ ] Contaminated pads. Caused by contamination with oil, grease, brake fluid, etc. Renew pads. Clean disc thoroughly with brake cleaner (Chapter 7).
- [ ] Brake fluid deteriorated. Fluid is old or contaminated. Drain system, replenish with new fluid and bleed the system (Chapter 7).
- [ ] Master cylinder internal parts worn or damaged causing fluid to bypass (Chapter 7).
- [ ] Master cylinder bore scratched by foreign material or broken spring. Repair or replace master cylinder (Chapter 7).
- [ ] Disc warped. Replace disc (Chapter 7).

Brake lever or pedal pulsates

- [ ] Disc warped. Replace disc (Chapter 7).
- [ ] Wheel axle bent. Replace axle (Chapter 7).
- [ ] Brake caliper bolts loose (Chapter 7).

- [ ] Brake caliper sliders damaged or sticking, causing caliper to bind. Lube the sliders or replace them if they are corroded or bent (Chapter 7).
- [ ] Wheel warped or otherwise damaged (Chapter 7).
- [ ] Wheel bearings damaged or worn (Chapter 7).

Brakes drag

- [ ] Master cylinder piston seized. Caused by wear or damage to piston or cylinder bore (Chapter 7).
- [ ] Lever balky or stuck. Check pivot and lubricate (Chapter 7).
- [ ] Brake caliper binds. Caused by inadequate lubrication of caliper slider pins (Chapter 7).
- [ ] Brake caliper piston seized in bore. Caused by wear or ingestion of dirt past deteriorated seal (Chapter 7).
- [ ] Brake pad damaged. Pad material separated from backing plate. Usually caused by faulty manufacturing process or from contact with chemicals. Replace pads (Chapter 7).
- [ ] Pads improperly installed (Chapter 7).
- [ ] Rear brake pedal freeplay insufficient. Check pedal height (Chapter 1).

13 Electrical problems

Battery dead or weak

- [ ] Battery faulty or worn out. Renew battery (Chapter 9).
- [ ] Battery leads making poor contact (Chapter 9).
- [ ] Load excessive. Caused by addition of high wattage lights or other electrical accessories.
- [ ] Ignition switch defective. Switch either grounds (earths) internally or fails to shut off system. Check the switch (Chapter 9).
- [ ] Regulator/rectifier defective (Chapter 9).
- [ ] Stator coil open or shorted (Chapter 9).

- [ ] Wiring faulty. Wiring grounded (earthed) or connections loose in ignition, charging or lighting circuits (Chapter 9).

Battery overcharged

- [ ] Regulator/rectifier defective. Overcharging is noticed when battery gets excessively warm (Chapter 9).
- [ ] Battery defective. Replace battery with a new one (Chapter 9).
- [ ] Battery amperage too low, wrong type or size. Install manufacturer's specified amp-hour battery to handle charging load (Chapter 9).

Note: *References throughout this index are in the form - "Chapter number" • "Page number"*

Preserving Our Motoring Heritage

< The Model J Duesenberg
Derham Tourster.
Only eight of these
magnificent cars were
ever built – this is the
only example to be found
outside the United States
of America

Almost every car you've ever loved, loathed or desired is gathered under one roof at the Haynes Motor Museum. Over 300 immaculately presented cars and motorbikes represent every aspect of our motoring heritage, from elegant reminders of bygone days, such as the superb Model J Duesenberg to curiosities like the bug-eyed BMW Isetta. There are also many old friends and flames. Perhaps you remember the 1959 Ford Popular that you did your courting in? The magnificent 'Red Collection' is a spectacle of classic sports cars including AC, Alfa Romeo, Austin Healey, Ferrari, Lamborghini, Maserati, MG, Riley, Porsche and Triumph.

A Perfect Day Out

Each and every vehicle at the Haynes Motor Museum has played its part in the history and culture of Motoring. Today, they make a wonderful spectacle and a great day out for all the family. Bring the kids, bring Mum and Dad, but above all bring your camera to capture those golden memories for ever. You will also find an impressive array of motoring memorabilia, a comfortable 70 seat video cinema and one of the most extensive transport book shops in Britain. The Pit Stop Cafe serves everything from a cup of tea to wholesome, home-made meals or, if you prefer, you can enjoy the large picnic area nestled in the beautiful rural surroundings of Somerset.

John Haynes O.B.E.,
Founder and
Chairman of the
museum at the wheel
of a Haynes Light 12.

< The 1936 490cc
sohc-engined
International
Norton – well known
for its racing success

The Museum is situated on the A359 Yeovil to Frome road at Sparkford, just off the A303 in Somerset. It is about 40 miles south of Bristol, and 25 minutes drive from the M5 intersection at Taunton.
Open 9.30am - 5.30pm (10.00am - 4.00pm Winter) 7 days a week, *except Christmas Day, Boxing Day and New Years Day*
Special rates available for schools, coach parties and outings Charitable Trust No. 292048